OCR Law
for AS

Jacqueline Martin

Editor: Sue Teal

Third Edition

HODDER
EDUCATION
AN HACHETTE UK COMPA

Orders: please contact Bookpoint Ltd, 130 Milton Park, Abingdon, Oxon
OX14 4SB. Telephone: (44) 01235 827720. Fax: (44) 01235 400454. Lines are
open from 9.00 - 5.00, Monday to Saturday, with a 24 hour message
answering service. You can also order through our website
www.hoddereducation.co.uk

If you have any comments to make about this, or any of our other titles,
please send them to educationenquiries@hodder.co.uk

British Library Cataloguing in Publication Data
A catalogue record for this title is available from the British Library

ISBN: 978-1-4441-9274-2

First Edition Published 2008
Second Edition Published 2011
This Edition Published 2013
Impression number 10 9 8 7 6 5 4 3 2 1
Year 2017 2016 2015 2014 2013

Hachette UK's policy is to use papers that are natural, renewable and
recyclable products and made from wood grown in sustainable forests.
The logging and manufacturing processes are expected to conform to the
environmental regulations of the country of origin.

Illustrations by Barking Dog Art
Cover illustration by Peter Gudynas/Zap Art
Typeset by Integra Software Services Pvt. Ltd., Pondicherry, India.
Printed and bound in Dubai for Hodder Education, an Hachette UK
Company, 338 Euston Road, London NW1 3BH

Contents

Preface

This book is aimed at the OCR specification for AS Law. The topics are covered in the order in which they appear in that specification.

The first chapter is an introductory one. It deals with the differences between civil and criminal law and gives a brief introduction to human rights. I have included this chapter as it is important that students grasp that civil and criminal cases are dealt with in different ways and in different courts. A brief account of human rights has been included as they affect so many aspects of our legal system.

The order of topics then starts with those set out for Unit 1 of the AS. Civil courts, alternative dispute resolution, police powers, pre-trial matters on criminal cases, the magistrates' courts and the Crown Court, appeals in criminal cases, sentencing, the judiciary, the legal profession, lay magistrates, juries and funding. The book then covers the topics needed for Unit 2: judicial precedent, Acts of Parliament, delegated legislation, statutory interpretation, European law and law reform.

Throughout the text I have used my best-selling book, *The English Legal System*, which many teachers of OCR AS Law are already familiar with, as the basis for this textbook. I have kept to the principles of explaining points simply and clearly, but at the same time providing some depth for the more able students. As well as covering the factual material, each chapter contains critical analysis at a level suitable for AS students.

The text is broken up into manageable 'bites' with the use of sub-headings. There are also diagrams and charts to help students with their understanding of topics. Key facts charts are included for each topic to enable students to have an overview of the topics. These charts are also helpful as revision aids.

Newspaper articles, cases and other 'live' material are provided in most chapters to illustrate the legal system at work today. Many of these items are also used as a basis for activities and exercises for students to do. There are also application tasks for students based on scenario style questions. Examination questions from the new specification for OCR AS Law are also given at the end of each chapter.

This third edition has been thoroughly updated and includes important changes which have occurred in the legal system since the last edition was published. These include the changes to sentencing and legal aid made by the Legal Aid, Sentencing and Punishment of Offenders Act 2012.

The law is as I believe it to be on 1 January 2013.

Jacqueline Martin

Acknowledgements

Every effort has been made to trace the copyright holders of material reproduced here, but if any have been inadvertently overlooked the Publishers will be pleased to make the necessary arrangements at the first opportunity. The authors and publishers would like to thank the following for permission to reproduce copyright illustrations:

p.21 © Andrew Holt/Alamy; **p.26** © Gareth Fuller/PA Wire/Press Association Images; **p.41** © Rex Features; **p.75** © Photofusion Picture Library/Alamy; **p.78** MARTYN HAYHOW/AFP/Getty Images; **p.98** © Dan Atkin/Alamy; **p.111** © TOBY MELVILLE/Reuters/Corbis; **p.112** © PSL Images/Alamy; **p.131** © Stockdisc/Corbis; **p.134** © Peter Dazeley/Photographer's Choice/Getty Images; **p.215** © rnl – Fotolia.com; **p.267** © F1 online/Super Stock.

Crown copyright material in this book is reproduced under the terms of the Open Government Licence.

Table of Acts of Parliament

Table of Cases

UNIT 1

English legal system

Chapter 1

Introduction to law

Murderer jailed for life

Burglar caught

Newspaper headlines like these are what many people think of when 'law' is mentioned. The other main source of information for the ordinary person is television, with real-life programmes such as *Crimewatch* and fictional series about the police. The headlines and these television programmes all involve criminal cases.

This does not give a complete picture of the law. In fact, the law deals with a very wide variety of different cases and situations. As well as all the criminal cases that we hear so much of, the law also deals with what is called civil law.

The OCR specification you are studying requires you to understand the different ways in which civil and criminal cases are dealt with.

1.1 Civil law

Civil law is about private disputes between individuals and/or businesses. There are several different types of civil law. Some important areas of civil law are:

- contract law
- law of tort
- family law
- employment law
- company law.

This book does not deal with the actual legal rules for any of these areas. It deals only with the system for resolving disputes. However, it is sensible to have some idea of the types of dispute that may be involved in these areas of law.

Law of contract

Consider the following situations:

(a) a family complain that their package holiday did not match what was promised by the tour operator and that they were put into a lower grade of hotel than the one they had paid for

(b) a woman has bought a new car and discovers that the engine is faulty

(c) a man who bought a car on hire-purchase has failed to pay the instalments due to the hire-purchase company.

All these situations come under the law of **contract**. There are also many other situations in which contracts may be involved. A contract is an agreement between two or more people and that agreement can be enforced by the courts. If a court case is successfully taken for breach of contract, the court will try to put the parties back into the position they would have been in if the contract had not been broken. This is usually done by ordering the person who broke the contract to pay a sum of money in compensation to the other person. This sum of money is called an award of damages. In a very small number of contracts the court may order the person in breach to carry out the contract. This is called specific performance.

Law of tort

Now look at the next list. These also involve disputes between individuals and/or businesses but there is no contract or agreement between them:

(a) a child pedestrian crossing a road is injured by a car whose driver is travelling too fast (the tort of negligence)

(b) a family complain that their health is being affected by the noise and smoke from a factory which has just been built near their house (the tort of nuisance)

(c) a man complains that a newspaper has written an untrue article about him which has damaged his reputation (the tort of defamation).

All these case come under the law of **tort**. This area of law recognises that there are situations where one person owes a legal responsibility to another. If there is a breach of this responsibility, then the person affected can make a claim under the law of tort. If successful the court will award them damages – a sum of money in compensation for any injury to them, their property or their reputation. Where there is a situation which is continuing (such as in (b) above), it is also possible for the court to order the person causing the problem not to do certain things. The above examples show possible breaches of different torts.

Other areas of law

Other divisions of civil law concentrate on specific topics. **Family law** covers all disputes that may arise within families. A major part of this is divorce law and who should have the day-to-day care of any children of the family. **Employment law** covers all aspects of employment. For example, any disputes about unfair dismissal or redundancy come under this area of law. **Company law** is very important in the business world: it regulates how a company should be formed, sets out the formal rules for running a company, and deals with the rights and duties of shareholders and directors.

As well as these areas of civil law, there are also laws relating to land, to copyright, to marine law and many other topics. So it can be seen that civil law covers a wide variety of situations.

1.2 Criminal law

Criminal law sets out the types of behaviour which are forbidden at risk of punishment. A person who commits a crime is said to have offended against the State and so the State has the right to prosecute them. This is so even though there is often an individual victim of a

Activity

On this page and the next page there are four newspaper articles. Two are about civil cases and two are about criminal cases. Read the articles and answer the questions at the end.

After you have done this activity, read section 1.3 to get a clearer understanding of the differences between the ways civil cases and criminal cases are dealt with in the courts.

Source A

Council worker ran in national sprints while signed off sick

A sprinter who raced in national competitions while signed off sick has been branded a 'common criminal' for defrauding his employers and made to pay the money back.

Matthew Thomas, 34, was given four months' jail suspended for two years and ordered to repay nearly £12,000 he had taken from his employer, Newham council.

Thomas, of Purley, south London, was ordered to carry out 250 hours of unpaid work and pay £8,000 in costs.

In August a jury at Inner London Crown Court found the runner guilty of seven counts of defrauding his employers by false representations. He was cleared of a further three counts of false representation and one of failing to disclose information relating to his athletics coaching.

Adapted from an article in *The Guardian*, 30 September 2010

Source B

Couple sue wedding photographer

A newly-married couple have successfully sued their wedding photographer after paying £1,450 for a 'woefully inadequate' service.

Marc and Sylvia Day were presented with a disc full of pictures from the big day with heads chopped off, inattentive guests and random close-ups of vehicles.

The cutting of the cake was missed and of the 400 images they were sent, only 22 met with their approval.

They have now been awarded compensations by a judge after winning a case for breach of contract against the photographer.

Deputy District Judge Keith Nightingale, found in favour of the Days at Pontefract County Court and criticised Mr Bowers for providing 'inappropriate' photos and a 'woefully inadequate' service.

He ordered him to pay back £500 from the £1,450 to the Days with £450 in damages, £100 for their loss of earning and £170 in court fees.

Adapted from an article by Paul Stokes in *The Daily Telegraph*, 5 October 2009
© Telegraph Media Group Limited 2009

Source C

Gun found next to baby

Mohammed Arif was convicted of possessing a firearm and jailed for six years at Birmingham Crown Court on Friday following the discovery in May.

Police were called to a house in the Bordesley Green area of Birmingham in the early hours after reports of a domestic dispute. They found the baby alone inside.

The antique, fully operational, Russian Smith and Wesson .44 revolver, loaded with six bullets, was wrapped in a blanket in the cot. Alongside was a machete.

Arif, 42, initially denied all knowledge of the weapons but his DNA was found on the gun and ammunition.

Taken from an article in *The Daily Express*, 30 September 2012

Source D

High Court uses Twitter to issue injunction

The High Court has ordered an injunction to be served through the social networking site Twitter for the first time.

In yesterday's ruling, the court said issuing the writ over the micro-blogging site was the best way to get to an anonymous tweeter who was impersonating a right-wing commentator.

The Twitter account, blaneysbarney, was impersonating Donal Blaney, a lawyer and Conservative blogger. The account, which was opened last month, features a photograph of Mr Blaney followed by a number of messages purporting to be by him.

The Court said that the unknown impostor should stop their activities and that they should reveal themselves to the court. The owner of the fake account will receive the writ next time they enter the site.

Taken from an article in *The Times*, 2 October 2009

Source E

Angry drinker poured half a pint of ale over 'grizzling' toddler because the noise disturbed his lunch

A grandfather poured beer over a crying toddler in a pub because the noise ruined his lunch plans, a court heard today.

Danny Polak, 64, lost his temper when 15-month-old Finlay White started making 'grizzling' sounds in the Ernehale pub in Arnold, Nottinghamshire.

He soaked the toddler in ale and then kicked the boy's mother, Rachel Atkin, in the backside when she went to confront him.

Polak was fined £355 and ordered to pay £50 in compensation when he appeared at Nottingham Magistrates' Court and admitted two counts of assault.

Taken from an article by Rob Preece in the *Daily Mail*, 15 October 2012

crime as well. For example, if a defendant commits the crime of burglary by breaking into someone's house and stealing money and other property, the State will prosecute the defendant for that burglary. But there is also an individual, the person living in the house, who is the victim of the crime. If the State does not prosecute then that individual has the right to prosecute. This happens only rarely in cases where the victim is an individual, but it is common in cases such as cruelty to animals where the RSPCA will often prosecute the offender.

The criminal courts have the right to punish those who break the criminal law. So, at the end of a case where the defendant is found guilty, that defendant will be given a punishment. Such punishments include imprisonment, a community sentence such as unpaid work, a fine, or a ban from driving.

Any individual victim of the crime will not necessarily be given compensation, though where possible the courts do order a defendant to pay compensation as well as punishing him or her.

1.3 Differences between civil and criminal law

There are many differences between civil cases and criminal cases. The newspaper articles on the previous pages show some of these differences. There are other differences as well and it is important to understand fully the distinctions between civil and criminal cases.

1.3.1 Purpose of the law

Civil law upholds the rights of individuals and the courts can order compensation in an effort at putting the parties in the position they would have been in if there had not been any breach of the civil law.

Criminal law is aimed at trying to maintain law and order. So, when a person is found guilty of an

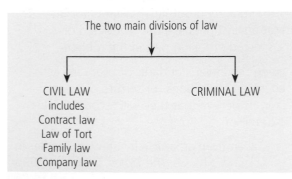

Figure 1.1 The main divisions of law

offence, that offender will be punished. There is also the aim of trying to protect society and this is the justification for sending offenders to prison.

1.3.2 Person starting the case

In civil cases the person starting the case is the individual or business which has suffered as a result of the breach of civil law.

Criminal cases are taken on behalf of the State, and so there is a Crown Prosecution Service responsible for conducting most cases. However, there are other State agencies which may prosecute certain types of offence, for example the Environment Agency which prosecutes pollution cases.

The person starting the case is given a different name in civil and criminal cases. In civil cases they are called the claimant, while in criminal cases they are referred to as the prosecutor.

1.3.3 Courts

The cases take place in different courts. In general, civil cases are heard in the High Court or the County Court. The High Court deals with more serious cases while the County Court deals with cases of lower value. (Note that some civil matters, especially family cases, can be dealt with in the Magistrates' Courts – see section 11.5 for further details.)

In both the High Court and the County Court a judge will try the case. It is very rare to have a case tried by a jury in a civil matter. See Chapter 12 for details of when a jury might be used in a civil case.

Criminal cases will be tried in either the Magistrates' Courts or the Crown Court. The Magistrates' Courts deal with less serious offences and the case is tried by a panel of lay magistrates or by a single legally qualified District Judge. Serious offences are tried in the Crown Court. The case is tried by a judge sitting with a jury. The judge decides points of law and the jury decide the verdict of 'guilty' or 'not guilty'.

1.3.4 Standard of proof

Criminal cases must be proved 'beyond reasonable doubt'. This is a very high standard of proof, and is necessary since a conviction could result in the defendant serving a long prison sentence.

Civil cases have to be proved 'on the balance of probabilities'. This is a much lower standard of proof, where the judge decides who is most likely to be right. This difference in the standard of proof means that it is possible for a defendant who has been acquitted in a criminal case to be found liable in a civil case based on the same facts. Such situations are not common, but one is illustrated in the following article.

Judgment overtakes Brink's-Mat accused 11 years later

Eleven years after a man was acquitted of the £26 million Brink's-Mat bullion robbery, a High Court judge ruled that he was involved and must repay the value of the gold.

Anthony White, acquitted at the Old Bailey in 1984 of taking part in Britain's biggest gold robbery, was ordered to repay the £26,369,778 value and £2,188,600 in compensation. His wife Margaret was ordered to pay £1,084,344. Insurers for Brink's-Mat had sued the couple for the value of the proceeds.

Mr Justice Rimmer told Mr White that his acquittal did not mean that the Old Bailey jury had been satisfied he was innocent; only that he was not guilty according to the standard of proof required in criminal cases ...

The case against the Whites is the latest and almost the last in a series of actions since the 1983 robbery brought by insurers for Brink's-Mat against people either convicted or suspected of taking part in the robbery.

Using the lower standards of proof in civil courts and in actions for seizure of assets, lawyers believe that they will recoup at least £20 million.

Taken from an article by Stewart Tendler in *The Times*, 2 August 1995

	CIVIL CASES	CRIMINAL CASES
Purpose of the law	To uphold the rights of individuals	To maintain law and order; to protect society
Person starting the case	The individual whose rights have been affected	Usually the State, through Crown Prosecution Service
Legal name for that person	Claimant	Prosecutor
Courts hearing cases	County Court or High Court Some cases dealt with in tribunals	Magistrates' Court or Crown Court
Standard of proof	The balance of probabilities	Beyond reasonable doubt
Person/s making the decision	Judge Very rarely a jury	Magistrates in Magistrates' Courts OR A judge and jury at the Crown Court
Decision	'Liable' or 'not liable'	'Guilty' (convicted) or 'not guilty' (acquitted)
Powers of the court	Usually an award of damages. Also possible: injunction, specific performance of a contract, rescission or rectification	Prison, community sentence fine, discharge, driving ban

Figure 1.2 Differences between civil and criminal cases

1.3.5 Outcome of case

A defendant in a civil case is found 'liable' or 'not liable'. A defendant in a criminal case is found 'guilty' or 'not guilty'. Another way of stating this in criminal cases is to say that the defendant is 'convicted' or 'acquitted'.

At the end of a civil case, anyone found liable will be ordered to put right the matter as far as possible. This is usually done by an award of money in compensation, known as damages, though the court can make other orders such as an injunction to prevent similar actions in the future or an order for specific performance (where the defendant who broke a contract is ordered to complete that contract).

At the end of a criminal case a defendant found guilty of an offence may be punished.

Exam tips

The table above gives some key terms and ways of describing legal personnel and matters connected with the legal process which will be important throughout your study of Law. You should try to master them as your script will appear more confident to an examiner if you can use these terms accurately in the right context. These terms will also be important in the second year of the course; the ones you use will vary depending on whether you are studying Criminal Law, Contract Law or the Law of Tort, so it's worth getting them right now!

1.4 Double liability

It is possible for the same incident to give rise to both civil and criminal liability. This occurs most often where someone is injured as a result of another person's bad driving. The driver can then be prosecuted in the criminal courts for a driving offence and also the injured person can claim against the driver in the civil courts. This next newspaper article shows a case where this happened.

Record £8.5 million for woman hit by car

A 22-year-old woman who suffered serious brain damage in a road accident nine years ago has been awarded £8.5 million, believed to be a record for a personal injury case (Frances Gibb writes).

Leanne Evans was hit by a 79-year-old driver on a pelican crossing in Birmingham when she was 13. The driver was fined £75 and convicted of careless driving.

Leanne now needs round-the-clock attention from eight carers, has severe memory impairment and uses a wheelchair.

Her father, Ivor Evans, said: 'We are very pleased for Leanne. This award will at least give her a limited quality of life and allow her to enjoy some of the things that every other 22-year-old likes to do, like going to pop concerts, going to the theatre and having a holiday, as well as making sure she has all the medical care that she needs.'

The Times, 15 March 2007
© The Times/NI Syndication

In this article the criminal case was the one in which the driver was convicted of careless driving. The civil case is the one in which the injured girl was awarded £8.5 million.

Activity

Look through newspapers to find articles about court cases. When you have found an article, use your knowledge about civil and criminal cases to decide what type of case it is.

If you are having difficulty finding civil cases, try searching for the phrase 'High Court' or 'County Court' in newspapers online at the following websites:

www.express.co.uk
www.dailymail.co.uk
www.telegraph.co.uk

Self-Test Questions

1 Who will start the case in:
   (a) a civil case
   (b) a criminal case?
2 Which courts try:
   (a) civil cases
   (b) criminal cases?
3 What is the standard of proof in:
   (a) a civil case
   (b) a criminal case?
4 Give two types of law that are part of the civil law.
5 Explain what is meant by 'double liability'.

1.5 Human rights and the English legal system

The Human Rights Act 1998 incorporated the European Convention on Human Rights into UK law. This is important, as it has affected many areas of the English legal system. This section explains key rights under the Convention and also gives a brief summary of some of the effects on our legal system.

1.5.1 The European Convention on Human Rights

The Convention sets out the rights that the people of Europe should have. These are:

- the right to life (Art 2), though it is recognised that states may impose the death penalty for certain crimes
- the right not to be tortured or subjected to inhumane or degrading treatment (Art 3)
- the forbidding of slavery (Art 4)
- the right to liberty (Art 5), although limitations on this right are permitted so that people who are lawfully arrested or held in custody for trial or given a prison sentence by a court can be detained
- the right to a fair trial (Art 6)
- the right not to be punished except according to law (Art 7)
- the right to respect for private and family life (Art 8).

The Convention also sets out freedoms which people should be able to enjoy. These include freedom of:

- thought, conscience and religion
- expression
- assembly and association.

1.5.2 Effect on the English legal process

Before the Convention was incorporated into our law by the Human Rights Act 1998, anyone who wanted to complain of a breach of human rights had to take their case to the European Court of Human Rights. If the United Kingdom was found to be in breach of the Convention, the Government did not have to change the law. However, in some cases it did do so. An example is *T v United Kingdom; V v United Kingdom* (1999) (see Criminal trials, below).

Since the Convention was incorporated, people can rely on the rights it gives in our courts. In addition, there have been some changes in our legal system in order to comply with the Convention. Some of these are explained below.

These points are not the only way in which the English legal system has been affected by the European Convention on Human Rights. However, they give some illustration of how wide-ranging the effect has been on our legal system.

Civil cases

An appeal route for small claims cases was created. Previously there had been no appeal for small claims cases. This would have breached Art 6 of the Convention – the right to a fair trial.

Criminal trials

In the case of *T v United Kingdom; V v United Kingdom* (1999), the European Court of Human Rights had ruled that there was a breach of Art 6. In the case, a boy of 10 and a boy of 11 were tried in the Crown Court for murder. The European Court of Human Rights held that the formality of a Crown Court trial would have made it difficult for the boys to understand what was happening. This meant that the trial was not fair and there was a breach of the European Convention.

Following this decision, trials of juveniles at the Crown Court were altered to make the trial process less formal.

Sentencing

Where an offender is sentenced to prison for life, it is usual to set a minimum period which must be served before the offender can be considered for parole. This minimum sentence used to be set by the Home Secretary (a Government Minister). The European Court of Human Rights held that this was a breach of the European Convention. This has been changed so that judges are now responsible for setting any minimum period.

Judicial appointment

Part-time judges in this country used to be appointed for a period of three years. After this time they could then be appointed for further periods of three years. In addition, the appointment was made by the Lord Chancellor (a Government Minister). The length of appointment was changed to five years as it was thought that the shorter period meant that there was a risk of the judges not being sufficiently independent from the Government. This would have been a breach of the European Convention.

1.5.3 Effect on sources of law

As well as affecting our legal system, the Human Rights Act 1998 sets out three important matters for the way our law is made and interpreted. These affect the making of Acts of Parliament, decisions on points of law by judges and the way in which judges interpret new laws. Each of these is explained below.

Acts of Parliament

When a new potential Act of Parliament (known as a Bill) is put before Parliament, there must be a statement as to whether it is compatible with the Convention rights or not.

Precedent

Section 2(1)(a) of the Human Rights Act 1998 states that our courts must take into account any judgment or decision of the European Court of Human Rights. This means that judges, when deciding a case, must look at human rights cases, as well as our own English law.

Statutory interpretation

Section 3 of the Act states that, so far as it is possible to do so, all legislation (that is, Acts of Parliament and other laws made in this country) must be given effect so that it is compatible with the European Convention. For example, if the wording of an Act of Parliament has two possible meanings, then the meaning which fits with the European Convention is the one that must be used.

Self-Test Questions

1 List three rights or freedoms which are given by the European Convention on Human Rights.
2 Which Act incorporates the Convention into English law?
3 Give an example of a change that has had to be made in the English legal system so that it complies with the Convention.
4 What statement has to be included in a new Act of Parliament in respect of human rights?
5 What effect does the Convention have on the system of judicial precedent?

Exam tips

The OCR specification will not require you to answer a question based directly on the material in this chapter but it does give you a vital overview of the way the law works and the inter-relationships between its different branches. It is very important for you to realise that the Law touches people's lives in many different ways and it gives you a sense of its role in a democratic society. Once you understand that you are better placed to learn about specific types of Law and to appreciate, for example, how the process of sentencing a defendant in a criminal case has to take account of several different elements, and that there may also be wider consequences as the legal rules need to be applied consistently and make some attempt to do justice.

Chapter 2

Civil cases

As already stressed in Chapter 1, it is important to understand the differences between civil cases and criminal cases. Civil cases cover a wide range of matters, so there cannot be a very specific definition which will cover all of them. However, a basic definition for civil claims is to say that these arise when an individual or a business believes that their rights have been infringed in some way. Some of the main areas of civil law are contract law, the law of tort, family law, employment law and company law.

As well as dealing with different areas of law, the types of dispute that can arise within the field of civil law are equally varied. A company may be claiming that money is owed to it (contract law); this type of claim may be for a few pounds or for several million. An individual may be claiming compensation for injuries suffered in an accident (the tort of negligence), while in another tort case the claim might not be for money but for another remedy, such as an injunction to prevent someone from building on disputed land. Other types of court orders include the winding-up of a company which cannot pay its debts or a decree of divorce for a marriage that has failed. The list is almost endless.

2.1 Negotiation

In most civil matters people regard a court case as a last resort and will try to resolve the problem without going to court, so that when a dispute arises it is likely that some form of negotiation will take place. The most usual situation is that the person making the complaint will either go to see the other side and explain the problem (this is common where shoppers take back sub-standard goods) or they will write to the other side, setting out the complaint. Many cases will be resolved at this stage by the other party agreeing to refund money, change goods, pay the debt or take some other desired action.

In fact, research in 2007 found that 89 per cent of people try some form of alternative way of resolving the dispute before starting a court case.

The need to try to settle any dispute is stressed in the leaflets issued by the Court Service on taking action in court.

Their leaflet, *I'm in a dispute – what can I do?*, includes the following:

> Do all disputes have to be settled in court?
>
> No. Going to court should always be a last resort. It can be expensive, stressful and time consuming.
>
> Before going to court you should always try to reach an agreement. For example, if you are in dispute with an organisation, you should use the organisation's complaints procedure before thinking of making a claim through the court.
>
> If you make a claim through the court without making any effort to reach an agreement first, you may find that the judge will hold this against you when considering payment of costs in the cases. You may not get your costs back, or the court may order you to pay the other party's costs, even if you win the case.
>
> Other ways you might try to reach an agreement include processes like negotiation, mediation and arbitration. They are often more informal than the court process.

Legal advice

If the other party will not settle the claim, then the aggrieved person must decide whether they are prepared to take the matter further. The most common next stage is to obtain legal advice and perhaps have a solicitor write to the other person. This may lead to a 'bargaining' situation where a series of letters is written between the parties and eventually a compromise is reached. However, if, after all this, the other side refuses to pay the debt or compensation or whatever else is claimed,

then the aggrieved person must decide if the matter is worth pursuing any further. This may involve starting a court case or using an alternative form of dispute resolution (ADR); these alternatives are considered in the next chapter.

Going to court

Taking a case to court can be an expensive exercise, even if you decide to 'do it yourself' and not use a lawyer. There will be a court fee based on the type and size of the claim. This can be claimed back from the other party if you win the case, but there is always the risk that you will lose the case and have to pay the other side's costs. Even if you win, your problems may not be over as the other person may not have enough money to pay the claim and refund your costs. If the case is complicated it could take years to complete and may cost thousands of pounds.

Given these problems, it is not surprising that many people who believe they have a good claim decide not to take court action.

Starting a court case does not mean that it will actually go to court. The vast majority of cases are settled out of court, so that fewer than five per cent of all cases started in the civil courts get as far as a court hearing. This is because the dispute is a private one between the parties involved and they can settle their own dispute at any time, even after court proceedings have been started.

2.2 Starting a court case

The civil justice system was reformed in 1999 following the Woolf Report (see section 2.6).

Parties are encouraged to give information to each other, in an attempt to prevent the need for so many court cases to be started. So, before a claim is issued, especially in personal injury cases, a pre-action 'protocol' should be followed. This is a list of things to be done. If the parties do not follow the procedure and give the required information to the other party, they may be liable for certain costs if they then make a court claim.

The information is usually in a letter explaining brief details of how the claim arises; why it is claimed that the other party is at fault; details of injury or other damage; and any other relevant matters. The defendant is then given three months to investigate the claim and must then reply, setting out if liability is admitted or if it is denied, with the reasons for the denial.

If expert evidence is going to be needed, then the parties should try to agree to use one expert. This should lead to many claims being settled, but there will still be some which need to go to court.

2.2.1 Which court to use

Where the decision is made to go to court, then the first problem is which court to use. The two courts which hear civil cases are:

- the County Court and
- the High Court.

For cases where the claim is for £25,000 or less, the case must be started in the County Court. For larger claims the claimant can usually choose to start a case in either the County Court or the High Court. However, there are some restrictions. These are that:

- personal injury cases for less than £50,000 must be started in the County Court, and
- all defamation actions must be started in the High Court.

So, for most cases over £25,000 a claimant will be able to choose the most convenient court for starting the case. The main points to consider in making the decision are the amount that is being claimed and whether the case is likely to raise a complex issue of law.

Jurisdiction

The type of case a court deals with is referred to as the jurisdiction of the court. The jurisdiction of the County Court is very wide, as it can hear cases of any amount. Also, it can hear claims about almost every type of civil law. This means it can hear contract cases, tort cases and land law cases (such as a claim for unpaid rent or a claim to get possession of land back from a tenant). The court can also deal with family cases, especially divorce and any related disputes about custody of the children, property or maintenance. Jurisdiction of the County Court is dealt with further in section 2.4.

If the High Court is chosen, then there is the question of which division to use. There are three divisions dealing with different types of law. These are:

- the Queen's Bench Division
- the Chancery Division and
- the Family Division.

The jurisdiction of the three divisions of the High Court is explained at section 2.5. The jurisdiction of all the courts is also shown in Figure 2.3.

2.2.2 Issuing a claim

If you are using the County Court, then you can choose to issue the claim in any of the 220 or so County Courts in the country. If you are using the High Court, then you can go to one of the 20 District Registries or the main court in London.

You need a claim form called 'N1' (see Figure 2.1). The court office will give you notes explaining how to fill in the form.

Court staff can help to make sure that you have filled in the claim form properly, or you may receive help from advice centres or a Citizens' Advice Bureau. To issue the claim, the completed form must be taken to the court office. A court fee for issuing the claim has to be paid. This fee varies according to how much the claim is for.

At the beginning of 2013 the fee for a claim of up to £300 was £35, with the maximum fee for a small claim (under £5,000) being £120. At the top end of the scale, claims of over £300,000 had a fee of £1,670.

Claim Form

In the

	for court use only
Claim No.	
Issue date	

Claimant

Defendant(s)

SEAL

Brief details of claim

Value

Defendant's name and address

	£
Amount claimed	
Court fee	
Solicitor's costs	
Total amount	

The court office at

is open between 10am and 4pm Monday to Friday. When corresponding with the court, please address forms or letters to the Court Manager and quote the claim number.

NI Claim form (CPR Part 7) (01.02)

Printed on behalf of The Court Service

Claim No.

Does, or will, your claim include any issues under the Human Rights Act 1998? ☐ Yes ☐ No

Particulars of Claim (attached)(to follow)

Statement of Truth
*(I believe)(The Claimant believes) that the facts stated in these particulars of claim are true.
*I am duly authorised by the claimant to sign this statement

Full name _____

Name of claimant's solicitor's firm _____

signed_____ position or office held _____
*(Claimant)(Litigation friend)(Claimant's solicitor)   (if signing on behalf of firm or company)

*delete as appropriate

Claimant's or claimant's solicitor's address to which documents or payments should be sent if different from overleaf including (if appropriate) details of DX, fax or e-mail.

Figure 2.1 Form N1

Internet Research

Look up court forms such as N1 on the website **www.courtservice.gov.uk**.

Also use that website to find guidance on starting cases in the County Court.

2.2.3 Defending a claim

When the defendant receives the claim form there are several routes which can be taken. They may admit the claim and pay the full amount. Where this happens, the case ends; the claimant has achieved what was wanted.

In other cases the defendant may dispute the claim. If the defendant wishes to defend the claim, he must send either an acknowledgement of service (Form N9) or a defence to the court within 14 days of receiving the claim. If only an acknowledgement of service is sent, then the defendant has an extra 14 days in which to serve the defence.

If the defendant does not do either of these things, then the claimant can ask the court to make an order that the defendant pays the money and costs claimed. This is called an order in default.

Self-Test Questions

1   What is normally tried instead of starting a civil court case?
2   What problems are there in taking a civil case to court?
3   What is a pre-action protocol?
4   Which are the two courts that hear civil cases?
5   How is a claim issued in a civil case?

2.2.4 The three tracks

Once a claim is defended, the court will allocate the case to the most suitable 'track' or way of dealing with the case. The decision on which track should be used is made by the District Judge in the County Court or the Master (a procedural judge) in the High Court. The tracks are:

1. **The small claims track**
    This is normally used for disputes under £5,000, except for personal injury cases and housing cases where the limit is usually £1,000.

2. **The fast track**
    This is used for straightforward disputes of £5,000–£25,000.

3. **The multi-track**
    This is for cases over £25,000 or for complex cases under this amount.

Note that the limit for small claims is likely to be increased to at least £10,000.

Allocation questionnaire

To help the judge consider to which track a claim should be allocated, both parties are sent an allocation questionnaire. This asks which track the parties think is suitable, and also for details of the case. The judge uses this information to decide which track is the most suitable.

Transfer of cases

For claims over £25,000 there may also be a decision to transfer the case from the County Court to the High Court or *vice versa*. Usually, claims of less than £25,000 are tried in the County Court, while claims for between £25,000 and £50,000 are generally tried in the court in which the proceedings were started. Claims for over £50,000 are usually tried in the High Court. This is shown in Figure 2.2.

We will now go on to consider the different courts and tracks.

2.3 Small claims

Clearly, it is important to have a relatively cheap and simple way of making a claim for a small amount of money, otherwise the costs of the action will be far more than the amount in dispute. For that reason, the small claims

Value of claim	Court in which case will usually be tried
Under £5,000	County Court small claims procedure
£5,000–£25,000	County Court fast-track procedure
£25,000–£50,000	Either High Court or County Court multi-track procedure
Over £50,000	High Court multi-track procedure

Figure 2.2 Summary of where cases are likely to be tried

procedure was started in 1973, and originally only claims of up to £75 could be made there. The limit has since been raised several times, especially in 1991 when the limit was increased to £1,000; in 1996, after the Woolf Report, the limit was increased to £3,000; and in 1999 it became £5,000. This is the current limit, but this is likely to be increased to at least £10,000 in the near future.

2.3.1 Small claims procedure

People are encouraged to take their own case so that costs are kept low. However, under the rules, small claims cases are started in the same way as all other cases. The use of lawyers is discouraged. It is possible to have a lawyer to represent you at a small claims hearing, but the winner cannot claim the costs of using a lawyer from the losing party.

Small claims cases are usually heard in private, but they can be heard in an ordinary court. The procedure allows the District Judge to be flexible in the way he hears the case. District Judges are encouraged to be more inquisitorial and are given training in how to handle small claims cases, so that they will take an active part in the proceedings, asking questions and making sure that both parties explain all their important points.

2.3.2 Advantages of small claims

1. The cost of taking proceedings is low, especially for claims under £1,000.
2. If you lose, you will not have to pay the other person's lawyers' costs.
3. People do not have to use lawyers, but can take the case themselves.

4. The procedure is quicker than for other cases.
5. The District Judge should help the parties to explain their case.

2.3.3 Disadvantages of small claims

1. Legal funding for paying for a lawyer is not available, though it may be possible to fund the case through a 'no win, no fee' arrangement (see Chapter 13).
2. Where the other side is a business, they are more likely to use a lawyer. This can put an unrepresented claimant at a disadvantage.
3. Research by John Baldwin has shown that District Judges are not always very helpful to unrepresented claimants.
4. Even when you win your case, it does not mean that you will get your money from the defendant. Only about 60 per cent of successful claimants actually received all the money awarded by the court.

Self-Test Questions

1 What is the lowest amount for which a claim can be started in the High Court?
2 In which court must claims for personal injury of less than £50,000 be started?
3 What are the three tracks and the normal financial limits on cases they hear?
4 Give three advantages of the small claims procedure.
5 Give three disadvantages of the small claims procedure.

2.4 County Court

There are about 220 County Courts; most major towns have a court. The courts can try nearly all civil cases. The main types of cases are:

- all contract and tort claims
- all cases for the recovery of land
- disputes over partnerships, trusts and inheritance up to a value of £30,000
- divorce cases.

Note that the Crime and Courts Bill 2012–13 has provision to create a new separate Family Court. All family matters currently dealt with in the County Court will be eventually transferred to this new court.

The County Court can try small claims, fast-track and multi-track cases. Its workload is much greater than that of the High Court. About two million cases are started in the County Courts each year.

Despite the large number of cases started, only a small number of cases actually proceed to a trial. Most cases settle, especially those involving claims in contract or tort. This means that the parties come to an agreement, so there is no need for the case to continue.

Cases will nearly always be heard in open court and members of the public are entitled to attend. The exceptions to this are cases involving family matters, for example maintenance hearings, and proceedings under the Children Act 1989, which are heard in private. The whole hearing is more formal and many claimants and defendants will be represented, usually by a solicitor but sometimes by a barrister.

The winner of a case may claim costs, including the cost of legal representation. All this makes a case in the County Court much more expensive than one in the small claims track.

Cases are usually heard by Circuit Judges, although District Judges hear lower-value cases. In rare cases it is possible for a jury of eight to sit with the judge. (For further information on the use of juries in civil cases, see Chapter 12.)

2.4.1 Fast-track cases

Claims between £5,000 and £25,000 needed a faster and cheaper method of being dealt with. In 1998, before the Woolf reforms, the statistics showed that the average wait for cases in the County Court was 85 weeks from the issue of the claim to the actual hearing in court. As well as delay, cases were too expensive. Indeed, the Woolf Report found that the costs of cases were often higher than the amount claimed.

'Fast track' means that the court will set down a very strict timetable for the pre-trial matters. This is aimed at preventing one or both sides from wasting time and running up unnecessary costs. Once a case is set down for hearing, the aim is to have the case heard within 30 weeks. After 1999, there was a great improvement, with cases heard more quickly. However, after reaching a low of 48 weeks' waiting time in 2009, the average wait in 2011 for a hearing increased to 56 weeks.

The actual trial will usually be heard by a District Judge and take place in open court with a more formal procedure than for small claims. In order to speed up the trial itself, the hearing is limited to a maximum of one day and the number of expert witnesses restricted, with usually only one expert being allowed.

The Government's consultation paper, *Solving Disputes in the County Court* (2011) pointed out that for lower level claims, the cost of a case was often greater than the amount claimed.

2.4.2 Multi-track cases

Claims for more than £25,000 are usually allocated to the multi-track. If the case was started in a County Court then it is likely to be tried there, though it can be sent to the High Court. The case will be heard by a Circuit Judge who will also be expected to 'manage' the case from the moment it is allocated to the multi-track route. The judge can set timetables and also ask the parties to try an alternative method of dispute resolution in an effort to avoid a full court hearing.

2.5 High Court

The High Court is based in London but also has judges sitting at 26 towns and cities throughout England and Wales. It has the power to hear any civil case and has three divisions, each of which specialises in hearing certain types of case. These divisions are the Queen's Bench Division, the Chancery Division and the Family Division.

2.5.1 Queen's Bench Division

The President of the Queen's Bench Division is the Lord Chief Justice and there are about 70 judges sitting in the division. It deals with contract and tort cases where the amount claimed is over £50,000, though, as seen earlier in this chapter, a claimant can start an action for any amount of £25,000 and above. Only multi-track cases are dealt with in the High Court.

Usually cases are tried by a single judge but there is a right to jury trial for fraud, libel, slander, malicious prosecution and false imprisonment

The Royal Courts of Justice

cases. When a jury is used there will be 12 members.

Cases in the High Court are expensive and can take a long time. The average time between issuing a claim and the trial is about three years. Cases are expensive because of court fees and the need to use lawyers. It can cost over £1,000 to issue a claim in the High Court and another £1,000 to set the case down for a hearing.

Judicial review

The Queen's Bench Division also has important supervisory functions over inferior courts and other bodies with decision-making powers, such as Government Ministers or local councils. Judicial review is concerned with whether a decision-making process has been carried out legally, as distinct from the merits of the decision in question.

2.5.2 Chancery Division

The Chancellor of the High Court is technically the head of the division. There are about 17 High Court judges assisting in the division. The main business of this division involves disputes concerned with such matters as insolvency, for both companies and individuals, the enforcement of mortgages, disputes relating to trust property, copyright and patents, intellectual property matters and contested probate actions. There is also a special Companies Court in the division which deals mainly with winding up companies.

Juries are never used in the Chancery Division and cases are heard by a single judge. The criticisms of cost and delay which apply to the Queen's Bench Division apply equally to the Chancery Division.

2.5.3 Family Division

The head of this division is the President, and 17 High Court judges are assigned to the division. It has jurisdiction to hear wardship cases and all cases relating to children under the Children

Key facts

County Court	**Financial limits**	• small claims – usually under £5,000 (likely to be increased to £10,000) • fast-track – between £5,000 and £25,000 • multi track – usually under £50,000 but parties can agree to a claim for any amount being heard in County Court.
	Types of case	• contract claims, eg for failure to pay agreed amount • tort claims, eg personal injury caused through negligence • land law cases, especially for recovery of possession of land • disputes over partnerships, trusts and inheritance up to a value of £30,000. • divorce cases.
High Court	**Financial limits**	• only claims over £25,000 • personal injury cases over £50,000 • any other multi-track claim.
	The three divisions	**Queen's Bench Division** • mainly contract and tort cases • applications for judicial review. **Chancery Division** • insolvency, for both companies and individuals • enforcement of mortgages • disputes relating to trust property • copyright and patents • intellectual property matters • contested probate cases. **Family Division** • wardship cases • all cases relating to children under the Children Act 1989 • declarations of nullity of marriage • grants probate in non-contested probate cases.

Figure 2.3 Key facts chart on the jurisdiction of the County Court and High Court

Act 1989. It also deals with other matters regarding the family, such as declarations of nullity of marriage, and grants probate in non-contentious probate cases.

Cases are heard by a single judge and, although juries were once used to decide defended divorce cases, they are not now used in this division.

Note that the Crime and Courts Bill 2012–13 has provision to create a new, separate Family Court. All family matters currently dealt with in the Family Division will be eventually transferred to this new court.

Self-Test Questions

1 What are the monetary limits on a fast-track claim?
2 In which court will fast-track cases be dealt with?
3 How does the court try to make sure that fast-track cases proceed quickly?
4 In which courts can multi-track cases be dealt with?
5 What are the three divisions of the High Court?

Activity

Advise the people in the following situations:

1. Sarah has bought a combined TV and DVD player costing £270 from a local electrical superstore. The DVD player has never worked properly, but the store has refused to replace it or to refund the purchase price to Sarah. She wishes to claim against the store. Advise her as to which court to start the case in and how she should go about this. Also explain to her the way in which the case will be dealt with if the store defends it and there is a court hearing.

2. Thomas has been badly injured at work and alleges that the injuries were the result of his employer's failure to take proper safety precautions. He has been advised that his claim is likely to be worth £200,000. Advise him as to which court or courts could hear his case.

3. Imran wishes to start an action for defamation against a national newspaper. Advise him as to which court he should use and explain to him who tries defamation cases.

2.6 The Woolf reforms

The present system of civil justice is based on the reforms recommended by Lord Woolf in his report *Access to Justice* (1996).

In 1995 Lord Woolf stated that a civil justice system should:

- be just in the results it delivers
- be fair in the way it treats litigants
- offer appropriate procedures at a reasonable cost
- deal with cases at a reasonable speed
- be understandable to those who use it
- provide as much certainty as the nature of particular cases allows
- be effective, adequately resourced and organised.

The Report found that virtually none of these points was being achieved in the civil courts, and criticised the system for being unequal, expensive, slow, uncertain and complicated. The report contained 303 recommendations. The most important ones proposed were:

- extending small claims up to £3,000 (brought in at £5,000)
- a fast track for straightforward cases up to £10,000 (brought in at £15,000 and now £25,000)
- a multi-track for cases over £10,000, with capping of costs
- encouraging the use of alternative dispute resolution
- giving judges more responsibility for managing cases
- more use of information technology
- simplifying documents and procedures and having a single set of rules governing proceedings in both the High Court and the County Court
- shorter timetables for cases to reach court and for lengths of trials.

2.6.1 The Civil Procedure Rules

From 26 April 1999, new Civil Procedure Rules (CPR) were brought into effect. These use much simpler language than previous rules. They also changed the vocabulary used in court cases. For example, anyone starting a civil case is now called the 'claimant'; previously the term used in most cases was the 'plaintiff'. The document used to start cases is a 'claim form', rather than a 'writ' or a 'summons'. The new terms are used in this book, but the old terms still appear in reports of cases decided before April 1999.

Overriding objective

Rule 1.1 of the Civil Procedure Rules states that the overriding objective is to enable the court to deal with cases justly. This means that courts should try to:

- ensure that the parties in any case are on an equal footing
- save expense

- deal with cases in a way which is proportionate to:
  - the amount involved (that is avoid the costs of the case being more than the amount claimed)
  - the importance of the case (for example, is there a major point of law involved?)
  - the complexity of the issues in the case
- ensure that the case is dealt with quickly and fairly
- allocate an appropriate share of the court's resources (so smaller claims do not take up more time than they justify).

Judicial management of cases

Judges have more control over proceedings than previously. They can set timetables and make sure that the parties do not drag out a case unnecessarily. Rule 1.4 of the Civil Procedure Rules explains that as well as fixing timetables, 'active case management' by judges includes:

- identifying the issues at an early stage
- deciding which issues need investigation and trial
- encouraging the parties to use alternative dispute resolution if this is appropriate
- dealing with any procedural steps without the need for the parties to attend court
- giving directions to ensure that the trial of a case proceeds quickly and efficiently.

2.6.2 The effects of the Woolf reforms

Research into the effect of the Woolf reforms has found that:

- the culture of litigation has changed for the better, with cooperation between the parties improving
- delay between issuing a claim and the court hearing has been reduced, but pre-action protocols and other pre-issue work mean that, overall, delay has not really improved
- case management conferences are felt to be one of the major successes of the CPR
- there is a more uniform procedure across the country

- there is a very high rate of settlement, often more than 60 per cent and in some courts over 80 per cent
- there has been little or no increase in ADR and out of court mediation: in practice judges rarely stay cases for mediation, and ADR has not become incorporated into the court process
- costs have increased overall as a result of being front-loaded. In particular, costs in fast-track cases are disproportionate
- the courts are still under-resourced and the IT systems 'primitive' compared with those used by practitioners.

In 2011, the Government in their consultation paper, *Solving Disputes in the County Court,* pointed out that it was 15 years since the Woolf Report and the system has not kept pace with the 'major economic and social shifts that have taken place since'. They believe that the system needs to focus more on dispute resolution and debt recovery, rather than the ideals of 'justice'. In particular, they pointed out that the costs of taking a case to court are often more than the amount claimed. The ideal is that disputes:

 should be resolved in the most appropriate forum, so that processes and costs are commensurate with the complexity of the issues involved.

They proposed a range of options to achieve this, including:

- fixed costs (already used for traffic accidents under £10,000) to be extended to other personal injury claims for up to £25,000 or even £50,000
- requiring all cases below the small claims limit to have attempted settlement by mediation, before being considered for a hearing
- introducing mediation information/assessment sessions for claims above the small claims limit to try to divert more cases into alternative dispute resolution
- increasing the upper level for small claims to at least £10,000.

Key facts

Courts dealing with civil cases	● County Court ● High Court
Different tracks for claims	● small claims ● fast track ● multi-track
Problems of civil cases	● cost ● delay ● complexity
1999 reforms	● encourage use of ADR ● simpler forms and language ● increase small claims limit to £5,000 ● fast track for claims between £5,000 and £15,000 (now £25,000) ● judges responsible for case management ● strict timetables
Effect of 1999 reforms	● cases settle earlier ● initial costs are high ● delays are getting shorter ● courts strict on timetables

Figure 2.4 Key facts chart on civil justice

Self-Test Questions

1 What did Lord Woolf state should be the ideals for a civil justice system?
2 What were the problems that the Woolf Report identified in the civil court system?
3 What is the overriding objective of the Civil Procedure Rules?
4 Give two positive factors that the Woolf reforms have brought.
5 Give two problems that still exist in the civil court system.

Exam tips

Many candidates avoid questions on the civil courts, mistakenly believing them to be difficult. If you are good at learning figures and are the sort of student who can visualise how the courts work then this could be the question for you! You need to be confident with the structure of the civil courts, including the financial limits found in each court, and you also need to be able to describe the track system clearly. This type of question will also require you to discuss the civil justice system so you need to have some things which are good and bad at your fingertips.

The question might focus on a particular court or it might deal with more general areas such as the effectiveness of the current system or the problems which exist. It's a good idea to think about all these issues before you get to the exam room – this makes for clearer and more confident analysis which will always impress an examiner.

Be aware that a question might cover the civil courts and appeals, so do not lose easy marks by not learning both parts of this topic.

2.7 Appellate courts

These are courts which hear appeals from lower courts. The main appellate courts are the Divisional Courts, the Court of Appeal and the Supreme Court.

2.7.1 Divisional Courts

Each division of the High Court has what is called a Divisional Court which has the power to hear appeals from inferior courts and tribunals. For most appeals, two or three of the judges from the particular division will sit together to hear the case.

Queen's Bench Divisional Court

The most important of the Divisional Courts is the Queen's Bench Divisional Court. This has two main functions:

1. It hears appeals by way of case stated from criminal cases decided in the Magistrates' Court. This is dealt with more fully in Chapter 7.

2. It has supervisory powers over inferior courts and tribunals and also over the actions and decisions of public bodies and Government Ministers. This process is known as 'judicial review' and for this purpose the court has the power to make what are called 'prerogative orders'. These orders are a mandatory order, which is a command to perform a duty; a prohibition order, which is an order to prevent an inferior court from hearing a case which it has no power to deal with; and a quashing

The Supreme Court

order, which removes the decision to the Queen's Bench Division so that its legality can be enquired into and the decision quashed if it is found to be invalid.

The Queen's Bench Divisional Court also hears applications for *habeas corpus* from those who allege that they are being unlawfully detained. This is an important way of protecting the right to liberty.

2.7.2 Court of Appeal (Civil Division)

The Court of Appeal has two divisions: civil and criminal. There are 38 Lords Justices of Appeal and each division is presided over by its own head. The Court of Appeal (Civil Division) is the main appellate court for civil cases and it is headed by the Master of the Rolls.

The Court of Appeal (Civil Division) mainly hears appeals from the following courts:

- all three divisions of the High Court
- the County Court for multi-track cases
- the Upper Tier Tribunal.

Permission to appeal

Permission to appeal is required in most cases. It can be granted by the lower court where the decision was made, or by the Court of Appeal. Permission to appeal will only be granted where the court considers that an appeal would have a real prospect of success or that there was some other compelling reason why the appeal should be heard.

Permission to appeal is not required in cases where the liberty of the individual is in issue; for example in an appeal against a committal to prison for breaking an injunction.

2.7.3 Supreme Court

This is the final court of appeal in the English legal system. It hears appeals from:

- the Court of Appeal
- the Divisional Courts

- the High Court under the 'leapfrog' provisions – this is very rare (see section 2.8.2).

Appeals are heard by the Justices of the Supreme Court. They have to sit as an uneven number panel, so there can be three, five, seven or even nine judges sitting to hear an appeal.

Prior to 2009, the final court of appeal was the House of Lords. So, when looking at judgments in cases before October 2009, they will have been decided by the House of Lords.

Permission to appeal

On an appeal from the Court of Appeal or the Divisional Courts, it is necessary to be given permission to appeal to the Supreme Court. This permission can be given by either the Supreme Court or the lower court. It is difficult to get leave to appeal, with only about one in three cases being granted leave.

In leapfrog cases from the High Court, not only must the Supreme Court give permission to appeal, but the trial judge must also grant a certificate of satisfaction. This will be done only if the case involves a point of law of general public importance which *either* involves the interpretation of a statute *or* is one where the trial judge is bound by a previous decision. Leapfrog appeals are rare, with permission to appeal being asked for in only two or three cases each year.

The number of appeals heard by the Supreme Court is small; usually about 60 cases per year involving civil law, with about three-quarters of these involving a question of statutory interpretation.

@ Internet Research

Use the internet to look up cases in which there has been an appeal to the Supreme Court and which are waiting for the appeal to be heard. This can be found on **www.supremecourt.gov.uk**.

2.8 Appeal routes in civil cases

Although the detail on the appellate courts is given in section 2.7, it is probably helpful to have a list of the normal appeal routes from both the County Court and the High Court.

2.8.1 Appeals from the County Court

The normal routes of appeal from a decision in the County Court are as follows:

- for fast-track cases dealt with by a District Judge, the appeal is heard by a Circuit Judge
- for fast-track cases dealt with by a Circuit Judge, the appeal is heard by a High Court Judge
- for final decisions in multi-track cases heard in the County Court (whether by a Circuit Judge or by a District Judge), the right of appeal is to the Court of Appeal.

Appeals from small claims

Since October 2000 appeals against decisions in small claims cases have been possible. This right of appeal was introduced in order to comply with Art 6 (the right to a fair trial) of the European Convention on Human Rights. The appeal routes are the same as for fast-track cases. This means that the appeal is to the next judge up in the hierarchy, so if the case was tried by a District Judge the appeal is to a Circuit Judge; if the case was dealt with by a Circuit Judge then the appeal is to a High Court Judge.

Second appeals

In exceptional cases there is a possible further appeal to the Court of Appeal. However, this will only happen rarely, as s 55 of the Access to Justice Act 1999 states that:

 no appeal may be made to the Court of Appeal ... unless the Court of Appeal considers that

(a) the appeal would raise an important point of principle or practice, or

(b) there is some other compelling reason for the Court of Appeal to hear it.

These appeal routes are shown in Figure 2.5.

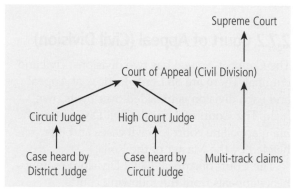

Figure 2.5 Appeal routes from the County Court

2.8.2 Appeals from the High Court

1. From a decision in the High Court the appeal usually goes to the Court of Appeal (Civil Division).

2. In rare cases there may be a 'leapfrog' appeal direct to the Supreme Court under the Administration of Justice Act 1969. Such an appeal must involve a point of law of general public importance which either concerns the interpretation of a statute or involves a binding precedent of the Court of Appeal or the Supreme Court which the trial judge must follow. In addition, the Supreme Court has to give permission to appeal.

These appeal routes are shown in Figure 2.6.

2.8.3 Further appeals

From a decision of the Court of Appeal there is a further appeal to the Supreme Court, but only if the Supreme Court or Court of Appeal gives

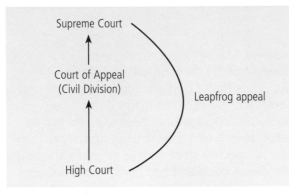

Figure 2.6 Appeal routes from the High Court

permission to appeal. Also note that if a point of European law is involved, the case may be referred to the European Court of Justice under Art 267 of the Treaty of the Functioning of the European Union. Such a referral can be made by any English court.

2.9 Tribunals

Tribunals operate alongside the court system and have become an important part of the legal system. Many tribunals were created in the second half of the twentieth century, with the development of the Welfare State. They were created in order to give people a method of enforcing their entitlement to certain social rights. However, unlike alternative dispute resolution where the parties decide not to use the courts, the parties in tribunal cases cannot go to court to resolve their dispute. The tribunal must be used instead of court proceedings.

There is now a unified structure for tribunals, with a First-tier Tribunal to hear cases at first instance and an Upper Tribunal to hear appeals. The First-tier Tribunal has seven chambers (divisions) and deals with about 300,000 cases each year. It has nearly 200 judges and 3,600 lay members.

Self-Test Questions

1   To where can an appeal in a small claim be made?

2   To where can an appeal in a multi-track case be made?

3   From which courts does the Court of Appeal (Civil Division) hear appeals?

4   Which is the final court of appeal?

5   What is a 'leap-frog' appeal?

Examination Questions

(a) Describe the jurisdiction of the civil courts and the three track system at first instance.
18 marks

(b) Discuss whether the track system and other recent reforms have improved the running of the civil courts.
12 marks

OCR G151 June 2012

Exam tips

Questions about civil appeals are not difficult as long as you have a very clear sense of the route a case will take and the detail at each stage. Clarity is important and drawing a diagram as part of your answer is perfectly acceptable (to obtain good marks, the diagram will need to be detailed). If you are not good at being precise in your explanation then perhaps this is not the best type of question for you.

Firstly, you will be required to give a clear, accurate and relevant description of factual material. The key word is 'relevant' – for example, if the question asks you to write about the High Court and higher appellate courts you will not gain marks if you write about the County Court. Secondly, you will be asked to look at a specific issue from more than one perspective so be sure to do that – there are always good and bad points and when you are revising it's a good idea to put these points into columns or boxes in your notes to help you recall them more easily.

Chapter 3

Alternative methods of dispute resolution

I n Chapter 2 we saw that using the courts to resolve disputes can be costly, in terms of both money and time. It can also be traumatic for the individuals involved and may not lead to the most satisfactory outcome for the case. An additional problem is that court proceedings are usually open to the public and the press, so there is nothing to stop the details of the case being published in local or national newspapers. It is not surprising, therefore, that people and businesses are increasingly seeking other methods of resolving their disputes. Alternative methods are referred to as 'ADR', which stands for 'Alternative Dispute Resolution', and include any method of resolving a dispute without resorting to using the courts. There are many different methods which can be used, ranging from very informal negotiations between the parties, to a comparatively formal commercial arbitration hearing.

3.1 Negotiation

Anyone who has a dispute with another person can always try to resolve it by negotiating directly with them. This has the advantage of being completely private, and is also the quickest and cheapest method of settling a dispute. If the parties cannot come to an agreement, they may decide to take the step of instructing solicitors, and those solicitors will usually try to negotiate a settlement. In fact, even when court proceedings have been commenced, the lawyers for the parties will often continue to negotiate on behalf of their clients, and this is reflected in the high number of cases which are settled out of court. Once lawyers are involved, there will be a cost element – clearly, the longer negotiations go on, the higher the costs will be. One of the worrying aspects is the number of cases that drag on for years, only to end in an agreed settlement literally 'at the door of the court' on the morning that the trial is due to start. Alternative dispute resolution methods aim to avoid this situation.

To encourage more use of ADR, the judges in the civil courts can ask the parties to consider using an alternative method.

3.2 Mediation

This is where a neutral mediator helps the parties to reach a compromise solution. The role of a mediator is to consult with each party and see how much common ground there is between them. He will explore the position with each party, looking at their needs and carrying offers to and fro, while keeping confidentiality. A mediator will not usually tell the parties his own views of the merits of the dispute; it is part of the job to act as a 'facilitator', so that an agreement is reached by the parties. However, a mediator can be asked for an opinion of the merits, and in this case the mediation becomes more of an evaluation exercise, which again aims at ending the dispute.

Mediation is only suitable if there is some hope that the parties can cooperate. Companies who are used to negotiating contracts with each other are most likely to benefit from this approach. Mediation can also take different forms, and the parties will choose the exact method they want. The important point in mediation is that the parties are in control: they make the decisions.

3.2.1 Formalised settlement conference

This is a more formal method of approaching mediation. It involves a 'mini-trial' where each side presents its case to a panel composed of a decision-making executive from each party, and a neutral party. Once all the submissions have been made, the executives, with the help of the neutral adviser, will evaluate the two sides' positions and try to come to an agreement. If the executives cannot agree, the neutral adviser will act as a mediator between them. Even if the whole matter is not resolved, this type of procedure may be able to narrow down the issues so that if the case does go to court, it will not take so long.

3.2.2 Mediation services

There are a growing number of commercial mediation services. One of the main ones is the Centre for Dispute Resolution which was set up in London in 1991. It has many important companies as members including almost all of the big London law firms. Businesses say that using the Centre to resolve disputes has saved several thousands of pounds in court costs. The typical cost of a mediator is about £1,000 to £1,500 a day. This compares with potential litigation costs which are frequently over £100,000 and sometimes may even come to more than £1 million, especially in major commercial cases.

There are also mediation services aimed at resolving smaller disputes, for example those between neighbours. An example of such a service is the West Kent Independent Mediation Service. This offers a free service that will try to help resolve disagreements between neighbours arising from such matters as noise, car-parking, dogs or boundary fence disputes. The Service is run by trained volunteers who will not take sides or make judgements on the rights and wrongs of an issue. They will usually visit the party who has made the complaint to hear their side of the matter; then, if that party agrees, they will ask to visit the other person and get their point of view. Finally, if both parties are willing, the mediator arranges a meeting between them in a neutral place. The parties are in control and can withdraw from the mediation process at any time.

The latest idea is Online Dispute Resolution. There are an increasing number of websites offering this, such as **www.e-mediator.co.uk** and **www.mediate.com/odr**.

3.2.3 Advantages of mediation

An advantage of mediation and mini-trials is that the decision need not be a strictly legal one sticking to the letter of the law: it is more likely to be based on commercial commonsense and compromise. The method also makes it easier for companies to continue to do business with each other in the future, and it may include agreements about the conduct of future business between the parties. This is something that cannot happen if the court gives judgment, as the court is only concerned with the present dispute.

Mediation avoids the adversarial conflict of the court room and the winner/loser result of court proceedings. It has been said that with mediation, everyone wins.

A high number of cases are resolved through mediation. The Centre for Dispute Resolution claims that over 80 per cent of cases in which it is asked to act are settled. It has also been found that even if the actual mediation session did not resolve the dispute, the parties were more likely to settle the case without going to court than in non-mediated cases. There is also the possibility that the issues may at least have been clarified, and so any court hearing will be shorter than if mediation had not been attempted.

3.2.4 Disadvantages of mediation

The main disadvantage of using mediation services is that there is no guarantee the matter will be resolved, and it will then be necessary to go to court after the failed attempt at mediation. In such situations there is additional cost and delay to resolution.

Another problem is that successful mediation requires a skilled mediator with 'natural talent, honed skills and accumulated experience'. If these qualities are not present, mediation can become a bullying exercise in which the weaker party may be forced into a settlement. This was recognised by one mediator who said:

 Leaning on people is the only way that you will get a settlement. If you lean on two halves of a see-saw it is usually the weaker half that will break and that is where you should apply your effort.

A final disadvantage is that amounts paid in mediated settlements are often lower than the amounts agreed in other settlements, and considerably lower than amounts awarded by the courts.

3.3 Conciliation

Conciliation is similar to mediation in that a neutral third party helps to resolve the dispute, but the main difference is that the conciliator will usually play a more active role. He will be expected to suggest grounds for compromise, and the possible basis for a settlement. In industrial disputes the Advisory Conciliation and Arbitration Service (ACAS) can give an impartial opinion on the legal position. As with mediation, conciliation does not necessarily lead to a resolution, and it may be necessary to continue with a court action.

Self-Test Questions

1 Why is an alternative form of dispute resolution often preferable to going to court?
2 Explain what is meant by negotiation.
3 Give two advantages of negotiation rather than taking a court case.
4 What is the role of a mediator?
5 Give an example of a mediation service.
6 Explain two advantages of mediation.
7 Explain two disadvantages of mediation.
8 How does the role of a conciliator differ from that of a mediator?

3.4 Arbitration

The word 'arbitration' is used to cover two quite different processes. The first is where the courts use a more informal procedure to hear cases; this is the way in which proceedings in the Commercial Court of the Queen's Bench Division are described. The second meaning of the word 'arbitration' is where the parties agree to submit their claims to private arbitration; this is the type of arbitration that is relevant to alternative dispute resolution, as it is another way of resolving a dispute without the need for a court case.

Negotiation	Parties themselves
Mediation	Parties with help of neutral third party
Conciliation	Parties with help of neutral third party who plays an active role in suggesting a solution
Arbitration	Parties agree to let third party make a binding decision
Litigation	Parties go to court and a judge decides the case

Figure 3.1 Methods of dispute resolution

Private arbitration is now governed by the Arbitration Act 1996, and s 1 of that Act sets out the principles behind it. This says that:

 (a) the object of arbitration is to obtain the fair resolution of disputes by an impartial tribunal without unnecessary delay or expense;

(b) the parties should be free to agree how their disputes are resolved, subject only to such safeguards as are necessary in the public interest.

So, arbitration is the voluntary submission by the parties, of their dispute, to the judgment of some person other than a judge. Such an agreement will usually be in writing, and indeed the Arbitration Act 1996 applies only to written arbitration agreements. The precise way in which the arbitration is carried out is left almost entirely to the parties' agreement.

3.4.1 The agreement to arbitrate

The agreement to go to arbitration can be made by the parties at any time. It can be before a dispute arises or when the dispute becomes apparent. Many commercial contracts include what is called a *Scott v Avery* clause, which is a clause where the parties in their original contract agree that in the event of a dispute arising between them, they will have that dispute settled by arbitration. Figure 3.2 shows a *Scott v Avery* clause in the author's contract for writing this book.

Where there is an arbitration agreement in a contract, the Arbitration Act 1996 states that the court will normally refuse to deal with any dispute; the matter must go to arbitration as agreed by the parties. However, the rules are different for consumer claims where the dispute is for an amount which can be dealt with in the small claims track. In such circumstances the consumer may choose whether to abide by the agreement to go to private arbitration, or to insist that the case be heard in the small claims track.

An agreement to go to arbitration can also be made after the dispute arises. Arbitration is becoming increasingly popular in commercial cases.

3.4.2 The arbitrator

Section 15 of the Arbitration Act 1996 states that the parties are free to agree on the number of arbitrators, so that a panel of two or three may be used or there may be a sole arbitrator. If the parties cannot agree on a number then the Act provides that only one arbitrator should be appointed. The Act also says that the parties are free to agree on the procedure for appointing an arbitrator. In fact most agreements to go to arbitration will either name an arbitrator or provide a method of choosing one, and in commercial contracts it is often provided that the president of the appropriate trade organisation will appoint the arbitrator.

There is also the Institute of Arbitrators which provides trained arbitrators for major disputes. In many cases the arbitrator will be someone who has expertise in the particular field involved in the dispute, but if the dispute involves a point of law,

---

Arbitration

24. If any difference shall arise between the PROPRIETOR and the PUBLISHERS touching the meaning of this Agreement or the rights and liabilities of the parties hereto, the same shall in the first instance be referred to the informal Disputes Settlement Scheme of the Publishers' Association, and failing agreed submission by both parties to such Scheme shall be referred to the arbitration of two persons (one to be named by each party) or their mutually agreed umpire in accordance with the provisions of the Arbitration Act 1996, or any amending or substituted statute for the time being in force.

Figure 3.2 Arbitration clause from author's contract

D Complaints

3. Disputes arising out of, or in connection with, this contract which cannot be amicably settled may (if you so wish) be referred to arbitration under a special scheme devised by arrangement with the Association of British Travel Agents (ABTA) but administered independently by the Chartered Institute of Arbitrators. The scheme provides for a simple and inexpensive method of Arbitration on documents alone, with restricted liability on you in respect of costs. The scheme does not apply to claims greater than £1,500 per person or £7,500 per booking form or to claims which are solely or mainly in respect of physical injury or illness or the consequences of such injury or illness. If you elect to use the scheme, written notice requesting arbitration must be made within nine months after the scheduled date of return from holiday.

Figure 3.3 Optional arbitration clause in a consumer contract

the parties may decide to appoint a lawyer. If there is no agreement on who or how to appoint, then, as a last resort, the court can be asked to appoint an appropriate arbitrator.

3.4.3 The arbitration hearing

The actual procedure is left to the agreement of the parties in each case, so that there are many forms of hearing. In some cases the parties may opt for a 'paper' arbitration, where the two sides put all the points they wish to raise into writing and submit this, together with any relevant documents, to the arbitrator. He will then read all the documents, and make his decision. Alternatively, the parties may send all these documents to the arbitrator, but before he makes his decision both parties will attend a hearing at which they make oral submissions to the arbitrator to support their case. Where necessary, witnesses can be called to give evidence. If witnesses are asked to give evidence orally then this will not normally be given on oath, that is, the person will not have to swear to tell the truth. However, if the parties wish, then the witness can be asked to give evidence on oath and the whole procedure will be very formal. If witnesses are called to give evidence, the Arbitration Act 1996 allows for the use of court procedures to ensure the attendance of those witnesses.

The date, time and place of the arbitration hearing are all matters for the parties to decide in consultation with the arbitrator. This gives a great degree of flexibility to the proceedings; the parties can chose what is most convenient for all the people concerned.

3.4.4 The award

The decision made by the arbitrator is called an 'award' and is binding on the parties. It can even be enforced through the courts if necessary. The decision is usually final, though it can be challenged in the courts on the grounds of serious irregularity in the proceedings or on a point of law (s 68, Arbitration Act 1996).

3.4.5 Advantages of arbitration

There are several advantages which largely arise from the fact that the parties have the freedom to make their own arbitration agreement, and decide exactly how formal or informal they wish it to be. The main advantages are:

- the parties may chose their own arbitrator, and can therefore decide whether the matter is best dealt with by a technical expert, a lawyer or a professional arbitrator
- if there is a question of quality this can be decided by an expert in the particular field, saving the expense of calling expert witnesses and the time that would be used in explaining all the technicalities to a judge
- the hearing time and place can be arranged to suit both parties
- the actual procedure used is flexible and the parties can choose that which is most suited to the situation; this will usually result in a more informal and relaxed hearing than in court

- the matter is dealt with in private and there will be no publicity
- the dispute will be resolved more quickly than through a court hearing
- arbitration proceedings are usually much cheaper than going to court
- the award is normally final and can be enforced through the courts.

3.4.6 Disadvantages of arbitration

There are some disadvantages of arbitration, especially where the parties are not on an equal footing as regards their ability to present their case. This is because legal aid is not available for arbitration and this may disadvantage an individual in a case against a business; if the case had gone to court, a person on a low income would have qualified for legal aid and so had the benefit of a lawyer to present their case. The other main disadvantages are that:

- an unexpected legal point may arise in the case which is not suitable for decision by a non-lawyer arbitrator
- if a professional arbitrator is used, his fees may be expensive
- it will also be expensive if the parties opt for a formal hearing, with witnesses giving evidence and lawyers representing both sides
- the rights of appeal are limited
- the delays for commercial and international arbitration may be nearly as great as those in the courts if a professional arbitrator and lawyers are used.

This problem of delay and expense has meant that arbitration has, to some extent, lost its popularity with companies as a method of dispute resolution. More and more businesses are turning to the alternatives offered by centres such as the Centre for Dispute Resolution or, in the case of international disputes, choosing to have the matter resolved in another country.

Prior to 1996, the law on arbitration had become complex, and the Arbitration Act 1996 was an attempt to improve the process. In general it can be said that certain types of dispute are suitable for arbitration, particularly commercial disagreements between two businesses where the parties have little hope of finding sufficient common ground to make mediation a realistic prospect, providing there is no major point of law involved.

Self-Test Questions

1 When can an agreement to arbitrate be made?
2 What is a *Scott v Avery* clause?
3 Who makes the decision in arbitration?
4 Explain three advantages of using arbitration to resolve a dispute.
5 Explain three disadvantages of using arbitration to resolve a dispute.

Activity

Find an arbitration clause in a consumer contract, for example for a package holiday or insurance or for a mobile phone.

 ## Internet Research

Look up websites for ADR organisations. Try:

www.adrgroup.co.uk
www.cedr.com.

Try to find what sort of dispute resolution services they offer.

Examination Questions

1(a) Describe and illustrate the different methods of Alternative Dispute Resolution available to deal with civil cases.   18 marks

1(b) Discuss the advantages of using Alternative Dispute Resolution to solve civil disputes rather than using the courts.

OCR G151 January 2013

Exam tips

This topic requires a good breadth of knowledge and suits candidates who do not enjoy learning a lot of very specific facts.

It is also a good topic to research on the internet and an examiner will always like to see one or two up-to-date examples of how ADR works; references to well chosen statistics will make your answer stand out from other candidates.

However, the broad range of this topic does have a downside in that you must commit to learning about all the different types of ADR. A question may require you to explain how all the different types of ADR work but then to discuss the relative merits of perhaps only two specific methods. This means you need to have comments about every type at your fingertips as the best way to score high marks is to make points that are specific to the type of ADR you have been asked to discuss rather than having to rely on very general comments relating to the topic as a whole.

Chapter 4

Police powers

Parliament grants special powers to the police to be used in certain circumstances when investigating crime. These powers include the right to stop suspects, to search them, to arrest and interview people, and to take fingerprints and DNA samples.

Without these powers it would be impossible to investigate crimes. However, it is important that people are not unnecessarily harassed by the police and that suspects are protected from unfair treatment. The law, therefore, also sets out certain rights that all suspects have.

Most of the police powers are set out in the Police and Criminal Evidence Act 1984. This is usually abbreviated to PACE. There are eight codes of practice giving more detail on the use of the various powers. These Codes are:

- Code A on stop and search powers
- Code B on powers to search premises and seize property
- Code C dealing with the detention and questioning of suspects
- Code D on the rules for identification procedures
- Code E on the tape-recording of interviews with suspects
- Code F on visual recording with sound of interviews (that is, videoing interviews)
- Code G on powers of arrest
- Code H on detention, treatment and questioning of those arrested under s 41 of the Terrorism Act 2000.

4.1 Powers to stop and search

The purpose of stop and search powers is to enable police officers to check out their suspicions without having to arrest the suspect. If officers find nothing through the stop and search, it has been a quick way of checking, rather than having to arrest the individual and take them to a police station.

4.1.1 Powers under PACE

Section 1 of PACE gives the police the right to stop and search people and vehicles in a public place. 'Public place' not only means the street, but also includes areas such as car parks. It can even include a garden if the police office has a good reason for believing that the person does not live at that address.

To stop and search under PACE, a police officer must have reasonable grounds for suspecting that the person is in possession of (or the vehicle contains) stolen goods or prohibited articles. Prohibited articles include items such as offensive weapons (this includes knives and other sharp objects) and articles for use in connection with burglary or theft or criminal damage.

Safeguards

As these powers are very wide, safeguards are in place. PACE states that the police officer must give his name and station. If this is not done then the search may be unlawful.

Osman v DPP (1999)

Officers who stopped and searched Mr Osman did not give their names or station. The Queen's Bench Divisional Court held this made the search of Mr Osman unlawful and so he could not be guilty of assaulting the police in the execution of their duty.

This was shown in *Osman v DPP* (1999). Also, if the officer fails to give the reason for the search, then that search is unlawful.

The need for the officers to inform the suspect of their name and the name of their police station before they began a search was also emphasised in *Michaels v Highbury Corner Magistrates' Court* (2009). This case involved a search under the Misuse of Drugs Act 1971.

Michaels v Highbury Corner Magistrates' Court (2009)

Michaels first of all tried to hide from police officers. He then walked towards the officers and was seen to put something in his mouth. The officers asked him to open his mouth, which he did, and they saw he had a wrap of drugs there. They then took hold of him and told him not to swallow the drugs, but he did swallow them. At no time during this did the police give their names or station.

Michaels was charged with obstructing the police and convicted at the magistrates' court. He appealed on the basis that the police had not taken reasonable steps to inform him of their names and station before the search began. The court allowed the appeal and quashed the conviction because the information had to be given for a subsequent search to be lawful.

Searches

If the search is in public, then the police can only request that the suspect removes outer coat, jacket and gloves (s 2(9) of PACE). The police officer must also make a written report as soon as possible after the search.

If the officer wishes to make a more thorough search, for example asking the suspect to take off their shoes or their T-shirt, then this must be done out of public view. It can be done in a police van.

Police conducting a stop and search

Detention for the purposes of a search must take place at or near the location of the stop.

4.1.2 Code A

Police Code of Practice A under PACE contains guidance on when the powers to stop and search should be used. The Code stresses that powers to stop and search must be used fairly, responsibly, with respect for people being searched and without unlawful discrimination.

Paragraph 2.2 of the code says:

 Reasonable suspicion can never be supported on the basis of personal factors alone. It must rely on intelligence or information about or specific behaviour by the person concerned.

For example, unless the police have a description of a suspect, a person's physical appearance (including any of the 'protected characteristics' set out in the Equality Act 2010), or the fact that a person is known to have a previous conviction, cannot be used alone or in combination with each other, or in combination with any other factor, as the reason for searching that person.

Reasonable suspicion cannot be based on generalisations or stereotypical images of certain groups or categories of people as more likely to be involved in criminality.

The protected characteristics set out in the Equality Act are age, disability, gender reassignment, race, religion or belief, sex and sexual orientation, marriage and civil partnership, pregnancy and maternity.

The Code stresses that there must be an objective basis for stopping and searching someone. This will normally be from information, such as information describing an article being carried, or the fact that a person has been seen carrying a type of article known to have been stolen recently in the area. Reasonable suspicion can also come from the behaviour of the suspect, for example if an officer encounters someone on the street at night who is obviously trying to hide something.

Appearance

There is one situation when a police officer may base his suspicions on appearance. This is where there is reliable information that members of a group or gang habitually carry knives unlawfully or weapons or controlled drugs, and wear a distinctive item of clothing or other means of showing that they are members of the group or gang. In these circumstances that distinctive item of clothing or other means of showing membership may provide reasonable grounds to stop and search a person.

Voluntary searches

A voluntary search is where a person is prepared to be searched voluntarily. Since 2004, Code of Practice A has made it clear that a voluntary search can only be made where a power to search already exists. All voluntary searches must be made in accordance with the law and the provisions of Code A. This includes the fact that voluntary searches must be recorded in writing.

4.1.3 Other powers to stop and search

As well as PACE there are also other Acts of Parliament which give the police the right to stop and search people. Two important powers are given under:

- the Misuse of Drugs Act 1971 which gives the police the power to stop and search for controlled drugs, and
- the Terrorism Act 2000 which gives the police powers to stop and search where there is reasonable suspicion that the person is involved in terrorism.

Terrorism Act 2000

There are powers to stop and search under ss 43 and 44 of the Terrorism Act. Under this Act the police have more powers of search than under PACE. In particular, the police can ask a suspect to remove their headgear and their shoes.

Criminal Justice and Public Order Act 1994

Section 60 of the Criminal Justice and Public Order Act 1994 gives the police the right to stop and search in anticipation of violence. This type of stop and search can only take place where it has been authorised by a senior police officer who reasonably believes that serious violence may take place in the area.

An interesting feature of this right to stop and search is that once it has been authorised, any police officer acting under it does not have to have reasonable suspicion about the individual he stops. Section 60(5) says that:

> " A constable may, in the exercise of those powers, stop any person or vehicle and make any search he thinks fit whether or not he has any grounds for suspecting that the person or vehicle is carrying weapons or (dangerous) articles ... "

This right to stop and search without any reason to suspect the individual who is stopped can be seen as an infringement of civil liberties. However, at least such rights are of limited duration as the senior police officer authorising such and stop and search powers can only do so for a period of 24 hours.

Another interesting power is given by s 60AA of the Criminal Justice and Public Order Act 1994. This allows police officers to ask a person to remove any item that they have reasonable grounds for believing is being worn to conceal that person's identity. This would include asking for the removal of a scarf or any item covering the face.

Self-Test Questions

1 What does PACE stand for?
2 Which section of PACE gives the police powers to stop and search individuals in public places?
3 What items of clothing can an officer ask the suspect to remove in public?
4 What information must the officer give the suspect before a search in order for the search to be lawful?
5 Name a case where the search was held to be unlawful because the information was not given.
6 Which Code of Practice gives the police guidance on using the powers of stop and search?
7 Name two others Acts which give the police the right to stop and search people.

4.1.4 Problems of stop and search powers

From 2005, there was a steady increase in the number of stop and searches, reaching a peak in 2008–9 of one and a half million. Much of the increase was due to extra stop and searches under s 60 of the Criminal Justice and Public Order Act 1994 and searches under terrorism laws. Although the overall number of stop and searches has decreased in the last few years, the number under PACE has increased. In 2010–11 there were over 1,200,000 such stop and searches recorded.

It is often said that the police overuse their powers to stop and search. In particular, records show that the Metropolitan Police in London carry out over 40 per cent of stops and searches under PACE. Even though this police force covers a large area, this seems a very high percentage.

Statistics also show that black people are seven times more likely than white people to be stopped and searched.

Figure 4.1 shows the number of stops and searches under PACE, with the section under which the search was carried out.

Balance of interests

The main difficulty with using stop and search powers is achieving the balance between crime prevention and interfering with human rights. A very sensitive area is in relation to items worn for religious reasons. This is why the normal stop and search powers under PACE do not allow the police to ask for the removal of headgear in public.

However, the importance of being able to ask people to remove items that may be concealing their identity was shown by the case of one of the failed bombers in the London bombing of July 2005. It was discovered that the man had initially avoided detection by leaving the city dressed in a burka which covered him completely.

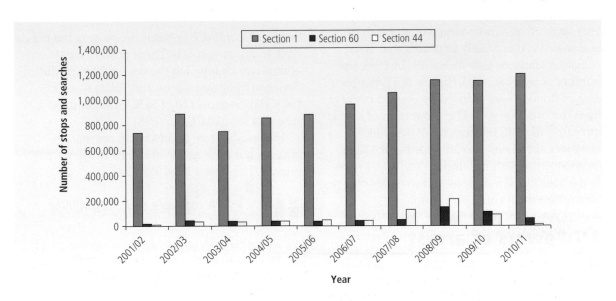

Figure 4.1 Number of stops and searches under PACE by reasons for search

Activity

State whether there has been a lawful stop and search in the following situations. Give reasons for your answers.

1. A member of the public tells a police officer that Zak has been holding a shiny object which looked like a knife. The officer stops Zak and tells Zak he will be searched as the officer believes he is carrying a knife. The officer does not tell Zak his identity or station.
2. Yan, who has six previous convictions for theft and burglary, is stopped by a police officer when he is walking home late one night. The officer tells Yan that he is going to search Yan. When Yan asks why, the officer says, 'With your history, there's always a reason'.
3. The police have a report of a burglary late at night. As two officers drive to the scene of the burglary, they see Sean walking along a nearby road carrying a holdall. The police stop Sean. They identify themselves and tell Sean they want to search him for stolen goods. They look in the holdall, but find it only contains clothes. Then they tell Sean to take off his jacket and his shoes. Sean does this. The police find nothing and let Sean go.

Does stop and search lead to arrest?

Although there are so many stops and searches, only a small number of these lead to an arrest. In 2010/11 only 9 per cent of those stopped and searched were arrested.

Statistics show that when there are fewer stops and searches, then the proportion leading to an arrest is higher. During the period 2000 to 2005 when there were only 850,000 stops and searches each year, on average 13 per cent lead to an arrest. This shows that a more targeted approach to stop and search is more likely to produce an arrest.

Earlier statistics also show this. In 1996, the number of stops and searches in the Tottenham area of London was reduced by over 50 per cent from the previous year. The proportion of arrests increased from 10 per cent to 17 per cent. However, there was also an increase of 17 per cent in crimes such as burglary and street robbery in the area. So, fewer stops and searches may not be as effective in crime prevention.

4.2 Powers of arrest

Where an offence has been or may have been committed, or is being or may be being committed, or is about to be committed, then the police have powers to arrest anyone they reasonably suspect of the offence. The powers of arrest under PACE were completely changed at the end of 2005. Powers to arrest are clearly necessary for protection of the public and prevention of crime. The problem is whether the powers introduced at the end of 2005 are too wide. The powers are explained in the next section.

4.2.1 Powers of arrest under PACE

Section 24 of PACE sets out the powers the police have to arrest suspects. These powers were completely changed at the end of 2005 by the Serious Organised Crime and Police Act 2005 (SOCPA). Section 110 of SOCPA substituted a new s 24 into PACE.

Previously there had to be an arrestable offence, but now an arrest can be made for any offence. The new s 24 of PACE says:

> s 24(1) 'A constable may arrest without a warrant –
>
> (a) anyone who is about to commit an offence;
>
> (b) anyone who is in the act of committing an offence;

(c) anyone whom he has reasonable grounds for suspecting to be about to commit an offence;

(d) anyone whom he has reasonable grounds for suspecting to be committing an offence.'

s 24(2) 'If a constable has reasonable grounds for suspecting that an offence has been committed, he may arrest anyone without a warrant whom he has reasonable grounds to suspect of being guilty of it.'

s 24(3) 'If an offence has been committed, a constable may arrest without a warrant –

(a) anyone who is guilty of the offence;

(b) anyone whom he has reasonable grounds for suspecting to be guilty of it.

It is easier to think of these powers by considering whether the offence (or possible offence) has been committed in the past, is being committed in the present or is about to be committed in the future. Figure 4.2 gives a summary of these powers.

These are very wide powers of arrest, but there is a 'necessity' test which sets limits on when an officer has the power to arrest. However, these limitations are not thought to be adequate.

TIMING	EVENT	SECTION
PAST **Actual offence**	anyone who is guilty of the offence	24(3)(a)
	anyone whom the constable reasonably suspects to be guilty	24(3)(b)
PAST **Suspected offences**	where a constable has reasonable grounds for suspecting that an offence has been committed he can arrest anyone whom he reasonably suspects to be guilty of it	24(2)
PRESENT	anyone who is in the act of committing an offence	24(1)(b)
	anyone whom the constable has reasonable grounds for suspecting to be committing an offence	24(1)(d)
FUTURE	anyone who is about to commit an offence	24(1)(a)
	anyone whom the constable has reasonable grounds for suspecting to be about to commit an offence	24(1)(c)

Figure 4.2 Police powers of arrest

Necessity test

An arresting officer can only arrest if he has reasonable grounds for believing that it is necessary to make the arrest for one of the following reasons:

- to enable the person's name or address to be ascertained
- to prevent the person:
  - causing physical injury to himself or any other person
  - suffering physical injury
  - causing loss of or damage to property
  - committing an offence against public decency
  - causing an unlawful obstruction of the highway
- to protect a child or other vulnerable person
- to allow the prompt and effective investigation of the offence or of the conduct of the person
- to prevent any prosecution for the offence from being hindered by the disappearance of the person in question.

These last two grounds are themselves open to abuse as they could be claimed to exist in many cases. The test for 'necessary' was considered in *Richardson v Chief Constable of West Midlands* (2011).

Richardson v Chief Constable of West Midlands (2011)

Richardson, a teacher of good character, had attended voluntarily by appointment at a police station to be interviewed about a possible common assault on a pupil. Because the full facilities at the police station were not open, he was asked to travel to another police station and meet the police officer there. When he arrived at the second police station he was arrested. After hearing his explanation of the incident, the police decided to take no further action. Richardson then sued the police for false imprisonment.

The judge at the High Court hearing found that the arrest had not been necessary. Richardson had attended voluntarily to be interviewed and had even gone to another police station because it was more convenient for the police. The reason the police put forward for the arrest was that it was necessary 'to allow the prompt and effective investigation of the offence'. The judge held that there was no reason to think that Richardson would not stay to be questioned, so the arrest was not justified. Richardson was awarded £1,000 damages.

4.2.2 PACE Code of Practice G

Code of Practice G gives guidelines for arrest under these powers. It stresses that a lawful arrest requires two elements:

- a person's involvement or suspected involvement or attempted involvement AND
- reasonable grounds for believing that the person's arrest is necessary.

The Code also states that arresting officers are 'required to inform the person arrested that they have been arrested, even if this fact is obvious and of the relevant circumstances in respect to both elements'.

The Code points out that the power to arrest is only exercisable if the constable has reasonable grounds for believing that it is necessary to arrest the person. It remains an operational decision at the discretion of the arresting officer as to:

- what action he may take at the point of contact with the individual
- the necessity criteria, if any, which apply
- whether to arrest, report for summons, grant street bail, issue a fixed penalty notice or take any other action open to the officer.

This part of the Code shows how much discretion is given to police officers.

4.2.3 Other powers of arrest
Arrest for breaching police bail

The Criminal Justice and Public Order Act 1994 added an extra power of arrest into PACE. This is now in s 46A of PACE and gives the police the right to arrest without a warrant anyone who, having been released on police bail, fails to attend at the police station at the set time.

Arrest for breach of the peace

As well as rights given by Acts of Parliament, the police retain a common law right to arrest where there has been or is likely to be a breach of the peace. This applies even if the behaviour complained of was on private premises, as demonstrated by the case of *McConnell v Chief Constable of the Greater Manchester Police* (1990). In this case the manager of a carpet store had asked McConnell to leave, but he had refused to do so. A police officer had then taken McConnell outside, but he attempted to re-enter, so the office arrested him for conduct whereby a breach of the peace might be occasioned. McConnell later sued the police for false imprisonment arguing that the arrest was unlawful as a breach of the peace could not occur on private premises, but the Court of Appeal held that it could do so and the arrest was lawful.

In *Bibby v Chief Constable of Essex Police* (2000), the Court of Appeal summarised the conditions that must apply for this common law power of arrest to be used. The conditions are:

- there must be a sufficiently real and present threat to the peace
- the threat must come from the person to be arrested
- the conduct of that person must clearly interfere with the rights of others and its natural consequence must be 'not wholly unreasonable' violence from a third party
- the conduct of the person to be arrested must be unreasonable.

Arrest with a warrant

The police may make an application to a magistrate for a warrant to arrest a named person. Such a warrant is issued under s 1 of the Magistrates' Court Act 1980 which requires written information, supported by evidence on oath showing that a person has committed or is suspected of committing an offence.

A warrant for arrest allows the police to enter and search the suspect's home for the purpose of making the arrest.

Arrest by private citizens

The Serious Organised Crime and Police Act 2005 also created a new s 24A in PACE. This sets out the rights of private citizens to make an arrest. The first point is that private citizens can only make an arrest in respect of indictable offences.

The arrest can be made if someone is in the act of committing an indictable offence or where the citizen has reasonable grounds for suspecting the person to be committing an indictable offence. A private citizen can also arrest where there has been an indictable offence and there are reasonable grounds for suspecting the person to be guilty of it.

However, there are also limitations. It must appear that it is not reasonably practicable for a constable to make the arrest, and it must be necessary because the citizen has reasonable grounds to believe the arrest is necessary to prevent the person:

- causing physical injury to himself or any other person
- suffering physical injury
- causing loss of or damage to property
- making off before a constable can assume responsibility for him.

4.2.4 Comment on powers of arrest
Manner of arrest

Whenever the police make an arrest, they should at the time of the arrest, or as soon as practicable afterwards, tell the person arrested that they are under arrest and the reason for it, even if it is perfectly obvious why they are being arrested. There is no set form of words to be used and, as is often portrayed in television dramas, it is sufficient if the arresting officer says something like 'You're nicked for theft'.

Where necessary, both the police and private citizens making an arrest may use reasonable force.

Lawful arrest

In *Taylor v Chief Constable of Thames Valley Police* (2004) the Court of Appeal held that the test whether the words of arrest were sufficient is:

 was the person arrested told in simple non-technical language that they could understand the essential legal and factual grounds for his arrest?

Taylor v Chief Constable of Thames Valley Police (2004)

Taylor was a 10-year-old boy who had been throwing stones during an anti-vivisection demonstration. When he was present at a later protest he was identified by a police officer who said, 'I am arresting you on suspicion of violent disorder on April 18th, 1998 at Hillgrove Farm.'

The Court of Appeal held that this was understandable and so there was a lawful arrest.

Activity

State whether there has been a lawful arrest in the following situations. Give reasons for your answers.

1. After an incident in which a man was stabbed and seriously hurt, a police officer grabs hold of Damon. When Damon protests and asks why, the police officer says, 'You know what it's for'. The police officer did not see the incident but was told by someone else at the scene that Damon was responsible.
2. Tony, a taxi driver, sees Gary climbing out of the window of a house. Tony catches hold of Gary and takes him to a nearby police station.
3. Amanda is stopped by the police for speeding. When one of the police officers asks for her name, she replies, 'Superwoman'. She is then asked for her address and refuses to give it. The police officer arrests her and takes her to the police station.

Self-Test Questions

1 Which section of PACE sets out the police powers to arrest?
2 If an officer suspects that an offence has been committed, can he lawfully arrest someone he suspects, even if it is later discovered there has been no offence?
3 Briefly outline the necessity test under which police can lawfully make arrest.
4 In addition to the powers under PACE, the police also have the right to make an arrest in other situations. Name two of these situations.
5 Can the police use reasonable force to make an arrest?
6 When the police have arrested a person, what rights do they have to search that person?

The right to search an arrested person

Where a person has been arrested the police have a right to search that person for anything which might be used to help an escape or anything which might be evidence relating to an offence. If such a search takes place in public the police can only require the suspect to remove outer coat, jacket and gloves.

4.3 Powers of detention

Once a person has been arrested and taken to a police station, there are rules setting out very strict time limits on how long they may be held there. There are also rules about the treatment of people in detention; these are contained in PACE and Code of Practice C.

Anyone brought to a police station must be brought before the custody officer as soon as practicable after their arrival at the police station. The custody officer must start a custody record in which all events at the police station in relation to the suspect must be written down. This will include the time of arrival and the reason why they have been brought to the police station and any reviews of the detention. The custody officer must also record any visits to the detainee in the cell in which he is detained or any other event which occurs.

4.3.1 Time limits under PACE

The length of time for which a person can be detained following arrest depends on the seriousness of the offence. Where a person has been arrested on suspicion of a summary offence (a less serious offence), then the police can only detain them for a maximum of 24 hours.

Where the person has been arrested on suspicion of an indictable offence (a more serious offence), the police can detain the suspect for another 12 hours (making a total of 36 hours). This can, however, only be done with the permission of a senior officer (superintendent or above).

To detain a person beyond 36 hours for an indictable offence, the police must apply to the Magistrates' Court. The magistrates can order detention for up to a maximum total of 96 hours. The detainee has the right to be represented and oppose such an application. Applications for the right to detain someone beyond the 36-hour period are only made in about one per cent of cases.

During the period of detention there must be regular reviews by the custody officer. The first review must be not later than six hours after the detention. Reviews must then take place at intervals of not less than nine hours. If at any time the custody officer decides that there are no grounds for continuing the detention, then he is under a duty to order that the detainee be immediately released from custody.

Terrorism cases

Longer periods of detention are allowed where the suspect has been arrested for terrorism offences. The period of detention may be extended to 14 days by a District Judge (Magistrates' Court).

After 14 days the suspect must be charged or released.

Figure 4.3 sets out the time limits on detention of suspects.

4.3.2 Rights of a detained person

Detainees must be told their rights by the custody officer. These rights include:

- having someone informed of his arrest
- being told that independent legal advice is available free, and being allowed to consult privately with a solicitor
- being allowed to consult the Code of Practice.

TIME FACTOR	EVENT(S)
Start of detention	Arrested person arrives at police station and the custody officer decides there is reason to detain him
Six hours	First review by custody officer
15 hours and every nine hours thereafter	Second and subsequent reviews by custody officer
24 hours	Summary offence – must charge or release. For indictable offences, after 24 hours the permission of a superintendent or above is needed to extend the detention to 36 hours
36 hours	For indictable offences the police may apply to magistrates to extend the period of detention
96 hours	Maximum time for detaining an arrested person (except under the Terrorism Act 2000). Police must charge or release the suspect

Figure 4.3 Time limits on detention of a suspect

Code C states that each detainee must be given a written notice setting out these three rights.

The right to have someone informed of the arrest

The right to have someone informed of the arrest is given by s 56 of PACE. The arrested person can nominate any friend, relative or any other person whom they think is likely to take an interest in their welfare. The person nominated by the detainee must be told of the arrest and where the person is being held.

This should normally be done as soon as practicable, but, in the case of an indictable offence, a senior police officer may authorise that there be a delay of up to 36 hours. This can only be done if there are reasonable grounds for believing that telling the named person will lead to interference or harm to evidence or to other persons or the alerting of others involved in the offence or hinder the recovery of property obtained through the offence.

Code C states that, in addition to the right to have someone informed of the arrest, a detained person should be allowed to speak on the telephone 'for a reasonable time to one person'. If the suspect is under the age of 17 the police must also contact a person 'responsible for his welfare' and inform them of the arrest.

The right to legal advice

A detained person may either contact their own solicitor or they can use the system of duty solicitors which is provided free for anyone under arrest. In fact, the Code of Practice tries to make sure that detained people are aware of their right to legal advice. Under the Code the custody officer, when he authorises the detention of someone at the police station, must ask the suspect to sign the custody record at that time, saying whether he wishes to have legal advice. Police stations must have posters 'prominently displayed' advertising the right to free legal advice and an arrested suspect must not only be told orally of this right, but also given a written notice of it.

It is possible for a senior police officer to authorise a delay to a suspect's right to see a solicitor in the case of an indictable offence for up to 36 hours. However, this can only occur if there are reasonable grounds for believing that giving access to a solicitor will lead to interference with or harm to evidence or to other persons or the alerting of others involved in the offence or hinder the recovery of property obtained through the offence. The case of *R v Samuel* (1988) stressed that it would only be on rare occasions that such a delay was justified and that it must be based on specific aspects of the case, not a general assumption that access to a solicitor might lead to the alerting of accomplices.

Key facts

Right	Source	Comment
To have someone informed of detention	s 56 PACE	Can be delayed for up to 36 hours for an indictable offence
To be told of right to legal advice	s 58 PACE	Can be delayed for up to 36 hours for an indictable offence BUT only in exceptional circumstances *R v Samuel* (1988)
To consult the Codes of Practice	Code C	
Suspect must be given written notice of these three rights listed above		
To have an appropriate adult present at interview	Code C	Applies to those under 17 and also to people who are mentally disordered and mentally vulnerable *R v Aspinall* (1999)
To speak to someone on the telephone	Code C	Not compulsory – police can refuse this
To have adequately lit and ventilated accommodation To have regular meals To be allowed a continuous period of eight hours' rest in 24 hours	Code C	

Figure 4.4 Key facts chart on rights of suspects in police detention

R v Samuel (1988)

The defendant was a 24-year-old man, whose mother had already been informed of her son's arrest some hours before he was refused access to a solicitor. The Court of Appeal felt that if anyone was likely to be alerted then it would already have happened and that there was no reason to deny Samuel his 'fundamental freedom' of consulting with a solicitor. As his final interview with the police had taken place after his solicitor had been refused access, the evidence of what was said at that interview was inadmissible in court and so Samuel's conviction for robbery was quashed.

In *R v Grant* (2005) the Court of Appeal held that the court would not tolerate illegal conduct by the police.

R v Grant (2005)

In this case there had been deliberate interference by the police with the detained suspect's right to the confidence of privileged communication with his solicitor. This was such a serious abuse of process that it justified his conviction for murder being quashed.

Other rights

Code C states that cells must be adequately heated, cleaned, lit and ventilated. A suspect should be offered at least two light meals and one main meal in any 24 hours. Drinks should be provided at mealtimes and upon reasonable request between meals. In any period of 24 hours a detainee must also be allowed a continuous period of at least eight hours' rest.

4.4 Police interviews of suspects

Any detained person may be questioned by the police. All interviews at a police station must be tape-recorded and some are video-recorded rather than just audio-taped.

Suspects have the right to have a solicitor present at any interview, unless it is one of the rare occasions referred to in *R v Samuel* (see section 4.3.2 above). However, if the suspect does not ask for a solicitor, the police may conduct the interview without one being present. In addition, if the matter is urgent or the solicitor likely to be delayed for some time, the police have the right to start questioning a suspect before a solicitor arrives.

Interviews should take place in interview rooms which are adequately heated, lit and ventilated. The person being interviewed must be offered a seat. Pace Code C points out that they shall not be required to stand. There must be breaks from interviews at mealtimes and also short refreshment breaks about every two hours.

4.4.1 Tape recording

Two copies of the tape recording are made. One is a master copy which is sealed. The other is the working copy which can be checked by the suspect or his lawyers.

At the start of each interview the police must start the tape by recording the time and who is present at the interview. At the end of the recording, the police must state the time it finishes.

4.4.2 Appropriate adult

If the suspect is under the age of 17 or is mentally disordered or mentally vulnerable, then there must be an 'appropriate adult' present during all interviews. This right is in addition to the right to legal advice.

> *R v Aspinall* (1999)
>
> The defendant suffered from schizophrenia. The Court of Appeal ruled that he should have had an appropriate adult present when interviewed by the police. This was so, even though the defendant appeared to be able to understand the police questions. As no appropriate adult had been present, the interview was not admissible as evidence.

4.4.3 Right to silence

Until the Criminal Justice and Public Order Act 1994 was enacted, defendants could refuse to answer any questions without any adverse conclusion being drawn on their silence. In fact, the previously used caution given before a police interview commenced contained the phrase 'you do not have to say anything'. However, the Government decided that this rule was allowing guilty people to go free and that the right to silence should be restricted. This was done by ss 34–39 of the Criminal Justice and Public Order Act 1994.

These sections allow inferences to be made from the fact that a defendant has refused to answer questions. As a result, the wording of the caution given to suspect before interviewing commences now states:

You do not have to say anything. But it may harm your defence if you do not mention when questioned something which you later rely on in court. Anything you do say may be given in evidence.

This does not mean that the defendant can be forced to speak; he can still remain silent. However, at any trial which follows the judge may comment on the defendant's failure to mention a crucial matter and this failure can form part of the evidence against him. It is argued that this alters the basic premise of criminal trials that the prosecution must prove the defendant's guilt.

However, a defendant's silence is not enough for a conviction on its own; there must be prosecution evidence as well.

4.4.4 Protection of suspects

The law gives some protection to suspects on the way in which they should be treated while being detained and questioned. Section 76 of PACE states that the court shall not allow statements which have been obtained through oppression to be used as evidence.

'Oppression' is defined as including torture, inhuman or degrading treatment and the use of or threat of violence. As pointed out above, Code C also gives protection to suspects who are being questioned in regard to the physical conditions of the interview. For example, the Code states that interview rooms must be adequately lit, heated and ventilated and that suspects must be given adequate breaks for meals, refreshments and sleep.

In theory, the treatment of a suspect is monitored by the custody officer who is supposed to keep accurate records of all happenings during the detention period. This should include the length and timing of interviews and other matters such as visits of police officers to the defendant's cell, so that if there are any breaches of the rules this will be obvious. However, research by Sanders and Bridge suggests that a substantial minority of custody records (about ten per cent) are falsified.

4.5 Searches, fingerprints and body samples

4.5.1 Searches

When a person is being held at a police station the police have no automatic right to search them. However, the custody officer has a duty to record everything a person has with him when he is brought to the police station, and if the custody officer thinks a search is necessary to carry out this duty, then a non-intimate search may be made.

Strip searches

These are defined in Code C as searches 'involving the removal of more than outer clothing'. The code stresses that a strip search may only take place if it is necessary to remove an article which a person in detention should not be allowed to keep, and there is reasonable suspicion that the person might have such an article concealed on their person.

Such searches should not take place in an area where the search can be seen by any person who does not need to be present. No member of the opposite sex should be present during a strip search. Suspects should not normally be required to remove all their clothing at the same time. A man should be allowed to put his shirt back on before he removes his trousers and a woman should be given a robe or similar garment to wear once she has removed her top garment.

Intimate searches

In addition, a high-ranking police officer can authorise an intimate search if there is reason to believe that the person has with him an item which he could use to cause physical injury to himself or others, or that he is in possession of a Class A drug.

An intimate search is defined as 'a search which consists of the physical examination of a person's body orifices other than the mouth'. If it is a drugs-related search then it may only be carried out by a suitably qualified person, for example a doctor or nurse. If it is a search for other items then, if practicable, it should be carried out by a suitably qualified person, but can be by another person if a high-ranking police officer authorises it.

4.5.2 Fingerprinting

Taking of fingerprints prior to arrest

Fingerprints can be taken prior to arrest away from the police station as it is now possible to check against the National Automated Fingerprint Identification System in a matter of minutes. This power can only be used where:

- the officer reasonably suspects that the person is committing or attempting to commit an offence, or has committed or attempted to commit an offence, and
- either the name of the person is unknown to, and cannot be readily ascertained by, the officer, or the officer has reasonable grounds for doubting whether the name given by the person is his real name.

Taking of fingerprints at the police station

At the police station, fingerprints can be taken by the police. The police will ask the detainee to agree to this, but if they do not consent the police have the right to use reasonable force to take fingerprints.

4.5.3 Samples

Non-intimate samples

At the police station, non-intimate samples can be taken by the police. As with fingerprints, the police will try to get the person's consent to this, but if they do not consent then the police have the right to use reasonable force to take the samples.

Intimate samples

There are different rules for intimate samples. These are defined by PACE as:

> (a) a sample of blood, semen or any other tissue fluid, urine or pubic hair;
>
> (b) a dental impression;
>
> (c) a swab taken from any part of a person's genitals or from a person's body orifice other than the mouth.

These can only be taken by a doctor or a nurse, with the permission of the suspect. Although a sample will only be taken where there is reasonable ground for suspecting involvement in a particular recordable offence, the sample may then be checked against information held on other crimes.

This has led to the solving of old crimes. In one case a woman who was arrested for drink-driving had a DNA sample taken. When the sample was checked against the database, it was a close match to the DNA profile of a rape suspect. This meant that the rapist was likely to be a close relative of the woman. The police checked her family and this led to the arrest of the rapist.

4.5.4 Retention of samples

Until 2001, fingerprints and samples were only kept where the suspect was found guilty of an offence. However, the Criminal Justice and Police Act 2001 inserted s 64(1A) into the Police and Criminal Evidence Act 1984. This section stated that fingerprints and samples:

> may be retained after they have fulfilled the purposes for which they were taken but shall not be used by any person except for purposes related to the prevention or detection of crime.

This meant that any fingerprints or samples could be kept, even though the suspect was not even charged with an offence. All DNA samples are put onto the national database. This was challenged in *S and Marper v United Kingdom* (2008).

Key facts

Power	Sections in PACE or other Act	Code of Practice	Comments
Stop and search	ss 1–7 of PACE Also other Acts, eg Misuse of Drugs Act 1971	A	Must be in a public place and must have reasonable grounds for suspecting person
Arrest	With a warrant OR under s 24 of PACE	C	Magistrates issue warrant Must have reasonable grounds for suspicion and must believe arrest is necessary
Detention	ss 34–46 PACE Normal limit 24 hours Can be extended to 36 hours by senior police officer Can be extended to 96 hours for indictable offence	C	Detainee has rights to: ● have someone told; ● to be told of availability of legal advice ● to see Code of Practice
Searches	ss 54, 55 PACE	C	Intimate search must be by person of same sex
Fingerprints	ss 61 PACE		
Samples	ss 62, 63 PACE		Intimate samples must be taken by qualified person
Police interviews	s 53 PACE Also ss 34–39 Criminal Justice and Public Order Act 1994 re 'silence'	D	● Police must caution ● Should tape-record ● Appropriate adult present for those under 17

Figure 4.5 Key facts chart on police powers

S and Marper v United Kingdom (2008)

S was aged 11 at the time of his arrest, and had been found not guilty of attempted robbery. Marper was charged with harassment of his partner, but the case had been later discontinued. The defendants argued that the retention of their samples was contrary to their right to respect for private and family life under Art 8(1) of the European Convention on Human Rights. The European Court of Human Rights held that the indefinite detention of DNA samples of people who had not been convicted was a breach of Art 8.

Following this decision, the law was changed. Initially, the time limit for keeping records where a person was either not charged or not convicted was six years. Now under the Protection of Freedoms Act 2012, the time limit for retention of fingerprints and DNA profiles is three years. In addition, where the person has not even been charged, there is an extra safeguard that the permission of the Commissioner for the Retention and Use of Biometric Material must be obtained.

An exception to the three year rule is where the person, although either not charged or not convicted of the offence for which the samples were taken, has a previous conviction for a recordable offence. In this instance, the records may be kept indefinitely.

Human rights groups are still critical of these rules, pointing out that it means that completely innocent people may still have their DNA record on the national database, even though it is for a limited time.

Self-Test Questions

1 When can the police interview a suspect without a solicitor present?
2 Which categories of people have the right to have an appropriate adult present during the interview?
3 What protection does s 76 of PACE provide for suspects?
4 What rules are there for strip searches?
5 Can fingerprints lawfully be taken by force?
6 What categories of people may take an intimate sample?
7 Which case decided that keeping DNA records where the suspect has not been charged was a breach of human rights?

Activity

Advise whether or not in the following situations there have been breaches of the rules in PACE and the Codes of Practice.

1 Leroy, aged 23, has been arrested on suspicion on murder. He is taken to the police station at 7.00 am on 6 June. The custody officer tells him that he will not be allowed to see a lawyer. Leroy is interviewed for eight hours that day about the alleged murder. He continually denies any involvement and demands to see a lawyer. The police take his fingerprints and a sample of saliva for DNA testing. Leroy spends the night in the police station cells. The following morning the police finally allow him to make a telephone call to his brother at 11.00 am (7 June).

2 Martin, aged 16, has been arrested for breaking into an office and stealing money. The police believe he may have been responsible for several other burglaries and that he has an accomplice. On the way to the police station they question him about this. At the police station he is taken into an interview room and told that the police have enough evidence 'to lock him up for years' but that if he tells them who was with him, the police will only caution him. Martin asks if he can see his father but the police refuse to call his father until Martin signs a confession.

4.6 The balance between police powers and individual rights

This chapter has shown that the police have a wide variety of powers to help them investigate crime. These powers are necessary otherwise it would not be possible to solve crimes and convict offenders. For example, the vast majority of people would agree that a DNA test ought to be taken from a suspected rapist. However, it is also important that the rights of the individual are protected.

In the previous sections of this chapter we have seen that, for each of the powers the police have, there are also limits on when and how they can use these powers. We have also seen that suspects are given rights, particularly when being detained by the police. It is important that there is a reasonable balance between the police having powers to investigate crime and protecting the rights of the individual.

The chart in Figure 4.6 summarises the police powers, limits on their powers and the relevant rights of the suspect. The final column then gives comments on the balance between the two. Note that this is only a summary. Fuller details are given in the earlier sections.

POLICE POWER	LIMITATIONS ON POWER	SUSPECT'S RIGHTS	COMMENT
Stop and search	Must have reasonable grounds for suspecting possession of stolen goods or prohibited articles. Must not stop only on basis of personal factors (eg age, race, known previous convictions). Must have real reason.	Police must give name and station. Police must state reason for search. If search is in public, can only ask suspect to remove outer coat, jacket and gloves.	If these are breached the search is unlawful. Only about 13 per cent of those stopped are arrested, suggesting that too many stop and searches are made. When there are fewer searches crime rates go up.
Arrest	There must be involvement or suspected involvement in an offence AND the police officer must have reasonable ground for believing the person's arrest is necessary.	Suspect must be told of arrest and reason for it. Police can only use reasonable force in making the arrest. Suspect must be taken to a police station as soon as possible after arrest.	The powers of arrest now apply to all offences. The necessity test is very wide. The police have considerable discretion in making the decision of whether to arrest or not.
Detention	Can only detain for 24 hours for summary offences. Can detain for 36 hours for indictable offences and can apply to magistrates for an extension to 96 hours. In terrorism cases the limit is 14 days.	Right to: ● have someone informed of detention ● have legal advice ● consult the Code of Practice. Cells must be adequately heated, cleaned, lit and ventilated. Must be given food and drink.	Custody officer reviews detention regularly. Custody record is kept BUT it is believed that 10 per cent of records are not accurate. The police need to be allowed to hold a suspect while investigations are on-going, eg waiting for results of a DNA test or while premises are searched.
Interview	Must tape-record interview.	Right to have solicitor present. Suspects under 17 or mentally ill must have an appropriate adult present. Must be given a break about every two hours. Must be allowed eight hours continuous rest in 24-hour period.	If urgent, interview can be started without solicitor present. Suspect can remain silent but this can be commented on at any later trial. Main protection is s76 PACE under which courts do not allow statements obtained through oppression to be used as evidence.

Figure 4.6 Police powers and the rights of the suspect

Searches	Custody officer can carry out a search if he thinks it is necessary. An intimate search must be authorised by a high-ranking officer if there is reason to believe the suspect has an item which could cause him damage, or that he is in possession of Class A drugs.	Strip search must be by member of same sex and suspects should not have to remove all their clothing at the same time. An intimate search should be carried out by a suitably qualified person, eg a doctor or nurse.	Right to privacy is reasonably protected.
Fingerprinting	Fingerprints prior to arrest can only be taken where there is reasonable suspicion of involvement in an offence and the name of the person is not known or there are reasonable grounds for believing the name given is false. After arrest police have right to fingerprint.	Suspect will be asked to consent to fingerprinting. If he does not consent, reasonable force can be used to take the prints.	Fingerprints may be kept indefinitely even if the person is not charged, but this may be changed.
Samples	After arrest police have the right to take samples.	Suspect will be asked to consent to samples being taken. If he does not consent, reasonable force can be used to take the samples. Intimate samples must be taken by a doctor or a nurse.	Where a defendant is not charged or found not guilty, DNA records obtained from samples can only be kept on the national database for three years. In *S and Marper v UK* (2008), it was held to be a breach of human rights to keep the records indefinitely.

Figure 4.6 Police powers and the rights of the suspect (continued)

4.7 Complaints against the police

Citizens who believe that the police have exceeded their powers can complain to the police authorities. Any complaint about police behaviour must be recorded.

The type of complaint then determines how it is dealt with, although in all instances, the police are under a duty to take steps to obtain and/or preserve evidence which is relevant to the complaint. Minor complaints will be dealt with informally, and if the complaint is proved, the individual will receive an apology and that will probably be an end of the matter. If disciplinary action is thought to be necessary, then the complaint should be investigated by the police force concerned, or by the Independent Police Complaints Commission.

4.7.1 The Independent Police Complaints Commission

The Independent Police Complaints Commission (IPCC) was set up in April 2004 to supervise the handling of complaints against the police and police staff such as Community Support Officers. The IPCC sets down standards for the police to follow when dealing with complaints. They also monitor the way that complaints are dealt with by local police forces.

In addition, the IPCC itself investigates serious issues. These include:

- any incident involving death or serious injury
- allegations of serious or organised corruption
- allegations against senior officers
- allegations involving racism
- allegations of perverting the course of justice.

The fact that the IPCC can carry out its own investigations into such matters is an improvement on the previous system, where police from one area would be asked to investigate complaints about police in another area. This was felt not to be sufficiently independent. The IPCC is totally independent of the police.

Who can make a complaint?

Any member of the public who:

- has been a victim of misconduct by a person serving with the police
- was present when the alleged misconduct took place and suffered loss, damage, distress or inconvenience, or was put in danger or at risk
- is a friend or relative of the victim of the alleged misconduct, or
- has witnessed the alleged misconduct.

A complaint can be made directly to the police force concerned or through the IPCC, any advice organisation such as the Citizens Advice Bureau, the Council for Racial Equality or a Youth Offending Team. Instead of making the complaint direct, it is also possible to ask a solicitor or your MP to make the complaint for you.

Examples of cases investigated

One example of the IPCC investigating was in relation to the death of Jean Charles de Menezes at Stockwell underground station in 2005. The police mistakenly believed that de Menezes was a terrorist,

but they had made mistakes in their conduct of the case. The police were criticised for their procedures.

Another case was the investigation into the death of Ian Tomlinson who collapsed and died during the G20 protests in London in 2009. Evidence suggested that there might have been direct contact between a police officer and Mr Tomlinson. The IPCC conducted a very thorough review, interviewing nearly 200 members of the public, as well as police officers. They also looked at more than 1,200 hours of CCTV film. As a result, a police officer was eventually charged with assaulting Mr Tomlinson.

Yet another case was the death of Sean Rigg in custody at Brixton police station. Mr Rigg suffered from mental illness. The police failed to respond quickly enough to calls from hostel staff where Mr Rigg was living saying he was behaving in a way that was a danger to himself and others. He was arrested after an incident away from the hostel and the police failed to recognise the signs of mental illness or to take sufficient care of him. This investigation led to some improvements in the recognition and care of mentally ill offenders. However, the IPCC points out that half of deaths in police custody are still of mentally ill offenders and more needs to be done to prevent this.

4.7.2 Court actions

Where the police have committed a crime in the unlawful execution of their duties, criminal proceedings may be brought against them. Such proceedings are usually for assault and may be commenced by a private prosecution or, as seen above, by the State.

If there is a breach of civil rights, citizens may also be able to take proceedings in the civil courts against the police. This can be done under a claim in tort for trespass to property, as would be the case if the police entered premises without a search warrant or other permission, or for trespass to the person where any arrest is unlawful. There can also be civil proceedings for false arrest or malicious prosecution.

Examination Questions

1(a) Describe the powers of the police under Police and Criminal Evidence Act 1984 (as amended) to stop and search a person on the street and make further searches at the police station.   18 marks

1(b) Paul has been arrested on suspicion of theft of a pair of earrings. Fingerprints are taken by force. He is strip searched by a male officer accompanied by a female officer. He is told to remove all his clothes. As nothing is found, an intimate search is done by a doctor and the earrings are found.
Explain whether or not Paul's treatment at the police station was lawful.   12 marks

OCR G151 June 2012

2(a) Describe the powers of the police to stop and search in the street.   18 marks

2(b) Discuss whether the balance of interests between crime prevention and individual rights is maintained by the current rules on stop and search in the street.
12 marks

OCR G151 June 2010

3(a) Describe the powers of the police to arrest a person on the street and any limitations on those powers.   18 marks

3(b) Raymond has been reported to the police by members of the public who say they have seen him selling drugs. Two police officers approach Raymond and, without identifying themselves, they arrest him. Raymond asks why he has been arrested and one of the police officers says "You know why!" Raymond is cautioned but then attempts to escape and is tackled to the ground.

Explain whether or not Raymond's arrest is lawful.   12 marks

OCR G151 January 2013

Exam tips

In Section B questions you are required to show different skills as you need to have both a wide range of detailed knowledge which you can use selectively and to be able to apply what you know to a set of facts.

In the exam, underline and identify the relevant pieces of information you need to consider. Then you need to be disciplined to write about those in preference to other material you might have spent a long time revising.

It is important to use the information you are given and to look at the issues from the perspective the question requires – this could be of a lawyer talking to a client. The best answers respond to the focus of the question. However, to do this well you need to be confident with all aspects of police powers, which makes this a challenging topic to master.

Making flow charts and mind maps can really help order the material and get it into a format where it is easier to learn and where you can make a simple plan at the start of your answer to keep you on track.

Chapter 5

Pre-trial procedure in criminal cases

The criminal law is set down by the State. A breach of the criminal law can lead to a penalty such as imprisonment or a fine being imposed on the defendant in the name of the State. Therefore, bringing a prosecution for a criminal offence is usually seen as part of the role of the State. Indeed, the majority of criminal prosecutions are conducted by the Crown Prosecution Service which is the State agency for criminal prosecutions (the role of the Crown Prosecution Service is covered in section 5.3).

It is also possible for a private individual or business to start a prosecution. Bodies such as the RSPCA regularly bring prosecutions. However, it is unusual for a private individual to bring a prosecution. This will only happen in rare cases where the police have refused to act to investigate a complaint, or where the Crown Prosecution Service has decided to drop a case after the police had brought charges.

5.1 Pre-trial hearings

All criminal cases will first go to the Magistrates' Court. It is unusual for a case to be completed at this first hearing, although it is possible for minor offences to be dealt with at this point. This would only be where the defendant pleads guilty and is either already legally represented or does not want legal representation. For most driving offences there is a special procedure which allows the defendant to plead guilty by post, so that no attendance at court is necessary. Even in these cases the magistrates may need to adjourn the case to obtain further information about the defendant.

5.1.1 Categories of offences

The type of offence that is being dealt with affects the number and type of pre-trial hearings, and where the final trial will take place. Criminal offences are divided into three main categories. These are:

1. Summary offences
   These are the least serious offences and are always tried in the Magistrates' Court. They include nearly all driving offences, common assault and criminal damage which has caused less than £5,000 worth of damage.
2. Triable either way offences
   These can be regarded as the middle range of

crimes and they include a wide variety of offences, such as theft and assault causing actual bodily harm. As the name implies, these cases can be tried in either the Magistrates' Court or the Crown Court.

3. Indictable offences
   These are the more serious crimes and include murder, manslaughter and rape. All indictable offences must be tried at the Crown Court, but the first hearing is dealt with at the Magistrates' Court. After this the case is transferred to the Crown Court.

Figure 5.1 summarises the three categories of offence.

5.1.2 Pre-trial procedure for summary offences

It is possible for cases to be dealt with on a first appearance in court, but often an adjournment may be needed. This could be because the Crown Prosecution Service does not possess all the information required to complete the case, or because the defendant wants to receive legal advice. Another reason for adjourning a case is where the magistrates want pre-sentence reports on a defendant who pleads guilty, before they decide what sentence to impose. When a defendant wishes to plead not guilty, there will almost always have to be an adjournment, as

CATEGORY OF OFFENCE	PLACE OF TRIAL	EXAMPLES OF OFFENCES
Summary	Magistrates' Court	Driving without insurance Taking a vehicle without consent Common assault
Triable either way	Magistrates' Court OR Crown Court	Theft Assault causing actual bodily harm Obtaining property by deception
Indictable	Crown Court	Murder Manslaughter Rape Robbery

Figure 5.1 The three categories of offence

witnesses will have to be brought to court. One of the main points to be decided on an adjournment is whether the defendant should be remanded on bail or in custody (see section 5.2).

Early administrative hearings

In order to prevent unnecessary delays, the first hearing is now an early administrative hearing (EAH). The hearing can be dealt with by a single lay magistrate, or even by the clerk of the court. The hearing is aimed at discovering if the defendant wants to apply for legal aid and, if so, enquiring into whether he is eligible for it; requesting pre-sentence or medical reports if these are appropriate; and deciding if the defendant should be remanded in custody or on bail.

5.1.3 Pre-trial procedure for triable either way offences

Plea before venue

The plea before venue procedure applies only to triable either way offences. Under this procedure, the defendant is first asked whether he pleads guilty or not guilty. If the plea is guilty then the defendant has no right to ask for the case to be heard at the Crown Court. However, the magistrates may decide to send the defendant to the Crown Court for sentence.

Mode of trial

If the defendant pleads not guilty then the magistrates must carry out 'mode of trial' proceedings to decide whether the case will be tried in the Magistrates' Court or the Crown Court.

The magistrates first decide if they think the case is suitable for trial in the Magistrates' Court and whether they are prepared to accept jurisdiction (they have the power to deal with the case).

Under s 19 of the Magistrates' Court Act 1980 they must consider the nature and seriousness of the case, their own powers of punishment and any representations of the prosecution and defence.

Cases involving complex questions of fact or law should be sent to the Crown Court. Other relevant factors which may make a case more suitable for trial at the Crown Court include:

- where there was a breach of trust by the defendant
- where the crime was committed by an organised gang
- where the amount involved is more than twice the amount that the magistrates can fine the defendant.

In rare cases where the Attorney-General, Solicitor-General or the Director of Public Prosecutions is the prosecutor, the magistrates must, under s 19(4) of the Magistrates Court Act 1980, send the case to the Crown Court if that is what the prosecution wants. In other cases the prosecution's wishes are just part of the matters to be considered by the magistrates before they decide whether they are prepared to hear the case or whether it should be tried at the Crown Court.

Defendant's election

If the magistrates are prepared to accept jurisdiction, the defendant is then told he has the right to choose trial by jury, but may be tried by the magistrates if he agrees to this course. However, he is also warned that if the case is tried by the magistrates and at the end of the case he is found guilty, the magistrates can send him to the Crown Court for sentence if they feel their powers of punishment are insufficient.

A main point for discussion is whether defendants should be allowed to choose where they will tried. This involves the right to trial by jury.

5.1.4 The right to trial by jury

Cases where the defendant pleads not guilty to a summary offence can never be tried by a jury. These are always tried by magistrates.

Cases where the defendant pleads not guilty to an indictable offence are always tried by jury.

The only offences for which there is a choice of who should try the case are triable either way offences. The choice is made at the mode of trial proceedings (explained at section 5.1.3) in cases where the defendant is pleading not guilty to a triable either way offence. If the magistrates decide that the case is suitable for them to try, then they must offer the defendant the choice of court for the trial.

In this type of case most defendants choose to be tried by magistrates in the Magistrates' Courts. However, there are some reasons why defendants may prefer to be tried by a jury in the Crown Court.

Reasons for choosing trial by jury

Defendants are more likely to be acquitted (found not guilty) at the Crown Court than in the Magistrates' Court. Only about 15 per cent of

defendants who plead not guilty in the Magistrates' Courts are found not guilty. At the Crown Court, over 60 per cent of defendants are acquitted.

An interesting point on the number of acquittals in the Crown Court is that most are as a result of the judge discharging the case or directing that the defendant be found not guilty. This will happen where the prosecution drops the case or witnesses fail to attend court, so there is no evidence against the defendant.

However, juries do acquit in more cases than magistrates. They acquit in about 35 per cent of cases, compared with the 15 per cent acquittal rate in the Magistrates' Courts.

Research conducted into the reasons why defendants chose trial at the Crown Court found that most did so on the advice of their lawyers. The main factor in the choice was the higher chance of an acquittal.

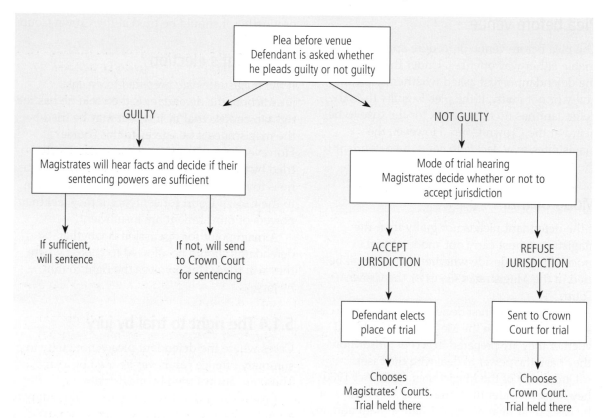

Figure 5.2 Flow chart of procedure for triable either way offences

However, there were other factors influencing the choice, including (where defendants were held in custody awaiting trial) a wish to serve part of the sentence in a remand prison!

Another reason for choosing trial at the Crown Court is that the defendant is more likely to receive legal aid. This means that the State will pay for his legal representation.

The legal representative at the Crown Court must have a certificate of advocacy giving the right to present cases at the Crown Court. This is likely to mean that the lawyer is more experienced at presenting cases in court.

Disadvantages of trial by jury

There is usually a longer wait before the case is dealt with than for cases in the Magistrates' Courts. If the defendant is not given bail, this waiting period is spent in prison. However, waiting times for trials in the Crown Court have been reduced in recent years. Nearly half of cases where the defendant is pleading not guilty are now dealt with within 16 weeks from the case being sent to the Crown Court.

The costs of the case are much great than those in the Magistrates' Court. If the defendant has to pay for their own lawyers, this will be expensive. In addition, if the defendant is ordered to pay part of the prosecution costs, this will be a greater amount than in the Magistrates Court.

The other disadvantage is that, for defendants who are found guilty, the judge at the Crown Court has the power to give a greater sentence than the magistrates.

5.1.5 Pre-trial procedure for indictable offences

Even for the most serious offences, the first hearing is in the Magistrates' Court. This deals with whether the defendant wants to apply for legal aid and issues of bail. All indictable offences are then sent to the Crown Court immediately after the early administrative hearing in the Magistrates' Court.

All other pre-trial matters are dealt with by a judge at the Crown Court.

5.2 Bail

An important pre-trial matter to be decided is whether the defendant should stay in custody while awaiting the trial, or whether bail should be granted. A person can be released on bail at any point after being arrested by the police. Being given bail means that the person is allowed to be at liberty until the next stage in the case.

5.2.1 Police powers to grant bail

The police may release a suspect on bail while they make further enquiries. This means that the suspect is released from police custody on the condition that they return to the police station on a specific date in the future.

The police can also give bail to a defendant who has been charged with an offence. In this case the defendant is bailed to appear at the local Magistrates' Court on a set date. The decision on whether to grant bail or not is made by the custody officer under s 38 of PACE as amended by the Criminal Justice and Public Order Act

1994. The custody officer can refuse bail if the suspect's name and address cannot be discovered, or if there is a doubt as to whether the name and address given are genuine. Apart from this, the normal principles as to when bail should be granted apply. These are set out in the Bail Act 1976 and are given in section 5.2.2.

If any person granted bail by the police fails to surrender to that bail (that is, attend at the next stage of the case) then the police are given the right to arrest them. About 84 per cent of people charged with offences are given bail by the police.

Conditional bail

The police have the power to impose conditions on a grant of bail. The types of conditions include asking the suspect to surrender his passport, report at regular intervals to the police station or ask another person to stand surety for him. These conditions can be only imposed in order to make sure that the suspect surrenders to bail, does not commit an offence while on bail and does not interfere with witnesses or interfere in any other way with the course of justice.

No police bail

Where, having charged a defendant with a crime, the police are not prepared to allow bail, they must bring the defendant in front of the Magistrates' Court at the first possible opportunity. If (as usually happens) the magistrates cannot deal with the whole case at that first hearing, the magistrates must then make the decision as to whether the defendant should be given bail or remanded in custody. The question as to whether bail should be given can also be considered by a court at any later stage of the criminal proceedings.

Statistics published by the Home Office show that the majority of those prosecuted are summonsed to court, rather than charged. This means that the question of bail or custody is not relevant: they are automatically at liberty. Of those who are charged, about five out of every six are released on bail by the police pending the

court proceedings, so in fact only a small number of defendants are refused bail by the police. In these cases the courts must then decide whether to grant bail.

5.2.2 The Bail Act 1976

This is the key Act. It starts with the assumption that an accused person should be granted bail, though this right is limited for certain cases (see section 5.2.3). Section 4 of the Bail Act 1976 gives a general right to bail. However, the court need not grant a defendant bail if it is satisfied that there are substantial grounds for believing that the defendant, if released on bail, would:

1. fail to surrender to custody
2. commit an offence while on bail
3. interfere with witnesses or otherwise obstruct the course of justice.

The court can also refuse bail if it is satisfied that the defendant should be kept in custody for his own protection.

In deciding whether to grant bail, the court will consider various factors including:

- the nature and seriousness of the offence (and the probable method of dealing with it)
- the character, antecedents (past record), associations and community ties of the defendant
- the defendant's record with respect to the fulfilment of his obligations under previous grants of bail in criminal proceedings; in other words whether he has turned up (surrendered to his bail) on previous occasions
- the strength of the evidence against him.

If a defendant is charged with an offence which is not punishable by imprisonment, bail can only be refused if the defendant has previously failed to surrender to bail and there are grounds for believing that he will not surrender on this occasion.

A court can make conditions for the granting of bail. These are similar to conditions which can be set by the police and may include the

Key facts

Bail can be granted by	• police • magistrates • Crown Court
Bail Act 1976	There is a presumption in favour of bail BUT • for an offence while already on bail, bail can only be given if the court is satisfied there is no significant risk of further offending • must be exceptional circumstances for bail to be granted for murder, attempted murder, manslaughter, rape or attempted rape where the defendant has already served a custodial sentence for such an offence
In all cases bail can be refused if there are reasonable grounds for believing the defendant would:	• fail to surrender • commit further offences • interfere with witnesses
Conditions can be imposed	• sureties • residence in bail hostel • curfew • hand in passport, etc.
Comment	Many of those in prison are awaiting trial and could have been given bail Problem of balancing this against need to protect public

Figure 5.3 Key facts chart on bail

surrender of passport and/or reporting to a police station. The court can also make a condition on where the accused must reside while on bail; this could be at a home address or at a bail hostel.

The court can also order that the defendant is placed on a curfew. This means that he has to be at his home address at set times, for example for the evening and night. As part of the curfew order the defendant is usually required to wear an electronic tag so that it is known where he is at all times.

Where there is no real prospect that a defendant will be given a custodial sentence if convicted, then that defendant must be granted bail.

Sureties

The court (and the police) can require a surety for bail. A surety is another person who is prepared to promise to pay the court a certain sum of money if the defendant fails to attend court. Note that no money is paid unless the defendant fails to answer to his bail. This system is different from those of other countries. For example, in the USA the surety must pay the money into court before the defendant is released on bail, but gets the money back when the defendant attends court as required.

Renewed applications and appeals

If bail is refused, then normally only one further application can be made to the magistrates, unless there is a change of circumstance. The defendant can appeal against a refusal to grant bail. Such an appeal is made to a judge at the Crown Court. A defendant who has been sent for trial to the Crown Court can also apply there for bail.

5.2.3 Restrictions on bail

The right to liberty is a human right and the right to bail is therefore part of that right. This means that, even for serious offences, bail must available in suitable cases. However, in some situations the public need to be protected from a potentially dangerous person. In such circumstances the right to bail is restricted.

Repeat serious offences

Where a person is charged with murder, attempted murder, manslaughter, rape or attempted rape and they have already served a custodial sentence for a similar offence, they only have the right to bail if the court thinks that there are exceptional circumstances.

Offence committed while on bail

Where a defendant, aged 18 or over, was on bail when the present alleged offence was committed, s 14 of the Criminal Justice Act 2003 amended the Bail Act 1976 to read:

> he may not be granted bail unless the court is satisfied that there is no significant risk of his committing an offence on bail (whether subject to conditions or not).

Restrictions on bail for adult drug users

Section 19 of the Criminal Justice Act 2003 amended the Bail Act 1976 to place restrictions on bail for adult offenders who have tested positive for specified Class A drugs where:

- the offender is either charged with possession or possession with intent to supply a Class A drug, or
- the court is satisfied that there are substantial grounds for believing that the misuse of a Class A drug caused or contributed to the offence OR that the offence was motivated wholly or partly by his intended misuse of such a drug, and

- the defendant has refused to agree to participate in an assessment or follow-up in relation to his dependency upon or propensity to misuse specified Class A drugs.

Such a defendant may not be granted bail unless the court is satisfied that there is no significant risk of his committing an offence on bail (whether subject to conditions or not).

Murder cases

Where the defendant is charged with murder, bail can only be granted by a judge at the Crown Court. Magistrates no longer have the power to grant bail in murder cases.

5.2.4 Prosecution appeals

The Bail (Amendment) Act 1993 gave the prosecution the right to appeal to a judge at the Crown Court against the granting of bail. Originally this only applied where the offence involved carried a maximum of at least five years' imprisonment. However, the Criminal Justice Act 2003 extended the prosecution's power to appeal to all offences punishable with imprisonment.

Self-Test Questions

1 What does 'being given bail' mean?
2 Which Act sets out the guidelines for making decisions in respect of bail?
3 What three main factors mean that a court need not grant bail?
4 Give three issues that will be taken into consideration in making the decision of whether to grant bail or not.
5 What is a surety?
6 Give three other conditions which can be imposed on the person bailed.
7 Can a person charged with murder be granted bail?

5.2.5 Balancing conflicting interests

Denying people bail is an interference with their right to liberty, which is why there is a presumption in favour of bail. However, it is important to protect the public from potentially dangerous criminals, and restrict the use of bail. Getting the right balance between these two conflicting interests can be difficult.

Prisoners on remand account for about nine per cent of the prison population. This means that about 8,000 people are held on remand in custody at any one time. About 20 per cent of these are actually sent to prison at the end of the case. So, over 6,000 people a year are remanded in custody, and either found not guilty or found guilty but not given a custodial sentence. These people's right to liberty has been seriously interfered with; these figures suggest that too many people are being remanded in custody. However, it is important to note that this number has been considerably reduced in the last few years.

Public protection

To protect the public, there are methods of trying to ensure that someone who is given bail will not commit offences while on bail. There are bail hostels where those on bail who have no home address can live and be supervised.

Recently there has been an increase in the use of curfews enforced by electronic tagging for those released on bail. However, there are doubts as to whether this is always successful in preventing re-offending. A *Panorama* programme in July 2007 claimed that there had been six murders committed by people who were tagged, and over 1,000 violent crimes. But it must be noted that, as tagging is also used for early release prisoners, not all these offences will have been committed by those on bail.

There are also a number of offenders who fail to answer to bail (attend at court when required).

These facts suggest that the balance may be tipping too far in favour of the individual who has been charged; you can see how difficult it is to get the balance right.

Activity

Consider each of the following situations and explain with reasons whether you think bail would be granted or not.

1. Alex, aged 19, is charged with a robbery in which he threatened a shopkeeper with a gun and stole £2,000. He has no previous convictions and lives at home with his mother.
2. Homer, aged 43, is charged with three offences of burglary. He has been convicted of burglary on two occasions in the past.
3. Melanie, aged 21, is charged with theft of items from a sportswear shop. She is currently unemployed and living rough. She has no previous convictions.

5.3 Crown Prosecution Service (CPS)

Before 1986, prosecutions brought by the State were normally conducted by the police. This led to criticism as it was thought that the investigation of crime should be separate from the prosecution of cases. The Royal Commission on Criminal Procedure (the Phillips Commission), whose report led to the enactment of PACE, had also pointed out that there was no uniform system of prosecution in England and Wales. The Commission thought it was desirable to have an independent agency to review and conduct prosecutions. Eventually, the Crown Prosecution Service was established by the Prosecution of Offences Act 1985 and began operating in 1986.

5.3.1 Organisation of the CPS

The head of the CPS is the Director of Public Prosecutions (DPP), who must have been qualified as a lawyer for at least ten years. The DPP is appointed by, and is subject to supervision by, the Attorney-General. Below the DPP are

Chief Crown Prosecutors who each head one of the 13 areas into which the country is divided.

There is also a separate CPS Direct section headed by a Chief Crown Prosecutor. This section advises on out-of-hours charging of suspects.

Each area is sub-divided into branches, which are headed by Senior District Crown Prosecutors. Within each branch, there are several lawyers and support staff, who are organised into teams and given responsibility for cases. Overall more than 8,000 lawyers are employed in the CPS.

5.3.2 The functions of the CPS

These involve all aspects of prosecution and can be summarised as:

- deciding on what offence(s) should be charged. This used to be done by the police, but sometimes inappropriate charges were brought which meant that the case had to be discontinued
- reviewing all cases passed to them by the police to see if there is sufficient evidence for a case to proceed, and whether it is in the public interest to do so; this is to avoid weak cases being brought to court
- being responsible for the case after it has been passed to them by the police
- conducting the prosecution of cases in the Magistrates' Court; this is usually done by

lawyers working in the CPS as Crown Prosecutors or Associate Prosecutors
- conducting cases in the Crown Court. This can either be by instructing an independent lawyer to act as prosecuting counsel at court or a Crown Prosecutor with the appropriate advocacy qualification.

On a practical level, once a defendant has been charged or summonsed with an offence the police role is at an end. They must send the papers for each case to the CPS – each case is then assigned to a team in the local branch of the CPS, and that team will be responsible for the case throughout the prosecution process. This is aimed at ensuring continuity and better communication in each case.

5.3.3 Prosecuting cases in court

The CPS has lawyers and non-lawyers who prosecute cases in the courts.

In the Crown Court those prosecuting are Crown Prosecutors – lawyers with the right to present cases in the Crown Court. In the Magistrates' Courts, cases may be presented by either a Crown Prosecutor or an Associate Prosecutor. Associate Prosecutors are non-lawyers employed by the CPS who have been especially trained to conduct cases in court.

Examination Questions

1(a) Describe how both the police and the courts decide on matters relating to the granting of bail since the Bail Act 1976.
18 marks

1(b) Simon is charged with the burglary of an antiques shop. He has three previous convictions for theft. He has previously complied with bail conditions. He lives locally with his wife and two children but plans to move to Spain.

Explain which factors are likely to be considered when making a decision whether or not to grant bail to Simon and what conditions may be imposed.
12 marks

OCR G151 January 2011

Exam tips

Bail is a relatively straightforward topic as long as you learn the relevant statutory provisions carefully. It helps if you can refer to key statutes and their significance. An example is the Bail Act 1976, which contains a presumption in favour of bail. This means that there is a general right to bail, although it is limited in some cases.

Matching the right section, and sub-section if necessary, to the correct material will certainly help to impress an examiner. It also helps if you can remember the dates of key statutes.

You need to be able to describe the process clearly so learning this topic as a flow chart can be very helpful. As you learn the material, make a list of the advantages and disadvantages of bail. Including some figures about the use of bail, and some of the problems associated with it, will make a discussion answer seem more confident and thorough in its approach.

If bail appears in a Section B question you will need to be able to explain how the statutory provisions relate to a scenario; you will probably be given some key pieces of information to guide you so make use of your highlighter to help you focus on what it important.

In a scenario question the most important skill is applying what you know to the facts – a good tip is to refer to the name of the person in the scenario to show the examiner that you are thinking about this particular individual rather than just making general comments about bail.

Chapter 6

Criminal courts

The two courts which hear criminal trials are the Magistrates' Court and the Crown Court. As already explained in Chapter 5, the actual court for the trial is decided by the category of crime involved in the charge. Summary offences can only be tried at the Magistrates' Court; indictable offences can only be tried at the Crown Court; and triable either way offences may be tried at either court.

At the Magistrates' Courts, cases are always tried by magistrates. At the Crown Court, cases are tried by a judge and jury.

In both the Magistrates' Court and the Crown Court, the majority of defendants plead guilty to the charge against them. In these cases the role of the court is to decide what sentence should be imposed on the defendant. Where the accused pleads not guilty, the role of the court is to try the case and decide whether the accused is guilty or not guilty; the burden of proof is on the prosecution who must prove the case beyond reasonable doubt. The form of the trial is an adversarial one, with prosecution and defence presenting their cases and cross-examining each other's witnesses, while the role of the magistrate or judge is effectively that of referee, overseeing the trial and making sure that legal rules are followed correctly. Magistrates and judges cannot investigate the case or ask to see additional witnesses.

6.1 Magistrates' Courts

There are about 330 Magistrates' Courts in England and Wales. They are local courts, so there will be a Magistrates' Court in many towns, while big cities will have several courts. Each court deals with cases that have a connection with its geographical area. Magistrates have jurisdiction over a variety of matters involving criminal cases. Cases are heard by magistrates, who may be either qualified District Judges or unqualified lay justices (see Chapter 11 for further details on magistrates). There is also a legally qualified clerk attached to each court to assist the magistrates.

6.1.1 Jurisdiction of the Magistrates' Courts

So far as criminal cases are concerned, the courts have jurisdiction in a variety of matters. Jurisdiction means that the court has the legal right to hear the case. Magistrates have a very large workload and they do the following:

1. Try all summary cases. There are over half a million cases heard each year.

2. Try any triable either way offences which it is decided should be dealt with in the Magistrates' Court (see section 6.1.3). There are about 400,000 such cases heard each year.

3. Deal with the first hearing of all indictable offences. These cases are then sent to the Crown Court.

4. Deal with all the side matters connected to criminal cases, such as issuing warrants for arrest and deciding bail applications.

5. Deal with motoring offences. There are over 600,000 of these each year.

6. Try cases in the Youth Court where the defendants are aged 10–17 inclusive. There are about 150,000 youth defendants dealt with each year.

With all these categories, Magistrates' Courts deal with over one and a half million cases per year.

Civil jurisdiction

The Magistrates' Courts also have some civil jurisdiction. Strictly speaking, this side of their work belongs in Chapter 2 – however, for completeness, and to illustrate the wide variety of work carried out by Magistrates' Courts, this aspect of their work is listed below. It includes:

- enforcing council tax demands and issuing warrants of entry and investigation to gas and electricity authorities
- family cases including orders for protection against violence and maintenance orders (note that Magistrates' Courts cannot grant divorces)
- proceedings concerning the welfare of children under the Children Act 1989
- hearing appeals against the refusal of a licence to sell alcohol.

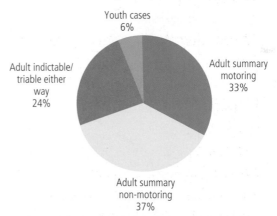

Figure 6.1 Defendants proceeded against in Magistrates' Courts (excluding adult breaches), by offence type, 2011

6.1.2 Summary trials

These are the least serious criminal offences and are sub-divided into offences of different 'levels' – level one being the lowest level and level five the highest. The use of levels allows a maximum fine to be set for each level which is increased in line with inflation from time to time. The current maximum fines date from the Criminal Justice Act 1991 and are level one: maximum £200; level two: £500; level three: £1,000;

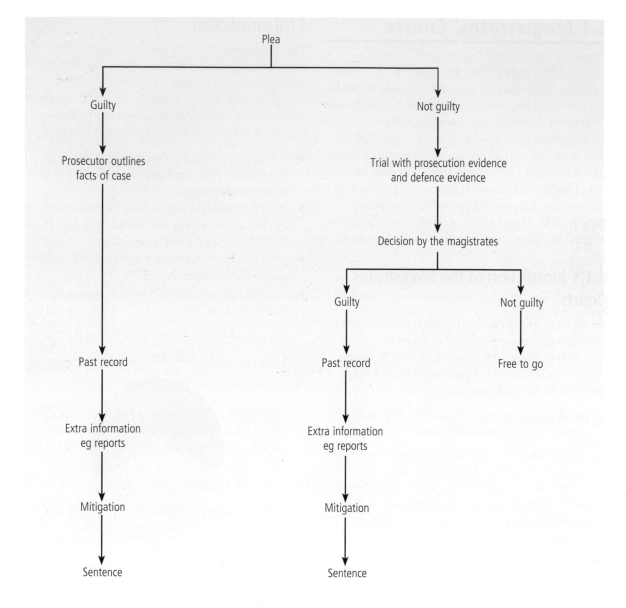

Figure 6.2 Flow chart of proceedings for a summary offence in the Magistrates' Court

level four: £2,500; and level five: £5,000. However, for certain breaches of environmental law and health and safety legislation, business can be fined up to £20,000 by the magistrates. The maximum prison sentence that can be given on summary trial is six months for one offence or twelve months for two or more triable either way offences.

At the start of any case, the clerk of the court will check the defendant's name and address and then ask whether he pleads guilty or not guilty. Over 90 per cent of defendants in the Magistrates' Court plead guilty and the process is then concerned with establishing an appropriate penalty for the case.

Giving evidence to a Magistrates' Court

Guilty plea

The usual sequence of events where the defendant pleads guilty to a summary offence is as follows:

1. The Crown Prosecutor or lay presenter from the CPS will give the court a resumé of the facts of the case.

2. The defendant is asked if he agrees with those facts (if he does not, the magistrates may have to hold an inquiry, called a Newton hearing, to establish the facts).

3. The defendant's past record of convictions, if any, is given to the court.

4. Other information about the defendant's background, especially his financial position, is given to the court.

5. Any relevant reports are considered by the magistrates; these may include a pre-sentence report prepared by a probation officer and/or a medical report on the defendant's mental health.

6. The defendant or his lawyer can then explain any matter which might persuade the magistrates to give a lenient sentence. This is called making a speech in mitigation.

7. The magistrates decide the sentence.

This is shown in flow chart form in Figure 6.2.

Not guilty plea

When a defendant pleads not guilty, the procedure is longer and more complicated, as both sides produce evidence to the court. Since the burden of proof is on the prosecution, it will begin the case – usually by making a short speech outlining what the case is about and what it hopes to prove. The prosecution witnesses will then be called one at a time to give evidence, and the prosecutor will question each to establish what he saw and heard. This is called the examination-in-chief. After the prosecution finishes the examination-in-chief of a witness, the defence will then cross-examine that witness to test their evidence and try to show that it is not reliable. The prosecution may also produce relevant exhibits, such as property found in the possession of the defendant or documents which help establish the case.

No case to answer

At the end of the prosecution case the defence can submit to the magistrates that there is no case to answer and that the case should be dismissed at this point. This is because the prosecution has to prove the case and if its evidence does not establish that case, then it must be dismissed.

Only a very small number of cases will be dismissed at this stage. In the vast majority the case will continue and the defence will have to give their evidence to the court.

Defence case

The defendant himself will usually give evidence, though he does not have to. However, since the Criminal Justice and Public Order Act 1994, the magistrates can draw their own conclusions from the fact that the accused stays silent and does not explain his side of the matter. If the defendant does give evidence, he can be cross-examined by the prosecutor, as can any defence witnesses. The defence can call any witnesses and produce any evidence that it believes will help to disprove the prosecution's case.

Once all the evidence has been given, the defence has the right to make a speech pointing out the weaknesses of the case to the magistrates and try to persuade them to acquit the defendant. Further speeches are not usually allowed unless there is a point of law to be argued. The magistrates then decide whether the defendant is guilty or not guilty. If they convict, they will then hear about his past record and may also look at reports and hear a speech in mitigation from the defence. They will then pass sentence.

If the magistrates dismiss the case, the defendant is free to go and cannot usually be tried for that offence again. There is, however, one exception when the defendant can be retried. This

is where the prosecution successfully appeals against the acquittal in a 'case stated' appeal (see Chapter 7, section 7.1.2 for the rules on these).

6.1.3 Triable either way offences

As already explained in Chapter 5, two preliminary matters have to be decided before there can be a trial in a triable either way offence: firstly, whether the defendant pleads guilty or not guilty, and secondly, where the trial should take place.

Guilty plea

If the defendant pleads guilty, then the case will be dealt with in the Magistrates' Court using the same procedure as for a guilty plea to a summary offence (see section 6.1.2). The only difference is that at the end of hearing all the facts the magistrates can decide to send the defendant to the Crown Court for sentencing. The magistrates can only do this if they feel that their powers of punishment are not sufficient.

Not guilty plea

If the defendant pleads not guilty then it has to be decided where the trial should take place – Magistrates' Court or Crown Court? The case will only be tried by the magistrates if they accept that it is a suitable case for them to try AND the defendant elects to be tried in the Magistrates' Court.

If the case is tried in the Magistrates' Court, the procedure is then the same as for a not guilty plea to a summary offence.

6.1.4 Sending cases to the Crown Court

Where the trial is going to be held at the Crown Court, the magistrates must officially send the case to the Crown Court.

For indictable offences the case is transferred to the Crown Court immediately after the first hearing at the Magistrates' Court. This is under s 51 of the Crime and Disorder Act 1998.

For triable either way offences, magistrates will hold a plea before venue hearing and, if the defendant pleads not guilty, a mode of trial hearing. If, at this hearing it is decided that the case is to be tried in the Crown Court, the magistrates will then transfer the case to the Crown Court.

6.1.5 The role of the clerk

Every bench of magistrates is assisted by a clerk who is also known as legal adviser. The senior clerk in each Magistrates' Court area has to be a barrister or solicitor of at least five years' standing. The role of the clerk is to guide the magistrates on questions of law, practice and procedure. The clerk makes sure that the correct procedure is followed in court. For example, at the start of a case it is the clerk who will ask the defendant whether he pleads guilty or not guilty. The clerk is not meant to take part in the decision-making process; that is the magistrates' role. This means that the clerk should not retire with the justices when they leave the court at the end of a case to consider their verdict.

The senior clerk has been granted greater powers to deal with routine matters which previously had to be done by magistrates. For example, clerks can now issue warrants for arrest, extend police bail, adjourn criminal proceedings (where the defendant is on bail and the terms on the bail are not being changed) and conduct early administrative hearings.

6.2 Youth Courts

Young offenders aged from 10 to 17 are dealt with in the Youth Court which is a branch of the Magistrates' Court. Children under the age of ten cannot be charged with a criminal offence.

There are some exceptional cases in which young offenders can be tried in the Crown Court. These are cases where the defendant is charged with murder or manslaughter, rape and causing death by dangerous driving. In addition, it is possible for those aged 14 and over to be sent to the Crown Court for trial in any case where they are charged with a serious offence (usually one which for an adult carries a maximum prison sentence of at least 14 years).

The Youth Court sits in private, with only those who are involved in the case allowed into the court room. Members of the press may be present, but they cannot publish the name of any young offender or other information which could identify him, such as address or school.

The magistrates who sit on the bench in these courts must be under 65 and have had special training to deal with young offenders. There must be at least one female magistrate and one male magistrate on the bench. The procedure in the court is less formal than in the adult courts and the parents or guardian of any child under 16 are required to be present for the proceedings. The court can also ask parents of those aged 16 or 17 to attend.

6.3 The Crown Court

The Crown Court currently sits in 77 different centres throughout England and Wales. There are three kinds of centre:

1. **First tier**
   These exist in main centres throughout the country, for example there are first-tier Crown Courts in Bristol, Birmingham, Leeds and Manchester. At each court there is a High Court and a Crown Court with separate judges for civil and criminal work. The Crown Court is permanently staffed by High Court judges as well as Circuit Judges and Recorders, and the court can deal with all categories of crime triable on indictment.

2. **Second tier**
   This is a Crown Court only, but High Court judges sit there on a regular basis to hear criminal cases, as well as Circuit Judges and Recorders. All categories of crime triable on indictment can be tried here.

3. **Third tier**
   This is staffed only by Circuit Judges and Recorders. The most serious cases, such as murder, manslaughter and rape, are not usually tried here as there is no High Court Judge to deal with them.

Maidstone Crown Court

DONBRIDGE CROWN COURT

The Queen v John Wilkie charged as follows:

STATEMENT OF OFFENCE
Murder contrary to the common law

PARTICULARS OF OFFENCE
John Wilkie on the 4th day of April 2011 murdered Abraham Lincoln

Figure 6.3 Sample indictment

The overriding objective of the Rules is that 'criminal cases be dealt with justly'.

The Crown Court deals with about 100,000 cases each year. This is a very much smaller number than are dealt with in the Magistrates' Courts. However, the Crown Court deals with serious cases and some cases will last several weeks or even months.

6.3.1 Preliminary matters

The indictment

This is a document which formally sets out the charges against the defendant. Although the defendant will have been sent for trial charged with specific crimes, the indictment can be drawn up for any offence that the witness statements reveal. In more complicated cases the indictment may be for several counts. Figure 6.3 shows a sample indictment.

Criminal Procedure Rules

Criminal Procedure Rules to deal with all aspects of criminal cases came into force in April 2005.

Disclosure by prosecution and defence

The Criminal Procedure and Investigations Act 1996 places a duty on both sides to make certain points known to the other. The prosecution, who have already given the defence statements of all the evidence they propose to use at the trial, must also disclose previously undisclosed material 'which in the prosecutor's opinion might reasonably be considered capable of undermining the case for the prosecution against the accused'.

The 1996 Act also imposes a duty on the defence in cases which are to be tried on indictment. In these, after the prosecution's primary disclosure, the defence must give a written statement to the prosecution, setting out:

- the nature of the accused's defence, including any particular defences on which he intends to rely
- the matters of fact on which he takes issue with the prosecution and why he takes issue
- any point of law which he wishes to take, and the case authority on which he will be relying.

The defendant also has to give details about any alibi, and the witnesses he intends calling to support that alibi. This information allows the prosecution to run police checks on the alibi witnesses.

Plea and case management hearing

Under the Criminal Procedure Rules, most cases sent to the Crown Court are dealt with first at a plea and case management hearing (PCMH). The first purpose of a PCMH is to find out whether the defendant is pleading guilty or not guilty. All the charges on the indictment are read out to the defendant in open court, and he is asked how he pleads to each charge. This process is called the 'arraignment'.

Guilty plea

If the defendant pleads guilty, the judge will, if possible, sentence the defendant immediately. This means that defendants who plead guilty will not have an unnecessarily long wait for their case to come to court.

Not guilty plea

Where a defendant pleads not guilty, the case will be tried by a jury. In order to get the case ready for hearing, the judge will require the prosecution and defence to identify the key issues, both of fact and law, that are involved in the case. He will then give any directions that are necessary to organise the actual trial; for instance, the prosecution and defence may agree that certain witnesses need not attend court as their evidence is not in dispute. Other points, such as whether it will be necessary to use a video link for any witnesses, are also agreed on. The aim of the PCMH is to speed up the actual trial process and to ensure that time will not be wasted on unnecessary points. It also allows the court to plan its lists.

The Criminal Procedure Rules encourage active case management. Case management in the Crown Court includes:

- the early identification of the real issues
- the early identification of the needs of witnesses
- achieving a certainty as to what must be done, by whom, and when, in particular by the early setting of a timetable for the progress of a case
- monitoring the progress of the case and compliance with directions
- ensuring that the evidence, whether disputed or not, is presented in the shortest and clearest way

- discouraging delay, dealing with as many aspects of the case as possible on the same occasion, and avoiding unnecessary hearings
- encouraging the participants to cooperate in the progression of the case, and
- making use of technology.

The full Criminal Procedure Rules are available online on the Ministry of Justice website: **www.justice.gov.uk**.

Self-Test Questions

1 Who hears cases in the Magistrates' Courts?
2 What criminal cases can be tried in the Magistrates' Courts?
3 Give two types of civil case that can be heard in the Magistrates' Court.
4 What role do magistrates have in respect of indictable offences?
5 Defendants of what ages are dealt with in the Youth Court?
6 Who tries cases in the Crown Court?

6.3.2 The trial

It is normal for a defendant appearing at the Crown Court to be represented, usually by a barrister, although solicitors who have a certificate of advocacy can also appear at the Crown Court. Defendants can also represent themselves.

At the trial where the defendant pleads not guilty, the order of events will normally be as follows:

1. The jury is sworn in to try the case (for further information on juries, see Chapter 12).

2. The prosecution will make an opening speech to the jury explaining what the case is about and what they intend to prove.

3. The prosecution witnesses give evidence and can be cross-examined by the defence; the prosecution will also produce any other evidence such as documents or video recordings.

4. At the end of the prosecution case the defence may submit that there is no case to go to the jury; if the judge decides there is no case, he will direct the jury to acquit the defendant.

5. The defence may make an opening speech provided they intend calling evidence other than the defendant.

6. The defence witnesses give evidence and are cross-examined by the prosecution; the defendant does not have to give evidence personally but the judge may comment on the failure to do so in his summing-up to the jury.

7. The prosecutor makes a closing speech to the jury pointing out the strengths of the prosecution case.

8. The defence makes a closing speech to the jury pointing out the weaknesses of the prosecution.

9. The judge sums up the case to the jury and directs them on any relevant law.

10. Members of the jury retire to consider their verdict in private.

11. The jury's verdict is given in open court.

12. If the verdict is guilty, the judge then sentences the accused; if the verdict is not guilty, the accused is discharged. Normally, once a defendant is found not guilty he can never be tried for that offence again. However, the Criminal Justice Act 2003 removed this 'double jeopardy' rule for serious cases if 'new and compelling evidence' comes to light, so that a defendant can be tried a second time.

Examination Questions

1(a) Describe how it is decided in which court a criminal trial will be heard. Include all categories of offence.   18 marks

1(b) Discuss the advantages and disadvantages of choosing to be tried in the Crown Court when charged with a triable either way offence.   12 marks

OCR G151 June 2011

2(a) Describe and illustrate the different categories of criminal offence and the procedure for deciding where a triable either way offence should be heard.   18 marks

2(b) Discuss the advantages and disadvantages of being tried in the Magistrates' Court for a triable either way offence.   12 marks

OCR G151 January 2013

Exam tips

The early stages of a criminal trial is an area which you can revise using graphic forms of learning. You need to be clear on the three categories of offences and the detail that goes with them but it is a less complicated body of material than some of the more figure-heavy areas of the specification. Section A questions are likely to focus on your knowledge of offences, followed by a discussion focused on a specific aspect such as the factors a defendant charged with a triable either way offence needs to consider when deciding the court in which they want their case to be heard. This topic area also works well in Section B questions where there will be a need to explain and evaluate a scenario. To do well you need to be confident that you can place an offence in the correct category and then apply the principles you have learnt to the facts, weighing up the advantages and disadvantages associated with the relevant type of offence as you go.

Chapter 7

Criminal appeals

The appeal rights of the defendant and the prosecution are completely different. Originally only the defendant had a right of appeal, but in the last 20 years various rights have also been given to the prosecution.

7.1 Appeals from the Magistrates' Court

The appeal routes from the Magistrates' Courts are completely different from appeals from the Crown Court. The appeal route from the Magistrates' Court will depend on whether the appeal is only on a point of law, or whether it is for other reasons. The two appeal routes are to the Crown Court, or to the Queen's Bench Divisional Court.

7.1.1 Appeals to the Crown Court

This is the normal route of appeal and is only available to the defence. If the defendant pleaded guilty at the Magistrates' Court, then he can only appeal against sentence. If the defendant pleaded not guilty and was convicted, then the appeal can be against conviction and/or sentence. In both cases the defendant has an automatic right to appeal and does not need to get leave (permission) to appeal.

At the Crown Court the case is completely re-heard by a judge and two magistrates. They can come to the same decision as the magistrates and confirm the conviction, or they can decide that

the case is not proved and reverse the decision. In some cases it is possible for them to vary the decision and find the defendant guilty of a lesser offence.

Where the appeal is against sentence, the Crown Court can confirm the sentence or they can increase or decrease it. However, any increase can only be up to the magistrates' maximum powers for the case.

Over the last few years there have been about 14,000 appeals to the Crown Court each year. Of these, half are against verdict and half against sentence. About two out of every five appeals are successful.

If it becomes apparent that there is a point of law to be decided, then the Crown Court can decide that point of law, but there is the possibility of a further appeal by way of a case stated appeal being made to the Queen's Bench Divisional Court (see section 7.1.2). A diagram setting out the appeal routes from the Magistrates' Court is shown in Figure 7.1.

7.1.2 Case stated appeals

These are appeals on a point of law which go to the Queen's Bench Divisional Court. Both the

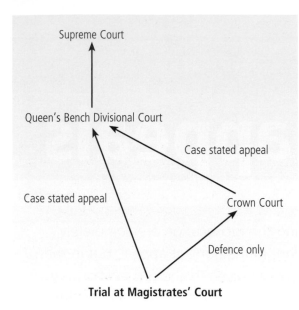

Figure 7.1 Appeal routes from the Magistrates' Court

Further appeal to the Supreme Court

From the decision of the Queen's Bench Divisional Court there is a possibility of a further appeal to the Supreme Court (formerly the House of Lords). Such an appeal can only be made if:

1. the Divisional Court certifies that a point of law of general public importance is involved
2. the Divisional Court or the Supreme Court gives permission to appeal because the point is one which ought to be considered by the Supreme Court.

Example

An example of a case which followed this appeal route was *C v DPP* (1994). This case concerned the legal point about the presumption of criminal responsibility of children from the age of ten up to their fourteenth birthday. Until this case, it had been accepted that a child of this age could only be convicted if the prosecution proved that the child knew he was doing wrong. The Divisional Court held that times had changed and that children were more mature and the rule was not needed. They decided that children of this age were presumed to know the difference between right and wrong, and that the prosecution did not need to prove 'mischievous discretion'.

The case was then appealed to the House of Lords who overruled the Divisional Court, holding that the law was still that a child of this

prosecution and the defence can use this appeal route and it can be direct from the Magistrates' Court, or following an appeal to the Crown Court.

The magistrates (or the Crown Court) are asked to state the case by setting out their findings of fact and their decision. The appeal is then argued on the basis of what the law is on those facts; no witnesses are called. The appeal is heard by a panel of two or three High Court Judges from the Queen's Bench Division, though in some cases a judge from the Court of Appeal may form part of the panel.

This route is only used by the defendant against a conviction or by the prosecution against an acquittal. It cannot be used to challenge the sentence. The appeal is made because they claim the magistrates came to the wrong decision having made a mistake about the law. The Divisional Court may confirm, vary or reverse the decision or remit (send back) the case to the Magistrates' Court for the magistrates to implement the decision on the law.

There are only about 100 case stated appeals every year.

Self-Test Questions

1 To which court is the normal appeal made from the Magistrates' Courts?
2 Who hears this appeal?
3 To which court can an appeal be made on a point of law?
4 What is an appeal on a point of law known as?
5 There is the possibility of a further appeal on a point of law. Which court hears this final appeal?

age was presumed not to know he was doing wrong, and therefore not to have the necessary intention for any criminal offence. A child of this age could only be convicted if the prosecution disproved this presumption by bringing evidence to show that the child was aware that what he was doing was seriously wrong. The House of Lords ruling was on the basis that it was for Parliament to make such a major change to the law, not the courts. The courts were bound by precedent.

7.2 Appeals from the Crown Court

7.2.1 Appeals by the defendant

The defendant has the possibility of appealing against conviction and/or sentence to the Court of Appeal (Criminal Division). So, at the end of any trial in which a defendant has been found guilty, his lawyer should advise him on the possibility of an appeal. This must be done verbally at the court, or in writing within 14 days of the trial. It is intended to make sure that each defendant has advice within the time limits for making an appeal. In order to appeal, a notice of appeal must be filed at the Court of Appeal (Criminal Division) within 28 days of conviction.

Leave to appeal

The rules on appeals are set out in the Criminal Appeal Act 1995, and in all cases the defendant must get leave to appeal from the Court of Appeal, or a certificate that the case is fit for appeal from the trial judge. The idea of having to get leave is that cases which are without merit are filtered out and the court's time saved.

The Criminal Appeal Act 1995

The Criminal Appeal Act 1995 simplified the grounds under which the court can allow an appeal. The Act states that the Court of Appeal:

> (a) shall allow an appeal against conviction if they think that the conviction is unsafe; and
>
> (b) shall dismiss such an appeal in any other case.

Since the European Convention on Human Rights has been incorporated into our law by the Human Rights Act 1998, the Court of Appeal has taken a broad approach to the meaning of 'unsafe'. In particular, a conviction has been held to be 'unsafe' where the defendant has been denied a fair trial.

New evidence

Any new evidence must appear to be capable of belief and would afford a ground for an appeal. This has to be considered together with whether it would have been admissible at the trial and why it was not produced at that trial.

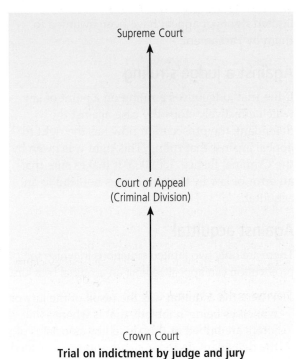

Supreme Court

↑

Court of Appeal
(Criminal Division)

↑

Crown Court
Trial on indictment by judge and jury

Figure 7.2 Appeal routes from the Crown Court

Court of Appeal's powers

The Court of Appeal can allow a defendant's appeal and quash the conviction. Alternatively, it can vary the conviction to that of a lesser offence of which the jury could have convicted the defendant. As far as sentencing is concerned, the court can decrease (but not increase) it on the defendant's appeal. Where the appeal is not successful, the court can decide to dismiss the appeal.

The Court of Appeal also has the power to order that there should be a re-trial of the case in front of a new jury. The power was given to it in 1988, but initially was not often used; in 1989 only one re-trial was ordered. However, its use has increased, with between 50 and 70 re-trials being ordered each year.

7.2.2 Appeals by the prosecution

Originally the prosecution had no right to appeal against either the verdict or sentence passed in the Crown Court. Gradually, however, some limited rights of appeal have been awarded to them by Parliament.

Against a judge's ruling

If the trial judge gives a ruling on a point of law which effectively stops the case against the defendant, the prosecution now has the right to appeal against that ruling. This right was given by the Criminal Justice Act 2003. It makes sure that an error of law by the judge does not lead to an acquittal.

Against acquittal

There are only two limited situations in which the prosecution can appeal against an acquittal by a jury.

1. Where the acquittal was the result of the jury or witnesses being 'nobbled', that is where some jurors are bribed or threatened by associates of the defendant. In these circumstances, provided there has been an actual conviction for jury 'nobbling', the Criminal Procedure and Investigations Act 1996 allows an application to be made to the High Court for an order

quashing the acquittal. Once the acquittal is quashed, the prosecution could then start new proceedings for the same offence. As yet, this power has never been used.

2. Where there is new and compelling evidence of the acquitted person's guilt and it is in the public interest for the defendant to be retried.

This second power is given by the Criminal Justice Act 2003 and is only available for some 30 serious offences, including murder, manslaughter, rape and terrorism offences. It is known as 'double jeopardy', since the defendant is being tried twice for the same offence.

The DPP has to consent to the re-opening of investigations in the case. Once the evidence has been found, then the prosecution has to apply to the Court of Appeal for the original acquittal to be quashed.

This power has been used in cases where new techniques of DNA testing now show that a defendant who was acquitted is in fact the offender. The first case in which this power was used is shown in the below article.

In 2011, two defendants who had been previously acquitted of the murder of black teenager, Stephen Lawrence, were retried and convicted some 19 years after the murder. Part of the new evidence was a DNA match with Stephen's blood found on the clothing of one of them. This evidence became available due to improved DNA testing techniques.

Man admits murder in first UK double jeopardy case

Fifteen years after he was cleared of murder, the first person in Britain to face a retrial under new double jeopardy rules admitted today that he killed his victim.

Billy Dunlop, 43, pleaded guilty to murdering pizza delivery girl Julie Hogg, 22, in Billingham, Teeside, when he appeared at the Old Bailey today.

Dunlop stood trial twice in 1991 for her murder but each time a jury failed to reach a verdict. He was formally acquitted under the convention that the prosecution do not ask for a third trial in such circumstances.

But in April last year the double jeopardy rule – which prevented a defendant who had been acquitted from being tried again for the same offence – was changed under the Criminal Justice Act 2003.

The following November the Director of Public Prosecutions announced the legal process to re-try Dunlop had begun. The case was sent to the Act of Parliament where his acquittal was quashed.

Taken from an article in the *Daily Mail*, 11 September 2006

Key facts

Party	Court which hears appeal	Reason for appealing	Relevant Act of Parliament
Defence	Court of Appeal	• against sentence and/or conviction • need leave to appeal • conviction 'unsafe'	Criminal Appeal Act 1995
Defence	Further appeal to Supreme Court	• on point of law of general public importance • need leave to appeal	
Prosecution	Court of Appeal	against a judge's ruling on a point of law	Criminal Justice Act 2003
Prosecution	High Court	asking for order to quash acquittal because of interference with witness or jury	Criminal Procedure and Investigations Act 1996
Prosecution	Court of Appeal	to have acquittal quashed because of new and compelling evidence	Criminal Justice Act 2003
Prosecution	Court of Appeal	Attorney-General's reference on a point of law: does not affect acquittal	Criminal Justice Act 1972
Prosecution	Court of Appeal	Attorney-General against lenient sentence	Criminal Justice Act 1988
Prosecution	Further appeal to Supreme Court	• on point of law of general public importance • need leave to appeal	

Figure 7.3 Key facts chart on appeal rights from the Crown Court

Referring a point of law

However, the prosecution have a special referral right in cases where the defendant is acquitted. This is under s 36 of the Criminal Justice Act 1972 which allows the Attorney-General to refer a point of law to the Court of Appeal, in order to get a ruling on the law. The decision by the Court of Appeal on that point of law does not affect the acquittal but it creates a precedent for any future case involving the same point of law.

Against sentence

Under s 36 of the Criminal Justice Act 1988 the Attorney-General can apply for leave to refer an unduly lenient sentence to the Court of Appeal for re-sentencing. This power was initially available for indictable cases only, but was extended in 1994 to many triable either way offences, provided that the trial of the case took place at a Crown Court. This power is used successfully in a number of cases each year. There has recently been an increase in the number of such referrals.

One case in 2007 was of a 14-year-old school boy who set fire to a school in West Yorkshire and caused £3 million worth of damage. His original sentence was a supervision order. The Court of Appeal held that this was 'unduly lenient' and changed the sentence to a four-year detention order.

In 2011, 118 cases referred by the Attorney-General were heard by the Court of Appeal. The sentences in 98 of these cases were increased. The case included one defendant whose sentence for two offences of rape was increased from 3½ years' imprisonment to 11 years' imprisonment.

7.2.3 Appeals to the Supreme Court

Both the prosecution and the defence may appeal from the Court of Appeal to the Supreme Court, but it is necessary to have the case certified as involving a point of law of general public importance, and to get permission to appeal, either from the Supreme Court or from the Court of Appeal. There are very few criminal appeals heard by the Supreme Court, usually between ten and twenty per year.

7.2.4 References to the Court of Justice of the European Union

Where a point of European law is involved in a case it is possible for any court to make a reference to the European Court of Justice under Art 267 of the Treaty of the Functioning of the European Union (see Chapter 18). However, this is a fairly rare occurrence in criminal cases, as most of the criminal law is purely 'domestic' and not affected by European Union law.

Self-Test Questions

1 When a defendant is tried in the Crown Court, to which court can an appeal be made?
2 What is the test used to decide if such an appeal will be successful?
3 When can the prosecution appeal against an acquittal?
4 Which Act gave the Attorney-General the power to refer an unduly lenient sentence to the Court of Appeal?
5 There is the possibility of a further appeal:
   (a) To which court would this appeal lie?
   (b) What conditions must be met before such an appeal will be heard?

7.3 The Criminal Cases Review Commission

Before 1997 there was no independent body to review possible miscarriages of justice. If the defendant's appeal failed, then there was little that he could do. The Home Secretary did have the power to review cases, but this was not sufficiently independent from the Government. In fact, the Home Secretary only used this power in a small number of cases.

To provide a better system for investigating possible miscarriages of justice, the Criminal Cases Review Commission was set up by the Criminal Appeal Act 1995.

The Commission has the power to investigate possible miscarriages of justice (including summary offences) and to refer cases back to the courts. In addition the Court of Appeal may direct the Commission to investigate and report to the court on any matter which comes before it in an appeal if it feels an investigation is likely to help the court resolve the appeal.

The members of the Commission are appointed by the Queen – at least one-third are legally qualified and at least two-thirds have relevant experience of the criminal justice system. They have about 60 support staff, treble the number previously used in the Home Office for such work. However, most of the re-investigation work is done by the police. This is felt to be unsatisfactory as it does not really make such a re-investigation independent, although it is true to say that many of the past miscarriages of justice have come to light as the result of investigation by other police forces.

Work

The Criminal Cases Review Commission took over the investigation of miscarriages of justice at the beginning of April 1997.

The main bulk of cases it investigates are brought to its attention by defendants themselves or by defendants' families, though some cases have been referred by the Court of Appeal and others have been identified by the Commission itself.

Some of the first cases it investigated were alleged miscarriages of justice from over 50 years ago, such as the case of Derek Bentley. Bentley was hanged for murder in 1953, while his co-defendant, Craig, who actually fired the fatal shot, was not hanged due to his youth. Over the years there had been many attempts to have the case re-opened but it was not until the Criminal Cases Review Commission took over the investigation that the case was referred back to the Court of Appeal. In July 1998 the Court of Appeal held that the summing-up of the judge at the trial had not been fair and it quashed the conviction.

In order for the Commission to be able to refer a case, there must normally have already been an appeal to the Court of Appeal, although the Commission has a discretion to refer a case where 'there are exceptional circumstances'.

Referrals to the Court of Appeal

By the beginning of 2013 the Criminal Cases Review Commission had received over 15,000 applications. The Commission had referred over 500 cases to the Court of Appeal – 470 of these had been heard and the convictions quashed in just over 300 cases.

Some cases have attracted much publicity. In 2003, Sally Clark's conviction for murdering her two babies was quashed after the scientific evidence was shown to be flawed. Similarly, in 2004 Sion Jenkins' conviction for the murder of his foster daughter was quashed, because of flawed scientific evidence.

In 2012, the conviction of Sam Hallam in 2005 for a murder committed in a gang attack was quashed. Sam, who was only 17 when convicted, had always insisted that he was not part of the gang and was not in the area when the murder was committed, although he could not remember exactly where he was. The Commission's review of the evidence revealed that Sam's mobile phone records and pictures showed that he was not present at the attack. The police had failed to examine his mobile phone during their investigation into the murder. The Commission also showed that the witnesses who identified Sam on the basis of a 'fleeting glimpse' were unreliable.

Activity

Check the website for the Criminal Cases Review Commission (**www.ccrc.gov.uk**) and find out:

1. How many cases has the Commission now dealt with?
2. How many cases has it referred to the Court of Appeal?
3. In how many cases has the defendant's conviction been quashed?

Examination Questions

(a) Describe the various appeals and other mechanisms for challenging the outcome of a Crown Court trial.   18 marks

(b) Lucas has been convicted at his trial in the Magistrates' Court. He was sentenced to five months' imprisonment. He wishes to appeal against his conviction as he believes the law was not applied properly in his case. He also wishes to appeal against his sentence as he feels it was too harsh. Explain the possible routes of appeal to Lucas.   12 marks

OCR G151 January 2012

Exam tips

This is another of those areas of the specification where you can do well if you are able to learn and then explain clearly how the system works. Revising this material using a flow chart, with different colours to indicate the courts, the role of the prosecution and the defence and the grounds for appeal can really help you get to grips with this topic.

It is not always popular with students so if you can do it well it's a good topic to have tucked away. It is acceptable to use a diagram in an exam answer as long as it is very clearly labeled and amplified by the accompanying text.

Section B application scenarios are quite often where appeals-based questions are found and once you have described the appeal routes you are likely to have to explain how the system would work for a defendant about whom you have been given some information.

Tips for a top quality answer include writing about the correct court then working upwards through the appeal structure, and reading the question carefully to see whether you need to write about the appeals available to both sides or just to one party, usually the defendant.

Chapter 8

Sentencing

8.1 The role of the courts

Whenever a person pleads guilty or is found guilty of an offence, the role of the court is to decide what sentence should be imposed on the offender. Judges and magistrates have a fairly wide discretion as to the sentence they select in each case, although they are subject to certain restrictions. Magistrates can only impose a maximum of six months' imprisonment for one offence (twelve months' for two) and a maximum fine of £5,000. Judges in the Crown Court have no such limits; they can impose up to life imprisonment for some crimes and there is no maximum figure for fines.

Figure 8.1 shows the percentages of different sentences imposed in Magistrates' Courts and at the Crown Court in 2011–12. The differing percentages of offenders given an immediate custodial sentence stresses that the Crown Court is dealing with more serious offences.

8.1.1 Restrictions on the courts' powers

However, there are other restrictions, both in the Magistrates' Court and the Crown Court. Each crime has a maximum penalty for that type of offence set by Parliament – for example, the crime of theft has a fixed maximum of seven years' imprisonment, so that no matter how much has been stolen, the judge can never send an offender to prison for longer than this.

Some offences have a maximum sentence of life imprisonment: these include manslaughter and rape. In such cases the judge has complete

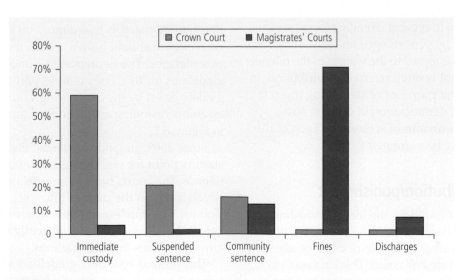

Source: Adapted from Sentencing Statistics for England and Wales 2011–12

Figure 8.1 Sentencing in the Magistrates' Courts and Crown Court

discretion when sentencing; the offender may be sent to prison for life or given a shorter prison sentence, or a non-custodial sentence may even be thought appropriate. Murder is the exception as it carries a mandatory life sentence; in other words, the judge has to pass life imprisonment as there is no other sentence available.

8.2 Aims of sentencing

When judges or magistrates have to pass a sentence they will not only look at the sentences available, they will also have to decide what they are trying to achieve by the punishment they give. Section 142 of the Criminal Justice Act 2003 sets out the purposes of sentencing for those aged 18 and over, saying that a court must have regard to:

- the punishment of offenders
- the reduction of crime (including its reduction by deterrence)
- the reform and rehabilitation of offenders
- the protection of the public, and
- the making of reparation by offenders to persons affected by their offences.

For young offenders, s 142A of the Criminal Justice Act 2003 states that, as well as the aims of punishment, reform and rehabilitation, protection of the public and reparation, the court must have regard to the principal aim of the youth justice system. This is to prevent offending (or re-offending) by persons aged under 18. The court must also have regard to the welfare of the offender.

Punishment is often referred to retribution. In addition to the purposes of sentencing given in the 2003 Act, denunciation of crime is also recognised as an aim of sentencing. Each of the aims will now be examined in turn.

8.2.1 Retribution/punishment

Retribution is based on the idea of punishment – the offender deserves punishment for his or her acts. It does not seek to reduce crime or alter the offender's future behaviour. This idea was expressed in the nineteenth century by Kant in *The Metaphysical Elements of Justice* when he wrote:

> " Judicial punishment can never be used merely as a means to promote some other good for the criminal himself or for civil society, but instead it must in all cases be imposed on him only on the ground that he has committed a crime. "

Retribution is therefore concerned only with the offence that was committed and making sure that the punishment inflicted is in proportion to that offence.

The crudest form of retribution can be seen in the old saying 'an eye for an eye and a tooth for a tooth and a life for a life'. This was one of the factors used to justify the death penalty for the offence of murder. In America, at least one judge has been known to put this theory into practice in other offences, by giving victims of burglary the right to go, with a law officer, to the home of the burglar and take items up to the approximate value of those stolen from them. In other crimes it is not so easy to see how this principle can operate to produce an exact match between crime and punishment.

Tariff sentences

Retribution, today, is based more on the idea that each offence should have a certain tariff or level of sentencing. The Sentencing Council produces guidelines for this. For example, part of the guidelines set by the Sentencing Council for assault occasioning actual bodily harm are given in Figure 8.2.

Since 2009, all guidelines must include a starting point for sentencing and a range for the offence. The courts have to impose a sentence which is within the offence range set by the new Council. The only exception is where the case before the court does not sufficiently resemble any of the cases in the guidelines.

This present system of guidelines should lead to consistency in sentencing. However, they leave

Step one: Determining the offence category

The court should determine the offence category using the table below.

Category 1	Greater harm (serious injury must normally be present) **and** higher culpability
Category 2	Greater harm (serious injury must normally be present) **and** lower culpability; **or** lesser harm **and** higher culpability
Category 3	Lesser harm **and** lower culpability

The guidelines then give factors which indicate higher or lower culpability. They also give factors to help decide the level of harm.

Step two: Starting point and category range

Having determined the category, the court should use the corresponding starting points to reach a sentence within the category range below. The starting point applies to all offenders irrespective of plea or previous convictions. A case of particular gravity, reflected by multiple features of culpability in step one, could merit upward adjustment from the starting point before further adjustment for aggravating or mitigating features, set out below.

Offence category	Starting point (applicable to all offenders)	Category range (applicable to all offenders)
Category 1	1 year 6 months' custody	1–3 years' custody
Category 2	26 weeks' custody	Low level community order – 51 weeks' custody
Category 3	Medium level community order	Band A fine – high level community order

Figure 8.2 Adapted from guidelines for assault occasioning actual bodily harm

very little discretion in sentencing for judges, and it may be difficult for courts to impose sentences aimed at reforming offenders.

8.2.2 Deterrence

This can be individual deterrence or general deterrence. Individual deterrence is intended to ensure that the offender does not re-offend, through fear of future punishment. General deterrence is aimed at preventing other potential offenders from committing crimes. Both are aimed at reducing future levels of crime.

Individual deterrence

Several penalties can be imposed with the aim of deterring the individual offender from committing similar crimes in the future. These include a prison sentence, a suspended sentence or a heavy fine. However, prison does not appear to deter as about 55 per cent of adult prisoners re-offend within two years of release. With young offenders, custodial sentences have even less of a deterrent effect. Over 70 per cent of young offenders given a custodial sentence re-offend within two years.

Critics of the theory of deterrence point out that it assumes that an offender will stop to consider the consequences of his action. In fact most crimes are committed on the spur of the moment, and many are committed by offenders who are under the influence of drugs or alcohol. These offenders are unlikely to stop and consider the possible consequences of their actions.

It is also pointed out that fear of being caught is more of a deterrent, and that while crime detection rates are low, the threat of an unpleasant penalty, if caught, seems too remote. Fear of detection has been shown to be a powerful deterrent by the success rate of closed circuit televisions used for surveying areas. In one scheme on London's District Line of the underground system there was an 83 per cent reduction in crime in the first full year that surveillance cameras were used.

General deterrence

The value of general deterrence is even more doubtful, as potential offenders are rarely deterred by severe sentences passed on others. However, the courts do occasionally resort to making an example of an offender in order to warn other potential offenders of the type of punishment they face.

General deterrence also relies on publicity so that potential offenders are aware of the level of punishment they can expect. Deterrent sentences will, therefore, be even less effective in cases of drug smuggling by foreign nationals, yet this is one of the crimes in which the courts seem tempted to resort to the hope that a severe sentence passed on one (or more) offender, will somehow deter other potential offenders.

General deterrence is in direct conflict with the principle of retribution, since it involves sentencing an offender to a longer term than is deserved for the specific offence. It is probably the least effective and least fair principle of sentencing.

8.2.3 Reform/rehabilitation

For this aspect, the main aim of the penalty is to reform the offender and rehabilitate him or her into society. It is a forward-looking aim, with the hope that the offender's behaviour will be altered by the penalty imposed, so that he or she will not offend in the future (it aims to reduce crime in this way). This principle of sentence came to the fore in the second half of the twentieth century with the development of community sentences.

As the abuse of drugs is the cause of many offences, there are also community sentences aimed at trying to rehabilitate drug abusers – Drug Rehabilitation Requirements.

Reformation is a very important element in the sentencing philosophy for young offenders, but it is also used for some adult offenders. The court will be given information about the defendant's background, usually through a pre-sentence report prepared by the probation service. Where relevant, the court will consider other factors, such as school reports, job prospects, or medical problems.

Individualised sentences

Where the court considers rehabilitation, the sentence used is an individualised one aimed at the needs of the offender. This is in direct contrast to the concept of tariff sentences seen in the aim of retribution. One of the criticisms of this approach is, therefore, that it leads to inconsistency in sentencing. Offenders who have committed exactly the same type of offence may be given different sentences because the emphasis is on the individual offender. Another criticism is that is tends to discriminate against the underprivileged. Offenders from poor home backgrounds are less likely to be seen as possible candidates for reform.

8.2.4 Protection of the public

The public need to be protected from dangerous offenders. For this reason, life imprisonment or a long term of imprisonment are given to those who commit murder or other violent or serious sexual offences.

The Criminal Justice Act 2003 introduced a provision for serious offences that where the court is of the opinion that there is a significant risk to members of the public of serious harm being caused by the defendant in the future, the court must send the defendant to prison for the protection of the public.

The Criminal Justice Act 2003 also has provision for extended sentences to be given where it is thought necessary to protect the public. This adds an extra period to the defendant's sentence during which he is freed on licence.

For less serious offences there are other ways in which the public can be protected; for example, dangerous drivers are disqualified from driving. Another method is to include an exclusion order as a requirement in a community order. This will ban the offender from going to places where he is most likely to commit an offence. The use of such a banning order is shown in *R v Winkler* (2004).

In this case the defendant committed an affray in Manchester when attending a football match in which Oldham Athletic, the team he supported, was playing. The judge banned the defendant from going into Oldham town centre on home match days and also banned him from approaching within half a mile of any football stadium. Both bans were for a period of six years.

Another method of protecting the public is to impose a curfew order on the offender, ordering him to remain at home for certain times of the day or night. The curfew can be monitored by an electronic tag, which should trigger an alarm if the offender leaves his home address during a curfew period.

8.2.5 Reparation

This is aimed at compensating the victim of the crime usually by ordering the offender to pay a sum of money to the victim or to make restitution, for example, by returning stolen property to its rightful owner. The idea that criminals should pay compensation to the victims of their crimes is one that goes back before the Norman Conquest to the Anglo-Saxon courts.

In England today, the courts are required to consider ordering compensation to the victim of a crime, in addition to any other penalty they may

Key facts

Theory	Aim of theory	Suitable punishment
Retribution/ Punishment	Punishment imposed only on ground that an offence has been committed	• tariff sentences • sentence must be proportionate to the crime
Deterrence	Individual – the offender is deterred through fear of further punishment General – potential offenders warned as to likely punishment	• prison sentence • heavy fine • long sentence as an example to others
Rehabilitation	Reform offender's behaviour	• individualised sentence • community order
Protection of the public	Offender is made incapable of committing further crime Society is protected from crime	• long prison sentences • tagging • banning orders
Reparation	Repayment/reparation to victim or to community	• compensation order • unpaid work • reparation schemes
Denunciation	Society expressing its disapproval Reinforces moral boundaries	• reflects blameworthiness of the offence

Figure 8.3 Key facts chart on aims of sentencing

think appropriate. Under s 130 of the Powers of Criminal Courts (Sentencing) Act 2000 courts are under a duty to give reasons if they do not make a compensation order. There are also projects to bring offenders and victims together, so that the offenders may make direct reparation.

The concept of restitution also includes making reparation to society as a whole. This can be seen mainly in the use of an unpaid work requirement where offenders are required to do many hours' work on a community project under the supervision of the probation service.

8.2.6 Denunciation

This is society expressing its disapproval of criminal activity. A sentence should indicate both to the offender and to other people that society condemns certain types of behaviour. It shows people that justice is being done. Lord Denning when giving written evidence to the Royal Commission on Capital Punishment put it in this way:

> Punishment is the way in which society expresses its denunciation of wrongdoing: and in order to maintain respect for the law it is essential that the punishment inflicted for grave crimes should adequately reflect the revulsion felt by the great majority of citizens for them.

Denunciation also reinforces the moral boundaries of acceptable conduct and can mould society's views on the criminality of particular conduct – for example, drink-driving is now viewed by the majority of people as unacceptable behaviour. This is largely because of the changes in the law and the increasingly severe sentences that are imposed. By sending offenders to prison, banning them from driving and imposing heavy fines, society's opinion of drink driving has been changed.

Self-Test Questions

1 What is the maximum period of imprisonment which magistrates can impose for one offence?
2 What are the six aims of sentencing?
3 What is meant by a 'tariff sentence'?
4 What are the two types of deterrence?
5 For what age group is reform/rehabilitation particularly important?
6 Which sentences are aimed at protecting the public?
7 Which orders or sentences are aimed at reparation?

Activity

Read the following article and answer the questions below.

Tougher jail terms DO deter criminals, admits Home Office

A Home Office report has concluded that stiffer prison sentences deter crime … the study found that convicts jailed for less than a year are almost 50 per cent more likely to commit a fresh crime within two years of their release than those locked up for between one and four years.

And they are twice as likely to break the law as those jailed for at least four years.

The report is embarrassing for the Government. Only this month [May 2007], Lord Falconer, newly-created Justice Secretary, announced that tens of thousands of burglars and other thieves would receive community punishments instead of jail sentences under plans to ease chronic prison overcrowding.

In March [2007] the Prime Minister signalled that there should be greater emphasis on rehabilitating offenders, tougher community sentences and crime prevention …

Figures show that 70 per cent of convicts jailed for under 12 months re-offended within two years, compared with 49 per cent of those convicted to between one and four years and 36 per cent of those serving as least four years.

The report said prisoners released from longer sentences were less likely to re-offend because they were older, had time to be rehabilitated and had been convicted of more serious 'one-off' offences.

Taken from an article by Ian Drury in the *Daily Mail*, 19 May 2007

Questions

1. What sentencing aim does this article suggest that stiffer prison sentences promote?
2. What sentencing aim did the Prime Minister want to emphasise?
3. What sentencing aim does the Home Office Report say had an effect on longer term prisoners?
4. Name and explain two other sentencing aims.

Exam tips

Sentencing is a very common topic on the exam paper and so it is worth making sure you have a good grasp of it. To do well you need to be confident and accurate in your knowledge. The aims of sentencing are an important part of the criminal justice process but it is very risky to think that you will be able to write about these aims without also knowing the range of sentences available and the factors that are taken into account when the courts are deciding on the most appropriate way forward for a defendant.

The aims of sentencing can appear in either Section A or B questions – in the former you will need to give factual information and then be able to discuss the relative merits of one or more sentencing aims. This means you need to have some points of comment ready on each of the aims. It is also worth remembering that sentencing principles can be different for adult and young offenders.

This could be especially relevant if the question appears in Section B as your response will then depend on the information you are given about the person to be sentenced. If you are asked to consider an adult offender you will not gain marks for writing about the aims which would have been relevant had they been a young offender, for example.

8.3 Sentencing Practice in the courts

The court will usually consider both the offence and the background of the offender, as well as the aims of sentencing. In order to do this, the court must know details of the offence, so where the defendant pleads guilty the prosecution will outline the facts of the case. As seen in Chapter 6, section 6.1.2, the defendant is asked if he agrees with those facts and, if not, a Newton hearing will be held for the facts to be established. This is important as the details of the offence can affect the sentence. Where the defendant has pleaded not guilty and been convicted after a trial, the court will have heard full information about the case during the trial.

8.3.1 Factors surrounding the offence

In looking at the offence, the most important point to establish is, how serious was it, of its type? This is now set out in s 143(1) of the Criminal Justice Act 2003 which states that:

> In considering the seriousness of the offence, the court must consider the offender's culpability in committing the offence and any harm which the offence caused, or was intended to cause or might reasonably foreseeably have caused.

The Act lists certain factors which are considered as aggravating, making an offence more serious. These are:

- previous convictions for offences of a similar nature or relevant to the present offence
- the fact that the defendant was on bail when he committed the offence
- racial or religious hostility being involved in the offence
- hostility to disability or sexual orientation being involved in the offence.

Other points the courts will want to know may include, for example in a case of theft, how much was stolen, and was the defendant in a position of trust? In a case of assault, the court will need to know what injuries were inflicted and whether the assault was premeditated, or was the victim particularly vulnerable (perhaps elderly).

Where the offender was in a position of trust and abused that trust, then the offence will be considered as being more serious and meriting a longer than usual sentence.

Where several defendants are convicted of committing a crime jointly, the court will want to know what part each played in the offence. Those who played a leading role are likely to receive heavier sentences while those with only a minor part (such as being a lookout) will receive lighter sentences.

8.3.2 Reduction in sentence for a guilty plea

There can be a reduction in sentence for a guilty plea, particularly when it is made early in the proceedings. The reduction for a guilty plea at the first reasonable opportunity is up to one-third, unless the evidence of guilt is overwhelming when it will be 20 per cent. A plea of guilty after the trial has started will only be given a one-tenth reduction. The amount of reduction is on a sliding scale, as shown in Figure 8.4.

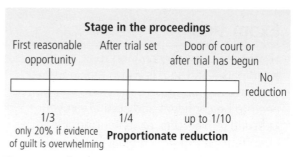

Figure 8.4 Reduction in sentence for a guilty plea

The concept of reducing the level of sentence imposed on a defendant just because he has pleaded guilty has caused controversy. Many people believe that if someone has 'done the crime, they should do the time'. However, there are good reasons for given a discount in sentence for a guilty plea. These include the fact that a guilty plea:

- avoids the need for a trial
- shortens the time between charge and sentence
- saves considerable cost
- saves victims from having to give evidence.

8.3.3 The offender's background
Previous convictions

The court will want to know whether the offender has any previous convictions. Those with no previous convictions are likely to receive lighter sentences than those with previous convictions. Failure to respond to previous sentences can make the present offence more serious. The past record of the offender will also determine whether he has to receive a minimum sentence or an automatic life sentence for certain offences.

Another important factor is whether the offender was on bail when he committed the offence. If this is the case, the court must treat that fact as an aggravating factor.

Pre-sentence reports

These are prepared by the probation service. The court does not have to (but usually will) consider such a report before deciding to impose a custodial sentence, though for very serious offences such a report may not be relevant.

Where the court is considering a community sentence, they are likely to have a report before they decide on the sentence. The report will give information about the defendant's background and suitability, or otherwise, for a community-based sentence. The defendant's background may be important in showing both why the offender committed a crime, and if he is likely to respond to a community-based penalty.

Medical reports

Where the offender has medical or psychiatric problems, the court will usually ask for a report to be prepared by an appropriate doctor. Medical conditions may be important factors in deciding the appropriate way of dealing with the offender; the courts have special powers where the defendant is suffering from mental illness. The treatment of mentally ill defendants is considered further in section 8.6.

The financial situation of the offender

Where the court considers that a fine is a suitable penalty, it must inquire into the financial circumstances of the offender, and take this into account when setting the level of the fine.

8.3.4 Sentencing Council

In 2003 the Sentencing Guidelines Council was set up to issue guidelines on any aspect of sentencing. There was also a Sentencing Advisory Panel which could make proposals to the Council that there should be guidelines for a particular offence or aspect of sentencing, and which conducted research on sentencing. In 2010 both of these bodies were replaced by the Sentencing Council.

The Sentencing Council has responsibility for:

- developing sentencing guidelines and monitoring their use;
- assessing the impact of guidelines on sentencing practice; and
- promoting awareness amongst the public regarding the realities of sentencing and publishing information regarding sentencing practice in Magistrates' and Crown Courts.

The Sentencing Council has more powers than the previous Council. In particular, the courts are now under a duty to impose a sentence which is within the offence range set out by the Council. The courts should only depart from the range when it is in the interests of justice to do so.

@ **Internet Research**

Look for sentencing guidelines on the Sentencing Council's website at http://sentencingcouncil.judiciary.gov.uk.

Self-Test Questions

1 Give three factors that make an offence more serious for the purposes of sentencing.
2 What is the maximum reduction in a sentence that an offender can be given for pleading guilty? What are the arguments for giving a reduction in sentence for a guilty plea?
3 Name three factors in the offender's background that may be considered when sentencing.
4 Who issues sentencing guidelines?
5 Why are sentencing guidelines issued?

8.4 Powers of the courts

As already indicated, the courts have several different types of sentences available to them. There are four main categories: custodial sentences, community sentences, fines and discharges. The courts also have the power to make additional orders such as compensation orders, and in motoring offences have other powers such as disqualification from driving.

8.4.1 Custodial sentences

A custodial sentence is the most serious punishment that a court can impose. Custodial sentences range from a few weeks to life imprisonment. They include:

● mandatory and discretionary life sentences
● fixed-term sentences
● suspended sentences.

Custodial sentences are meant to be used only for serious offences. Section 152 of the Criminal Justice Act 2003 says that the court must not pass a custodial sentence unless it is of the opinion that the offence (or combination of offences):

> **"** was so serious that neither a fine alone nor a community sentence can be justified. **"**

The age of the offender is also important as young offenders should only be given a custodial sentence as a last resort. Where a young offender is given a custodial sentence they are always held in separate units from adults.

The court must state its reason for imposing a custodial sentence, and in the case of the Magistrates' Court, that reason must be written on the warrant of commitment and entered in the court register.

Inside Winchester prison

Mandatory life sentences

For murder, the only sentence a judge can impose is a life sentence. However, the judge is allowed to state the minimum number of years' imprisonment that the offender must serve before being eligible for release on licence. This minimum term is now governed by the Criminal Justice Act 2003. This gives judges clear starting points for the minimum period to be ordered. The starting points range from a full-life term down to 12 years.

A whole-life term should be set where the offence falls into one of the following categories:

- the murder of two or more persons, where each murder involves a substantial degree of premeditation or planning, the abduction of the victim, or sexual or sadistic conduct
- the murder of a child if involving the abduction of the child or sexual or sadistic motivation
- a murder done for the purpose of advancing a political, religious or ideological cause, or
- a murder by an offender previously convicted of murder.

Cases which have a starting point of 30 years include where:

- the murder is of a police or prison officer in the course of his duty
- a murder was committed using a firearm or explosive
- the murder was the sexual or sadistic murder of an adult
- a murder was racially or religiously aggravated.

For any offence of murder which is not specifically given a starting point of a whole-life term or 30 years, a starting point of 15 years is given. Where the offender was under the age of 18 at the time of the offence, this period is 12 years. Once the judge has decided on the starting point, any aggravating or mitigating factors must then be considered.

Aggravating factors which can increase the minimum term ordered by the judge include the fact that the victim was particularly vulnerable because of age or disability, or any mental or physical suffering inflicted on the victim before death.

Mitigating factors include the fact that the offender had an intention to cause grievous bodily harm rather than an intention to kill, a lack of premeditation or the fact that the offender acted to some extent in self-defence (though not sufficient to give him a defence). Where there are mitigating factors, the judge can set a minimum term of less than any of the starting points.

Discretionary life sentences

For other serious offences such as manslaughter, rape and robbery the maximum sentence is life imprisonment, but the judge does not have to impose it. The judge has discretion in sentencing and can give any lesser sentence where appropriate. This could be a community order or even a fine or a discharge.

Fixed-term sentences

For other crimes, the length of the sentence will depend on several factors, including the maximum sentence available for the particular crime, the seriousness of the crime and the defendant's previous record. Imprisonment for a set number of months or years is called a 'fixed-term' sentence.

Prisoners do not serve the whole of the sentence passed by the court. Anyone sent to prison is automatically released after they have served half of the sentence. Only offenders aged 21 and over can be given a sentence of imprisonment.

Home Detention Curfew

The Crime and Disorder Act 1998 allows early release from prison on condition that a curfew condition is included. The curfew is enforced by electronic tagging. The period of curfew is increased with the length of sentence. There is no automatic right to be released on curfew; each prisoner is assessed to see if he or she is suitable. If a Home Detention Curfew order is not made, then the prisoner must serve half the sentence before release on licence.

The reason for introducing Home Detention Curfews is to encourage recently released prisoners to structure their lives more effectively, as well as prevent re-offending. Also, the prison population is reduced by releasing prisoners early in this way.

Extended sentences

Section 85 of the Powers of Criminal Courts (Sentencing) Act 2000 gives the sentencing court the power to pass an extended sentence for a sexual or violent offence. This means that the offender is given a custodial sentence plus a further period (the 'extension period') during which the offender is at liberty on licence. The extension period cannot exceed ten years for a sexual offence or five years for a violent offence.

The idea behind this sentence is to have greater control over sexual offenders when they leave prison. Such offenders are also required to register with the police so that it is known where they are living.

Minimum sentences

There is a minimum sentence of seven years for anyone aged 18 or over who is convicted on three separate occasions of dealing in Class A drugs. There is also a minimum sentence of three years for those convicted of burglary of a residential building for a third time. In both cases, judges can impose a shorter sentence if there are exceptional circumstances.

Prison population

Prisons in England and Wales are overcrowded. There has been a big increase in the number of

 Internet Research

Look up the current prison population on the internet. It can be found at www.justice.gov.uk/about/hmps.

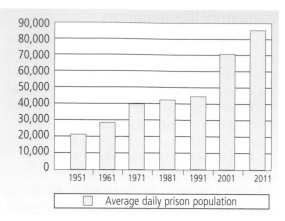

Figure 8.5 Average daily prison population for England and Wales 1951–2011

people in prison, and there are not enough prison places. Figure 8.5 shows the increase in the prison population between 1951 and 2011.

Suspended prison sentences

An adult offender may be given a suspended prison sentence of up to two years (six months' maximum in the Magistrates' Court). This means that the sentence does not take effect immediately. The court will fix a time during which the sentence is suspended; this can be for any period up to two years. If, during this time, the offender does not commit any further offences, the prison sentence will not be served. However, if the offender does commit another offence within the period of suspension, then the prison sentence is 'activated' and the offender will serve that sentence together with any sentence for the new offence.

A suspended sentence should only be given where the offence is so serious that an immediate custodial sentence would have been appropriate, but there are exceptional circumstances in the case that justify suspending the sentence.

The suspended sentence can be combined with any of the requirements used in a community order (see section 8.4.3). If the offender fails to meet the requirements, the suspended sentence may be 'activated'. This

Activity

Read the following extracts from a parliamentary briefing paper giving statistics on prisoners and answer the questions below.

- Over 25 per cent of prisoners had been taken into care as a child compared to 2 per cent of the population.
- 81 per cent of prisoners were unmarried prior to imprisonment, rising to 85 per cent since imprisonment. Almost 10 per cent had been divorced. These figures are twice as high as those found in the general population.
- One half of male and one third of female sentenced prisoners were excluded from school. One half of male and seven out of ten female prisoners have no qualifications.

- Two-thirds of prisoners have numeracy skills at or below a level expected of an 11 year old. One half have a reading ability and 82 per cent have writing ability at or below this level.
- Two-thirds of prisoners were unemployed in the four weeks before imprisonment.
- Around 70 per cent of prisoners suffer from two or more mental disorders. In the general population, the figures are 5 per cent for men and 2 per cent for women.
- Prisoners are more likely to be abusers of illegal drugs and alcohol than other sectors of the community.

Taken from *Prison Population Statistics,*
House of Commons Library,
24 May 2012

Questions

1. What problems did many prisoners have when they were children?

2. What other problems do many of those who are convicted have prior to their conviction?

3. What percentage of prisoners suffer from two or more mental disorders?

4. Which factor(s) in the above list do you think would be most likely to lead to a person committing offences?

5. Discuss ways in which offenders could be helped not to reoffend.

means that the offender will be made to serve the term of imprisonment. Prior to the Criminal Justice Act 2003, a suspended sentence could only be combined with a fine or a compensation order, leaving the offender unsupervised. As a result, a suspended sentence was seen as a 'soft option' and rarely used by the courts.

As it can now be combined with any order the court thinks appropriate, it is used more often, especially in the Crown Court where it is used in about 20 per cent of sentences.

8.4.2 Community orders

The Criminal Justice Act 2003 created one community order under which the court can combine any requirements they think are necessary. These requirements are listed below. The sentences can 'mix and match' requirements, allowing them to fit the restrictions and rehabilitation to the offender's needs. The sentence is available for offenders aged 16 and over. The full list of requirements available to the courts is set out in s 177 of the Criminal Justice Act 2003. This states:

177(1) Where a person aged 16 or over is convicted of an offence, the court by or before which he is convicted may make an order imposing on him any one or more of the following requirements:

   (a) as unpaid work requirement

   (b) an activity requirement

   (c) a programme requirement

   (d) a prohibited activity requirement

   (e) a curfew requirement

   (f) an exclusion requirement

   (g) a residence requirement

   (h) a mental health treatment requirement

   (i) a drug rehabilitation requirement

   (j) an alcohol treatment requirement

   (k) a supervision requirement, and

   (l) in the case where the offender is aged under 25, an attendance centre requirement.

Each of these is defined within the Criminal Justice Act 2003. Most are self-explanatory from their name, such as drug rehabilitation and alcohol treatment. Much crime is linked to drug and alcohol abuse and the idea behind these two requirements is to tackle the causes of crime, and hopefully prevent further offences. Mental health treatment is also aimed at the cause of the offender's behaviour. The main other requirements are explained briefly below.

Unpaid work requirement

This requires the offender to work for between 40 and 300 hours on a suitable project organised by the probation service. The exact number of hours will be fixed by the court, and those hours are then usually worked in eight-hour sessions, often at weekends. The type of work involved will vary, depending on what schemes the local probation service have running. The offender may be required to paint school buildings, help build a play centre or work on conservation projects. When Eric Cantona, the French footballer, was found guilty of assaulting a football fan, the court ordered that he help at coaching sessions for young footballers.

One criticism is that the number of hours is not enough – other countries which run similar schemes can impose much longer hours. However, re-offending rates are lower than for other community sentences.

Prohibited activity requirement

This requirement allows a wide variety of activities to be prohibited. The idea is to try to prevent the defendant from committing another crime of the type he has just been convicted of. Often the defendant is forbidden to go into a certain area where he has caused trouble. In some cases the defendant has been banned from wearing a 'hoodie'. In 2006, a defendant who was found guilty of criminal damage was banned from carrying paint, dye, ink or marker pens.

Curfew requirement

Under this requirement, an offender can be ordered to remain at a fixed address for between two and sixteen hours in any 24-hour period. This order can last for up to six months and may be enforced by electronic tagging (where suitable). Courts can only make such an order if there is an arrangement for monitoring curfews in their area. Such monitoring can be done by spot-checks, with security firms sending someone to make sure that the offender is at home, or offenders may be electronically tagged. There are also pilot schemes on using satellite technology to track those who are tagged.

The cost of tagging is quite expensive, but it is much cheaper than keeping an offender in prison.

Initially tagging appeared to be a successful method of preventing re-offending. However, as the use of electronic tagging has increased (its use doubled between 2005 and 2011), the failure rate has increased.

A report in 2012 by the Chief Inspector of Probation showed that over half of offenders ordered to wear an electronic tag broke the terms of their curfew. Twenty per cent were minor violations where the offenders were warned and then successfully completed their order. However, in 37 per cent of cases, there was a serious violation which required further action by the courts.

Exclusion requirement

Offenders are ordered not to go to certain places. The order can specify different places for different periods or days. This is intended to keep offenders away from areas where they are most likely to commit crime; for example, a persistent shoplifter could be banned from certain shopping areas. The order can be for up to two years for

offenders aged 16 and over, and a maximum of three months for those under 16.

Supervision requirement

For this requirement the offender is placed under the supervision of a probation officer for a period of up to three years. During the period of supervision the offender must attend appointments with the supervising officer or with any other person decided by the supervising officer.

The Criminal Justice Act 2003 states that a supervision requirement may be imposed for the purpose of 'promoting the offender's rehabilitation'.

8.4.3 Fines

This is the most common way of disposing of a case in the Magistrates' Court where the maximum fine is £5,000 for an individual offender. The magistrate can impose a fine of up to £20,000 on businesses who have committed offences under certain regulations, such as health and safety at work. In the Crown Court only a small percentage of offenders are dealt with by way of a fine.

8.4.4 Discharges

These may be either a conditional discharge or an absolute discharge.

Conditional discharge

A conditional discharge means that the court discharges an offender on the condition that no further offence is committed during a set period of up to three years. It is intended to be used where it is thought that punishment is not necessary. If an offender re-offends within the time limit, the court can then impose another sentence in place of the conditional discharge, as well as imposing a penalty for the new offence. Conditional discharges are widely used by Magistrates' Courts for first-time minor offenders.

Activity

Look at the bar chart on the opening page of this chapter which shows the types of sentence used in the Magistrates' Court and the Crown Courts and answer the following questions.

1. What type of sentence are offenders most likely to be given at the Crown Court?
2. What type of sentence are offenders most likely to be given at the Magistrates' Courts?
3. Why do you think the sentences used most frequently are different for the two courts?
4. Which two types of sentence show the biggest difference in percentages given at the Crown Court and at the Magistrates' Courts?
5. Why do you think the percentages for these two types of sentence are different in the Magistrates' Court and the Crown Court?

Absolute discharge

An absolute discharge means that, effectively, no penalty is imposed. Such a penalty is likely to be used where an offender is technically guilty but morally blameless. An example could be where the tax disc on a vehicle has fallen to the floor – it is technically not being displayed and an offence has been committed. So, in the unlikely situation of someone being prosecuted for this, the magistrates, who would have to impose some penalty, would most probably decide that an absolute discharge was appropriate.

8.4.5 Disqualification from driving

Where a defendant is charged with a driving offence, the courts may also have the power to disqualify that person from driving for a certain period of time. The length of the disqualification will depend on the seriousness of the driving

offence. Usually the courts will impose a fine as well as disqualification. For a first-time drink-driving offence the courts have to disqualify the defendant for a minimum of 12 months, unless there are very exceptional reasons not to disqualify. If an offender has a previous drink-drive conviction, then the minimum is usually three years' disqualification.

The courts can use this power to disqualify in any other crime where the offender has used a vehicle to commit an offence. For example, a defendant who drives a car in order to do a burglary could be disqualified from driving, but this power is not often used.

8.4.6 Other powers available to the courts

The courts have other powers which are aimed at compensating victims and/or making sure that the defendant does not benefit from his or her crimes.

Compensation orders and restitution orders

Courts can make an order that the defendant pay a sum of money to his victim in compensation. They are encouraged to use this order by the fact that they must give reasons if they do *not* make a compensation order, in any case in which they have the power to do so. In the Magistrates' Court the maximum amount of compensation is £5,000.

If the defendant still has the property he obtained from the victim, then the courts can make an order that the property is returned. This is called a restitution order.

Deprivation and forfeiture orders

A court can order an offender to be deprived of property he has used to commit an offence; for example, a person convicted of drink-driving could be ordered to lose his car. There are special powers to order forfeiture in drug-related cases. The Proceeds of Crime Act 1995 also gives the courts powers to take from criminals all profits from crime for up to six years before conviction.

Internet Research

Try your hand at sentencing online. Go to http://ybtj.cjsonline.gov.uk and you will be given the facts of a real case. Decide what sentence you would give and then see what sentence the judge in the case gave.

8.5 Young offenders

This term includes all offenders under the age of 21. However, there are considerable variations in the different sentences available for those under 18, under 16, under 14 and under 12. The main aim in sentencing young offenders is reformation and rehabilitation. As already seen in Chapter 6, offenders under 18 are normally dealt with in the Youth Court.

8.5.1 Available sentences

Young Offenders' Institutions

Offenders aged 15 to 20 can be sent to a Young Offenders' Institution as a custodial sentence. The minimum sentence is 21 days and the maximum is the maximum allowed for the particular offence. If the offender becomes 21 years old while serving the sentence, he will be transferred to an adult prison.

Detention and training orders

The Crime and Disorder Act 1998 created a new custodial sentence, called a detention and training order, for young offenders. The sentence must be for a specified period with a minimum of four months and a maximum of 24 months. The offender is sent to a secure training centre. Half of the sentence is spent in custody and the other half in the community.

A detention and training order can be passed on offenders from the age of 12 to the age of 21, but for those under the age of 15 this order can only be made if they are persistent offenders.

Detention for serious crimes

For very serious offences, the courts have additional power to order that the offender be detained for longer periods. For 10- to 13-year-olds this power is only available where the crime committed carries a maximum sentence of at least 14 years' imprisonment for adults. For 14- to 17-year-olds, it is also available for causing death by dangerous driving, or for causing death by careless driving while under the influence of drink or drugs. The length of detention imposed on the young offender cannot be more than the maximum sentence available for an adult.

Detention at Her Majesty's Pleasure

Any offender aged 10–17 who is convicted of murder must be ordered to be detained during Her Majesty's Pleasure. This is an indeterminate sentence which allows the offender to be released when suitable. The judge in the case can recommend a minimum number of years that should be served before release is considered, and the Lord Chief Justice will then set the tariff.

If an offender reaches 21 while still serving a sentence, he will be transferred to an adult prison.

Youth Rehabilitation Order

For community sentences, there is now the Youth Rehabilitation Order. This was brought in by the Criminal Justice and Immigration Act 2008. It works on the same principle as a community order for an adult offender. The court can 'mix and match' requirements to suit the circumstances.

The requirements which can be attached to a youth rehabilitation order are:

(a) an activity requirement

(b) a supervision requirement

(c) in a case where the offender is aged 16 or 17 at the time of the conviction, an unpaid work requirement

(d) a programme requirement

(e) an attendance centre requirement

(f) a prohibited activity requirement

(g) a curfew requirement

(h) an exclusion requirement

(i) a residence requirement

(j) a local authority residence requirement

(k) a mental health treatment requirement

(l) a drug treatment requirement

(m) a drug testing requirement

(n) an intoxicating substance treatment requirement, and

(o) an education requirement.

Most of the requirements are similar to those for adults, but there are some aimed specifically at younger offenders. These include a local authority residence requirement under which an offender under 17 can be placed in the care of the local authority. An education requirement is aimed at those of school age. Attendance centre requirements are also used for young offenders.

Attendance centre requirement

This type of order is only for those under 25, and is available for all young offenders from the age of ten upwards. It involves attendance at a special centre for two or three hours a week – up to a maximum of 36 hours for 16- to 24-year-olds, and 24 hours for 14- to 15-year-olds. The minimum number of hours for these age groups is 12. Offenders under the age of 14 can only be given a maximum of 12 hours at an attendance centre. The centres used to be run by the police but are now under the supervision of the probation service; they are usually held on Saturday afternoons and will include organised leisure activities and training. An Attendance Centre Order cannot be made if the offender has served a period of detention previously.

Fines

The maximum amount of a fine varies with the age of the offender: 10- to 13-year-olds can only be fined a maximum of £250, while for 14- to 17-year-olds the maximum is £1,000. Those aged 18 and over are subject to the normal maximum of the Magistrates' Court of £5,000.

Discharges

Both a conditional discharge and an absolute discharge may be used for an offender of any age. Conditional discharges are commonly used for first-time young offenders who have committed minor crimes.

Reprimands and warnings

These are not sentences passed by a court, but methods by which the police can deal with offenders without bringing the case to court. For either a reprimand or warning to be given there must be evidence that a child or young person has committed an offence and admits it. In addition, the police must be satisfied that it would not be in the public interest for the offender to be prosecuted. A reprimand or warning can only be given if the offender has never been convicted of any offence.

There is a limit to the number of times and the occasions on which an offender can be 'cautioned'. The first step is the reprimand. This can only be given if the child or young person has not been previously reprimanded or warned. Even then it should not be used where the constable considers the offence to be so serious as to require a warning.

An offender may be warned only if he has not been warned before or if an earlier warning was more than two years before. When warned, the child or young offender must be referred to a Youth Offending Team. This team assesses the case and, unless it considers it inappropriate to do so, arranges for the offender to participate in a rehabilitation scheme.

8.5.2 Parental responsibility

If the parents agree, they can be bound over to keep their child under control for a set period of up to one year. If the child commits an offence during this period the parents will forfeit a sum of money up to a maximum of £1,000. If a parent unreasonably refuses to be bound over, the court has the power to fine that parent instead. Parents can also be bound over to ensure that a young offender complies with a community sentence.

Where an offender under 16 years old is fined or ordered to pay compensation, the court must

Key facts

Types of sentence	Age limitations
Custodial sentences	• Prison only for 21+ • Young Offenders' Institution 15- to 20-year-olds • Detention and training order for 12- to 20-year-olds • Powers of detention for 10- to 17-year-olds in serious cases
Community orders/ Youth rehabilitation orders	• May 'mix and match' different requirements to suit different offenders' needs
Fines	• Over-18s: Magistrates' Court, maximum £5,000 (Crown Court, no limit) • 14–17: maximum £1,000 • 10–13: maximum £250
Discharges	• Conditional discharge: 10+ • Absolute discharge: 10+
Other powers	• Disqualification from driving: 10+ • Compensation orders: 10+ • Reparation orders: 10–17

Figure 8.6 Key facts chart on sentencing powers of the courts

require the offender's parents to pay, and the financial situation of the parent is taken into account in deciding the amount of the order.

Parenting orders

This is intended to offer training and support to parents to help change their children's offending behaviour. In this way it is more practical than the existing provisions which merely make a parent responsible for their child's offending behaviour. Under such an order a parent can be required to attend counselling or guidance sessions for up to three months on a maximum basis of once a week.

In addition, the parent may be required to comply with conditions imposed by the courts; for example, escort the child to school or ensure that a responsible adult is present in the home in the evening to supervise the child. A court may make a parenting order where:

• the court makes a child safety order
• the court makes an anti-social behaviour order (or sex offender order) in respect of a child

• a child or young person is convicted of an offence
• a parent is convicted of an offence relating to truancy under the Education Act 1996.

An order should only be made if it is desirable in the interests of preventing the conduct which gave rise to the order. Where a person under the age of 16 is convicted of an offence, the court should make a parenting order unless it is satisfied that it is not desirable in the interests of preventing the conduct which gave rise to the order. In this case the court must state in open court that it is not satisfied and explain why not.

8.5.3 Youth Offending Teams

The Crime and Disorder Act 1998 made it the duty of each local authority to establish one or more Youth Offending Teams (YOTs) in their area. The main idea in establishing these teams is to build on cooperation between agencies involved, especially social services and the probation service. These teams are to coordinate the provision of youth justice services in the area.

A YOT must include a probation officer, a local authority social worker, a police officer, a representative of the local health authority and a person nominated by the chief education officer. Any other appropriate person may also be invited to join the team.

The role of YOTs is highlighted by the fact that, under s 66 of the Crime and Disorder Act 1998, any offender who is warned must be referred to the local YOT. Youth courts may also refer offenders to the YOT.

Activity

Suggest a suitable sentence for the following offenders and explain what the aim of the sentence would be.

1. Kevin, aged 22, has been found guilty by the magistrates of two charges of criminal damage. The amount of damage involved is estimated at £600. He is single, unemployed and has no previous convictions.
2. Melanie, aged 15, appeared before the local youth court and admitted shoplifting on five occasions. She also admitted two offences of taking and driving a car without the owner's consent. She has appeared before the youth court on two previous occasions for similar offences.
3. Andrew, aged 26, has been found guilty at the Crown Court of an assault causing grievous bodily harm. He committed this offence while on bail, charged with another offence of violence.

8.6 Mentally ill offenders

The law recognises that, so far as possible, mentally ill offenders should not be punished but should receive treatment. Where an offence has been committed by an offender who is mentally ill, the courts have a wider range of powers available to them. In addition to the ordinary sentences which can be given, there are special provisions aimed at treating such offenders in a suitable way.

The main additional powers available to the courts are to give the offender a community sentence, with a requirement that he or she attends for treatment, make a hospital order or make a restriction order under s 41 of the Mental Health Act 1983.

A community order requiring the offender to have treatment will be made where the court is satisfied that the mental condition is treatable, and that there is no need to make a hospital order. A hospital order will be made if the condition makes it appropriate that the offender should stay in hospital for treatment.

However, there are some cases in which the protection of the public is a key element. Under s 41 of the Mental Health Act 1983 offenders with severe mental problems, who are considered to be a danger to the community, can be sent to a secure hospital such as Broadmoor. Magistrates' Courts cannot make such an order; it can only be made by a Crown Court. The order can be that the offender be detained for a set period or, where necessary, for an indefinite period. If an offender is ordered to be detained for an indefinite period, the hospital can only discharge him with the permission of the Home Secretary or the Mental Health Review Tribunal.

Self-Test Questions

1 What is meant by a mandatory life sentence?
2 What is a Home Detention Curfew?
3 What is the minimum sentence which can be given to someone convicted of burglary for the third time?
4 Explain four requirements that can be attached to a community order.
5 What is the effect of a conditional discharge?
6 What custodial sentences can be passed on an offender aged between 18 and 20?
7 Name three non-custodial sentences that can be given to a young offender.

Examination Questions

1(a) Describe the different custodial sentences available for adult and young offenders.   18 marks

1(b) Bryn, who is 17 years old, has been convicted of the serious offence of robbery. He has several previous convictions for theft and has previously been fined, given a supervision order and been subject to a curfew whilst electronically tagged.

Explain what factors are likely to be taken into account when sentencing Bryn and what sentence he is likely to be given.   12 marks

OCR G151, January 2012

2(a) Describe the aims of sentencing and the factors that are taken into account when sentencing an individual.   18 marks

2(b) Discuss which sentences would be most appropriate when the main aim of sentencing is the prevention of crime.   12 marks

OCR G151 June 2010

Exam tips

The other part of sentencing is the practical aspect – what sentences are likely to be used in a particular case. Here it is really important that you read the question carefully so that the information you use is relevant.

The distinction between young and adult offenders is crucial and there is a lot of detailed information to master. This can make sentencing a difficult area to revise and you need to be organised in your approach.

Making charts and getting someone to test you can really help you sort out a lot of detail which is not necessarily hard to learn in itself but which must be used correctly to gain high marks. Sometimes, as with the Youth Rehabilitation Orders, you don't need to know every single possible condition which can be attached to one of these Orders – a selection that shows you understand how the courts will use these conditions will be enough.

Questions quite often use a scenario to direct your answer – tips to doing well include:

● consideration of the age of the offender;
● the type of offence they have committed;
● the court in which their case has been heard; and
● relevant information you are given about their background such as their past record and their family circumstances.

Make use of your highlighter so that you keep to the point as sentencing is a big topic. Because it takes time and effort to master, students can feel tempted to give a lot of information which isn't really needed because they want to show off all their revision – try not to fall into this trap as you will score higher marks by answering the specific question you have been set.

Chapter 9

The judiciary

When speaking of judges as a group, they are referred to as the 'judiciary'. There are many different levels of judges, but their basic function is the same. Their main role is to make decisions in respect of disputes. They must do this in a fair, unbiased way, applying the law and the legal rules of England and Wales.

The judiciary is divided into what are known as 'superior' judges (those in the High Court and above) and 'inferior' judges (those in the lower courts). This distinction affects training, work and, in particular, the terms on which they hold office. So it is important to start by understanding which judges sit in which court.

9.1 Types of judges

9.1.1 Superior judges

Superior judges are those in the Supreme Court, the Court of Appeal and the High Court. They are:

- the Justices of the Supreme Court who sit in the Supreme Court
- the Lord Justices of Appeal in the Court of Appeal
- High Court Judges (also known as puisne (pronounced 'pew-nay') judges) who sit in the three divisions of the High Court; judges in the Queen's Bench Division of the High Court also sit to hear serious cases in the Crown Court.

The head of the judiciary is the Lord Chief Justice.

9.1.2 Inferior judges

The inferior judges include:

- Circuit Judges, who sit in both the Crown Court and the County Court
- Recorders, part-time judges who usually sit in the Crown Court, though a few may hear cases in the County Court
- District Judges, who hear small claims and other matters in the County Court
- District Judges (Magistrates' Courts), who sit in Magistrates' Courts in London and other major towns and cities.

The parade of judges and silks on the first day of the legal year

9.2 Qualifications

To become a judge at any level it is necessary to meet the judicial-appointment eligibility condition relevant to that level. This means the applicant must have the relevant legal qualification and have gained experience in the law for a certain period. The qualifications to become a judge have been widened over the last 20 years.

Relevant qualification

The Tribunals, Court and Enforcement Act 2007 contains the most recent changes to the qualifications needed. This Act states that to apply to become a judge it is necessary to have the relevant legal qualification. This is normally as a barrister or solicitor, but for some levels the Act has opened up some judicial posts beyond solicitors and barristers for the first time. Fellows of the Institute of Legal Executives (ILEX), Registered Patents Attorneys and Trade Mark Attorneys may apply for certain lower level posts.

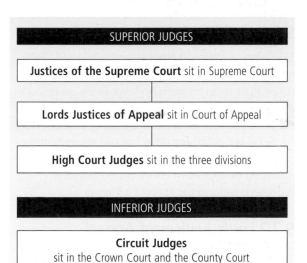

SUPERIOR JUDGES

Justices of the Supreme Court sit in Supreme Court

Lords Justices of Appeal sit in Court of Appeal

High Court Judges sit in the three divisions

INFERIOR JUDGES

Circuit Judges
sit in the Crown Court and the County Court

Recorders
sit part-time in the Crown Court and the County Court

District Judges
sit in County Court

District Judges (Magistrates' Courts) sit in Magistrates' Courts

Figure 9.1 The hierarchy of judges

Gain experience in law

The Tribunals, Court and Enforcement Act 2007 widened the ways in which applicants may have gained experience in law. As well as practising or teaching law, the Act recognises that activities such as acting as an arbitrator or mediator, advising on law or drafting legal documents are also methods by which an applicant can gain experience in law.

The Act also reduced the length of time that a person has to work in the law before they can apply to become a judge. Previously the minimum time was seven years for lower level posts and ten years for most senior posts. These time periods are now five and seven years respectively.

These changes have all helped to widen the pool of potential candidates for judgeships, and may eventually make the composition of the Bench a wider cross-section of society.

The qualifications for each level of judge are set out below.

9.2.1 Justices of the Supreme Court

These are appointed from those who hold high judicial office, such as a judge in the Court of Appeal, or from those who have been qualified to appear in the senior courts for at least 15 years. As the Supreme Court is the final appellate court for Scotland and Northern Ireland as well, judges can also be appointed from those who have qualified to appear in courts in Scotland or Northern Ireland for at least 15 years.

9.2.2 Lords Justices of Appeal

These must have been qualified as a barrister or solicitor and have gained experience in law for at least seven years, or to have been an existing High Court judge. In practice nearly all Lords Justices of Appeal have been appointed from existing High Court judges. Although solicitors are eligible for appointment, it was not until 2007, that the first solicitor Lord Justice of Appeal was appointed. He has since been

Middlesex Guildhall, home of the new Supreme Court

promoted and now sits as a Justice of the Supreme Court.

9.2.3 High Court judges

In order to be eligible to be appointed as a High Court judge it is necessary either to be qualified as a barrister or solicitor and have gained experience in law for at least seven years, or to have been a Circuit Judge for at least two years. Prior to 1990, only those who had practised as a barrister for at least ten years were eligible. The present qualification routes give solicitors the chance to become High Court judges. The first was appointed in 1993 and the second in 2000. This second solicitor judge (Sir Lawrence Collins) was later promoted to the Supreme Court. However, the vast majority of High Court judges have been barristers.

9.2.4 Circuit Judges

The applicant must be qualified as a barrister or solicitor and have gained experience in law for at least seven years. Those who have been Recorders, District Judges, or Tribunal Judges are also eligible for appointment. These provisions have widened the pool of potential judges and are gradually leading to a better cross-section among the judges at this level.

The usual route to becoming a Circuit Judge is to be appointed as a Recorder first and then be promoted to a Circuit Judge. About 18 per cent of Circuit Judges are former solicitors.

9.2.5 Recorders

This is a part-time post. The applicant must be qualified as a barrister or solicitor and have gained experience in law for at least seven years. Usually an applicant is appointed as a Recorder in training first and then after two or three years can apply to be appointed as a Recorder.

A Recorder sits as a judge for about 20 days a year, and continues with their ordinary work for the rest of the time. The appointment is for five years and most Recorders work in the Crown Court, though it is also possible for them to sit in the County Court.

9.2.6 District Judges

At this level an applicant must be qualified as a barrister or solicitor and have gained experience in law for at least five years or to have been a Deputy District judge. The vast majority of District Judges in the County Court are former solicitors.

District Judges in the Magistrates' Courts need the same qualifications. About two-thirds of these are former solicitors. It is usual to have sat part-time as a deputy District Judge before being considered for the position of District Judge. Under the Tribunals, Courts and Enforcement Act 2007, ILEX Fellows are now eligible to be appointed as Deputy District Judges.

9.3 Selection

9.3.1 History

Until 2005, the Lord Chancellor was the key f igure in the selection of superior judges. The Lord Chancellor's Department would keep information on all possible candidates. These files would contain confidential information and opinions from existing judges on the suitability of each person. The contents of these files were secret.

When there was a vacancy for a judicial position in the House of Lords (previously the highest court in the country – now replaced by the Supreme Court), the Court of Appeal or the High Court, the Lord Chancellor would consider the information in these files and decide which person he thought was the best for the post. That person would then be invited to become a judge.

Not surprisingly, this system of selection was seen as secretive. It was also felt that it favoured white males, as there were few women and, until 2004, no ethnic minority judges in the higher ranks of the judiciary.

The major role of the Lord Chancellor in appointment was also controversial, as the Lord Chancellor is a political appointment. It was thought that the appointment of judges should be independent from any political influence. So the method of appointment was changed by the Constitutional Reform Act 2005 and a Judicial Appointments Commission created to deal with selection of judges.

9.3.2 The Judicial Appointments Commission

Virtually all judges are now selected by the Judicial Appointments Commission. This was created under the Constitutional Reform Act 2005 and started work in April 2006. The Commission is responsible for selecting between about 500 and 700 people for appointment to judicial posts each year.

There are 15 members of this Commission. There must be:

- six lay members
- five judges – three of these from the Court of Appeal or High Court plus one Circuit Judge and one District Judge or equivalent
- one barrister
- one solicitor
- one magistrate
- one tribunal member.

The key features of the new process for appointing judges are:

- appointments are made solely on merit
- the Commission is entirely responsible for assessing the merit of the candidates and selecting candidates for appointment
- no candidate can be appointed unless recommended by the Commission
- the Commission must consult with the Lord Chief Justice and another judge of equivalent experience before recommending a candidate for appointment
- the Lord Chancellor has limited powers in relation to each recommendation for appointment. He can reject a candidate once or ask the Commission to reconsider once but he must give reasons in writing for this.

The power of the Lord Chancellor to reject a candidate or ask the Commission to reconsider has been criticised, as it infringes the independence of the judiciary.

The Crime and Courts Bill 2012–13 has provision to transfer the Lord Chancellor's power in respect of all judges below the High Court to the Lord Chief Justice. The Senior President of Tribunals will be given the power to appoint judges for the First-tier and Upper Tribunals. The Lord Chancellor will still be consulted on appointments to the High Court and Court of Appeal. However, for lower court judgeships, the process will be completely separate from the Government and Executive.

Judicial qualities

The Commission has listed five qualities that are desirable for a good judge. These are:

- intellectual capacity
- personal qualities including integrity, independence of mind, sound judgment, decisiveness, objectivity and willingness to learn
- ability to understand and deal fairly
- authority and communication skills
- efficiency.

The process

Positions are advertised widely in newspapers, legal journals and also online. To encourage a wide range of candidates to apply, the Commission runs roadshows and other outreach events designed to communicate and explain the appointments system to potential applicants.

All candidates have to fill in an application form. Candidates are also asked to nominate between three and six referees. In addition, the Commission has published a list of people whom it may consult about candidates. These include existing judges. For lower-level posts, applicants will also be asked to write an essay or do a case study.

The Commission will then select the best candidates to be interviewed. The interview process may include role play or taking part in a formal, structured discussion. After the interviews, the final selections will be made and recommended to the Lord Chancellor for appointment.

When the first vacancies for High Court judgeships were advertised through this system in 2006, there were 129 applicants, but only 18 of them were women and all the applicants were white. Since then more women and people from ethnic minorities have started to apply for judgeships, so the pool of potential judges is widening.

For example, in 2010 there were 90 applicants for High Court judgeships. Fifteen of these were women of whom two were recommended for appointment. Six were from black ethnic minorities and two of these were recommended for appointment.

More information can be found on the Judicial Appointments Commission's website at **http://jac.judiciary.gov.uk.**

@ Internet Research

Look at the Commission's website to see if any judicial posts are currently being advertised.

9.3.3 Justices of the new Supreme Court

When the Supreme Court was established in 2009, the judges from the House of Lords were automatically made judges of the Supreme Court. Judges for new appointments since then are selected according to the method set out in Part 3 of the Constitutional Reform Act 2005. This states that when there is a vacancy, the Office of the President of the Court must convene a Supreme Court selection commission.

This commission must include the President and the Deputy President of the Supreme Court and one member of the Judicial Appointments Commission. As the Supreme Court is also the final court of appeal for Scotland and Northern Ireland, the commission must also include a member from the Judicial Appointments Board for Scotland and from the Northern Ireland Judicial Appointments Commission.

The commission decides the selection process to be used. It then uses that process to select a candidate and report that selection to the Lord Chancellor.

Under s 29 of the Constitutional Reform Act 2005, the Lord Chancellor can reject that candidate or ask the commission to reconsider. This can only be done if the Lord Chancellor is of the opinion that the person selected is not suitable for the office or that there is evidence that the person is not the best candidate on merit. The Lord Chancellor must give his reasons for rejecting a candidate and ask the Commission to reconsider in writing.

Once the Lord Chancellor has accepted the Commission's nomination, he then notifies the Prime Minister and the Prime Minister must recommend to the Queen that she appoints that person. The Prime Minister will not be able to recommend another person for appointment. This prevents any reoccurrence of the situation in the 1980s when Mrs Thatcher, the then Prime Minister, once refused to nominate the first-choice candidate.

9.4 Appointment

Once a candidate has been selected and that selection accepted by the Lord Chancellor, the appointment is then made by the Queen for all judicial posts from District Judges up to the Justices of the Supreme Court.

Self-Test Questions

1 In which courts do the superior judges sit?
2 Give two types of inferior judge.
3 What qualifications does a High Court judge need?
4 What qualifications does a District Judge need?
5 Which body makes the selection of judges?
6 What judicial qualities are they looking for in candidates?
7 What power does the Lord Chancellor have in relation to the selection of judges?

9.5 Judicial roles

The work that a judge does depends on the level of court in which he works.

9.5.1 Justices of the Supreme Court

Judges in the Supreme Court hear about 70 cases each year. These are appeals. They can be in civil or criminal cases. However, every year there are far more civil appeals. A case can only be appealed to the Supreme Court if there is a point of law involved. Often civil cases involve complicated and technical areas of law such as planning law or tax law.

The Justices of the Supreme Court must sit as an uneven number panel, with a minimum of three judges to hear a case. In practice they usually sit as a panel of five or seven.

Any decision of the Supreme Court on a point of law becomes a precedent for all lower courts to follow.

All judgments by the Supreme Court are on put on their website at **www.supremecourt.gov.uk**.

9.5.2 Lords Justices of Appeal

There are about 38 Lords Justices of Appeal. They sit in both the civil and criminal divisions of the Court of Appeal, so they deal with both civil and criminal cases. Their workload is much heavier than that of the Supreme Court.

On the criminal side, they will hear over 7,000 applications for leave to appeal against sentence or conviction. These are dealt with by one judge. Less than a quarter of these get leave to appeal, so the full court then hears about 1,600 criminal appeals . In addition, they hear over 1,000 civil appeals every year. These may be appeals against the finding of liability or an appeal about the remedy awarded, such as the amount of money given as damages.

Court of Appeal Judges usually sit as a panel of three to hear cases. On rare occasions in important cases, there may be a panel of five. Decisions by the Court of Appeal on points of law become precedents which lower courts must follow.

Because the workload of the Court of Appeal is so large, High Court Judges are often used to form part of the panel. This means there may be one Lord Justice of Appeal sitting with two High Court Judges.

In law reports Court of Appeal Judges are referred to as 'Lord Justice' or 'Lady Justice', but when their judgments are being quoted it is usually abbreviated to the surname, followed by 'LJ'; for example 'Arden LJ'.

9.5.3 High Court Judges

Every judge in the High Court will be assigned to one of the Divisions. There are about 73 judges in the Queen's Bench Division, 18 in the Chancery Division and 19 in the Family Division.

There are also Deputy High Court Judges who sit to help with the workload.

The main function of High Court Judges is to try cases. These are known as cases at 'first instance' because it is the first time the case has been heard by a court. They will hear evidence from witnesses, decide what the law is and make the decision as to which side has won the case. If the claim is for damages (an amount of money) the judge decides how much should be awarded to the winning claimant. The type of work dealt with by each Division is more fully described in Chapter 2. When hearing first instance cases, judges sit on their own. In some rare cases in the Queen's Bench Division there may be a jury.

High Court Judges also hear some appeals. These are mainly from civil cases tried in the County Court. The judges in the Queen's Bench Division also hear criminal appeals from the Magistrates' Courts by a special case stated method. These are appeals on law only. When sitting to hear appeals, there will be a panel of two or three judges.

Judges from the Queen's Bench Division also sit to hear criminal trials in the Crown Court. When they do this, they sit with a jury. The jury decides the facts and the judge decides the law. Where a defendant pleads guilty or is found guilty by a jury, the judge then has to decide on the sentence.

@ Internet Research

Look up law reports on the internet. Try **www.bailii.org**.

Try to find:

1. A law report in which there was a female judge.

2. A report of the Court of Appeal in which one at least of the judges is only of High Court level.

3. A report from the High Court in which the judge sitting is only a Deputy High Court Judge.

Key facts

Court	Judges	Qualifications	Role
Supreme Court	Justices of the Supreme Court	15-year senior court qualification *or* have held high judicial office	Hear appeals on points of law Civil and criminal cases
Court of Appeal	Lords Justices of Appeal	Barrister or solicitor with seven years' legal experience *or* be an existing High Court Judge	Hear appeals Criminal appeals against conviction and/or sentence Civil cases on the finding and/or the amount awarded
High Court	High Court Judges Also know as puisne judges	Barrister or solicitor with seven years' legal experience *or* be a Circuit Judge for two years Some appeal work	Sit in one of the three Divisions Hear first-instance cases and decide liability and remedy
Crown Court	High Court Judges Circuit Judges Recorders	See above Barrister or solicitor with seven years' legal experience or be a Recorder or other lower level judge Barrister or solicitor with seven years' legal experience	Try cases with a jury Decide the law Pass sentence on guilty defendants
County Court	Circuit Judges District Judges	See above Barrister or solicitor with five years' legal experience	Civil cases – decide liability and remedy District Judges hear small claims
Magistrates' Courts	District Judges (Magistrates' Courts)	Barrister or solicitor with five years' legal experience NB ILEX fellows can be appointed Deputy District Judges	Criminal cases – decide law and verdict Pass sentence on guilty defendants Some family work

Figure 9.2 Key facts chart on judges

In law reports High Court Judges are referred to as 'Mr Justice' or 'Mrs Justice', but when their judgments are being quoted it is usually abbreviated to the surname, followed by 'J'; for example 'Dobbs J'.

9.5.4 Inferior judges

Circuit Judges sit in the County Court to hear civil cases and also in the Crown Court to try criminal cases. There are over 600 Circuit Judges. In civil cases they sit on their own (it is very rare to have a jury in a civil case in the County Court). They decide the law and the facts. They make the decision on who has won the case. They also decide the amount of damages (money) to be awarded to the winning party or any other remedy that is appropriate to the case.

In criminal cases they sit with a jury. The jury decides the facts and the judge decides the law. Where a defendant pleads guilty or is found guilty by a jury, the judge then has to decide on the sentence.

Recorders are part-time judges who are appointed for a period of five years. They are used mainly in the Crown Court to try criminal cases, but some sit in the County Court to help with civil cases.

District Judges sit in the County Court to deal with small claims cases (under £5,000) and can also hear other cases for larger amounts. There are over 400 District Judges.

District Judges (Magistrates' Courts) sit and try criminal cases in the Magistrates' Courts. They sit on their own and decide facts and law. When a defendant pleads guilty or is found guilty, they also have to decide on the sentence.

They may also sit to hear family cases, but this will usually be with two lay magistrates.

9.6 Training

The training of judges is carried out by the Judicial Studies Board, which was set up in 1979. There is training for new judges as well as ongoing training for experienced judges.

Once a lawyer has been appointed as a Recorder in training, they attend a one-week course run by the Judicial Studies Board, and then shadow an experienced judge for a week. For experienced judges one-day courses are occasionally available, especially on the effect of new legislation. The Judicial Studies Board publishes a list of seminars for the year and judges can apply to attend any of the seminars.

Critics point out that the training is very short, and that even if all the people involved are experienced lawyers, this does not mean that they have any experience of doing such tasks as summing-up to the jury or sentencing. There is also the fact that some Recorders will not have practised in the criminal courts as lawyers, so their expertise is limited, and a one-week course is a very short training period.

No compulsory training is given to new High Court Judges, although they are invited to attend the courses run by the Judicial Studies Board. The attitude of the judiciary to training has changed considerably over the last 20 years.

Training used to be seen as insulting to lawyers who had spent all their working lives in the courts, building up expertise in their field. It was also seen as a threat to judicial independence. However, the need for training is now fully accepted.

Human awareness training

Since 1993 judges have had to attend a course on racial awareness. This is designed to make them aware of what might be unintentionally discriminatory or offensive, such as asking a non-Christian for their Christian name. There is also training in human awareness, covering gender awareness and disability issues. The training explores the perceptions of unrepresented parties, witnesses, jurors, victims and their families, and tries to make judges more aware of other people's viewpoints.

9.6.1 Should there be a 'career' judiciary?

In many European countries becoming a judge is a career choice made by students once they have their basic legal qualifications. They will usually not practise as a lawyer first, but instead are trained as judges. Once they have qualified as a judge they will sit in junior posts and then hope to be promoted up the judicial ladder. This has two distinct advantages over the system in use in the UK:

- The average age of judges is much lower, especially in the bottom ranks. In the UK an assistant Recorder will normally be in their late thirties or early forties when appointed, and the average age for appointment to the High Court Bench tends to be late forties/early fifties.
- Judges have had far more training in the specific skills they need.

The disadvantage of the European system is that judges may be seen as too closely linked to the Government as they are civil servants. In this country, judges are generally considered to be independent from the Government. This point of judicial independence is explored more fully in section 9.10.

Exam tips

This is a big topic and exam questions will tend to focus on particular aspects, but it is likely that more than one facet will be examined so you need to have a good grasp of the whole topic. You must be sufficiently confident in your knowledge that you can mix and match what you know to suit the requirements of the question. It is important to read the question carefully and only write about the aspect indicated by the question.

As the judiciary usually appears in Section A of the paper, after explaining some factual material you will then need to embark on analysis and a discussion which could focus on a wide range of issues – ranging from selection and training to a comparison with the lay magistracy and anything in between! A revision mind map is a very helpful way to help you categorise lots of information and using colours and clear labelling will help you get an image in your mind that you can use as a plan in the exam room.

9.7 Tenure

It is important that judges should be impartial in their decisions. In particular, it is important that the Government cannot force a judge to resign if that judge makes a decision with which the Government disagrees. In the UK, judges are reasonably secure from political interference.

9.7.1 Security of tenure of superior judges

Superior judges have security of tenure in that they cannot be dismissed by the Government. This right originated in the Act of Settlement 1700 which allowed them to hold office while of good behaviour. (Before 1700, the Monarch could dismiss judges at will.) The same provision is now contained in the Senior Courts Act 1981 for High Court Judges and Lords Justices of Appeal, and in the Constitutional Reform Act 2005 for the Justices of the Supreme Court. As a result, they can only be removed by the Monarch following a petition presented to him or her by both Houses of Parliament. This gives superior judges protection from political whims and allows them to be independent in their judgments.

This power to remove a superior judge has never been used for an English judge, though it was used in 1830 to remove an Irish judge, Jonah Barrington, who had misappropriated £700 from court funds.

The Lord Chancellor, however, after consulting with the Lord Chief Justice, can declare vacant the office of any judge who (through ill-health) is incapable of carrying out his work and of taking the decision to resign.

In fact, what has happened on two occasions in the past is that pressure has been put on unsatisfactory High Court Judges to resign. The first of these was in 1959 when the Lord Chancellor asked Mr Justice Hallett to resign; the second in 1998 when Mr Justice Harman resigned after criticisms by the Court of Appeal.

9.7.2 Tenure of inferior judges

These do not have the same security of tenure of office as superior judges since the Lord Chancellor, with the consent of the Lord Chief Justice, has the power to dismiss inferior judges for incapacity or misbehaviour. A criminal conviction for dishonesty would obviously be regarded as misbehaviour and would lead to the dismissal of the judge concerned.

This happened in the case of Bruce Campbell, a Circuit Judge, who was convicted of evading Customs duty on cigarettes and whisky. The Lord Chancellor has also indicated that drunken driving would probably be seen as misbehaviour, as would racial or sexual harassment.

In addition, under the Constitutional Reform Act 2005, the Lord Chief Justice has the power to suspend a person from judicial office if they are subject to criminal proceedings or have been convicted. The Lord Chief Justice can only exercise this power if the Lord Chancellor agrees, and must use set procedures.

Complaints about the personal conduct of judges are investigated by the Office for Judicial Complaints. If a complaint is upheld, the Lord Chancellor and the Lord Chief Justice have the power to advise, warn or remove a judge for misconduct. In 2009, Judge Margaret Short was dismissed through this procedure for 'inappropriate, petulant and rude' behaviour.

Any judge who is suspended or disciplined in any other way can make a complaint to an Ombudsman if the procedures have not been carried out correctly and fairly.

9.7.3 Retirement

Since the Judicial Pensions and Retirement Act 1993 all judges retire at the age of 70. However, authorisation can be given for superior judges to continue beyond that age up to the age of 75. All inferior judges retire at 70.

Internet Research

Look on the judicial website **www.judiciary. gov.uk** (in the section 'About the judiciary') to find the ages of the Lords Justice of Appeal. Their dates of birth are given in the list of the judges. How many of them are over 70?

Self-Test Questions

1 What is the role of the judges in the Supreme Court?
2 What is the role of a judge in the Crown Court?
3 Which body carries out the training of judges?
4 What criticisms can be made of the training?
5 What advantages are there to having a career judiciary?
6 How can a superior judge be dismissed?
7 How can an inferior judge be dismissed?

Key facts

Judges	Court/s	Tenure
Justices of the Supreme Court	Supreme Court	'during good behaviour' (Constitutional Reform Act 2005, s 33)
Lords Justices of Appeal	Court of Appeal	'whilst of good behaviour' (Senior Courts Act 1981, s 11(3))
High Court Judges	High Court Crown Court for serious cases	'whilst of good behaviour' (Senior Courts Act 1981, s 11(3))
Circuit Judges	Crown Court County Court	Can be dismissed by Lord Chancellor, with consent of Lord Chief Justice, for incapacity or misbehaviour (Courts Act 1971, s 17(4))
District Judges	County Court Magistrates' Court	Can be dismissed by Lord Chancellor with consent of Lord Chief Justice
Recorders	Crown Court Some may sit in County Court	Appointed for period of five years; Lord Chancellor can decide not to re-appoint. (Under the Crime and Courts Bill 2012–13, this power NOT to re-appoint will be given to the Lord Chief Justice.)

Figure 9.3 Key facts chart on judges and their tenure

Activity

Read the following newspaper article and answer the questions below.

Do you fancy being a High Court judge? Forget the whisper over a drink at your Inn of Court or the traditional 'tap on the shoulder'. Dust off your CV and send in an application. And then prepare yourself for an 'interview' with a selection panel. This is the new world of appointing judges ...

The selection process will be undertaken by the Judicial Appointments Commission, the independent body set up under the Constitutional Reform Act in 2005 to take over responsibility for selecting judges from the Lord Chancellor's officials.

There has been advertising for High Court judges before – but they were selected on paper. This time, the candidates will undergo a face-to-face discussion – and that, with

references and their own application form, will combine to inform the selection.

Baroness Usha Prashar, who is chairman of the 15 lay and judicial commissioners and 105 staff, will now be responsible for 500 to 700 appointments a year, including the High Court ...

The aim she says is for a much more transparent process that will encourage a greater diversity of candidates. 'Up to now the process was perceived to be very secretive and not very open. There was a view that it was those who you knew who counted – and that probably deterred a lot of people who felt they would not get a fair deal. This will be objective and transparent and hopefully that will encourage more people to apply.'

Taken from an article by Frances Gibb,
The Times, 31 October 2006
© The Times/NI Syndication

Questions

1. Who was responsible for appointing judges under the old system?

2. Who is responsible for appointing judges now?

3. Describe the problems with the old system

of appointing judges.

4. Describe how the present system operates.

5. Explain whether you think that the present system encourages a wider range of applicants for judgeships.

9.8 Composition of the Bench

One of the main criticisms of the Bench is that it is dominated by elderly, white, upper-class males. There are very few women judges, and even fewer judges from ethnic minorities in the upper ranks of the judiciary. So far as the age of judges is concerned, it is unusual for any judge to be appointed under the age of 40, with superior judges usually being well above this age.

9.8.1 Women in the judiciary

The number of women in judicial posts is very small, although there has been an improvement

in recent years. Since 1990 there has been an increase in the number of women appointed to the High Court. The first woman judge in the Queen's Bench Division was appointed in 1992, and the first in the Chancery Division in 1993. By 2013, the total number of women judges in the High Court had increased to 17 out of over 100 judges.

The first woman in the Court of Appeal was appointed in 1988. This was Lady Butler-Sloss. The legal system was so unused to women in the higher levels of the judiciary that when she was appointed she had to be addressed in court as 'My Lord', and in law reports her title was written as 'Lord Butler-Sloss'! It was not until the Courts Act 2003 that the official title of women judges in the Court of Appeal became 'Lady Justice of Appeal'.

A second woman was appointed to the Court of Appeal in 1999, and a third in 2000. In February 2001 the first all-female Court of Appeal panel sat. The first woman judge in the House of Lords was appointed in 2004 and she is now a Justice of the Supreme Court. In 2012, there were four women Lord Justices of Appeal out of 38 judges in the Court of Appeal.

Lower down the judicial ladder, there are more women being appointed than in the past. In 2012, 16 per cent of Circuit Judges and 17 per cent of Recorders were female. The greatest number of female judges is at District Judges level, where about a third are women.

9.8.2 Ethnic minorities

In 2004 the first ethnic minority judge was appointed to the High Court and by 2010 there were three ethnic minority judges. But there are still none in the Court of Appeal or the Supreme Court. At the lower levels, ethnic minorities are slightly better represented. In 2012, 2.6 per cent of Circuit Judges and 6.5 per cent of Recorders were from an ethnic minority. About four per cent of District Judges are from ethnic minorities. These percentages have increased in the last few years. It may well be that the new appointments system is gradually creating greater diversity in the judiciary.

By 2012, the overall percentage of ethnic minority judges was 4 per cent. This is not representative of the community. However, it is representative of the percentage of BAME (Black, Asian and Minority Ethnic) lawyers who are eligible for appointment.

9.8.3 Educational and social background

At the higher levels judges tend to come from the upper levels of society, with many having been educated at public school and nearly all attending Oxford or Cambridge Universities. A survey by the magazine *Labour Research* found

that of the 85 judges appointed from 1997 to mid-1999, 73 per cent had been to public school and 79 per cent to Oxbridge. Judges (especially superior judges) will have spent at least 20 years of their careers working as barristers and mixing with a small group of like-minded people.

In 2007, Penny Darbyshire surveyed 77 judges from different levels of the judiciary. She found that there were marked differences in background between superior judges and those at a lower level. For example, none of the District Judges (Magistrates' Court) had been to private school, while 11 out of 16 High Court Judges and eight out of the ten Court of Appeal/House of Lords judges she interviewed had been privately educated.

There was also a major difference in the universities that senior judges had attended compared to judges at a lower level. Ninety per cent of Court of Appeal/House of Lords had been to Oxford or Cambridge, but only one of six District Judges (Magistrates' Court) and four out of thirteen District Judges (County Court) had attended Oxbridge. However, as the judges in the Court of Appeal and House of Lords (now Supreme Court) decide complex cases and law, Darbyshire points out that:

'It would surely be a matter of concern if senior judges were not highly educated and exceptionally intelligent.'

9.9 Theory of the separation of powers

The theory of separation of powers was first put forward by Montesquieu, a French political theorist, in the eighteenth century. The theory states that there are three primary functions of the State and that the only way to safeguard the liberty of citizens is by keeping these three functions separate. These functions are:

- legislative
- executive
- judiciary.

As the power of each is exercised by independent and separate bodies, each can keep a check on the others and thus limit the amount of power wielded by any one group. Ideally, this theory requires that individuals should not be members of more than one 'arm of the state'.

Some countries, for example the USA, have a written constitution which embodies this theory. In the United Kingdom there is no such written constitution, but even so the three organs of State are roughly separated. There is some overlap, especially in the fact that the Lord Chancellor is involved in all three functions of the State. However, the Lord Chancellor's role in relation to the judiciary was considerably reduced by the Constitutional Reform Act 2005 and is being reduced further by the Crime and Courts Bill 2012.

The three arms of the State identified by Montesquieu are:

1. The **legislature**
   This is the law-making arm of the State and in the UK system this is Parliament.

2. The **executive** or the body administering the law
   Under the British political system this is the Government of the day which forms the Cabinet.

3. The **judiciary** who apply the law
   In other words, the judges.

There is an overlap between the executive and the legislature, in that the Ministers forming the Government also sit in Parliament and are active in the law-making process. With the exception of the Lord Chancellor, there is very little overlap between the judiciary and the other two arms of the State. This is important because it allows the judiciary to act as a check and ensure that the executive does not overstep its constitutional powers. This is in accordance with Montesquieu's theory. However, it is open to debate whether the judiciary is truly independent from the other organs of government.

@ Internet Research

Look up the judicial website **www.judiciary.gov.uk** and look at the section 'About the judiciary'.

1. Look up the biographies of any two judges. Find out the following matters:

   (a) Which school did they go to?
   (b) At which university did they get their degree?
   (c) When did they first become a judge?
   (d) What court are they a judge in now?

2. Find out how many woman judges there are in the Court of Appeal.
3. Find out how many ethnic minority judges there are in the High Court.

9.10 Independence of the judiciary

As already stated, an independent judiciary is seen as important in protecting the liberty of the individual from abuse of power by the executive. Judges in the English system can be thought of as independent in a number of ways.

9.10.1 Independence from the legislature

Judges are generally not involved in the law-making functions of Parliament. Full-time judges are not allowed to be members of the House of Commons, although the rule is not as strict for part-time judges so that Recorders and Assistant Recorders can be Members of

Parliament. There used to be judges in the House of Lords when the Appellate Committee of the House of Lords was the final court of appeal. The main reason for the creation of the Supreme Court in 2009 was to separate the judiciary from the legislature. The judges of the Supreme Court are not allowed to be members of the House of Lords.

9.10.2 Independence from the executive

Superior judges cannot be dismissed by the Government and in this way they can truly be said to be independent of the Government. They can make decisions which may displease the Government, without the threat of dismissal. The extent to which judges are prepared to challenge or support the Government is considered in section 9.10.4.

Judicial independence is now guaranteed under s 3 of the Constitutional Reform Act 2005. This states that the Lord Chancellor, other Ministers in the Government and anyone with responsibility for matters relating to the judiciary or the administration of justice must uphold the continued independence of the judiciary.

The section also specifically states that the Lord Chancellor and other Ministers must not seek to influence particular judicial decisions.

Ministry of Justice

In 2007 a Ministry of Justice was created to bring together all the key elements of the justice system under one ministry. Previously two ministries, the Department for Constitutional Affairs and the Home Office, had had responsibility for separate parts of the justice system.

The Ministry of Justice has responsibility for:

- the civil courts
- the criminal courts
- the judiciary
- legal aid and funding of cases
- prisons
- the probation service
- sentencing.

There were fears that the budget of the new department would not be sufficient for all this

and that prisons would take a large part of the budget. The main area where the budget has been cut is legal aid.

Judges were also worried about the effect of the change on their independence. The Minister for Justice is also the Lord Chancellor. As the Minister for Justice is a key role in the executive, it was difficult to see how he could also maintain the independence of the judiciary. This problem has been to some extent overcome by removing more of the Lord Chancellor's powers of appointment of judges (see 9.3.2).

9.10.3 Freedom from pressure

There are several ways in which judges are protected from outside pressure when exercising their judicial functions.

1. They are given a certain degree of financial independence, as judicial salaries are paid out of the consolidated fund so that payment is made without the need for Parliament's authorisation. This does not completely protect them from parliamentary interference with the terms on which they hold office. As already seen, changes can be made to retirement ages and qualifying periods for pensions.

2. Judges have immunity from being sued for actions taken or decisions made in the course of their judicial duties. This was confirmed in *Sirros v Moore* (1975) and is a key factor in ensuring judicial independence in decision-making.

3. As already noted, the security of tenure of the superior judges protects them from the threat of removal.

9.10.4 Independence from political bias

This is the area in which there is most dispute over how independent the judiciary are. Writers, such as Professor Griffith, have pointed out that judges are too pro-establishment and conservative with a small 'c'.

Pro-Government decisions

Griffith cited cases such as the 'GCHQ case' in showing that judges tend to support the establishment. This case, *Council of Civil Service Unions v Minister for the Civil Service* (1984), concerned the Minister for the Conservative Government withdrawing the right to trades union membership from civil servants working at the intelligence headquarters in Cheltenham. The House of Lords upheld the Minister's right, and the decision was seen as anti-trade union.

Anti-Government decisions

There is, however, evidence that judges are not as pro-establishment as sometimes thought. Lord Taylor, when giving the Dimbleby Lecture in 1992, pointed out that this could be seen in the case of the Greenham Common women who had camped by an RAF base in protest against nuclear missiles. In *DPP v Hutchinson* (1990) some of the women were prosecuted under a bylaw for being on Ministry of Defence property unlawfully. The case went all the way to the House of Lords, where the Law Lords ruled in the women's favour, holding that the Minister had exceeded his powers in framing the bylaw so as to prevent access to common land.

Human rights

More recently, the courts have upheld challenges by asylum-seekers and by people held under the Anti-Terrorism, Crime and Security Act 2001. In *R (on the application of Q) v Secretary of State for the Home Department* (2003) Collins J in the High Court declared that the Home Secretary's power to refuse to provide assistance to asylum-seekers who had not immediately, on their entry to this country, declared their intention to claim asylum was unlawful. The Court of Appeal upheld this decision, although they did suggest how the relevant Act could be made compatible with human rights.

In *A and another v Secretary of State for the Home Department* (2004) the House of Lords declared that the Anti-Terrorism, Crime and Security Act 2001 was incompatible with the Convention. The Act allowed foreign nationals to be detained indefinitely without trial where there was suspicion that they were involved in terrorist

activity. The Lords held that this breached both Art 5 (the right to liberty) and Art 14 (no discrimination on basis of nationality). This decision forced the Government to change the law.

With the Human Rights Act 1998 incorporating the European Convention on Human Rights, judges can declare that an Act is incompatible with the Convention. This puts pressure on the Government to change the law. The first case in which this happened was *H v Mental Health Review Tribunal* (2001).

The courts also have a duty to interpret laws in a way which is compatible with the Convention.

So, while it is true that judges are still predominantly white, male, middle-class and elderly, it is possible to argue that they are not out of touch with the 'real world', and that they are increasingly prepared to challenge the establishment.

9.10.5 Independence from case

Judges must not try any case where they have any interest in the issue involved. The Pinochet case in 1998 reinforced this rule. In that case the House of Lords judges heard an appeal by the former Head of the State of Chile. There was a claim to extradite him to Chile to face possible trial for crimes involving torture and deaths which had occurred there while he was Head of State.

Amnesty International, the human rights movement, had been granted leave to participate in the case. After the House of Lords ruled that Pinochet could be extradited, it was discovered that one of the judges, Lord Hoffmann, was an unpaid director of Amnesty International Charitable Trust. Pinochet's lawyers asked for the decision to be set aside and to have the case re-heard by a completely independent panel of judges.

The Law Lords decided that their original decision could not be allowed to stand. Judges had to be seen to be completely unbiased. The fact that Lord Hoffmann was connected with Amnesty meant that he might be considered not to be completely impartial. The case was retried with a new panel of judges.

Human rights

The test for bias has been influenced by the European Convention on Human Rights. In *Re Medicaments (no 2), Director General of Fair Trading v Proprietary Association of Great Britain* (2001) the Court of Appeal followed decisions of the European Court of Human Rights. The court said that the test was an objective one of whether the circumstances were such as to lead a fair-minded and informed observer to conclude that there was a real possibility of bias.

Self-Test Questions

1 What criticisms can be made of the composition of the judiciary?
2 Briefly explain the theory of the separation of powers.
3 Why was the Supreme Court created?
4 Which Act has guaranteed the independence of the judiciary from the Government?
5 Give two examples of cases in which the decisions show that judges do act independently of the Government.

Exam tips

The area relating to the separation of powers, judicial independence and the constitutional place of the judges is another aspect of the topic which can be examined. It is possible that it can be combined with other more general issues, so do not fall into the trap of thinking that the independence of the judiciary is a topic that you can revise in isolation.

Judicial independence is an interesting and fast-moving area with plenty of case examples to show how these issues have been resolved so it is a good idea to have several examples you can write about, choosing ones that show the different facets of the relationship.

Remember that for a discussion question you need to have comments which look at this issue from more than one perspective. When you are considering the judges' relationship with human rights your answer will be more confident if you can refer to the correct Article of the European Convention on Human Rights.

Examination Questions

1(a) Describe the theory of the separation of powers and its application to the English legal system, using examples to illustrate your answer.   18 marks

1(b) Discuss the extent to which recent reforms in selection have strengthened the independence of the judiciary.   12 marks

OCR G151, June 2011

2(a) Describe the qualifications, selection and training of judges.   18 marks

2(b) Discuss whether or not the changes to the selection of judges is leading to a wider cross-section of people becoming judges.   12 marks

OCR G151 January 2010

Chapter 10

The legal profession

I n England and Wales there are two types of lawyers (barristers and solicitors), jointly referred to as 'the legal profession'. Most countries do not have this clear-cut division among lawyers: a person will qualify simply as a lawyer, although after qualifying it will be possible for them to specialise as an advocate, or in a particular area of law. This type of system is used in the medical profession in the UK, where all those wishing to become doctors take the same general qualifications. After they have qualified, some doctors go on to specialise in different fields, perhaps as surgeons, and will take further qualifications in their chosen field.

In the UK, not only are the professions separate, but there is no common training for lawyers, although there have been increasing calls for this. As far back as 1971 the Ormrod Committee was in favour of a common education for all prospective lawyers. In 1994, an advisory committee on legal education recommended that 'the two branches of the profession should have joint training'. Yet despite these recommendations, the training of the two professions remains separate. However, in 2012, another review of legal education and training took place and this may lead to changes (see 10.6).

10.1 Solicitors

There are over 120,000 solicitors practising in England and Wales. Of these, 87,000 are in private practice and the remainder are in employed work in industry or commerce, local government or the Crown Prosecution Service. Solicitors are represented by their own professional body: the Law Society.

10.1.1 Law Society

This organisation represents solicitors. On its website it states that:

'we are here to help, protect and promote solicitors across England and Wales'.

It used to regulate the profession, but this function has been given to the independent Solicitors' Regulation Authority. The Law Society also used to deal with complaints against solicitors, but this meant there was a conflict of interest. The Law Society could not represent solicitors and be impartial in its investigation of any complaint. This function is now overseen by an independent body, the Office for Legal Complaints.

Solicitors' Regulation Authority

This authority is now responsible for regulating the solicitors' profession. This includes setting down education, training and qualification requirements and the rules under which solicitors have to practise. The Authority also investigates allegations of professional misconduct.

10.1.2 Training

To become a solicitor it is usual to have a law degree, although those with a degree in a subject other than law can do an extra year's training in core legal subjects, and take the Common Professional Examination (CPE) or Graduate Diploma in Law (GDL).

The next stage is the one-year Legal Practice Course. This can be taken as a one-year full-time course or a two-year part-time course. It is practically based and includes training in skills such as client-interviewing, negotiation, advocacy, drafting documents and legal research. There is also an emphasis on business management, for example keeping accounts.

Training contract

Even when this course has been passed, the student is still not a qualified solicitor. He must next obtain a training contract under which he works in a solicitors' firm for two years, getting practical experience. This training period can also be undertaken in certain other legal organisations such as the Crown Prosecution Service, or the legal department of a local authority.

During this two-year training contract the trainee will be paid, though not at the same rate as a fully qualified solicitor, and will do his own work, supervised by a solicitor. He will also have to complete a 20-day Professional Skills Course which builds on the skills learned on the LPC.

At the end of the time, the trainee will be admitted as a solicitor by the Law Society and his name will be added to the roll (or list) of solicitors. Even after qualifying, solicitors have to attend continuing education courses to keep their knowledge up to date.

Non-graduate route

There is also a route under which non-graduates can qualify as solicitors by first becoming legal executives. This route is only open to mature candidates and takes longer than the graduate route. The three routes to becoming a solicitor are shown in Figure 10.1.

Criticisms of the training process

Several criticisms can be made of the training process.

Financial problems

Students usually have to pay the fees of the Legal Practice Course (about £12,000) and support themselves during this year. If they have a degree in a subject other than law and have to do the CPE/GDL, they will also have had to pay about £10,000 for that course. Fees have to be paid because the LPC and CPE/GDL are post-graduate courses, so students must pay all the cost.

The result of this policy is that students from poorer families may not be able to afford to take these courses and may be prevented from becoming solicitors, even though they may have obtained a good law degree. Other students may

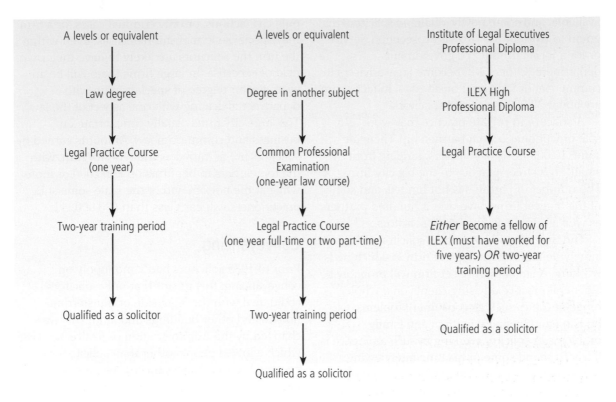

Figure 10.1 Training routes to become a solicitor

take out bank loans, so that although they qualify, they start the training period with a large debt. The financial problems have been made worse by the increasing fees charged by universities for the basic degree courses. These fees have been as high as £9,000 a year since 2012. This financial problem is also one faced by prospective barristers.

In order to help would-be solicitors, the CPE can be taken as a part-time course over two years, instead of the one-year full-time course. Doing the course part-time allows students to work as well, easing their financial problems. Often this work will be as a para-legal in a law firm, so that the student is also gaining practical experience at the same time.

Lack of legal knowledge

Non-law graduates do only one year of formal law for the CPE or GDL. There have been recommendations that the main entry route should be via a law degree, but in practice 25 per cent of solicitors will not have taken a law degree. One critic posed the question of whether the public would be satisfied with doctors who have only studied medicine for one year, concentrating on only six subjects. Yet this is precisely what is occurring in the legal profession.

Over-supply

A third problem is one of over-supply, so that students who have passed the LPC are unable to obtain a training contract. This can be a problem, particularly during times of economic crisis when legal firms will be cutting back rather than recruiting.

10.1.3 Solicitors' work

The majority of those who succeed in qualifying as a solicitor will then work in private practice in a solicitors' firm. However, there are other careers available, and some newly-qualified solicitors may go on to work in the Crown Prosecution Service or for a local authority or government department. Others will become legal advisers in commercial or industrial businesses. In fact, there are about 30,000 employed solicitors.

A solicitor in private practice may work as a sole practitioner or in a partnership. There are some 10,000 firms of solicitors, ranging from the small 'high street' practice to the big city firms. The number of partners is not limited, and some of the biggest firms have over a hundred partners as well as employing assistant solicitors.

The type of work done by a solicitor will largely depend on the type of firm in which he is working. A small high street firm will probably be a general practice advising clients on a whole range of topics such as consumer problems, housing and business matters and family problems. A solicitor working in such a practice is likely to spend some of his time interviewing clients in his office and negotiating on their behalf, and a large amount of time dealing with paperwork. This will include:

- writing letters on behalf of clients
- drafting contracts, leases or other legal documents
- drawing up wills
- dealing with conveyancing (the legal side of buying and selling flats, houses, office buildings and land).

The solicitor may also, if he wishes, act for some of his clients in court. Standing up in court, putting the client's case and questioning witnesses is known as advocacy. Some solicitors specialise in this and spend much of their time in court.

Specialising

Although some solicitors may be general practitioners handling a variety of work it is not unusual, even in small firms, for a solicitor to specialise in one particular field. The firm itself may only handle certain types of cases, perhaps only civil actions, or only criminal cases, or a firm may specialise in matrimonial cases. Even within the firm the solicitors are likely to have their own field of expertise. In large firms there will be an even greater degree of specialisation with departments dealing with one aspect of the law. The large city firms usually concentrate on business and commercial law. Amounts earned by solicitors are as varied as the types of firm, with the top earners in big firms on £500,000 or more, while at the bottom end of the scale some sole practitioners will earn less than £30,000.

Conveyancing

Prior to 1985 solicitors had a monopoly on conveyancing: this meant that only solicitors could deal with the legal side of transferring houses and other buildings and land. This was changed by the Administration of Justice Act 1985 which allowed people other than solicitors to become licensed conveyancers. As a result of the increased competition in this area, solicitors had to reduce their fees, but even so they lost a large proportion of the work. This led to a demand for wider rights of advocacy.

Rights of advocacy

All solicitors have always been able to act as advocates in the Magistrates' Courts and the County Courts, but their rights of audience in the higher courts used to be very limited. A solicitor could only act as advocate in the Crown Court on an appeal or a plea of guilty. They could not represent their client in a trial.

Until 1986, solicitors had no rights of audience in open court in the High Court, though they could deal with preliminary matters in preparation for a case. This lack of rights of audience was emphasised in *Abse v Smith* (1986) in which two Members of Parliament were contesting a libel action. They came to an agreed settlement, but the solicitor for one of them was refused permission by the judge to read out the terms of that settlement in open court. Following

A solicitor interviews a client

this decision the Lord Chancellor and the senior judges in each division of the High Court issued a Practice Direction, allowing solicitors to appear in the High Court to make a statement in a case that has been settled.

Certificate of advocacy

The first major alteration to solicitors' rights of audience came in the Courts and Legal Services Act 1990. Under this Act, a solicitor in private practice had the right to apply for a certificate of advocacy which enabled him to appear in the higher courts. Such a certificate was granted if the solicitor already had experience of advocacy in the Magistrates' Court and the County Court, took a short training course and passed examinations on the rules of evidence. The first certificates were granted in 1994 and by 2012 over 6,000 solicitors had qualified to be advocates in the higher courts.

The Access to Justice Act 1999 (s 36) provided that all solicitors will automatically be given full rights of audience. However, new training requirements to allow solicitors to obtain these rights have not been brought in.

Legal Disciplinary Practices (LDPs)

Section 66 of the Courts and Legal Services Act 1990 had provisions to allow solicitors to form partnerships with other professions, such as accountants. This would give clients a wider range of expertise and advice in a 'one-stop shop'. However, these provisions have not been brought into being.

Instead the Legal Services Act 2007 allows Legal Disciplinary Practices where up to 25 per cent of partners in a firm can be non-lawyers. The Act also allows Alternative Business Structures. So, instead of having to be a partnership, solicitors can form companies. Such companies do not have to be owned by solicitors.

10.1.4 Complaints against solicitors

A solicitor deals directly with clients and enters into a contract with them. This means that if the client does not pay, the solicitor has the right to sue for his fees. It also means that the client can sue his solicitor for breach of contract if the solicitor fails to do the work.

Key facts

Original rights	To present cases in County Court and Magistrates' Court, also at Crown Court on committal for sentence or appeal from Magistrates' Court
Practice Direction 1986	Following *Abse v Smith*, allowed to make statement in High Court in cases in which terms had been agreed
Courts and Legal Services Act 1990	Solicitors allowed to apply for certificate of advocacy to conduct cases in the higher courts. Must have experience of advocacy, take course and pass examinations
Access to Justice Act 1999	Solicitors to have full rights of audience

Figure 10.2 Key facts chart on solicitors' rights of audience

A client can also sue the solicitor for negligence in and out of court work. This happened in *Griffiths v Dawson* (1993) where solicitors for the plaintiff had failed to make the correct application in divorce proceedings against her husband. As a result the plaintiff lost financially and the solicitors were ordered to pay her £21,000 in compensation.

Other people affected by the solicitor's negligence may also have the right to sue in certain circumstances. An example of this was the case of *White v Jones* (1995) where a father wanted to make a will leaving each of his daughters £9,000. He wrote to his solicitors, instructing them to draw up a will to include this. The solicitors received this letter on 17 July 1986 but had done nothing about it by the time the father died on 14 September 1986. As a result, the daughters did not inherit any money and they successfully sued the solicitor for the £9,000 they had each lost.

Negligent advocacy

It used to be held that a solicitor presenting a case in court could not be sued for negligence. However, in *Hall v Simons* (2000), the House of Lords decided that advocates can be liable for negligence.

10.1.5 Complaints procedure

In-house procedure

All solicitors' firms must have a procedure for dealing with complaints from dissatisfied clients. All those who consult the firm must be given information about the complaints procedure. If the matter cannot be resolved in-house, then the client has the right to make a complaint to the Legal Ombudsman.

History of complaints procedure

The Law Society used to have its own complaints body to deal with disputes between solicitors and their clients. There were problems with this, as noted above. One of the main concerns was that one of the Law Society's main roles was to represent solicitors. By operating its own complaints procedure, there was a conflict between the interest of the solicitor and the interest of the client who was complaining.

The other difficulty for those complaining about poor service by a solicitor was that the complaints bodies run by the Law Society have been frequently criticised for delays and inefficiency. Because of these criticisms, the Law Society changed its complaints procedure several time. The last body was the Consumer Complaints Service. However, this body was not as efficient as it should have been. In most years only two out of every three complaints were handled satisfactorily. These problems were one of the factors which led to the Government reforming the complaints procedure and making it independent of the legal profession.

Office for Legal Complaints

The Legal Services Act 2007 created the Office for Legal Complaints. This is completely independent of the Law Society and any other sector of the legal profession. The Office has a non-lawyer as Chairman and the majority of members must also be non-lawyers. This Office has set up the Legal Ombudsman to deal with complaints about poor service by solicitors and other legal professionals.

The Legal Ombudsman

The office started work in October 2010. It is independent and impartial. When a complaint is received, the office will look at the facts in each case and weigh up both sides of the story. If the Legal Ombudsman agrees that a lawyer's service has been unsatisfactory, it can ask the lawyer and the law firm to:

- apologise to the client
- give back any documents that the client might need
- put things right if more work can correct what went wrong
- refund or reduce the legal fees, or
- pay compensation of up to £30,000.

In 2011–12, the Legal Ombudsman received 7,130 complaints against solicitors. About 20 to 25 per cent of complaints are about costs. Others are about delay, poor advice or poor practice. No statistics are available on the number of complaints which were upheld. There are, however, case studies on the Legal Ombudsman's website showing the type of complaint and stating whether it was upheld.

Activity

Look at the Legal Ombudsman's website **www.legalombudsman.org.uk** and find a case study of a complaint. You could use this as the basis of a presentation to your class.

Self-Test Questions

1 If a person has a non-law degree, what extra qualification must they take if they wish to become a lawyer?
2 What is the skills-based qualification which all would-be solicitors must pass?
3 What is a training contract?
4 What problems can arise when training to become a lawyer?
5 Explain three types of work that a solicitor's firm might carry out.
6 What is a certificate of advocacy?
7 Which body represents solicitors?
8 Which independent body now deals with complaints about poor service by a solicitor?

Exam tips

The legal profession gives rise to many exam questions and tends to be a popular topic with students. It is not too difficult to learn some material and so you might think this is a good question to rely on. To some extent that is true as the topic makes regular appearances, but you cannot guarantee that just one profession will come in isolation. This means that you take a big gamble if you don't learn about each profession to the same level. You also need to consider the possibility of a question which focuses on a particular aspect which is common to both professions – the work of both solicitors and barristers being an example.

Making flow charts that help you see the progression route for both professions in terms of their qualifications and training helps you become familiar with the order in which things happen and where there are any striking similarities or divergences.

Solicitors' Regulation Authority

This Authority investigates complaints about the professional misconduct of solicitors. If there is evidence of serious professional misconduct, they can put the case before the Solicitor's Disciplinary Tribunal. If the Tribunal upholds the complaint, it can fine or reprimand the solicitor or, in more serious cases, it can suspend a solicitor from the Roll, so that he or she cannot practise for a certain time. In very serious cases, the Tribunal can strike off a solicitor from the Roll.

10.2 Barristers

There are about 12,000 barristers in independent practice in England and Wales. In addition, there are another 3,000 barristers employed by organisations such as the Crown Prosecution Service, businesses, local government or the Civil Service. Collectively, barristers are referred to as 'the Bar' and they are represented by their own professional body – the General Council of the Bar. All barristers must also be a member of one of the four Inns of Court (Lincoln's Inn, Inner Temple, Middle Temple and Gray's Inn), all of which are situated near the Royal Courts of Justice in London.

10.2.1 Training

Entry to the Bar is normally degree-based, though there is a non-degree route for mature entrants, under which a small number of students qualify. As with solicitors, graduate students without a law degree can take the one-year course for the Common Professional Examination or Graduate Diploma in Law in the core subjects, in order to go on to qualify as a barrister. All student barristers have to pass the Bar Professional Training Course. On the course students study:

- case preparation
- legal research
- written skills
- opinion-writing (giving written advice)
- drafting documents such as claim forms
- conference skills (interviewing clients)

A barrister in robes

- negotiation
- advocacy (speaking in court).

Students also study specific areas of law related to their future profession, such as civil litigation, criminal litigation and the law of evidence.

All student barristers must join one of the four Inns of Court and used to have to dine there 12 times before being called to the Bar. Students may now attend in a different way, for example a weekend residential course. This helps students on courses outside London as travelling costs are lower. The idea behind the rule requiring all trainee barristers to dine was that they met senior barristers and judges and absorbed the traditions of the profession. In practice, few barristers dine at their Inns and students are unlikely to meet anyone except other students.

Once a student has passed the Bar Professional Training Course, he is then 'called to the Bar'. This means that they are officially qualified as a barrister. However, there is still a practical stage to their training which must be completed. This is called 'pupillage'.

Pupillage

After the student has passed the Bar Professional Training Course there is 'on-the-job' training where the trainee barrister becomes a pupil to a qualified barrister. This effectively involves 'work shadowing' that barrister, and can be with the same barrister for 12 months or with two different pupil masters for six months each. There is also a requirement that they take part in a programme of continuing education organised by the Bar Council. After the first six months of pupillage, barristers are eligible to appear in court and may conduct their own cases. During pupillage trainee barristers are paid a small salary – usually about half the amount paid to trainee solicitors.

The various training routes are shown in Figure 10.3.

10.2.2 Barristers' work

Barristers practising at the Bar are self-employed, but usually work from a set of chambers where they can share administrative expenses with other barristers. Most sets of chambers are fairly small, with about 15–25 barristers working there.

They will employ a clerk as a practice administrator – booking in cases and negotiating fees – and they will have other support staff. One of the problems facing newly qualified barristers is the difficulty of finding a tenancy in chambers. Many will do a third six-month pupillage and then 'squat' as an unofficial tenant before obtaining a place. The rule on having to practise from chambers has been relaxed, so that it is technically possible for barristers to practise from home. However, despite the fact that a tenancy in chambers is not essential, it is still viewed as the way to allow a barrister to build a successful practice.

The majority of barristers concentrate on advocacy, although there are some who specialise in areas such as tax and company law, and who rarely appear in court. Barristers have rights of audience in all courts in England and Wales. Even those who specialise in advocacy do a certain amount of paperwork, writing opinions on cases, giving advice and drafting documents for use in court.

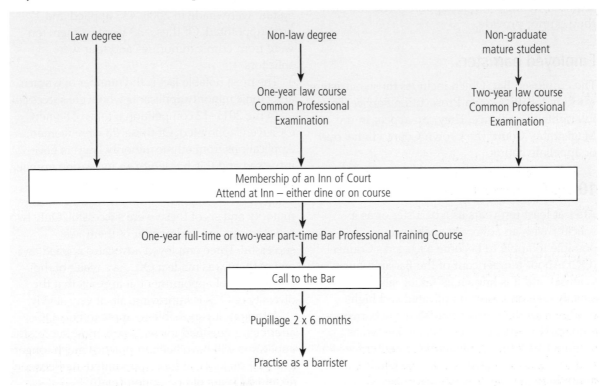

Figure 10.3 Training routes to becoming a barrister

Direct access

Originally it was necessary for anybody who wished to instruct a barrister to go to a solicitor first. The solicitor would then brief the barrister. This was thought to create unnecessary expense for clients, as it meant they had to use two lawyers instead of one. As a result of criticism the Bar has, since 2004, granted direct access to anyone (business or individual) in civil cases. It is no longer necessary to go to a solicitor in order to instruct a barrister for civil cases. However, direct access is still not allowed for criminal cases or family work.

Cab rank rule

Normally barristers operate what is known as the 'cab rank rule', under which they cannot turn down a case if it is on the area of law they deal with and they are free to take the case. However, where clients approach a barrister direct, the cab rank rule does not apply. Barristers can turn down a case which would require investigation or support services which they cannot provide.

Employed barristers

The employed Bar, which includes those barristers working for the Crown Prosecution Service, have full rights of audience. They can appear in the Magistrates' Court, the Crown Court, High Court or appellate courts.

10.2.3 Queen's Counsel

After at least ten years as a barrister or as a solicitor with an advocacy qualification, it is possible to apply to become a Queen's Counsel (QC). About ten per cent of the Bar are Queen's Counsel and it is known as 'taking silk'. QCs usually take on more complicated and high-profile cases than junior barristers (all barristers who are not Queen's Counsel are known as 'juniors'), and they can command higher fees for their recognised expertise. Often a QC has a junior barrister to assist with the case.

Until 2004 Queen's Council were appointed by the Lord Chancellor. However, the Lord Chancellor's criteria for selecting QCs was criticised as being too secretive. There was also the fact that fewer than ten per cent of QCs were women and only a very few were from ethnic minorities. In turn, this was likely to have an effect on the composition of the judiciary since senior judges are usually chosen from the ranks of Queen's Counsel.

These criticisms led to a change in the method of appointment.

Appointment system for QCs

Selection of who should become a QC is now made by an independent selection panel. Both barristers and solicitors may apply to become QCs. They have to pay a fee of £2,500. Applicants provide references (these can include references from clients) and are interviewed by members of the panel. The panel then recommends those who should be appointed to the Lord Chancellor.

The first appointments of QCs under the new system were made in 2006; 443 applied and 175 were appointed. Of these, 33 were women, ten were from ethnic minorities and four were solicitors.

The most notable fact is the number of women and ethnic minority applicants who were successful.

In the 2011–12 competition a total of 88 new QCs were appointed. Of these, 23 were women. Applications from ethnic minority lawyers have increased and this has led to an increasing number of successful applicants. In the 2011–12 competition 15 applicants were from an ethnic minority and six of these were successful. Only two solicitors applied and neither of them was successful. Three employed advocates applied and one of them was made a QC. As a result of the new system of appointment, it appears that the diversity of QCs is improving, albeit very slowly.

Although it is possible to apply to be a QC after being qualified for ten years, most successful applicants will have been in practice much longer. The vast majority of those appointed are between 40 and 55 years old on appointment.

10.2.4 Complaints against barristers

Where a barrister receives a brief from a solicitor, he does not enter into a contract with his client and so cannot sue if their fees are not paid. Similarly, the client cannot sue for breach of contract. However, they can be sued for negligence. In *Saif Ali v Sydney Mitchell and Co* (1980) it was held that a barrister could be sued for negligence in respect of written advice and opinions. In that case a barrister had given the wrong advice about who to sue, with the result that the claimant was too late to start proceedings against the right person.

In *Hall (a firm) v Simons* (2000) the House of Lords held that lawyers could also be liable for negligence in the conduct of advocacy in court. This decision overruled the earlier case of *Rondel v Worsley* (1969) in which barristers were held not to be liable because their first duty was to the courts and they must be 'free to do their duty fearlessly and independently'.

The Law Lords in *Hall (a firm) v Simons* felt that in light of modern conditions it was no

Key facts

	Solicitors	Barristers
Training	Degree, if not in law then must do Common Professional Examination or Graduate Diploma in Law	
	Legal Practice Course Training contract	Bar Professional Training Course Must join one of the four Inns of Court Pupillage
Role	Private practice in solicitors' firm Wide variety of work Contracts, leases, wills, conveyancing etc. Direct access by clients	Self-employed in chambers Mostly court work Also write opinions and draft documents Since 2004 direct access by clients in civil cases
	May be employed in CPS, CDS, local authority etc. or private commercial business	
Advocacy	Automatic rights in Magistrates' Courts and County Court Advocacy certificate for higher courts (Courts and Legal Services Act 1990) Plans for full rights (Access to Justice Act 1999)	Full rights in all courts
Queen's Counsel	Selection is now by an independent QC selection panel Applicants will be judged on seven competencies Applicants give referees and are interviewed by two members of the panel	
Representative body	Law Society	Bar Council
Regulatory body	Solicitors' Regulatory Authority	Bar Standards Board
Complaints body	Legal Ombudsman; Office for Supervision of Legal Complaints	

Figure 10.4 Key facts chart comparing solicitors and barristers

longer in the public interest that advocates should have immunity from being sued for negligence. They pointed out that doctors could be sued and they had a duty to an ethical code of practice and might have difficult decisions to make when treating patients. There was no reason why advocates should not be liable in the same way.

They also pointed out that allowing advocates to be sued for negligence would not be likely to lead to the whole case being re-argued. If an action against an advocate was merely an excuse to get the whole issue litigated again, the matter would almost certainly be struck out as an abuse of process.

Legal Ombudsman

This service now deals with complaints about poor service by a barrister (see section 10.1.5).

Bar Standards Board

This is the body which regulates the profession of barristers. It sets training and entry standards. It also sets out a Code of Conduct with which barristers should comply.

The Board investigates any alleged breach of the Code of Conduct. It can discipline any barrister who is in breach of the Code. If the matter is serious it will be referred to the Disciplinary Tribunal of the Council of the Inns of Court.

Council of the Inns of Court

Barristers can be disciplined by the tribunal of the Council of the Inns of Court if they fail to maintain the standards set out in their Code of Conduct. The tribunal can suspend a barrister from practice or, in extreme cases, the Senate can disbar a barrister from practising.

10.3 Legal Services Act 2007

This Act was passed following the Clementi Report. It set up the Legal Services Board, a new regulator, to oversee all legal professions. It also brought in the Office for Legal Complaints, a new complaints system, which deals with complaints against any of the legal professions.

10.3.1 Legal Services Board

The role of the Board is to have independent oversight regulation of the legal profession. It consists of a Chairman and seven to ten members appointed by the Secretary of State. The first Chairman must be a non-lawyer and the majority of members must also be non-lawyers.

The Solicitors' Regulatory Authority will continue to be the regulator for solicitors and the Bar Standards Board will continue to be the regulator for barristers. However, the Legal Services Board will oversee their work. For example, when either of the professions' regulatory bodies wish to make major changes to their Codes of Conduct or working practices, they must gain the approval of the Legal Services Board to do so.

10.3.2 Complaints about legal services

The Act established the Office for Legal Complaints to handle all complaints in respect of the legal profession. The Office has set up the Legal Ombudsman to perform the day-to-day handling of complaints. This work began in October 2010. The aim is to simplify the complaints structure for consumers. It is also completely independent of the legal professions.

10.3.3 Business structures

Prior to the Act there were restrictions on the types of business structures in the legal profession. The main restrictions were that:

- barristers and solicitors could not operate from the same business
- lawyers were not allowed to enter into partnership with non-lawyers
- non-lawyers could not be involved in the ownership or management of legal businesses
- legal practices could operate as a companies.

So, generally, barristers and solicitors could not work together, nor could lawyers and non-lawyers work together in legal businesses. The Legal Services Act changed this by allowing:

- legal businesses to include lawyers and non-lawyers

- legal businesses to include barristers and solicitors
- non-lawyers to own legal businesses
- legal businesses to operate as companies.

Since 2009 solicitors have been allowed to form Legal Disciplinary Practices (LDPs). In these firms up to 25 per cent of partners can be non-lawyers. In 2010, the rules on working practices for barristers were changed, so that they can be managers or work in LPDs. These practices are still owned by lawyers.

Alternative Business Structures

Alternative Business Structures (ABSs) have been allowed since October 2011. These can be owned by non-lawyers. So major companies, such as Tesco, could own an ABS. To set up an ABS a licence to operate has to be given. Access to justice must be considered when such a licence is applied for. This is to prevent commercial businesses choosing only the most profitable areas of law and possibly leaving an area without lawyers to do the less profitable types of law.

The first three licences were given in April 2012. Two of these were to 'high street' solicitors who wished to bring in a non-lawyer practice manager to their practices. The first 'big name' to be given a licence was the Co-operative Society.

As more ABSs are set up, the style of legal advice and services is likely to change considerably. Traditional solicitors' firms will face competition from commercial firms, such as the Co-op.

The way in which solicitors and barristers can work together now in an ABS is shown by the

@ Internet Research

Look up the Legal Services Act 2007 on **www.legislation.gov.uk**. At the start of the Act there is an index of contents. Use this to find which part of the Act deals with:

(a) The Legal Services Board

(b) Alternative Business Structures

(c) Legal complaints

group, Artesian Law. Six of the seven partners are barristers, the other being a solicitor. They also intend to have a non-lawyer practice manager. So, the firm can not only do the advocacy in court, but it can also do the solicitor's work involved in litigation. It can also bid for legal aid contracts.

10.4 Fusion

A major debate used to be whether the two professions should be merged into one profession. The advantages of fusion were thought to be:

- reduced costs, as only one lawyer would be needed instead of a solicitor and a barrister
- less duplication of work because only one person would be doing the work, instead of a solicitor preparing the case and then passing it on to a barrister
- more continuity, as the same person could deal with the case from start to finish.

The disadvantages of fusion were seen as:

- a decrease in the specialist skills of advocacy
- loss of the independent Bar and the lack of availability of advice from independent specialists at the Bar
- less objectivity in consideration of a case; at the moment the barrister provides a second opinion
- loss of the 'cab rank principle' under which barristers have to accept any case offered to them (except when they are already booked on another case for the same day). This principle allows anyone to get representation, even if their case is unpopular or unlikely to win.

The argument for fusion is no longer so important since the changes made by the Courts and Legal Services Act 1990 and the Access to Justice Act 1999 mean that barristers and solicitors can take a case from start to finish. Under the Access to Justice Act, barristers have the right to do litigation (that is, the preliminary work in starting a case) which has in the past always been done by solicitors. At the same time, solicitors have wider rights of advocacy and may represent clients in all courts.

Activity

Read the following article and answer the questions below.

Talent, not cash, should open the door to the Bar

The ancient buildings, paved courtyards and well-tended lawns of the Inns of Court shout privilege. But is the privilege of being a barrister one that anyone can attain – regardless of social background or wealth?

Concerns that it is now harder to enter the Bar have grown along with the costs of university and Bar training. Nearly one in three students arrive with debts of £20,000. The one-year vocational course can add another £15,000 – and non-law graduates have to fund an extra year on top of that.

But the barrier is not just financial. Geoffrey Vos, QC, whose father was a Bermondsey leather merchant, identifies other hurdles: lack of contacts or knowledge about the profession; its intimidating environment; the scramble to find a pupillage, or training place; and then the challenge of securing a seat in chambers. Finally, there is uncertainty of success or earning power.

The profession's entry profile is far more diverse that it was. But then what? Getting in is just the first hurdle. Perceived obstacles once inside can be a further deterrent. At the top the profession is still mostly male, white and privileged: 73 per cent of barristers in eight top commercial chambers went to private schools. At law firms, the proportion of women partners over ten years has risen slowly from 16.55 per cent to 23.2 per cent now. Women in the higher levels of the profession are nowhere near beginning to reflect the level of women entering the profession.

Adapted from an article by Frances Gibb in
The Times, 3 April 2007
© The Times/NI Syndication

Questions

1. The article mentions the Inns of Court. Name the four Inns of Court.

2. Briefly describe the contents of the Bar Vocational Course.

3. Why do non-law graduates have to study for an extra year?

4. What financial barriers are there to becoming a barrister?

5. What other barriers are there to becoming a barrister?

6. In which area have the legal professions become more diverse?

7. What are the problems at the higher levels of the legal professions?

@ Internet Research

The article states that the profession's entry is far more diverse than it was.

Try to find out what the current figures are for entrants to the legal professions. These are on the websites for the Law Society and the Bar: www.lawsociety.org.uk and www.barcouncil.org.uk.

With the implementation of the Legal Services Act there is even less need for the professions to be fused. Barristers and solicitors will be able to work together in the same legal business.

10.5 Women and ethnic minorities in the legal profession

The legal profession has an image of being dominated by white males. Both women and ethnic minorities are under-represented in the higher levels of the legal professions.

Women

As a result of the increasing numbers of women studying law, women now make up over half of new solicitors and barristers. This in turn means that there are now greater numbers of women practising in both professions: 32 per cent of members of the Bar and 46 per cent of solicitors are female.

Despite this there are very few women at the higher levels in either profession. For example, at the Bar only about 12 per cent of QCs are women. In the solicitors' profession, 25 per cent of women are partners, compared to 49 per cent of men. Women solicitors tend to be in junior positions as assistant solicitors or junior partners.

One of the reasons put forward to explain these low percentages of women at senior levels is that the increase in female entrants is a fairly recent phenomenon. Twenty years ago there were comparatively fewer women entering the legal professions, and so it is not so surprising that there are correspondingly fewer women in senior positions.

Women also tend to earn less than their male counterparts, even when they do achieve higher status, especially in the solicitors' ranks. Even the starting salaries of women are lower. The gap becomes bigger the higher up the profession, with men earning on average £15,000 more per year than women.

A report, *Obstacles and Barriers to the Career Development of Women Solicitors*, was published by the Law Society in 2010. The following factors were the main reasons why women were less likely than men to progress in the profession:

- lack of flexible working hours;
- the organisational culture which was perceived as being traditional, conservative and male-dominated;
- the long working hours with the 24/7 mindset;
- the fact that the measurement of success was strongly linked to the number of hours billed to clients – measuring quantity rather than quality;
- the fact that women are not prepared to challenge the status quo or push themselves forward for promotion.

These factors lead to many women leaving solicitors' firms, often to become an 'in-house' lawyer in another organisation where there is a different work culture.

Ethnic minorities

The number of people from ethnic minorities is also increasing in both legal professions. About 12 per cent of solicitors and 15 per cent of barristers in practice are from ethnic minorities. As with women, they are more likely to be in junior positions. An interesting fact is that ethnic minority lawyers are well represented in the Crown Prosecution Service, making up over 15 per cent of lawyers there.

Five per cent of QCs are from an ethnic minority and this figure is gradually increasing. However, only 25 per cent of ethnic minority solicitors are partners, compared to 38 per cent of white solicitors. Statistics also show that ethnic minority solicitors are more likely to work in smaller firms with only a few partners.

However, the figures are an improvement on previous years. In particular the new procedure for appointing QCs appears to have encouraged lawyers from ethnic minorities to apply.

This trend is important as it means there is likely to be an increase in judges appointed from ethnic minorities in future.

10.6 Future reforms

In 2012, the Legal Education and Training Review (LETR) was carried out by the Bar Standards Board, the Solicitors Regulation Authority and ILEX Professional Standards. The report should be published in 2013.

This review may well recommend some fundamental changes. Look at the LETR's website (**http://letr.org.uk**) to see their recommendations.

Self-Test Questions

1 Name the four Inns of Court.
2 What skills-based course must a barrister pass to be fully qualified?
3 What is pupillage?
4 What is meant by 'chambers'?
5 Explain two types of work a barrister might do.
6 What is meant by 'direct access', and which types of case is it NOT allowed for?
7 What is a QC?
8 Which body represents barristers?
9 Which case decided that barristers could be sued for negligence in their work?
10 Which body deals with complaints of poor service made against barristers?

Exam tips

Having got to the end of this chapter, you can see there is a lot of material to cover. When you are revising you need to separate it out into different areas, perhaps using a mind map to give you an overall summary, and then using revision cards or smaller mind maps for each of the individual areas. Once you have mastered the factual information you need to remember to give the information you are asked for – it's very tempting to write everything you know if you have worked really hard on the topic but try to resist doing that so that you can gain top marks. The second part of the question will ask for a discussion on a more specific area – perhaps training or the complaints system or the best way forward for the legal profession. Again it is a good idea to have some comments already thought out as part of your revision and remember to look at any issue from the point of view of its advantages and its disadvantages. To get top marks rather than listing all the points on one side of the argument and then repeating the process for the other point of view, try to give both sides of each point as you go along. This will seem much more coherent and thoughtful – the examiner will like to see this and be keen to give you more marks.

Examination Questions

1(a) Describe the education and training of barristers and how problems a client has with their barrister are dealt with.

18 marks

1(b) Discuss whether the 2010 changes have improved the way complaints about barristers and solicitors are dealt with.

12 marks

OCR G151 June 2012

2(a) Describe the qualifications and training of both barristers and solicitors.

18 marks

2(b) Discuss the problems associated with training for both barristers and solicitors.

12 marks

OCR G151 June 2010

Chapter 11

Magistrates

There is a tradition of using lay people (people who are not legally qualified) in the decision-making process in our courts. Today this applies particularly to the Magistrates' Courts and the Crown Court. However, in the past lay people were also frequently used to decide civil cases in the High Court and the County Court, and there are still some cases in which a jury can be used in the civil courts. There are also lay people with expertise in a particular field who sit as part of a panel as lay assessors. This occurs in the Patents Court and the Admiralty Court in the High Court as well as in tribunals.

11.1 Lay magistrates

There are about 25,000 lay magistrates sitting as part-time judges in the Magistrates' Courts; another name for lay magistrates is Justices of the Peace. They sit to hear cases as a bench of two or three magistrates. A single lay magistrate sitting on his or her own has very limited powers. They can, however, issue search warrants and warrants for arrest and conduct Early Administrative Hearings.

There are also District Judges (Magistrates' Courts) who work in Magistrates' Courts. These are not lay people but are qualified lawyers who can sit on their own to hear any of the cases that come before the court. They have the same powers as a bench of lay magistrates. Since the duties of these District Judges are the same as those of lay magistrates and since the history of the two is linked, details of District Judges

(formerly known as stipendiary magistrates) are also included in this chapter.

11.1.1 History of the magistracy

The office of Justice of the Peace is very old, dating back to the twelfth century at least. In 1195 Richard I appointed 'keepers of the peace'. By the mid-thirteenth century the judicial side of their position had developed and by 1361 the title Justice of the Peace was being used. Over the years they were also given many administrative duties, for example, being responsible for the poor law, highways and bridges, and weights and measures. In the nineteenth century, elected local authorities took over most of these duties, though some remnants remain, especially in the licensing powers of the Magistrates' Courts.

The poor quality of the local Justices of the Peace in London and the absence of an adequate police force became a matter of concern towards the end of the eighteenth century. This led to seven public offices with paid magistrates being set up in 1792. This was the origin of the modern stipendiary magistrate. Until 1839 they were in charge of the police as well as hearing cases in court.

Outside London, the first appointment of a paid magistrate was in Manchester in 1813. In 1835 the Municipal Corporations Act gave a general power for boroughs to request the appointment of a stipendiary magistrate. At the beginning a paid magistrate did not have to have any particular qualifications, but from 1839 they could only be appointed from barristers. Solicitors did not become eligible to be appointed as stipendiary magistrates until 1949.

11.2 Qualifications

11.2.1 Lay magistrates

Lay magistrates do not have to have any qualifications in law. There are, however, some requirements as to their character. There are six key qualities which candidates should have. These are:

- good character
- understanding and communication
- social awareness
- maturity and sound temperament
- sound judgement
- commitment and reliability.

They must have certain 'judicial' qualities – it is particularly important that they are able to assimilate factual information and make a reasoned decision upon it. They must also be able to take account of the reasoning of others and work as a team.

There are also formal requirements as to age and residence: lay magistrates must be aged between 18 and 65 on appointment. In reality, there are very few appointments of magistrates under the age of 30.

However, since the age for appointment was reduced to 18 in 2003 there have been a small

number of much younger magistrates appointed. In 2004 there were at least two appointments of young magistrates, one aged 21 in Shropshire and another aged 23 in West Yorkshire. In 2006 the youngest magistrate, age 19, was appointed in Pontefract.

Despite these appointments of young magistrates, only four per cent of magistrates are under the age of 40.

11.2.2 Area

The country is divided into local justice areas. These areas are specified by the Lord Chancellor and lay magistrates are expected to live or work within or near to the local justice area to which they are allocated.

11.2.3 Commitment

The other requirement is that lay magistrates must be prepared to commit themselves to sitting at least 26 half days each year. It is thought that this level of commitment deters many people from becoming lay magistrates.

11.2.4 Restrictions on appointment

Some people are not eligible to be appointed. These include people with serious criminal convictions, though a conviction for a minor motoring offence will not automatically disqualify a candidate. Others who are disqualified include undischarged bankrupts, members of the forces and those whose work is incompatible with sitting as a magistrate, such as police officers and traffic wardens.

Relatives of those working in the local criminal justice system are not likely to be appointed as it would not appear 'just' if, for example, the wife of a local police officer were to sit to decide cases. In addition people whose hearing is impaired, or who by reason of infirmity cannot carry out all the duties of a justice of the peace, cannot be appointed. Close relatives will not be appointed to the same Bench.

11.2.5 District Judges

These were previously known as stipendiary magistrates. They must be qualified as a barrister or solicitor or be Deputy District judge. They must also have five years' experience in the law. ILEX Fellows are now eligible to be appointed as Deputy District Judges.

District Judges are only appointed to courts in London or other big cities such as Birmingham, Liverpool and Manchester. Before becoming a District Judge they will usually be a Deputy District Judge sitting part-time for two years to gain experience of sitting judicially, and to establish their suitability for full-time appointment.

11.3 Appointment

About 1,500 new lay magistrates are appointed each year. The appointments are made by the Lord Chancellor. In order to decide who to appoint, the Lord Chancellor relies on recommendations made to him by the local advisory committees – this method of appointment is much criticised.

11.3.1 Local Advisory Committees

These committees have a maximum of 12 members. Most members will be existing magistrates, but at least a third of members must be non-magistrates.

Anyone aged 18 to 65 can apply to be a lay magistrate. To try to encourage as wide a range of potential candidates as possible, committees advertise in local newspapers for individuals to put themselves forward. Advertisements will sometimes be placed in newspapers aimed at particular ethnic groups. Some local committees have used other methods of publicising vacancies for magistrates, such as placing adverts on local buses or advertising on local radio. Open evenings may be organised at the local Magistrates' Court, so that people can find out more about magistrates and their role. All of this aims to attract as wide a spectrum of potential candidates as possible. The intention is to create a panel representative of all aspects of society.

A balance of occupations is aimed at. The Lord Chancellor has set down 11 broad categories of occupations, and advisory committees are recommended that they should not have more than 15 per cent of the bench coming from any single category. Other industrial and social groupings are also taken into consideration to try to achieve a Bench which is representative of the local community.

11.3.2 Interview panels

There is usually a two-stage interview process. At the first interview the panel tries to find out more about the candidate's personal attributes, in particular looking to see if they have the six key qualities required. The interview panel will also explore the candidate's attitudes on various criminal justice issues such as youth crime or drink-driving. The second interview is aimed at testing candidates' potential judicial aptitude and this is done by a discussion of at least two case studies which are typical of those heard regularly in Magistrates' Courts. The discussion might, for example, focus on the type of sentence which should be imposed on specific case facts.

The advisory committees will interview candidates and then submit names of those they think are suitable to the Lord Chancellor. He will then appoint new magistrates from this list. Once appointed, magistrates may continue to sit until the age of 70.

11.4 Composition of the Bench today

The traditional image of lay justices is that they are 'middle-class, middle-aged and middle-minded'. This image is to a certain extent true. Half of all lay magistrates are between 60 and 70 years old, with only four per cent under the age of 40. The majority are supporters of the Conservative Party; this is so even in areas where there is a high Labour vote. A report, *The Judiciary in the Magistrates' Courts* (2002), found that lay magistrates:

- were drawn overwhelmingly from professional and managerial ranks, and
- 40 per cent of them were retired from full-time employment.

However, in other respects the Bench is well balanced. The figures for 2012 show that 51.3 per cent of magistrates are women. This is much better than the percentage for professional judges. Also, ethnic minorities are reasonably well represented in the magistracy. The figures for 2012 show that just over 8 per cent of magistrates come from an ethnic minority. This also compares very favourably to the professional judiciary where only about 4 per cent are from ethnic minority backgrounds.

The relatively high level of ethnic minority magistrates is largely a result of campaigns to attract a wider range of candidates. In an effort to encourage people from ethnic minorities to apply, advertisements appear in such publications as the *Caribbean Times*, the *Asian Times* and *Muslim News*. This has led to an increase in the number of ethnic minority appointments.

The Lord Chancellor has encouraged disabled people to apply to become magistrates. This has included appointing blind persons as lay magistrates. In 2012, about 5 per cent of lay magistrates had a disability.

So, apart from the age range, the magistracy is very diverse.

@ Internet Research

Look at the Magistrates' Association website at **www.magistrates-association.org.uk**. You can find out more about how to become a magistrate.

11.5 Magistrates' duties

They have a very wide workload which is mainly connected to criminal cases, although they also deal with some civil matters, especially family cases. They try 97 per cent of all criminal cases and deal with preliminary hearings in the remaining three per cent of criminal cases. This will involve Early Administrative Hearings, remand hearings, bail applications and committal proceedings.

They also deal with civil matters which include the enforcing of debts owed to the utilities (gas, electricity and water), non-payment of the council tax and non-payment of television licences. In addition, they hear appeals from the refusal of a local authority to grant licences for the sale of alcohol and licences for betting and gaming establishments.

Youth Court and Family Court

Specially nominated and trained justices form the Youth Court panel to hear criminal charges against young offenders aged 10–17 years old. A panel must usually include at least one man and one woman.

There is also a special panel for the Family Court to hear family cases including orders for protection against violence, affiliation cases, adoption orders and proceedings under the Children Act 1989. This court will become part of the new Family Court which is to be set up under the Crime and Courts Bill 2012–13.

Appeals

Lay magistrates also sit at the Crown Court to hear appeals from the Magistrates' Court. In these cases the lay justices form a panel with a qualified judge.

11.6 Training of lay magistrates

The training of lay magistrates is supervised by the Magistrates' Committee of the Judicial Studies Board. This Committee has drawn up a syllabus of the topics which lay magistrates should cover in their training. However, because of the large numbers of lay magistrates, the actual training is carried out in local areas, sometimes through the clerk of the court, and sometimes through weekend courses organised by universities with magistrates from the region attending.

Since 1998, magistrates' training has been monitored more closely. There were criticisms prior to then that, although magistrates were required to attend a certain number of hours' training, there was no assessment of how much they had understood.

Competencies

The framework of training is divided into four areas of competence, the first three of which are relevant to all lay magistrates. The fourth competence is for Chairmen of the Bench. The four areas of competence are:

1. Managing yourself – this focuses on some of the basic aspects of self-management in relation to preparing for court, conduct in court and ongoing learning.
2. Working as a member of a team – this focuses on the team aspect of decision-making in the Magistrates' Court.
3. Making judicial decisions – this focuses on impartial and structured decision-making.
4. Managing judicial decision-making – this is for the Chairman's role and focuses on working with the legal adviser, managing the court and ensuring effective, impartial decision-making.

For delivering training there are Bench Training and Developmental Committees (BTDCs); s 19(3) of the Courts Act 2003 sets out a statutory obligation on the Lord Chancellor to provide training and training materials.

11.6.1 Training of new magistrates

The training in the first year for a new magistrate consists of:

1. Initial training before sitting in court, a new magistrate will undergo introductory training on the basics of the role. After this they will sit in court with two other experienced magistrates.
2. Mentoring: each new magistrate has a specially trained magistrate mentor to guide them through the first 12–18 months. There are six formal mentored sittings in the first 12–18 months, where the new magistrate will review his/her learning progress.
3. Core training: over the first year, further training, visits to prisons or Young Offenders' Institutions and observing other magistrates will take place.
4. Consolidation training: at the end of the first year, this training builds on the learning from sittings and the core training. This is designed to help magistrates to plan for ongoing development and prepare for their first appraisal.
5. First appraisal: about 12–18 months after appointment, when both mentor and the magistrate agree that he or she is ready, the new magistrate is appraised. When successful, the magistrate is deemed fully competent.

Any magistrate who cannot show that they have achieved the competencies will be given extra training. If they still cannot achieve the competencies, then the matter is referred to the local Advisory Committee, who may recommend to the Lord Chancellor that the magistrate is removed from sitting.

The training programme for new magistrates should normally follow the pattern set out in Figure 11.1.

Appointment

↓

Initial training

↓

First sitting

↓

Mentored sittings
Magistrates adjudicate in
court as wingers

↓

9–12 months consolidation training

↓

After 12–18 months appraisal

↓

Three year cycle continuation training
followed by approval

Figure 11.1 New magistrates' training

11.6.2 Training sessions

These are organised and carried out at local level within the 42 court areas. Much of the training is delivered by Justices' Clerks. The Judicial Studies Board intends that most training should still be delivered locally. However, they take into account the need to collaborate regionally and nationally where appropriate. In particular, the training of Youth and Family Panel Chairmen will be delivered nationally for areas which do not have enough such Chairmen requiring training to run an effective course locally.

11.6.3 Ongoing training

Magistrates continue training while they work. They have continuation training every three years, and they are also appraised every three years to ensure that they maintain their competency to sit. They will also have update training on changes in the law.

If they wish to sit in the Youth Court or in the Family Court they will be given extra training. They will also receive extra training if they wish to become a Chairman and will be appraised for this role.

This new scheme involves practical training 'on the job'. It also answers the criticisms of the old

system where there was no check made on whether the magistrate had actually benefited from the training session they attended.

11.7 Retirement and removal

The retirement age is 70, but when magistrates become 70 they do not officially retire – instead, their names are placed on the Supplemental List. This means that they can no longer sit in the Magistrates' Court. However, they can continue to carry out some administrative functions mainly connected with signing documents. Lay magistrates who move from the commission area to which they were appointed cannot continue as magistrates in that area. If they wish to continue as magistrates, their names will be placed on the Supplemental List until there is a vacancy in their new area. Lay magistrates may, of course, resign from office at any time and many will resign before reaching 70.

11.7.1 Removal

Section 11 of the Courts Act 2003 gives the Lord Chancellor the power to remove a lay justice for the following reasons:

- on the grounds of incapacity or misbehaviour
- on the grounds of a persistent failure to meet such standards of competence as are prescribed by a direction given by the Lord Chancellor, or
- if the Lord Chancellor is satisfied that the lay justice is declining or neglecting to take a proper part in the exercise of his functions as a justice of the peace.

Removal for misbehaviour usually occurs when a magistrate is convicted of a criminal offence. There are about ten such removals each year. However, on occasions in the past there have been removals for such matters as taking part in a CND march or transvestite behaviour. There was considerable criticism of the Lord Chancellor's use of his power of removal in such circumstances and it is unlikely that such behaviour today would lead to removal from the Bench.

Key facts

Qualifications	Live or work near court in which they sit Need common sense, integrity Disqualified for serious criminal record, bankruptcy or work that is incompatible
Appointment	By Lord Chancellor on the recommendation of local advisory committees
Training	Four basic competencies: Initial training Mentors and mentored sessions Core training Appraisal Ongoing training every three years
Composition	25,000 lay magistrates, 49 per cent men, 51 per cent women on Bench Good representation of ethnic minorities (8 per cent) 50 per cent age 60–70, only four per cent under 40
Work	Summary trials Ancillary matters, e.g. issuing warrants, bail applications Youth court Family court Sit in Crown Court on appeal from Magistrates' Court

Figure 11.2 Key facts chart on lay magistrates

11.8 The magistrates' clerk

Every Bench is assisted by a clerk. There will be one Magistrates' Clerk for each area. There will also be a legal adviser sitting with each Bench in court. The senior clerk in each court has to be qualified as a barrister or solicitor for at least five years. The clerk's duty is to guide the magistrates on questions of law, practice and procedure. This is set out in s 28(3) of the Justices of the Peace Act 1979 which says:

> It is hereby declared that the functions of a justices' clerk include the giving to the justices ... of advice about law, practice or procedure on questions arising in connection with the discharge of their functions.

The clerk or legal adviser is not meant to assist in the decision-making and should not normally retire with the magistrates when they go to make their decision. In *R v Eccles Justices, ex parte Farrelly* (1992) the Queen's Bench Divisional Court quashed convictions because the clerk had apparently participated in the decision-making process.

Clerks deal with routine administrative matters, and can issue warrants for arrest, extend police bail, adjourn criminal proceedings. They also have the powers to deal with Early Administrative Hearings.

Exam tips

Magistrates are a popular topic with students. It appears quite often on the exam paper which means that your revision will often be worthwhile.

The topic breaks down into several key factual areas and you need to cover the qualifications needed to be a magistrate, the selection process, the training and then the work that a magistrate does. It is well worth breaking your revision into chunks and making sure that you have all your factual information organised under the appropriate headings.

One way to bring the topic alive is to see what magistrates actually do. Of course this doesn't mean that you have to commit a crime but you can visit a magistrate's court and if you speak to the court usher they may be able to get the magistrates to spend a few minutes talking to you about their job. Magistrates will often come to schools and colleges to talk to students so see if your teacher or lecturer can organise this. You might be able to take part in a sentencing workshop, you will be able to ask all the questions you want.

Your revision will be easier when you have seen them in action or heard what they have to say on, for example, the qualities they had to show to be chosen or the kind of people they sit with on the local bench. Law is a living subject and this is an easy way to make it come alive for you.

@ Internet Research

Have a look at a magistrates court at www.judiciary.gov.uk/interactive-learning.

11.9 Advantages of lay magistrates

11.9.1 Cross-section of society

Lay magistrates provide a wider cross-section on the Bench than would be possible with the use of professional judges. This is particularly true of women, with just over half of magistrates being female. Also, ethnic minorities are well represented in the magistracy.

A former Lord Chancellor pointed out that the magistracy was very diverse:

 Magistrates come from a wide range of backgrounds and occupations. We have magistrates who are dinner ladies and scientists, bus drivers and teachers, plumbers and housewives. They have different faiths and come from different ethnic backgrounds, some have disabilities. All are serving their communities, ensuring that local justice is dispensed by local people. The magistracy should reflect the diversity of the community it serves.

Lay magistrates are more representative than District Judges in the Magistrates' Courts. Only 25 per cent of District Judges are women as against over 50 per cent of lay magistrates. People from ethnic minorities make up 4 per cent of District Judges, compared with 8 per cent of lay magistrates. However, District Judges are much younger on average than lay magistrates.

11.9.2 Local knowledge

Lay magistrates used to have to live within 15 miles of the area covered by the commission, in order that they would have local knowledge of particular problems in the area. Under the Courts Act 2003 there is no longer a formal requirement that they should live in or near the area in which they sit as a magistrate, although it is intended that normally magistrates will continue to sit in the local justice area in which they reside. However, if there is a good reason to do otherwise, for example where it is easier for the magistrate to sit in the area where he works, then this is allowed.

Even though lay magistrates live or work in the relevant justice area, it is sometimes argued that they do not have any real knowledge of the problems in the poorer areas. This is because most magistrates come from the professional and managerial classes and live in the better areas. However, their main value is that they will have more awareness of local events, local patterns of crime and local opinions than a professional judge from another area.

Another problem is that during the last ten years, nearly 150 Magistrates' Courts have been closed. This causes problems of access and attendance because in some areas people have long journeys to their 'local' court. It also means that the advantage of lay magistrates having local knowledge is being lost.

11.9.3 Cost

The use of unpaid lay magistrates is cheap. It is estimated that 1,000 extra District Judges would be needed to replace all the lay magistrates. This would be expensive. In addition, there would also be the problem of recruiting sufficient qualified lawyers.

The cost of a trial in the Magistrates' Court is also much cheaper than a trial in the Crown Court. This is partly because cases in the Crown Court are more complex and therefore likely to take longer. Even so, the cost both to the Government and to defendants who pay for their own lawyer would be much higher in the Crown Court.

11.9.4 Legal adviser

Since 1999, all magistrates' clerks have to be qualified as either a barrister or a solicitor. The legal advisers, who sit in each court, also have to have some legal qualifications, though they need not be a barrister or solicitor. This brings a higher level of legal skill to the Magistrates' Court. The availability of a legal adviser gives the magistrates access to any necessary legal advice on points that may arise in any case. This overcomes any criticism of the fact that lay magistrates are not themselves legally qualified. In addition, the training of lay magistrates is improving with the new training system and the strengthened role of the Judicial Studies Board in their training.

11.9.5 Few appeals

Comparatively few defendants appeal against the magistrates' decisions, and many of the appeals that are made are against sentence not against the finding of guilt. In 2011, the *Judicial Statistics Annual Report* showed that only some 13,000 appeals were made to the Crown Court from the Magistrates' Courts. Out of these, less than half were allowed. This was out of a total workload of over 1.5 million defendants dealt with in the Magistrates' Courts.

There are also very few instances where an error of law is made. This is shown by the fact that in 2011 there were only 79 appeals by way of case stated to the Queen's Bench Divisional Court. Of these appeals, less than half were allowed. From this it can be argued that despite the amateur status of lay magistrates, they do a remarkably good job.

Key facts

Advantages of using lay magistrates	Disadvantages of using lay magistrates
Cross-section of local people Good gender balance Good ethnic balance Much better cross-section than District Judges	Not a true cross-section 50 per cent are aged 60 or over Majority are from professional or managerial background Older than District Judges
Live (or work) locally and so know the area and its problems	Unlikely to live in the poorer areas and so do not truly know the area's problems
Cheaper than using professional judges as they are only paid expenses Cheaper than sending cases to the Crown Court	
Improved training with mentoring and appraisals	There are inconsistencies in sentencing and decisions on bail
Have legal adviser for points of law	Not legally qualified
Very few appeals	

Figure 11.3 Key facts chart on advantages and disadvantages of using lay magistrates

11.10 Disadvantages of lay magistrates

11.10.1 Middle-aged, middle class

Lay magistrates are often perceived as being middle-aged and middle class. The report *The Judiciary in the Magistrates' Courts* (2000) showed that this was largely true. They found that 40 per cent of lay magistrates were retired and also that they were overwhelmingly from a professional or managerial background. However, as already discussed at section 11.9.1, lay magistrates are from a much wider range of backgrounds than professional judges.

11.10.2 Prosecution bias

It is often said that lay magistrates tend to be biased towards the prosecution, believing the

police too readily. One fact supporting this theory is that there is a lower acquittal rate in Magistrates' Courts than in the Crown Court. There is also the fact that they will see the same Crown Prosecution Service prosecutor or designated case worker frequently and this could affect their judgement. However, part of their training is aimed at eliminating this type of bias.

11.10.3 Inconsistency in sentencing

Magistrates in different areas often pass very different sentences for what appear to be similar offences. This is something which has not really improved over the years, despite the training that lay magistrates receive.

For example, figures for 2004 showed that magistrates in Sunderland discharged 36.4 per cent of all defendants, whereas only 9.2 per cent of defendants in Birmingham were discharged.

In Newcastle, magistrates sentenced only 7.2 per cent of defendants to an immediate custodial sentence. In Hillingdon in West London, the magistrates sentenced 32 per cent of defendants to an immediate custodial sentence.

Figures for 2010 show similar discrepancies. The highest percentage of offenders being given a custodial sentence was in Bristol (11.1 per cent) and Peterborough (11.0 per cent). At the other end of the scale, only 0.1 per cent of offenders appearing in Dinefwr Magistrates' Courts were given custodial sentences.

Bristol also imposed the highest percentage of community sentences at 32.2 per cent, whilst in Dinefwr it was 6.6 per cent. The overall figures for Bristol show that out of 5,687 offenders sentenced, 630 were given a custodial sentence and 1,831 a community sentence. In Dinefwr, out of 1,169 offenders sentenced, only one was given a custodial sentence and 79 a community sentence.

These figures do not take into account what types of offences were involved, but the figures for Bristol seem to be excessively high. This is so even when compared to other city areas with similar number of offenders, such as Coventry where, out of 7,162 offenders, 492 were given a custodial sentence (6.8 per cent) and 1,043 were given community sentences (14.4 per cent).

An interesting point is that District Judges are more likely than lay magistrates to sentence an offender to imprisonment.

11.10.4 Reliance on the clerk

The lack of legal knowledge of the lay justices should be offset by the fact that a legally qualified clerk or adviser is available to give advice. However, this will not prevent inconsistencies in sentencing since the clerk is not allowed to help the magistrates decide on a sentence. In some courts it is felt that the magistrates rely too heavily on their clerk.

11.11 Comparing lay magistrates and District Judges

11.11.1 Qualifications and work

- Lay magistrates are not legally qualified. District Judges (DJs) must be qualified as a barrister or solicitor (or for a Deputy Judge they can be a Fellow of the Institute of Legal Executives).
- Lay magistrates sit only part-time (a minimum of 26 half days a year); DJs sit full-time.
- Lay magistrates are only paid expenses; DJs are paid a full salary.

11.11.2 Advantages of using District Judges

- DJs are younger than lay magistrates. The majority of DJs are aged between 35 and 55. Half of all lay magistrates are aged 60 or over.
- DJs deal with cases more speedily than lay magistrates.
- DJs are able to deal with more complex cases.
- One DJ could replace 30 lay magistrates.
- A survey found that court users had more confidence in DJs than in lay magistrates.
- DJs are more consistent and use the correct procedure.

11.11.3 Disadvantages of using District Judges

- DJs are not likely to be from the local community, unlike lay magistrates who must live or work in or near the area for the court they sit in. A survey found that the public thought lay magistrates would be better at representing the views of the community and sympathetic with the defendants' circumstances.

- The same survey found that court users considered lay magistrates better than DJs at showing courtesy, using simple language and showing concern to distressed victims.
- DJs are more likely to become 'case-hardened' as they hear so many similar cases. However, lay magistrates can also become case-hardened after a number of years.
- DJs are more likely than lay magistrates to refuse bail.
- DJs are more likely than lay magistrates to impose an immediate custodial sentence.
- The cost of replacing lay magistrates with DJs was estimated in 2000 to be over £23 million.

Self-Test Questions

1 What two types of 'judge' sit to hear cases in the Magistrates' Courts?
2 What qualifications (age, character) must lay magistrates have?
3 How are potential lay magistrates selected, and by whom?
4 Who appoints lay magistrates?
5 What types of cases do magistrates deal with in the Magistrates' Courts?
6 What does the Youth Court deal with?
7 How are lay magistrates trained?
8 At what age must lay magistrates retire?
9 Give three advantages of using lay magistrates.
10 Give three disadvantages of using lay magistrates.

Examination Questions

1(a) Describe **both** the selection and the training of lay magistrates.   18 marks

1(b) Discuss the **disadvantages** of using lay magistrates to deal with criminal cases.   12 marks

OCR G151 January 2011

Exam tips

The discussion aspect of this subject will be rooted in some aspect of the good and bad aspects of the magistracy, so you can make a chart with two columns to get you going with your revision. As in the factual aspect of the question, you might need to consider a particular aspect, perhaps training or selection, but you might also need to think about wider issues such as the advantages or otherwise of the magistracy compared to other types of judges.

To get top marks you need to make your points confidently but it is also necessary to develop them. For example, rather than simply saying that magistrates are good because they are local you could go on to say that this is important because it helps the community feel safer if they can see those who have done wrong being brought to account. This is an important element of living in a democratic society. In other words, try to think beyond the obvious!

Chapter 12

Juries

12.1 History of the jury system

Juries have been used in the legal system for over 1,000 years. There is evidence that they were used even before the Norman Conquest. However, in 1215 when trial by ordeal was condemned by the Church and (in the same year) the Magna Carta included the recognition of a person's right to trial by 'the lawful judgment of his peers', juries became the usual method of trying criminal cases. Originally they were used for providing local knowledge and information, and acted more as witnesses than decision-makers. By the middle of the fifteenth century, juries had become independent assessors and assumed their modern role as deciders of fact.

12.1.1 Independence of the jury

The independence of the jury became even more firmly established following *Bushell's Case* (1670). In that case several jurors refused to convict Quaker activists of unlawful assembly. The trial judge would not accept the not guilty verdict, and ordered the jurors to resume their deliberations without food or drink. When the jurors persisted in their refusal to convict, the court fined them and committed them to prison until the fines were paid. On appeal, the Court of Common Pleas ordered the release of the jurors, holding that jurors could not be punished for their verdict. This established that the jury were the sole arbiters of fact and the judge could not challenge their decision.

A more modern-day example demonstrating that judges must respect the independence of the jury is *R* v *McKenna* (1960). In that case the judge at the trial had threatened the jury that if they did not return a verdict within another ten minutes they would be locked up all night. The jury then returned a verdict of guilty, but the defendant's conviction was quashed on appeal because of the judge's interference.

12.2 Modern-day use of the jury

Only a small percentage of cases is tried by jury today. However, juries are used in the following courts:

- Crown Court for criminal trials on indictment
- High Court, Queen's Bench Division (but only for certain types of cases)
- County Court (for similar cases to the Queen's Bench Division)
- Coroners' Courts (in some cases).

12.2.1 Juries in criminal cases

The most important use of juries today is in the Crown Court where they decide whether the defendant is guilty or not guilty. Jury trials, however, account for less than one per cent of all criminal trials. This is because 97 per cent of cases are dealt with in the Magistrates' Court and of the cases that go to the Crown Court, about two out of every three defendants plead guilty. Also, some of the cases at the Crown Court, in which the defendant has entered a not guilty plea, will not go before a jury as the case will be discharged by judge without any trial. This occurs where the Crown Prosecution Service withdraws the charges, possibly because a witness refuses to give evidence.

A jury in the Crown Court has 12 members.

12.2.2 Juries in civil cases

Juries in civil cases are now only used in very limited circumstances, but where they are used they have a dual role. They decide whether the claimant has proved his case or not. Then, if they decide that the claimant has won the case, the jury also decides the amount of damages that the defendant should pay to the claimant.

Up to 1854 all common law civil cases were tried by jury, but from 1854 the parties could agree not to use a jury and gradually their use declined. Then in 1933 the Administration of Justice Act limited the right to use a jury, so that juries could not be used in disputes over breach of contract.

The present rules for when juries may be used in civil cases are set out in s 69 of the Senior Courts Act 1981 for High Court cases, and s 66 of the County Courts Act 1984 for cases in that court. These Acts state that parties have the right to jury trial only in the following types of case:

- defamation, in cases of libel and slander (this is the most frequent use of juries)
- false imprisonment
- malicious prosecution
- fraud.

All these cases involve character or reputation and it is for this reason that jury trial has been retained. Even for these cases a jury trial can be refused by the judge if the case involves complicated documents or accounts or scientific evidence and is therefore thought to be unsuitable for jury trial. Fewer than ten cases a year are tried by jury in the Queen's Bench Division and nearly all of these are defamation cases.

Where a jury is used in the High Court there will be 12 jurors.

Use of juries in personal injury cases

In other civil cases in the Queen's Bench Division of the High Court the parties can apply to a judge for trial by jury, but it is very rare for such a request to be granted. This follows the case of *Ward v James* (1966) where the plaintiff was claiming for injuries caused in a road crash. In this case the Court of Appeal laid down guidelines for personal injury cases. These were:

- personal injury cases should normally be tried by a judge sitting alone, because such cases involve assessing compensatory damages which have to have regard to the conventional scales of damages
- there have to be exceptional circumstances before the court will allow a jury to be used in such a case.

The decision in *Ward v James* effectively stopped the use of juries for personal injury cases. The following cases show how the courts have proved very reluctant to let juries be used.

Singh v London Underground (1990)

A request for a jury to try a personal injury case arising from the King's Cross Underground fire was refused. It was held that the case was unsuitable for jury trial because it involved such wide issues and technical points.

H v Ministry of Defence (1991)

The defendant was a soldier who had received negligent medical treatment necessitating the amputation of part of his penis. He applied for jury trial, but it was held that jury trial for a personal injury claim would only be allowed in very exceptional circumstances and this case was not such a one. The court said that an example of when jury trial might be appropriate was where the injuries resulted from someone deliberately abusing their authority and there might well be a claim for exemplary damages.

Key facts

Court	Type of case	Role	Number on jury
Crown Court	Serious criminal cases: e.g. murder, manslaughter, rape	Decide verdict 'Guilty' or 'Not guilty'	12
High Court	Defamation False imprisonment Malicious prosecution Any case alleging fraud	Decide liability If find for the claimant, also decide amount of damages	12
County Court	Defamation False imprisonment Malicious prosecution Any case alleging fraud	Decide liability If find for the claimant, also decide amount of damages	8
Coroners' Court	Deaths: • in custody and death was violent or cause unknown • as a result of a police act • caused by a notifiable accident, poisoning or disease	Decide cause of death	7–11

Figure 12.1 Key facts chart on the use of juries

County Court

Trial by jury in the County Court is very rare, but since 1991 with the changes in the jurisdiction (defamation actions can be transferred for trial to the County Court) there are occasionally cases in which a jury is used. Where a jury is used in the County Court there will be eight jurors. Use of jury is so rare in the County Court that when one was used in a County Court in the north of England, a newspaper article claimed that it was the first one for 40 years.

12.2.3 Coroners' Courts

In these courts a jury of between seven and eleven members may be used to enquire into deaths. Under the Coroners and Justice Act 2009 a jury will only be used if:

(a) there is reason to suspect that the deceased died while in custody and that either:

(i) the death was a violent or unnatural one, or
(ii) the cause of death is unknown,

(b) the death resulted from an act or omission of a police officer

(c) the death was caused by a notifiable accident, poisoning or disease.

12.3 Jury qualifications

12.3.1 Basic qualifications

The qualifications for jury service were revised in 1972 following the Morris Committee Report on jury service. Before this date there was a property qualification – in order to be a juror, it was necessary to be the owner or tenant of a dwelling. This restriction meant that women and young people who were less likely to own or rent property were prevented from serving on a jury. The Morris Committee thought that being a juror should be the counterpart of being a citizen. As a result, the qualifications for jury service were widened in the Criminal Justice Act 1972 and based on the right to vote. The present qualifications are set out in the Juries Act 1974 (as amended) so that to qualify for jury service a person must be:

● aged between 18 and 70
● registered as a parliamentary or local government elector
● ordinarily resident in the United Kingdom, the Channel Islands or the Isle of Man for at least five years since their thirteenth birthday.

However, certain people are not allowed to sit on a jury even though they are within these basic qualifications. These are people who are disqualified and those who are mentally disordered.

12.3.2 Disqualification

Some criminal convictions will disqualify a person from jury service. The type of sentence and the length of a prison sentence decide whether the person is disqualified and the period for which that disqualification lasts. Disqualified permanently from jury service are those who at any time have been sentenced to:

● imprisonment for life, detention for life or custody for life
● detention during Her Majesty's pleasure or during the pleasure of the Secretary of State

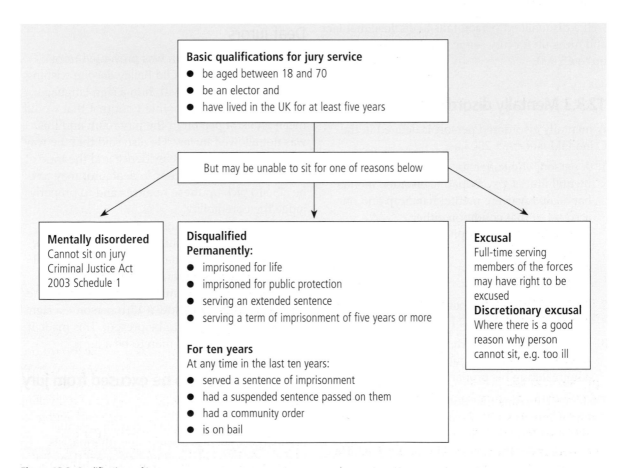

Basic qualifications for jury service
● be aged between 18 and 70
● be an elector and
● have lived in the UK for at least five years

But may be unable to sit for one of reasons below

Mentally disordered
Cannot sit on jury
Criminal Justice Act
2003 Schedule 1

Disqualified
Permanently:
● imprisoned for life
● imprisoned for public protection
● serving an extended sentence
● serving a term of imprisonment of five years or more

For ten years
At any time in the last ten years:
● served a sentence of imprisonment
● had a suspended sentence passed on them
● had a community order
● is on bail

Excusal
Full-time serving members of the forces may have right to be excused
Discretionary excusal
Where there is a good reason why person cannot sit, e.g. too ill

Figure 12.2 Qualifications of jurors

- to imprisonment for public protection or detention for public protection
- an extended sentence
- a term of imprisonment of five years or more or a term of detention of five years or more.

Those in the following categories are disqualified for ten years:

- at any time in the last ten years served a sentence of imprisonment
- at any time in the last ten years had a suspended sentence passed on them
- at any time in the last ten years had a community order or other community sentence passed on them.

In addition, anyone who is currently on bail in criminal proceedings is disqualified from sitting as a juror.

If a disqualified person fails to disclose that fact and turns up for jury service, they may be fined up to £5,000.

12.3.3 Mentally disordered persons

A 'mentally disordered person' is defined in the Criminal Justice Act 2003 as:

1. A person who suffers or has suffered from mental illness, psychopathic disorder, mental handicap or severe mental handicap and on account of that condition either:
   (a) is resident in a hospital or similar institution or
   (b) regularly attends for treatment by a medical practitioner.
2. A person for the time being under guardianship under s 7 of the Mental Health Act 1983.
3. A person who, under Part 7 of that Act, has been determined by a judge to be incapable of administering his property and affairs.

There are criticisms that this definition does not distinguish between those receiving treatment for mild depression from their GP and those sectioned under the Mental Health Act 1983. The definition of a 'mentally ill person' for the purposes of the Juries Act 1974 is likely to be amended in the future in answer to these criticisms.

12.3.4 Lack of capacity

A judge at the court may discharge a person from being a juror for lack of capacity to cope with the trial. This could be because the person does not understand English adequately or because of some disability which makes them unsuitable as a juror. This includes blind people, who would be unable to see plans and photographs produced in evidence. Section 9B(2) of the Juries Act 1974 (which was added into the Act by the Criminal Justice and Public Order Act 1994, s 41) makes it clear that the mere fact of a disability does not prevent someone from acting as a juror. The judge can only discharge the juror if he is satisfied that the disability means that that juror is not capable of acting effectively as a juror.

Deaf jurors

In June 1995 a deaf man was prevented from sitting on a jury at the Old Bailey despite wishing to serve and bringing with him a sign language interpreter. The judge pointed out that that would mean an extra person in the jury room and this was not allowed by law. He also said that the way in which witnesses gave evidence and the tone of their voice were important: 'a deaf juror may not be able to pick up these nuances and to properly judge their credibility'.

In November 1999 another deaf man challenged the ban on him sitting as a juror. The judge in this case felt that there was no practical reason why he should not sit, but the law only allowed the 12 jury members to be present in the jury room. It did not allow a 13th person – a sign-language interpreter – to be present. This made it impossible for the deaf man to be a juror.

12.3.5 The right to be excused from jury service

Prior to April 2004 people in certain essential occupations, such as doctors and pharmacists, had a right to be excused jury service if they did not want to do it. The Criminal Justice Act 2003 abolished this category. This means that doctors and other medical staff are no longer able to refuse to do jury service, though they can apply for a discretionary excusal.

Members of the forces

Full-time serving members of the forces may be excused from jury service if their commanding officer certifies that their absence from duty (because of jury service) would be prejudicial to the efficiency of the service.

12.3.6 Discretionary excusals

Anyone who has problems which make it very difficult for them to do their jury service, may ask to be excused or for their period of service to be put back to a later date. The court has a discretion to grant such an excusal but will only do so if there is a sufficiently good reason. Such reasons include being too ill to attend court or suffering from a disability that makes it impossible for the person to sit as a juror, or being a mother with a small baby. Other reasons could include business appointments that cannot be undertaken by anyone else, or examinations or holidays that have been booked.

In these situations the court is most likely to defer jury service to a more convenient date, rather than excuse the person completely. This is stated in the current guidance for summoning officers which is aimed at preventing the high number of discretionary excusals. The guidance states that:

❝ The normal expectation is that everyone summoned for jury service will serve at the time for which they are summoned. It is recognised that there will be occasions where it is not reasonable for a person summoned to serve at the time for which they are summoned. In such circumstances the summoning officer should use his/her discretion to defer the individual to a time more appropriate. Only in extreme circumstances, should a person be excused from jury service. ❞

If a person is not excused from jury service they must attend on the date set or they may be fined up to £1,000 for non-attendance.

12.3.7 Lawyers and police on juries

There used to be a category of people who were ineligible for jury service. This included judges and others who had been involved in the administration of justice within the previous ten years. This category was abolished by the Criminal Justice Act 2003. This means that judges, lawyers, police, etc. are now eligible to serve on juries. Many people feel that this could lead to bias or to a legally well-qualified juror influencing the rest of the jury.

In *R v Abdroikof, R v Green and R v Williamson* (2007) the House of Lords considered appeals where a police officer or prosecutor had been one of the jury members.

They held that the fact that one of the members of jury was a police officer did not of itself make a trial unfair. However, a majority of three of the five judges held that in the situation where a police officer on the jury had worked in the same station as a police officer giving evidence for the prosecution in the trial, then there was the risk of bias. The test to be applied in such cases was:

❝ whether the fair-minded and informed observer, having considered the facts, would conclude that there was a real possibility that the tribunal was biased. ❞

The House of Lords also quoted from the decision in *R v Sussex Justices, ex parte McCarthy* (1924) where the judge stated that justice must not only be done, but must be seen to be done.

The same three judges in a majority decision also held that the presence of a juror who was a local Crown Prosecutor in the Crown Prosecutor Service meant that justice was clearly not being seen to be done. Lord Bingham stated:

❝ It is, in my opinion, clear that justice is not seen to be done if one discharging the very important neutral role of juror is a full-time, salaried, long-serving employee of the prosecutor. **"**

In *Hanif v United Kingdom* (2012), the European Court of Human Rights ruled that having a police officer on the jury was a breach of Article 6(1) of the European Convention on Human Rights – the right to a fair trial. In this case, the police officer juror had immediately alerted the court to the fact that he knew one of the prosecution police witnesses. It was particularly important as the evidence of this witness was crucial to the case against the defendant. However, the trial judge had ruled that this did not matter.

The case continued with the police officer juror being the foreman of the jury and the defendant was convicted. The Court of Appeal, somewhat surprisingly, had upheld the conviction. This ruling of the Court of Appeal appears to be contrary to the judgment of the House of Lords in *Abdroikof* as it would appear that a fair-minded person would conclude there was a real possible risk of bias.

Judges on jury service

In June 2004 (just two months after the rules on jury service changed) a judge from the Court of Appeal, Lord Justice Dyson, was summoned to attend as a juror. This prompted the Lord Chief Justice, Lord Woolf, to issue observations to judges who are called for jury service. These point out that:

- a judge serves on a jury as part of his duty as a private citizen
- excusal from jury service will only be granted in extreme circumstances
- deferral of jury service to a later date should be sought where a judge has judicial commitments which make it particularly inconvenient for him to do jury service at the time he was called to do so
- at court if a judge knows the presiding judge or other person in the case, he should raise this

with the jury bailiff or a member of the court staff if he considers it could interfere with his responsibilities as a juror
- it is a matter of discretion for an individual judge sitting as a juror as to whether he discloses the fact of his judicial office to the other members of the jury
- judges must follow the directions given to the jury by the trial judge on the law and should avoid the temptation to correct guidance which they believe to be inaccurate as this is outside their role as a juror.

The point about letting the court know when someone involved in the case is personally known to the juror is also relevant to practising lawyers who are called for jury service.

Activity

Discuss whether you think the following people should sit on a jury:

1. A woman who was fined for shoplifting a month ago.
2. A man who was fined and disqualified from driving for taking cars without the consent of the owner.
3. A doctor who works in general practice.
4. A doctor who works in an accident and emergency unit of a busy city hospital.
5. A Circuit Judge who frequently tries cases in the Crown Court.

12.4 Selecting a jury

At each Crown Court there is an official who is responsible for summonsing enough jurors to try the cases that will be heard in every two-week period. This official will arrange for names to be selected at random from the electoral registers, for the area which the court covers. This is done through a computer selection at a central office. It is necessary to summons more than 12 jurors as most courts have more than one courtroom and it will not be known how many of those summonsed are disqualified – or will be excused. In fact, at the bigger courts up to 150 summonses may be sent out each fortnight.

Those summonsed must notify the court if there is any reason why they should not or cannot attend. All others are expected to attend for two weeks' jury service, though, of course, if the case they are trying goes on for more than two weeks they will have to stay until the trial is completed. Where it is known that a trial may be exceptionally long, such as a complicated fraud trial, potential jurors are asked if they will be able to serve for such a long period.

12.4.1 Vetting

Once the list of potential jurors is known, both the prosecution and the defence have the right to see that list. In some cases it may be decided that this pool of potential jurors should be 'vetted', that is, checked for suitability. There are two types of vetting:

- routine police checks
- wider background checks.

Routine police checks

Routine police checks are made on prospective jurors to eliminate those disqualified. This occurred in the following two cases.

R v Crown Court at Sheffield, ex parte Brownlow (1980)

The defendant was a police officer and the defence sought permission to vet the jury panel for convictions. The judge gave permission but the Court of Appeal, while holding that it had no power to interfere, said that vetting was 'unconstitutional' and a 'serious invasion of privacy' and not sanctioned by the Juries Act 1974.

R v Mason (1980)

It was revealed that the Chief Constable for Northamptonshire had been allowing widespread use of unauthorised vetting of criminal records, the Court of Appeal approved of this type of vetting. Lawton LJ pointed out that, since it is a criminal offence to serve on a jury while disqualified, the police were only doing their normal duty of preventing crime by checking for criminal records. Furthermore, the court said that, if in the course of looking at criminal records convictions were revealed which did not disqualify, there was no reason why these should not be passed on to prosecuting counsel, so that this information could be used in deciding to stand by individual jurors (see section 12.4.3 for information on the right of stand by).

Juror's background

A wider check may be made on a juror's background and political affiliations. This practice was brought to light by the 'ABC' trial in 1978 where two journalists and a soldier were charged with collecting secret information. It was discovered that the jury had been vetted for their loyalty. The trial was stopped and a new trial ordered before a fresh jury. Following this, the Attorney-General published guidelines on when political vetting of jurors should take place. These guidelines state that:

(a) vetting should only be used in exceptional cases involving:
- national security where part of the evidence is likely to be given *in camera*
- terrorist cases.

(b) vetting can only be carried out with the Attorney-General's express permission.

12.4.2 Selection at court

The jurors are usually divided into groups of 15 and allocated to a court. At the start of a trial the court clerk will select 12 out of these 15 at

Key facts

Court	Crown Court
Qualifications	Aged 18–70 Registered to vote Resident in UK for at least five years since age 13
Disqualified	Sentenced to five years' or more imprisonment – disqualified for life Served a prison sentence OR suspended sentence OR a community order – disqualified for ten years On bail – disqualified while on bail
Excusals	Members of the armed forces Discretionary – ill, business commitments, or other 'good reason'
Selection	A central office selects names from the lists of electors Summons sent to these people Must attend unless disqualified or excused
Vetting	May be checked for criminal record – *R v Mason* (1980) In cases of national security may be subject to a wider check on background subject to Attorney-General's guidelines
Challenges	Individual juror may be challenged for cause, e.g. knows defendant Whole panel may be challenged for biased selection – but no right to a multi-racial jury (*R v Ford* (1989)) Prosecution may 'stand by' any juror
Function	Decide verdict – 'Guilty' or 'Not guilty' Sole arbiters of fact but judge directs them on law
Verdict	Must try for a unanimous verdict BUT if cannot reach a unanimous verdict then a majority verdict can be accepted of 10:2 or 11:1

Figure 12.3 Key facts chart on the use of juries in criminal cases

random. All jurors are shown a DVD when they arrive at court. This explains the layout of the court and procedure in court. It also tells jurors how to behave. For example, they are told not to discuss the case with other people.

12.4.3 Challenging

Once the court clerk has selected the panel of 12 jurors, these jurors come into the jury box to be sworn in as jurors. At this point, before the jury is sworn in, both the prosecution and defence have certain rights to challenge one or more of the jurors. There are two challenges which can be made and, in addition, the prosecution has a special right. These are:

- to the array
- for cause
- prosecution right to stand by jurors.

To the array

This right to challenge is given by s 5 of the Juries Act 1974 and it is a challenge to the whole jury on the basis that it has been chosen in an unrepresentative or biased way. This challenge was used successfully against the 'Romford' jury at the Old Bailey in 1993 when, out of a panel of 12 jurors, nine came from Romford, with two of them living within 20 doors of each other in the same street. In *R v Fraser* (1987) this method of challenging a jury was also used, as the defendant

1   In which criminal court is a jury used?
2   In which civil courts may a jury be used?
3   What age limits are there for jury service?
4   What two other basic qualifications are there for jury service?
5   Give two situations in which a person is disqualified from jury service.
6   What special rule is there about jury service for serving members of the armed forces?
7   What is meant by a 'discretionary excusal' from jury service?
8   What is the name of the case in which the House of Lords considered the effect of a police officer or prosecutor sitting a jury member?
9   What test did the House of Lords state should be used in cases where a jury member was a police officer or prosecutor?
10 Why was it ruled that a deaf person could not sit on a jury?

was of an ethnic minority background but all the jurors were white. The judge in that case agreed to empanel another jury. However, in *R v Ford* (1989) it was held that if the jury was chosen in a random manner then it could not be challenged simply because it was not multi-racial.

For cause

This involves challenging the right of an individual juror to sit on the jury. To be successful, the challenge must point out a valid reason why that juror should not serve on the jury. An obvious reason is that the juror is disqualified, but a challenge for cause can also be made if the juror knows or is related to a witness or defendant. If such people are not removed from the jury there is a risk that any subsequent conviction could be quashed.

This occurred in *R v Wilson* and *R v Sprason* (1995).

R v Wilson and *R v Sprason* (1995)

The wife of a prison officer was summoned for jury service. She had asked to be excused attendance on that ground, but this request had not been granted. She served on the jury which convicted the two defendants of robbery. Both defendants had been on remand at Exeter prison where her husband worked. The Court of Appeal said that justice must not only be done, it must be seen to be done; the presence of Mrs Roberts on the jury prevented that, so that the convictions had to be quashed.

Prosecution right to stand by jurors

This is a right that only the prosecution can exercise. It allows the juror who has been stood by to be put to the end of the list of potential jurors, so that they will not be used on the jury unless there are not enough other jurors. The prosecution does not have to give a reason for 'standing by', but the Attorney-General's guidelines make it clear that this power should be used sparingly.

12.4.4 Criticisms of the selection of juries

Use of electoral register

The method of selecting jurors from the list of registered voters is open to criticism as it does not always give a representative sample of the population. It excludes some groups, such as homeless people who cannot register to vote. Also, not every one who is eligible registers to vote. This is especially true of young people and those who change address frequently.

One of the debates has always been whether random selection produces juries which are reasonably representative of the local population. Studies done in the 1970s and 1980s found that juries in some areas were not truly representative in gender (fewer women), age (fewer young people) and race (under-representative of ethnic minorities).

However, a study, *Diversity and Fairness in the Jury System* published in 2007 and looking at juries in 2003 and 2005, found that juries are now representative in gender, age and race. The only under-representation found by the study was of lower classes and unemployed people.

Disqualified jurors

Although some checks are carried out, many disqualified people fail to disclose this fact and sit on juries. One survey of Inner London juries estimated that one in every 24 jurors was disqualified. In one instance at Snaresbrook Crown Court, a man with 15 previous convictions sat as a juror in three cases and was the jury foreman in two of them. He later admitted that, as far as he was concerned, all defendants were not guilty unless they 'had been molesting kids'.

Excusals

If there are too many discretionary excusals it may lead to an unrepresentative jury. For this reason,

wherever possible, jury service is deferred instead of excusing the juror from service.

Prosecution's right of 'stand by'

The prosecution's right of stand by was kept even when the defence's peremptory challenge was withdrawn. This might be seen as giving the prosecution an advantage in 'rigging' the jury, particularly when combined with vetting. However, even when a jury has been vetted, it does not always give the prosecution an advantage. This was seen in *Ponting's Case* (1985), where the defendant was charged with an offence against the Official Secrets Acts and the jury was vetted. Despite the vetting the jury returned a not guilty verdict (see section 12.6.2 for further comment on this case).

12.5 The jury's role in criminal cases

The jury is used only at the Crown Court for cases where the defendant pleads not guilty. This means that a jury is used in about 20,000 cases each year.

12.5.1 Split function

The trial is presided over by a judge and the functions split between the judge and jury. The

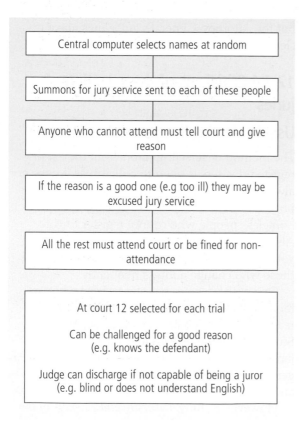

Figure 12.4 Selecting a jury

Activity

Read the following extract from *Diversity and Fairness in the Jury System* (2007) and answer the questions below.

The Criminal Justice Act 2003 removed ineligibility and the right of excusal from jury service for a number of groups (those aged 65–69, MPs, clergy, medical professionals and those in the administration of justice). But summoned jurors may still be disqualified or excused from jury service (due to age, residency, mental disability, criminal charges, language, medical or other reasons).

- The study found that the most significant factors predicating whether a summoned juror will serve or not are income and employment status, not ethnicity. Summoned jurors in the lower income brackets and those who are economically inactive are far less likely to serve than those in medium to high income brackets and those who are employed.

- In 2005, of all those who replied to their summonses, 64 per cent of jurors served, 9 per cent were disqualified or ineligible, 27 per cent were excused. Of those excused, most were for medical reasons that prevented serving (34 per cent) or child care (15 per

cent) and work reasons (12 per cent). Fifteen per cent of all the summonses in the survey were either returned as undeliverable or not responded to, which occurred most often in areas of high residential mobility.

- The report established that most current thinking about who does and does not do jury service is based on myth, not reality

Myth: Ethnic minorities are under-represented among those doing jury service.

Reality: Analysis showed that, in almost all courts (81 of the 84 surveyed), there was no significant difference between the proportion of black and ethnic minority jurors serving and the black and ethnic minority population levels in the local juror catchment area for each court.

Myth: Women and young people are under-represented among serving jurors, and the self-employed are virtually exempt for jury service.

Reality: The study establishes that jury pools at individual courts closely reflected the local population in terms of gender and age, and the self-employed are represented among serving jurors in direct proportion to their representation in the population.

Questions

1. What are the age limits for jury service?

2. What is the residency requirement to qualify for jury service?

3. What categories of people are disqualified from doing jury service?

4. What categories of people are less likely to serve on a jury?

5. What percentage failed to reply to their summons to do jury service?

6. For what types of reason were people excused from jury service?

7. What does the study show about the representative nature of juries?

judge decides points of law and the jury decides the facts. At the end of the prosecution case, the judge has the power to direct the jury to acquit the defendant if he decides that, in law, the prosecution's evidence has not made out a case against the defendant. This is called a directed acquittal and occurs in about ten per cent of cases.

Where the trial continues, the judge will sum up the case at the end, to the jury and direct them on any law involved. The jury retires to a private room and makes the decision on the guilt or innocence of the accused in secret. Initially the jury must try to come to a unanimous verdict, that is, one on which they are all agreed. The judge must accept the jury verdict, even if he does not agree with it. This long-established principle goes back to *Bushell's Case* (1670). The jury does not give any reasons for their decision.

12.5.2 Majority verdicts

If, after at least two hours (longer where there are several defendants), the jury have not reached a verdict, the judge can call them back into the courtroom and direct them that he can now accept a majority verdict. Majority verdicts have been allowed since 1967. Where there is a full jury of 12, the verdict can be 10–2 or 11–1, either for guilty or for not guilty. If the jury has fallen below 12 for any reason (such as the death or illness of a juror during the trial) then only one can disagree with the verdict. If there are 11 jurors, the verdict can be 10–1; if there are 10 jurors it can be 9–1. If there are only nine jurors the verdict must be unanimous. A jury cannot go below nine.

Majority verdicts were introduced because of the fear of jury 'nobbling', that is jurors being bribed or intimidated by associates of the defendant into voting for a not guilty verdict. When a jury had to be unanimous, only one member need be bribed to cause a 'stalemate' in which the jury was unable to reach a decision. It was also thought that the acquittal rates in jury trials were too high and majority decisions would result in more convictions.

Where the jury convicts a defendant on a majority verdict, the foreman of the jury must announce the

numbers both agreeing and disagreeing with the verdict in open court. This provision is contained in s 17(3) of the Juries Act 1974 and is aimed at making sure the jury has come to a legal majority, and not one, for example of eight to four, which is not allowed. However, in *R v Pigg* (1983), the Court of Appeal held that, provided the foreman announced the number who had agreed with the verdict, and that number was within the number allowed for a majority verdict, then the conviction was legal. It did not matter that the foreman had not also been asked how many disagreed with the verdict. About 20 per cent of convictions by juries each year are by majority verdict.

12.5.3 Secrecy

The jury discussion takes place in secret and there can be no inquiry into how the jury reached its verdict. This is because s 8 of the Contempt of Court Act 1981 makes disclosure of anything that happened in the jury room a contempt of court which is a criminal offence. It is a contempt 'to obtain, disclose or solicit any particulars of statements made, opinions expressed, arguments advanced or votes cast by members of a jury in the course of their deliberations in any legal proceedings'. The section was brought in because newspapers were paying jurors large sums of money for 'their story'. This is obviously not desirable, but the total ban on finding out what happens in the jury room means that it is difficult to discover whether jurors have understood the evidence in complex cases.

12.6 Advantages of jury trial

12.6.1 Public confidence

On the face of it, asking 12 strangers who have no legal knowledge and without any training to decide what may be complex and technical points is an absurd one. Yet the jury is considered as one of the fundamentals of a democratic society. The right to be tried by one's peers is a bastion of liberty against the state and has been supported by eminent judges. For example, Lord Devlin said juries are 'the lamp that shows that freedom lives'.

The tradition of trial by jury is very old and people seem to have confidence in the impartiality and fairness of a jury trial. This can be seen in the objection to withdrawing the right to jury trial from cases of 'minor' theft.

12.6.2 Jury equity

Since jurors are not legal experts, are not bound to follow the precedent of past cases or even Acts of Parliament, and do not have to give reasons for their verdict, it is possible for them to decide cases on their idea of 'fairness'. This is sometimes referred to as 'jury equity'. Several cases have shown the importance of this, in particular *Ponting's Case* (1985).

> *Ponting's Case* (1985)
>
> A civil servant was charged under the old wide-ranging s 2 of the Official Secrets Act 1911. He had leaked information to a Member of Parliament on the sinking of the ship, The General Belgrano, during the Falklands War. At his trial he pleaded not guilty, claiming that his actions had been in the public interest. The jury refused to convict him even though the judge ruled there was no defence. The case also prompted the Government to reconsider the law and to amend s 2.

More recently, a jury acquitted a mother of attempting to murder her daughter who committed suicide. Her daughter was aged 31 and had been ill for 17 years. She had injected herself with an overdose of morphine. The mother had given her daughter some medication to ease her suffering in her final hours. She had pleaded guilty to assisting the daughter's suicide, but the prosecution had insisted on continuing to prosecute her for attempted murder.

12.6.3 Open system of justice

The use of a jury is viewed as making the legal system more open. Justice is seen to be done as members of the public are involved in a key role and the whole process is public. It also helps to keep the law clearer as points have to be explained to the jury, enabling the defendant to understand the case more easily. Against this is the fact that the jury deliberates in private and that no one can inquire into what happened in the jury room. In addition, the jury does not have to give any reason for its verdict. When a judge gives a judgment he explains his reasoning and, if he has made an error, it is known and can be appealed against.

12.6.4 Secrecy of the jury room

This can be seen as an advantage, since the jury is free from pressure during discussions. Jurors are protected from outside influences when deciding on the verdict. This allows juries to bring in verdicts that may be unpopular with the public as well as allowing jurors the freedom to ignore the strict letter of the law. It has been suggested that people would be less willing to serve on a jury if they knew that their discussions could be made public.

12.6.5 Impartiality

A jury should be impartial as the jurors are not connected to anyone in the case. The process of random selection should result in a cross-section of society and this should also lead to an impartial jury, as they will have different prejudices and so should cancel out each other's biases. No single individual person is responsible for the decision. A jury is also not case-hardened since they sit for only two weeks and are unlikely to try more than three or four cases in that time. After the end of the case the jury dissolves and, as Sir Sebag Shaw said, it is 'anonymous and amorphous'.

12.7 Disadvantages of jury trial

12.7.1 Perverse decisions

In section 12.6.2 we looked at the idea of jury equity, the fact that the jury can ignore an unjust law. However, in some circumstances this type of decision can be seen as perverse and unjustified. Juries have refused to convict in other clear-cut cases such as *R v Randle and Pottle* (1991) where the defendants were charged with helping the spy George Blake to escape from prison. Their prosecution did not occur until 25 years after the escape, when they wrote about what they had done and the jury acquitted them, possibly as a protest over the time lapse between the offence and the prosecution.

Another case where the evidence was clear yet the jury acquitted the defendants, was *R v Kronlid and others* (1996). In this case, the defendants admitted they had caused £1.5 million damage to a plane. They pleaded not guilty on the basis that they were preventing the plane from being sent to Indonesia where it would have been used in attacks against the people of East Timor. The jury acquitted them.

12.7.2 Secrecy

In section 12.6.4 we considered how the secrecy of the jury protects jurors from pressure. However, the secrecy of the jury room is also a disadvantage. This is because no reasons have to be given for the verdict, so there is no way of knowing if the jury did understand the case and come to the decision for the right reasons.

In *R v Mirza* (2004) the House of Lords ruled that it could not inquire into discussions in a jury room. Two separate cases were considered in the appeal. These were *R v Mirza* and *R v Connor and Rollock* (2004).

R v Mirza (2004)

The defendant was a Pakistani man who settled in the UK in 1988. He had an interpreter to help him in the trial and during the trial the jury sent notes asking why he needed an interpreter. He was convicted on a 10–2 majority. Six days after the jury verdict, one juror wrote to the defendant's counsel alleging that from the start of the trial there had been a 'theory' that the use of an interpreter was a 'ploy'. The juror also said that she had been shouted down when she objected and reminded her fellow jurors of the judge's directions.

Connor and Rollock (2004)

A juror wrote to the Crown Court stating that while many jurors thought it was one or other of the defendants who had committed the stabbing, they should convict both to 'teach them a lesson'. This was five days after the verdict but before sentence was passed. As in Mirza, there was a majority verdict of 10–2. The complaining juror said that, when she argued that the jury should consider which defendant was responsible, her co-jurors had refused to listen and remarked that if they did that they could take a week to consider verdicts in the case.

Decision

The House of Lords held that s 8 of the Contempt of Court Act 1981 made it a contempt to disclose or obtain or solicit information about what had occurred in the jury room even for the purposes of an appeal. They also ruled that s 8 was compatible with Art 6 of the European Convention on Human Rights (the right to a fair trial). They pointed out that:

- confidentiality was essential to the proper functioning of the jury process
- there was merit in finality
- jurors had to be protected from harassment.

Exceptions

There are two exceptions where the courts will inquire into the conduct of the jury in coming to their verdict. The first is where there has been a complete repudiation of the oath taken by the jurors to try the case according to the evidence. In other words, they have used another method to make their decision.

The best known example of this is the case of *R v Young (Stephen)* (1995).

The second exception is where extraneous material has been introduced into the jury room. Examples have included telephone calls in and out of the jury room, papers mistakenly included in the set of papers given by the court to the jury and information from the internet. This last happened in *R v Karakaya* (2005).

Key facts

Advantages	Disadvantages
Public confidence Considered to be a fundamental part of a democratic society New qualifications for jury service mean that almost everyone can serve on a jury	High acquittal rates undermine confidence in the criminal justice system Doing jury service is unpopular
Jury equity *Ponting's Case*	Perverse verdicts *Randle and Pottle* *Kronlit*
Open system of justice Involves members of the public	Media influence Reporting may influence the decision *Taylor and Taylor*
Secrecy of the jury room protects jurors from pressure	Secrecy means that: ● the reasons for the decision are not known ● the jury's understanding of the case cannot be checked (*Mirza*) Exception: Complete repudiation of oath *Young (Stephen)* extraneous material used (*Karakaya*)
Impartiality Having 12 members with no direct interest in the case should cancel out any bias	Bias In some cases there has been racial bias *Sander v UK*

Figure 12.5 Key facts chart of advantages and disadvantages of jury trial

R v Young (Stephen) (1995)

The defendant was charged with the murder of two people. The jury had to stay in a hotel overnight as they had not reached a verdict by the end of the first day of deliberations. At the hotel, four of the jurors held a séance using a ouija board to try to contact the dead victims and ask them who had killed them. The next day, the jury returned a guilty verdict.

When the use of the ouija board became known, the Court of Appeal quashed the conviction and ordered a retrial. The Court also felt able to inquire into what had happened as it had occurred in a hotel and was not part of the jury room deliberations.

R v Karakaya (2005)

The defendant was accused of rape. A juror did an internet search at home and brought into the jury room the printed-out results of the search. The jury convicted Karakaya, but this conviction was quashed because of the outside information that the jury had access to during their deliberations. A retrial was ordered and Karakaya was acquitted by the jury in the second trial.

Jurors and the internet

Judges do direct jurors not to look at the internet for information, but it seems that the use of internet research by jurors is getting more common. In Cheryl Thomas' research, *Are Juries Fair?* (2010), she found that 12 per cent of jurors admitted they had looked on the internet for information about cases they were trying. The risk of using the internet is that the information may be prejudicial to the defendant. For example, doing a search on a defendant's name may find newspaper reports of previous convictions, which the jury should not know about. Also defendants have been known to upload highly personal information regarding their own behaviour and even crimes, on to social networking sites.

12.7.3 Bias

However, although jurors have no direct interest in a case, and despite the fact that there are 12 of them, they may still have prejudices which can affect the verdict. Some jurors may be biased against the police – this is one of the reasons that those with certain criminal convictions are disqualified from sitting on a jury. In particular there is the worry that some jurors are racially prejudiced.

This was considered in *Sander v United Kingdom* (2000).

Sander v United Kingdom (2000)

The European Court of Human Rights ruled that there had been a breach of the right to a fair trial under Art 6 of the European Convention on Human Rights. In the case one juror had written a note to the judge during the trial raising concern over the fact that other jurors had been making openly racist remarks and jokes. The judge asked the jury to 'search their consciences'. The next day the judge received two letters, one signed by all the jurors in which they denied any racist attitudes and a second from one juror who admitted that he may have been the one making the jokes. Despite the discrepancies between these two letters, the judge allowed the case to continue with the same jury. The European Court of Human Rights held that in these circumstances the judge should have discharged the jury as there was an obvious risk of racial bias.

Recent research

A report, *Are Juries Fair?*, by Cheryl Thomas (2010) looked at whether there was bias in cases where a defendant from a black ethnic minority was tried by an all-white jury. This was done by using two main methods:

- case simulations (mock trials) which used 41 juries with 478 jurors
- analysis of over half a million charges tried in the period 1 October 2006 to 31 March 2008.

In the mock trials no racial discrimination was shown. The verdicts from the real cases during 2006–2008 showed only small differences based on the defendant's ethnicity. White and Asian defendants both had a 63% jury conviction rate; Black defendants had a 67% jury conviction rate.

12.7.4 Media influence

Media coverage may influence jurors. This is especially true in high-profile cases, where there has been much publicity about police investigations into a case. This occurred in the case *R v West* (1996) in which Rosemary West was convicted for the murders of ten young girls and women, including her own daughter. From the time the bodies were first discovered, the media coverage was intense. In addition, some newspapers had paid large sums of money to some of the witnesses in order to secure their story after the trial was completed. One of the grounds on which Rosemary West appealed against her conviction was that the media coverage had made it impossible for her to receive a fair trial. The Court of Appeal rejected the appeal, pointing out that otherwise it would mean that if 'allegations of murder were sufficiently horrendous so as to inevitably shock the nation, the accused could not be tried'. They also said that the trial judge had given adequate warning to the jury to consider only the evidence they heard in court.

Another case which highlighted media influence on the jury's decision was *R v Taylor and Taylor* (1993) in which two sisters were charged with murder. Some newspapers published a still from a video sequence which gave a false impression of what was happening. After the jury convicted the two defendants, the trial judge gave leave to appeal because of the possible influence this picture could have had on the jury's verdict; the Court of Appeal quashed the convictions.

12.7.5 Lack of understanding

There are worries that jurors may not understand the case which they are trying. In particular, they may not understand the judge's direction on the law in the case. In one case at Snaresbrook Crown Court, after they had retired to consider their verdict, they sent a note to the judge asking what they had to do! The judge discharged that jury from the case. There has been recent research into jurors' understanding of cases, both in Australia and in England.

Australian research

Research into jury trials in New South Wales, Australia in 2006 has revealed that some jurors did not know what verdict had been given in the case they had just tried. The research was into 32 trials about child abuse. It involved aspects such as how jurors thought the child witness had been treated in the case.

The jurors were given a questionnaire immediately after the verdict had been given. In total, 277 jurors took part. The first question asked 'What was the verdict in this case?'. Only in a quarter of the trials did all the jurors give the correct answer. In the other cases at least one juror gave an incorrect version of the verdict. In one case four jurors said that the accused had been found guilty when he had actually been found not guilty.

The researchers point out that it is possible that jurors were expressing their own view of what they thought the verdict should have been. However, the research stated that it seems some jurors were confused, unclear or uncertain about the verdict. If jurors do not know what the verdict

was immediately after that verdict has been given, then it creates doubts about how much of the case the jurors had understood.

English research

A report, *Are Juries Fair?*, by Cheryl Thomas was published in 2010. This looked at various aspects of the use of juries. One area was jurors' understanding of cases. In order to test understanding a series of simulated trials were used. A total of 797 jurors in three different areas all saw the same simulated trial and heard exactly the same judicial directions on the law.

The jurors were first asked whether they thought they had understood the directions. In two of the areas, Blackfriars, London and Winchester, over two thirds of the jurors felt they were able to understand the directions. In Nottingham only just under half of the jurors felt they understood the directions.

The jurors' understanding of the directions was then tested. This discovered that only 31 per cent of the jurors had actually understood the directions fully in the legal terms used by the judge. When the jurors were given a written summary of the instructions, the number who fully understood increased to 48 per cent.

This study shows that, even with a written summary, less than half of jurors fully understood the judge's directions.

12.7.6 Fraud trials

Fraud trials with complex accounts being given in evidence can create special problems for jurors. Even jurors who can easily cope with other evidence may have difficulty understanding a fraud case. These cases are also often very long, so that the jurors have to be able to be away from their own work for months. A long fraud trial can place a great strain on jurors. Such cases also become very expensive, both for the prosecution and for the defendants.

The Roskill Committee in 1986 suggested that juries should not be used for complex fraud cases.

Two provisions have recently been made in Acts of Parliament for this to happen.

The Criminal Justice Act 2003 had provision for the prosecution to apply for trial by a judge alone in complex fraud cases. However, this was never brought into force and in 2012 the Legal Aid, Sentencing and Punishment of Offenders Act repealed the provision.

In the Domestic Violence, Crime and Victims Act 2004 there is a special provision for cases where there are a large number of counts on the indictment. This allows a trial of sample counts with a jury and then, if the defendant is convicted on those, the remainder can be tried by a judge alone.

12.7.7 Jury tampering

In a few cases friends of the defendant may try to interfere with the jury. This may be by bribing jury members to bring in a not guilty verdict or by making threats against jury members so that they are too afraid to find the defendant guilty. In such cases police may be used to try to protect the jurors but this may not be effective and is also expensive and removes the police from their other work.

To combat this, s 44 of the Criminal Justice Act 2003 provides that where there has already been an effort to tamper with a jury in the case, the prosecution can apply for the trial to be heard by judge alone. The first trial without a jury was approved in *R v Twomey and others* (2009).

R v Twomey and others (2009)

The defendants were charged with various offences connected to a large robbery from a warehouse at Heathrow. Three previous trials had collapsed and there had been a 'serious attempt at jury tampering' in the last of these. The prosecution applied to a single judge for the trial to take place without a jury. The judge refused but the Court of Appeal overturned this decision, ordering that the trial should take place without a jury.

The Criminal Procedure and Investigations Act 1996 allows for a retrial to be ordered if someone is subsequently proved to have interfered with the jury.

However, in other cases, the Court of Appeal has not granted trial by judge alone. In *KS v R* (2010), there had been several trials on various allegations of fraud committed by the defendant. It was not until the tenth trial that jury tampering occurred. It occurred because jurors and members of the public who wished to smoke during breaks were directed to the same area. During one of these breaks, a friend of the defendant approached a juror. The Court of Appeal refused an application for trial by judge alone. They pointed out that the casual arrangements at the Crown Court which had allowed the contact would not be repeated. Also the approach had been opportunistic rather than a deliberate targeting of jurors. For these reasons, there was no need to order trial by judge alone.

12.7.8 High acquittal rates

Juries are often criticised on the grounds that they acquit too many defendants. The figures usually quoted in support of this are that about 60 per cent of those who plead not guilty at the Crown Court are acquitted. However, this figure does not give a true picture of the workings of juries as it includes cases discharged by the judge and those in which the judge directed an acquittal.

The judicial statistics show that in most years more than half of acquittals are ordered by the judge without a jury even being sworn in to try the case. This happens where the prosecution drop the case at the last minute and offer no evidence against the defendant. Usually about 10–15 per cent of acquittals are by a jury but on the direction of a judge.. This occurs where the judge rules that there is no case against the defendant; it might be because of a legal point or because the prosecution evidence is not sufficient in law to prove the case. When these decisions are excluded from the statistics it is found that juries actually acquit in less than 40 per cent of cases.

12.7.9 Other disadvantages

The compulsory nature of jury service is unpopular, so that some jurors may be against the whole system, while others may rush their verdict in order to leave as quickly as possible.

Activity

Read the following extract from an article in the *Daily Mail* on 15 July 2010 by James White and use it as a base for a discussion on the disadvantages of jury trial.

Teenager almost wrecked two trials by texting gossip about defendant to fellow juror

A teenager jeopardised two Crown Court trials by texting gossip claiming a defendant was a paedophile to a fellow juror.

Danielle Robinson, 19, was serving on a jury at Hull Crown Court last week when she sent two messages to a woman juror sitting on another trial.

The first said: 'Hi it's Danielle from court. Are you doing the kid's case?' The woman replied: 'I can't talk to you.'

But Robinson, a single mother of a five-month-old boy, followed it up with gossip she heard outside court in a shop.

She appeared in court yesterday after admitting a charge of contempt of court … [and] the judge handed the defendant an eight-month suspended prison sentence.

[He said] 'On the first day of your jury service you watched a DVD by way of training and were told not to talk about your case with others until all 12 of you were together. You blatantly breached the DVD instructions about no communication with others'.

Jury service can be a strain, especially where jurors have to listen to horrific evidence. Jurors in the Rosemary West case were offered counselling after the trial to help them cope with the evidence they had had to see and hear.

The use of juries makes trials slow and expensive. This is because each point has to be explained carefully to the jury and the whole procedure of the case takes longer.

12.8 Special problems with using juries in civil cases

12.8.1 Amount of damages

Juries in civil cases decide both the liability of the parties in the case and also the amount of damages that will be awarded. The awards vary greatly as each jury has its own ideas and does not follow past cases. The amount is, therefore, totally unpredictable which makes it difficult for lawyers to advise on settlements. Judges look back to past awards when deciding awards of damages in personal injury cases, and then apply an inflation factor so that there is consistency between similar cases. Juries in defamation cases cause particular problems with very large awards; one judge called it 'Mickey Mouse' money.

The Court of Appeal has power to order a new trial or substitute such sum as appears proper to the court, if they feel the damages were excessive or inadequate. This power was first used in a case brought by the MP Teresa Gorman where the Court of Appeal reduced the damages awarded to her by the jury from £150,000 to £50,000. It was also used in *Rantzen v Mirror Group Newspapers* (1993) when the award to Esther Rantzen, the founder of 'Childline' (a charity set up to help abused children) over allegations that she had deliberately kept quiet about the activities of a suspected child abuser, was reduced from £250,000 to £110,000.

12.8.2 Unreasoned decision

The jury does not have to give a reason either for its decision or for the amount it awards. A judge always gives a judgment, which makes it easier to see if there are good grounds for an appeal.

12.8.3 Bias

The problems of bias in civil cases are different to those encountered in criminal cases. In some defamation cases the claimants and/or the defendants may be public figures so that jurors will know and possibly hold views about them. Alternatively there is the fact that the defendant in a defamation case is often a newspaper, and jurors may be biased against the press or may feel that 'they can afford to pay'.

12.8.4 Cost

Civil cases are expensive and the use of a jury adds to this as the case is likely to last longer. At the end of the case the losing party will have to pay all the costs of the case which may amount to hundreds of thousands of pounds. As a result of this, the Lord Chancellor has introduced some reforms so that defamation actions are less costly. Firstly, with the increase in County Court jurisdiction, parties can now agree that their case should be transferred to the County Court. Here, a jury of eight may be used and the trial is likely to be less expensive than one in the High Court. Secondly, the parties may also agree to the case being tried by a judge alone without a jury. The Defamation Act 1996 allows the claimant to seek a limited sum (up to £10,000) in a quick procedure dealt with by a judge. This allows those who want to clear their name and receive immediate compensation at a lower cost to do so.

12.9 Alternatives to jury trial

Despite all the problems of using juries in criminal cases, there is still a strong feeling that this is the best method available. However, if juries are not thought suitable to try serious criminal cases, what alternative form of trial could be used?

12.9.1 Trial by a single judge

This is the method of trial in the majority of civil cases which is generally regarded as producing a fairer and more predictable result. Trial by a single judge was used for some criminal trials in Northern Ireland until 2007. These were called the Diplock courts and were brought in on the recommendation of Lord Diplock to replace jury trial because of the special problems of threats and jury 'nobbling' that existed between the different sectarian parties.

However, there appears to be weaker public confidence in the use of judges to decide all serious criminal cases. The arguments against this form of trial are that judges become case-hardened and prosecution-minded. They are also from a very elite group and would have little understanding of the background and problems of defendants. Individual prejudices are more likely than in a jury where the different personalities should go some way to eliminating bias. But, on the other hand, judges are trained to evaluate cases and they are now being given training in racial awareness. This may make them better arbiters of fact than an untrained jury.

12.9.2 A panel of judges

In some other European countries, cases are heard by a panel of three or five judges sitting together. This allows for a balance of views, instead of the verdict of a single person. However, it still leaves the problems of judges becoming case-hardened and prosecution-minded and coming from an elite background. The other difficulty is that there are not sufficient judges and our system of legal training and appointment would need a radical overhaul to implement this proposal. It would also be expensive.

12.9.3 A judge plus lay assessors

Under this system the judge and two lay people would make the decision together. This method is used in the Scandinavian countries. It provides the legal expertise of the judge, together with lay participation in the legal system by ordinary members of the public. The lay people could either be drawn from the general public, using the same method as is used for selecting juries at present or a special panel of assessors could be drawn up as in tribunal cases. This latter suggestion would be particularly suitable for fraud cases.

Self-Test Questions

1 How are the names of potential jurors chosen?
2 What two types of vetting may take place?
3 When can a challenge be made to an individual juror?
4 What is the role of the jury in a criminal case?
5 What is meant by a majority verdict?
6 Which Act of Parliament makes it an offence for a juror to disclose what happened in the jury room?
7 Explain three advantages of using juries.
8 Explain three disadvantages of using juries.
9 Explain two problems of using a jury in a civil case.
10 Give two alternative methods of trial other than trial by jury.

12.9.4 A mini-jury

Finally, if the jury is to remain, then it might be possible to have a smaller number of jurors. In many continental countries when a jury is used there are nine members. For example, in Spain, which reintroduced the use of juries in certain criminal cases in 1996, there is a jury of nine. Alternatively a jury of six could be used for less serious criminal cases that at the moment can have a full jury trial, as occurs in some American states.

Examination Questions

1(a) Describe both the qualifications and the procedure for selecting a jury.   18 marks

1(b) Discuss the arguments against keeping the jury system.   12 marks

OCR, G151, June 2011

Exam tips

Part (b) questions on juries will require a discussion of a specific aspect. As always, read the question carefully and make sure you focus on the required area.

The topic of juries is an area in which some advantages and disadvantages can be illustrated with cases, so make sure you can do this. A good quality answer will include the case name with a brief resumé of what happened in the case, and will also explain why the case demonstrates the point you are trying to make.

Chapter 13

Funding of legal services

When faced with a legal problem, most people need expert help from a lawyer. Often the need is only for advice, but some people may need help in starting court proceedings and/or presenting their case in court. For the ordinary person seeking legal assistance, there are three main difficulties:

1. Lack of knowledge. Many people do not know where their nearest solicitor is located or, if they do know this, they do not know which solicitor specialises in the law involved in their particular case.

2. Fear of dealing with lawyers. People feel intimidated when dealing with lawyers.

3. Cost. Solicitors charge from about £100 an hour for routine advice from a small local firm, to over £600 an hour for work done by a top city firm of solicitors in a specialist field.

13.1 Access to justice

Where a person cannot get the help they need, they are being denied access to justice. Access to justice involves both an open system of justice and also being able to fund the costs of a case.

Various schemes have aimed at making the law more accessible to everyone. One of the earliest was the Citizens Advice Bureau which started in 1938 and now operates in most towns.

However, the problem of cost still remains a major hurdle. The cost of civil cases in the High Court may run into hundreds of thousands of pounds. Even in the cheaper County Court, the cost will possibly be more than the amount of money recovered in damages. There is the additional risk in all civil cases that the loser has to pay the winner's costs.

In criminal cases, a person's liberty may be at risk and it is essential that they should be able to defend themselves properly.

For these reasons, the Government has run schemes to help those in lower income brackets with funding cases. The first scheme was started in 1949 and altered many times over the years. In 2000, the Legal Services Commission was set up by the Government to run legal aid. However, in March 2010, the House of Commons Committee of Public Accounts criticised the Legal Services Commission for its financial management. In 2012, the Government decided to abolish the Legal Services Commission and bring legal aid under the control of the Ministry of Justice. This was done by passing the Legal Aid, Sentencing and Punishment of Offenders Act 2012.

13.2 The Legal Aid, Sentencing and Punishment of Offenders Act 2012

The Legal Aid, Sentencing and Punishment of Offenders Act 2012 abolished the Legal Services Commission. The administration of legal aid since April 2013 is operated by the Legal Aid Agency and comes under the umbrella of the Ministry of Justice.

An independent civil servant is the Director of Legal Aid Casework and the decisions on granting legal aid will be made by him and his team.

13.2.1 Service providers

The system works by the Government making contracts with providers of legal services so that the providers can do legal work and be paid from Government funds. Providers include law firms and not-for-profit organisations, such as the Citizens Advice Bureau offering advice on legal matters.

13.2.2 Criteria for civil legal aid services

The Act gives the Lord Chancellor the power to set criteria for making civil legal aid services

available. It also sets out the factors the Lord Chancellor must consider when setting the criteria. These factors are set out in s 10(3) of the Act. They include:

- the likely cost of providing the services and the benefit which may be obtained by them
- the availability of resources to provide the services
- the importance for the individual of the matters in relation to which the services would be provided
- the availability of other services, such as mediation
- where the services are sought by an individual in relation to a dispute, the individual's prospect of success in the dispute
- the public interest.

13.2.3 Availability of legal aid

Under previous legal aid systems, aid was available for all cases except those specifically excluded. There always were certain types of case excluded, for example small claims.

Under the new system, the starting point is that legal aid is not available for civil cases unless it is a category specifically mentioned in the Act or other regulations. The types of cases for which legal aid is allowed include those involving children's rights and those involving liberty of the individual. This includes cases being heard at Mental Health Tribunals, as these are about whether a person should continue to be detained in a mental hospital, and cases involving claims for asylum.

The result of this change to the availability of legal aid means that it is no longer granted for those injured through medical negligence. Also removed from legal aid are claims for trespass to the person, to land or to property. These previously were eligible for legal aid.

13.3 Government funding in civil cases

The funding for legal aid comes from the Government's budget. This means that a set amount is made available each year. Also the amount set has to be considered against all other claims on the budget, such as hospitals and health care and education. As a result, the Government cannot afford to make legal aid available to everyone. In order to qualify, there is a strict means test.

13.3.1 Means testing

A person applying for Government-funded advice or representation must show that they do not have enough money to pay for their own lawyer. In order to decide if the applicant is poor enough to qualify for government-funded help, their income and capital are considered.

People receiving Income Support or Income-Based Job Seekers' Allowance automatically qualify, assuming their disposable capital is below the set level. For all other applicants, their gross income is considered first. If a person's gross income is above a set amount per month, then they do not qualify.

Disposable income

If the person's gross income is below the set amount per month, then their disposable income has to be calculated by starting with their gross income and taking away:

- tax and National Insurance
- housing costs
- childcare costs or maintenance paid for children
- an allowance for themselves and for each dependant.

If the amount left after making all deductions is below a minimum level, the applicant does not have to pay any contribution towards their funding. If the amount left is above a maximum level, the person will not qualify for any of the schemes provided by the Legal Aid Agency.

Where the disposable income is between the minimum level and the maximum level, the person applying for legal help has to pay a monthly contribution. The more in excess of the minimum, the greater the amount of the contribution. This idea of minimum and maximum levels is shown in Figure 13.1.

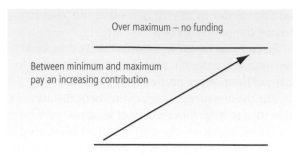

Figure 13.1 Minimum and maximum limits for legal aid

Note that the figures for the limits on income are increased slightly each year. You will be able to find the current figures on the Ministry of Justice's website **www.justice.gov.uk**.

Disposable capital

Disposable capital is the assets of the person, such as money in a bank or savings account, stocks and shares or expensive jewellery. In order to qualify for funding to take a court case, there is a maximum limit for disposable capital of £8,000.

If the assets are over £8,000, they must use their own money to fund any legal case, although once they have spent the money in excess of £8,000 they can become eligible for funding. Even where the disposable capital is below £8,000 they can be asked to pay a contribution towards their case.

Where a person owns a home, the value of that home is taken into account in deciding the disposable capital. This is the case even though the person may have a large mortgage. Only the first £100,000 of any mortgage is deducted from the value of the home. This rule means that people are regarded as having too much disposable capital because of the value of their house, but in reality they may have no spare money.

13.4 Problems with funding of civil cases

13.4.1 'Advice deserts'

There is evidence that not enough legal service providers have contracts. This is partly due to the smaller numbers of contracts made with providers by the Legal Services Commission (and now by the Legal Aid Agency) and also to the fact that many solicitors are finding that the rates of pay are so low, it is not economically viable for solicitors to continue in the scheme. This has created what have been called 'advice deserts'.

The problem of advice deserts was considered by the Constitutional Affairs Select Committee as long ago as 2004. In the evidence to the Committee, even the Legal Services Commission acknowledged that:

> It is clear that there are parts of England and Wales in which the need for publicly funded legal services is not currently being met.

In their report, the Select Committee gave the position in Northumberland as an example. There were no housing law advisers and no-one with a contract for immigration law in Northumberland. Furthermore, there were only two contracts for employment law in the area. People have to travel a long way to see a lawyer. This can be expensive and is difficult for people on low incomes, those caring for small children or those who have a disability which makes it difficult to travel.

Since 2004, the position has been getting worse as more solicitors have stopped doing government-funded legal work. With so few legal service providers in certain areas, people who want help may have to travel long distances to find it.

The continuing lack of lawyers to undertake certain types of case has been confirmed by a survey carried out in 2008–2009 by the Legal Action Group. For example, they quote one person from South Wales as saying she had:

> … contacted dozens of solicitors in the last month, but no help was forthcoming as none specialised in welfare benefits.

The annual report for the Legal Services Commission also showed how the numbers of law firms doing legal aid work had decreased. When the Legal Services Commission started in 2000, there were about 5,000 law firms doing legal aid work. By 2012, there were only 1,780 firms.

13.4.2 Eligibility levels

Even where there are enough legal services providers in an area, only people with very low levels of income and capital can qualify for help. As far back as 2004 the Select Committee on Constitutional Affairs, which investigated the adequacy of the provision of civil legal aid, pointed out that:

> At present, the legal aid system is increasingly being restricted to those with no means at all. There is a substantial risk that many people of modest means but who are home-owners will fall out of the ambit of legal aid. In many cases, this may amount to a serious denial of access to justice.

The financial limits have become increasingly restrictive so that this statement is even more true today.

13.4.3 Lack of funds

The fact that there is a limit on the amount given by the budget means that some cases will not be funded as there is no money left for them. Also, the fact that criminal cases take priority on funding means there may not be enough left for civil cases. This can lead to civil cases which have merit being refused funding just because the money has run out.

13.4.4 Non-availability

As set out in section 13.2.2, funding is not available for all civil claims. Claims for damages for personal injury are excluded from the scheme. Any such case has to be paid for privately or through a conditional

Key facts

Managing body	Legal Aid Agency
Different levels of help and representation available	● advice only ● legal representation – covers all aspects of case ● support funding – partial funding of a very high-cost case
Means test	Strict means test on gross income, disposable income and disposable capital for all services
Merits test for legal representation	Whether the case has a reasonable chance of success and the damages will be worth more than the costs. Other criteria including: ● can the matter be funded in another way? ● are there funds available?
Problems	● number of solicitors is decreasing ● financial level of eligibility exclude people of modest means ● capping of fund together with increasing criminal expenditure means that less is available for civil cases ● only available for specified types of cases, NOT available for personal injury cases and medical negligence or employment tribunal cases

Figure 13.2 Key facts chart on public funding in civil cases

fee agreement (see section 13.6). This works well where people have suffered minor injuries, but it can be argued that it creates difficulties for people who have been left with serious disabilities. They need all the help they can get to make sure they receive adequate compensation.

It can also be argued that people bringing employment claims against large companies are disadvantaged by being unable to receive public funding to bring their case. The company will be able to afford a lawyer and will be at an advantage in the case.

13.5 Private funding

Anyone who can afford it can pay for a solicitor and/or a barrister to deal with a legal matter. There are firms of solicitors in most towns. However, some solicitors specialise in certain types of work. If your legal problem is in an unusual area of law, then it may be necessary to travel to another town to find a solicitor who can deal with it.

The bigger firms of solicitors work in the major cities, in particular London. They often specialise in commercial law and the majority of their clients are businesses.

Consulting a solicitor can be expensive. The average cost of a solicitor outside London is about £150 an hour. For a big London firm of solicitors, the charges are usually at least £600 an hour and can be as much as £1,000 an hour.

On issues of civil law, it is also possible to consult a barrister directly, without going to a solicitor first. This can be cheaper than using a solicitor because barristers do not have such high business expenses as solicitors.

13.6 Conditional fees

One of the main problems of taking a case to court is that it is difficult to estimate how long it will last or how much it will cost. If a person is funding their own case, this is a major problem for them. Also, if they lose the case, they may have to pay the costs of the other party. The combined costs of the case can be many thousands of pounds. In order to overcome these problems, a conditional fee agreement (CFA) can be used in all civil cases, except family cases.

CFAs cannot be used in criminal cases.

13.6.1 How conditional fees work

The solicitor and client agree on the fee that would normally be charged for such a case. The agreement will also set out what the solicitor's success fee will be if he wins the case.

Many conditional fee agreements will be made on the basis that if the case is lost, the client pays nothing. Because of this sort of agreement, the scheme is often referred to as 'no win, no fee'. However, some solicitors may prefer to charge a lower level fee, for example half the normal fee, even if the case is lost.

If the case is won, the client has to pay the normal fee plus the success fee.

13.6.2 Success fee

The success fee could be up to 100 per cent of the normal fee. However, most agreements will include a 'cap' on the success fee, which prevents it from being more than 25 per cent of the

damages (amount of money) that the client wins as compensation. This protects the client from having to pay more than he or she won as compensation. Even so, it can mean that the client is left with very little of their damages. This is easier to understand by looking at the examples given in Figure 13.3.

Under the Legal Aid, Sentencing and Punishment of Offenders Act 2012, the Lord Chancellor is able to set a limit on the maximum percentage for the success fee, so it is unlikely that solicitors will be able set a success fee of 100 per cent in future.

A winning claimant used to be able to claim the success fee back from the losing defendant. This has been changed by the Legal Aid, Sentencing and Punishment of Offenders Act 2012 which states that:

> A costs order made in proceedings may not include provision requiring the payment by one party of all or part of a success fee payable under a conditional fee agreement.

So now the position is that a winning claimant will have to pay any success fee themselves.

Agreement

Normal fee	£4,000
Fee if case is lost	NIL
Success fee	£2,000
Cap on success fee	25% of damages

Possible results of case	**Client pays**
Case is lost	Nothing
Case is won: client gets £50,000 damages	£6,000 (£4,000 + £2,000)
Case is won: client gets £6,000 damages	£5,500 (£4,000 + £1,500*)

*This £1,500 is because the success fee cannot be more than 25% of the damages

Figure 13.3 Illustration of conditional fees

13.6.3 Insurance premiums

Although the client will often not have to pay anything to their own lawyer if the case is lost, they will usually have to pay the costs of the other side. This can leave the client with a very large bill to pay. To help protect against this, it is possible to insure against the risk. This type of insurance is known as 'after-the-event' (ATE) insurance. So, if the case is lost, your insurers will pay the other side's costs.

In order to get insurance, it is necessary to pay a premium (a sum of money) to the insurance company. Premiums for 'after-the-event' insurance are usually quite expensive. This premium usually has to be paid in advance of the decision in the case. This can cause problems to people who cannot afford the cost of the premium.

It used to be possible for a winning claimant to be able claim the cost of ATE back from the defendant. This has been changed by the Legal Aid, Sentencing and Punishment of Offenders Act 2012 and it can no longer be claimed back. The claimant has to fund it themselves.

13.6.4 Are conditional fees working?

Conditional fee agreements have helped thousands of people to bring cases to court and obtain justice. One area in which they have been particularly useful for claimants has been in defamation cases. Legal aid has never been available for such cases and only the rich could risk pursuing defamation claims. CFAs have enabled ordinary people to take such cases.

However, there are problems with CFAs. Low value cases are not attractive to lawyers who need to be able to make a profit for their legal business to survive. Lawyers are also more likely to take on cases where there is a very high chance of success.

The Legal Aid, Sentencing and Punishment of Offenders Act 2012 has made CFAs less attractive for two reasons:

1. The cost of after-the-event insurance can no longer be claimed back from the defendant by a claimant who wins the case.

2. Success fees can no longer be claimable from the defendant by a claimant who wins the case.

These two points mean that a winning claimant will have to bear more of the cost of taking a case. As a result, a large proportion of the amount of damages they receive may well be used up by their costs.

Key facts

How conditional fee agreements work	● The client and solicitor agree on the normal fee and on a success fee if the case is won ● The success fee can be up to 100% of the normal fee ● If the case is lost, most clients will pay nothing to their own solicitor ● After-the-event insurance is usually taken out to protect against the risk of paying the other's costs if the case is lost
Advantages of CFAs	● Provide access to justice for those who cannot get government funding and cannot afford to pay in the normal way ● Client will feel confident in solicitor's commitment to case ● Hopeless cases will not be taken on, saving court time
Disadvantages of CFAs	● Clients cannot afford to pay insurance premiums or other expenses ● Consumers may be subjected to high-pressure sales tactics ● Consumers do not understand the risks and liabilities of CFAs and may be misled by sales people ● Some claims end in 'zero gain' ● Solicitors do not want to take on high-risk claims or low-value claims: this can deny access to justice

Figure 13.4 Key facts chart on conditional fee agreements

13.7 Advice in civil cases

When people have a legal problem, the first thing they want is advice. The Legal Services Commission had developed a telephone help line for people to seek initial basic advice. Also it had a website offering advice. These two services are likely to continue under the new Legal Advice Agency.

13.7.1 Community Legal Advice Centres

The Legal Services Commission also established Community Legal Advice Centres (CLACs). These are a one-stop service providing advice on debt, welfare benefits, community care, housing and employment. The first two such centres were set up in Leicester and Gateshead. It was intended that there would eventually be about 75 CLACs.

13.7.2 Service providers

People can also get advice from a solicitor or a not-for-profit organisation that holds a contract with the Government to give advice in civil cases. To receive advice in this way, the person has to come within the financial limits explained in 13.3.1 above.

13.7.3 Other advice agencies

Apart from Government-funded schemes, there are a number of different advice schemes available. The main ones are Citizens Advice Bureaux and law centres. However, there are other agencies which offer advice on specific legal topics. These include trades unions which will help members with work-related legal problems. There are also charities, such as Shelter, which offer advice to people with housing problems.

These will offer advice free to anyone who has a problem of the type they deal in.

13.7.4 Citizens Advice Bureaux

Citizens Advice Bureaux (CABx) were first set up in 1938 and today there are about 1,000 throughout the UK with a bureau existing in most towns. They give general advice free to anyone on a variety of issues mostly connected to social welfare problems and debt, but they also advise on some legal matters. They can also provide information on which local solicitors do legal aid work or give cheap or free initial interviews. Many have arrangements under which solicitors may attend at the bureau once a week or fortnight to give more qualified advice on legal matters.

As well as being available for anyone to get advice, the Legal Services Commission has awarded contracts for some CABx to provide Government-funded advice.

13.7.5 Law Centres

These offer a free, non-means-tested legal service to people in their area. The first Law Centre opened in North Kensington in 1970. This stated its aims as providing:

> a first class solicitor's service to the people ... a service which is easily accessible, not intimidating, to which they can turn for guidance as they would to their family doctor, or as someone who can afford it would turn to his family solicitor.

Their aim is to provide free legal advice (and sometimes representation) in areas where there are few solicitors. Many of their clients are disadvantaged.

Funding

Law Centres have always struggled to secure enough funding. Recent cuts by local authorities in their budgets have meant the withdrawal or reduction of funding from this source. As a result some Law Centres have had to close. Funding also comes from the Legal Services Commission (when the Ministry of Justice takes over legal aid, it is to be hoped this funding will continue). Some centres have received funds from the Big Lottery Fund where the Law Centre is part of a community project.

As at the beginning of 2013, there were 55 Law Centres operating.

Key facts

Government-funded schemes	Advice agencies	Lawyers
Legal Aid Agency website offering advice	Citizens' Advice Bureaux	Some solicitors offer a free half-hour first interview
Telephone service	Law Centres	Bar Pro Bono Unit
Community Legal Advice Centres	Legal insurance	Pay privately for advice
Legal aid advice scheme – means tested and only available to those on low incomes		

Figure 13.5 Key facts chart on where to get advice in civil cases

Activity

Look at the website of the Law Centres Federation at **www.lawcentres.org.uk**. This should give you the present number of Law Centres. It will also give information about the work they do.

13.7.6 Schemes run by lawyers

Some solicitors offer a free half-hour first interview. Local CABx will have a list of solicitors who offer the service.

Another service by solicitors is the Accident Legal Advice Service (ALAS) which is aimed at helping accident victims claim compensation. In addition, the Law Society runs Accident Line – a free telephone service to put accident victims in contact with solicitors who do personal injury work.

Bar Pro Bono Unit

Since 1996, volunteer barristers have staffed the Bar Pro Bono Unit. This unit gives free advice to those who cannot afford to pay and who cannot get legal aid. They will give advice on any area of law and will also where necessary represent the client in court proceedings.

Free Representation Unit (FRU)

This is also staffed by volunteer barristers. It was founded in 1972 and provides representation for:

● cases in employment tribunals
● social security appeals, and
● claims for criminal injury compensation.

These are areas of law where legal aid is not available.

Until recently, the FRU operated only in London. However, they are trying to set up units in Nottingham, Birmingham and Manchester.

13.7.7 Insurance

Another way of funding a court case is by legal insurance. Most motor insurance policies offer cover (for a small extra cost) for help with legal fees in cases arising from road accidents and there are also policies purely for insurance against legal costs.

13.8 Legal aid in criminal cases

From 2013 criminal legal aid services have been under the Legal Aid Agency in the Ministry of Justice. The Director of Legal Aid Casework will supervise criminal legal aid, as well as civil legal aid. The agency will make contracts with law firms to provide legal services to people charged with criminal offences.

13.8.1 Advice and assistance for individuals in custody

Section 13 of Legal Aid, Sentencing and Punishment of Offenders Act 2012 states that:

 Initial advice and initial assistance are to be available … to an individual who is arrested and held in custody at a police station or other premises if the Director has determined that the individual qualifies for such advice and assistance …

The Director must have regard to the interests of justice when making that determination. There will be regulations setting out more precisely what is to be considered in making determinations under s 13.

Telephone advice

One of the problems in the 1990s with duty solicitor schemes was that, in many cases, the solicitor did not attend at the police station, but merely gave advice over the telephone. Although this was viewed as a defect in the scheme, telephone advice has now become the Government's preferred method of action for duty solicitors. Since 2004, solicitors cannot claim for attending at the police station unless they can show that attendance was expected to 'materially progress the case'.

Representation

In order to get representation, the defendant has to qualify under the 'interests of justice' test. There is also a means test.

13.8.2 Interests of justice

A defendant will only get help with legal funding for representation in court if he can show that he comes within at least one of the five 'interests of justice' factors. These factors are:

1. Whether, if any matter arising in the proceedings is decided against him, the individual would be likely to lose his liberty or livelihood or suffer serious damage to his reputation.

2. The case will involve consideration of a point of law.

3. The individual is unable to understand the proceedings in court or to state his own case.

4. The case may involve the tracing, interviewing or expert cross-examination of witnesses.

5. It is in the interests of another person that the individual be represented (such as in a rape case).

13.8.3 Magistrates' Court means testing

As well as having to qualify under the 'interests of justice' test, defendants who are being tried in the Magistrates' Courts are also means tested.

Those who are on income support, defendants under the age of 16 and those under 18 in full-time education automatically pass the means test. For everyone else, the test starts with a first-stage simple means test which is calculated on gross annual income. If their income is too high on this test, then the defendant does not qualify for legal aid. If a defendant's income is below a certain level, they qualify. For those in the middle bracket, they are further means tested to calculate their disposable income.

The levels allowed are very low. This means that about three-quarters of adults do not qualify for legal aid in criminal cases in the Magistrates' Courts.

13.8.4 Crown Court means testing

This was gradually introduced during 2010. The main difference from the Magistrates' Courts is that there is no upper limit on disposable income. All defendants can receive legal aid. It is free for those on low incomes.

Where a defendant has to pay, then the higher their income, the higher the contribution they will have to pay towards the case. The maximum amount they have to pay through contributions from their income is set by the type of case.

If a defendant is found guilty, they may also have to pay extra from their capital. This only applies where their capital is over £30,000.

If a defendant is found not guilty, any contributions paid will be normally be refunded.

13.9 Problems with funding of criminal cases

13.9.1 'Interests of justice' test

This test is applied very strictly. Even where a defendant is charged with an offence for which a prison sentence can be given, for example theft, it does not necessarily mean that he will pass the 'interests of justice' test. The rule is that there must be a real risk of imprisonment.

This has the effect that a defendant who has several previous convictions for theft will qualify for legal help as they are likely to be imprisoned. However, someone with no previous convictions is not likely to be sent to prison. So, if they are pleading not guilty they will have to represent themselves or pay for private legal help.

13.9.2 Means test

In the Magistrates' Courts, this is a strict test. The levels of income allowed are very low. About three-quarters of adults do not qualify for legal aid in criminal cases.

The limits are less severe in the Crown Court, but even here some defendants do not qualify for legal aid. As the cases are more serious and it is more expensive to defend a case, there is a real risk of injustice due to lack of availability of legal help.

13.9.3 Lack of lawyers

The Government has cut the fees paid to lawyers for criminal cases. Fixed fees are being brought in which do not take account of the true amount of work that may need to be done. As a result, fewer solicitors are taking on Government-funded legal work. This makes it more difficult for defendants to find a local solicitor to take their case. The annual reports for the Legal Services Commission emphasise the decrease in solicitors doing legal aid work. Prior to the year 2000, there were over 5,000 law firms doing criminal legal aid work, but by 2012 there were only 1,640 firms.

13.9.4 Budget

The budget given by the Government for legal funding has not risen in line with inflation. This means that there is less money to allocate for funding.

Key facts

Managing body	Legal Aid Agency
Different levels of help and representation available	● Duty solicitor at the police station ● Advice and assistance ● Legal representation
Merits test for representation	● Whether it is in the interests of justice ● Defendant at risk of losing liberty, livelihood or reputation ● Substantial point of law involved ● Defendant unable to understand proceedings ● Involves tracing, interview or expert cross-examination of witnesses ● Is in the interests of another person
Means test	● Duty solicitor free of charge and not means tested ● Means testing for representation in court
Problems	● Strict application of 'interests of justice' test ● Strict means test so that three-quarters of adults cannot qualify in Magistrates' Courts ● Lack of solicitors doing publicly funded criminal law work

Figure 13.6 Key facts chart on public funding in criminal cases

Exam tips

Legal funding and advice also comes under the wider umbrella of access to justice so you need to think about comments relating to this topic in both specific and more general terms. As this is an area which affects so many people, there are plenty of comments you can make and this makes the discussion element of the question a little easier to manage.

You need to be careful to write about the correct area of law and think about the issues from different perspectives. These include:

- the problems which face an individual who needs help
- the efficiency of the service provided from the point of those providing the help
- the broader issue of whether our society is succeeding in this key area.

All these might be themes you could consider as part of getting your thoughts into a coherent order.

The other advantage of thinking about more complex issues when you are revising is that you can check you have made the point correctly, and that you can get it across clearly. This will mean that you are less likely to feel under pressure when you are in the exam room and so avoid getting confused or having one of those dreadful moments where your mind goes completely blank! Think about it beforehand so you can be calm when it matters – this makes it much easier to do well.

Examination Questions

1(a) Describe both publicly funded legal representation in civil cases and conditional fee agreements. 18 marks

(b) Discuss how methods of funding affect access to justice. 12 marks

OCR G151 January 2011

UNIT 2

Sources of law

Chapter 14

Judicial precedent

Judicial precedent refers to the source of law where past decisions of the judges create law for future judges to follow. This source of law is also known as case law. It is a major source of law, both historically and today.

Exam tips

The remaining chapters of this book focus on material covered by G152. The name of this paper is Sources of Law and this gives you a clue as to where the emphasis of the questions will be placed. When you are studying and revising these topics you need to remember that the law is made in different ways, for a variety of reasons, and the purpose it is trying to achieve should underpin your consideration of these topic areas. The other difference with this paper is that it introduces you to materials which you have to read, understand and use as the basis of your answers in the exam, so you need to use different skills to do well. This paper is not based on success by simply learning a list of facts and a number of discussion points – you need to use the sources to focus, develop and support your answer. The sources can be varied and it is a good idea to look at past questions so that you are familiar with the type of materials and the legal language which they use. This paper introduces you to 'real law' which makes it interesting, and you can do well if you spend time working on your skills as well as revising your knowledge.

14.1 The doctrine of precedent

The English system of precedent is based on the Latin maxim *stare decisis et non quieta movere* (usually shortened to *stare decisis*). This means 'stand by what has been decided and do not unsettle the established'. This supports the idea of fairness and provides certainty in the law.

14.1.1 Judgments

Precedent can only operate if the legal reasons for past decisions are known, so at the end of a case there will be a judgment. This is a speech made by the judge (or judges) hearing the case giving the decision and explaining the reasons for the decision. In a judgment the judge usually gives a summary of the facts of the case, reviews the arguments put to him by the advocates in the case, and then explains the principles of law he is using to come to the decision.

These principles are the important part of the judgment and are known as the *ratio decidendi* which means 'the reason for deciding' (and is pronounced 'ray-she-o dess-id-end-i'). This is what creates a precedent for judges to follow in future cases. The rest of the judgment is known as *obiter dicta* ('other things said').

It is also worth realising that there can be more than one speech at the end of a case, depending on the number of judges hearing the case. In courts of first instance there will be only one judge and therefore one judgment. In the Divisional Courts and the Court of Appeal, cases are heard by at least two judges and usually three. In the Supreme Court, the panel has to consist of an uneven number of judges, so there could be three, five, seven or even nine judges. This means there can be more than one judgment.

The fact that there are two or more judges does not mean that there will always be several judgments as it is quite common for one judge to give the judgment and the other judge/judges simply to say 'I agree'!

However, in cases where there is a particularly important or complicated point of law, more than one judge may want to explain his legal reasoning on the point. This can cause problems in later cases as each judge may have had a different reason for his decision, so there will be more than one *ratio decidendi*.

14.1.2 *Ratio decidendi*

As already stated, this is the only part of the judgment which forms a precedent. A major problem when looking at a past judgment is to divide the *ratio decidendi* from the *obiter dicta*, as older judgments are usually in a continuous form, without any headings specifying what is meant to be part of the *ratio* and what is not. This means that the person reading the judgment (especially a judge in a later case) will have to decide what the *ratio* is. Sir Rupert Cross defined the *ratio decidendi* as:

 any rule expressly or impliedly treated by the judge as a necessary step in reaching his conclusion.

Michael Zander says that the *ratio decidendi* is:

 a proposition of law which decides the case, in the light or in the context of the material facts.

It depends on the level of the court making the decision as to whether the *ratio* has to be followed by a later court (a binding precedent) or whether it merely has to be considered by that court.

14.1.3 *Obiter dicta*

The remainder of the judgment is called *obiter dicta* ('other things said') and judges in future cases do not have to follow it. Sometimes a judge will speculate on what his decision would have been if the facts of the case had been different. This hypothetical situation is part of the *obiter dicta* and the legal reasoning put forward in it may be considered in future cases, although, as with all *obiter* statements, it is not binding precedent.

As well as learning the Latin phrases *ratio decidendi*, *obiter dicta* and *stare decisis* there are some English phrases which are important for understanding the concept of judicial precedent. These are 'original precedent', 'binding precedent' and 'persuasive precedent'.

14.1.4 Original precedent

If the point of law in a case has never been decided before, then whatever the judge decides will form a new precedent for future cases to follow. It is an original precedent. As there are no past cases for the judge to base his decision on, he is likely to look at cases which are the closest in principle and he may decide to use similar rules. This way of arriving at a judgment is called reasoning by analogy.

14.1.5 Binding precedent

This is a precedent from an earlier case which must be followed even if the judge in the later case does not agree with the legal principle. A binding precedent is only created when the facts of the second case are sufficiently similar to the original case and the decision was made by a court which is senior to (or in some cases the same level as) the court hearing the later case.

14.1.6 Persuasive precedent

This is a precedent that is not binding on the court, but the judge may consider it and decide that it is a correct principle so he is persuaded that he should follow it. Persuasive precedent comes from a number of sources, as explained below:

Courts lower in the hierarchy

Such an example can be seen in *R v R* (1991), where the House of Lords agreed with and followed the same reasoning as the Court of Appeal in deciding that a man could be guilty of raping his wife.

Decisions of the Judicial Committee of the Privy Council

This court is not part of the court hierarchy in England and Wales and so its decisions are not binding, but, since many of its judges are also members of the Supreme Court (formerly the House of Lords), their judgments are treated with respect and may often be followed. An example of this can be seen in the law on remoteness of damages in the law of tort and the decision made by the Privy Council in the case of *The Wagon Mound (No 1)* (1961). In later cases courts in England and Wales followed the decision in this case.

More recently, in *A-G for Jersey v Holley* (2005) the Privy Council ruled that in the defence of provocation a defendant was to be judged by the standard of a person having ordinary powers of self-control. This was contrary to an earlier judgment by the House of Lords. In cases in 2005 and 2006 the Court of Appeal followed the Privy Council decision rather than the decision of the House of Lords.

Statements made *obiter dicta*

This is clearly seen in the law on duress as a defence to a criminal charge, where the House of Lords in *R v Howe* (1987) ruled that duress could not be a defence to a charge of murder. In the judgment the Lords also commented, as an obiter statement, that duress would not be available as a defence to someone charged with attempted murder. When in *R v Gotts* (1992) a defendant charged with attempted murder tried to argue that he could use the defence of duress, the *obiter* statement from *Howe* was followed as persuasive precedent by the Court of Appeal.

A dissenting judgment

Where a case has been decided by a majority of judges (for example, 2–1 in the Court of Appeal), the judge who disagreed will have explained his reasons. If that case goes on appeal to the Supreme Court, or if there is a later case on the same point which goes to the Supreme Court, it is possible that the Supreme Court may prefer the dissenting judgment and decide the case in the same way. The dissenting judgment has persuaded them to follow it.

Decisions of courts in other countries

Where another country uses the same ideas of common law as in our system, their decisions may be considered. This especially applies to Commonwealth countries such as Canada, Australia and New Zealand.

14.2 The hierarchy of the courts

In England and Wales our courts operate a very rigid doctrine of judicial precedent which has the effect that:

- every court is bound to follow any decision made by a court above it in the hierarchy
- in general, appellate courts (courts which hear appeals) are bound by their own past decisions.

So the hierarchy of the courts is the next important point to clarify. Which courts come where in the hierarchy? Figure 14.1 shows this in the form of a cascade model and Figure 14.2 gives each court and its position in respect of the other courts. The position of each court is also considered in this section and in sections 14.3 and 14.4 below.

14.2.1 Appellate courts

Appellate courts are those hearing appeals.

The European Court of Justice

Since 1973, the highest court affecting our legal system is the European Court of Justice. For points of European law, a decision made by this court is binding on all other courts in England and Wales. However, there are still laws which are unaffected by European Union law and for these the Supreme Court is the most senior court. An important feature of the European Court of Justice is that it is prepared to overrule its own past decisions if it feels it is necessary. This flexible approach to past precedents is seen in other legal systems in Europe, and is a contrast to the more rigid approach of our national courts.

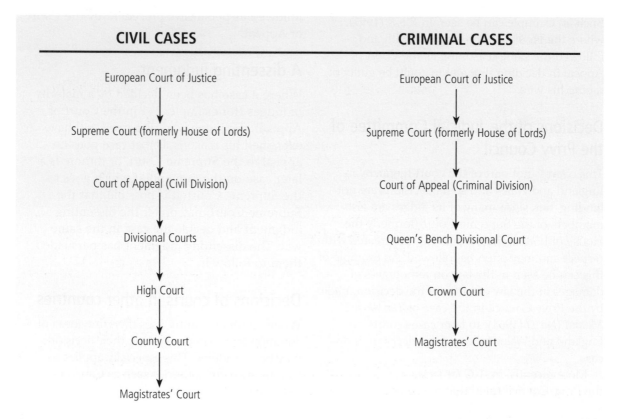

Figure 14.1 Cascade model of judicial precedent operating in the hierarchy of the courts

Supreme Court

The most senior national court is the Supreme Court and its decisions bind all other courts in the English legal system. The Supreme Court is not bound by its own past decisions, although it will generally follow them. This point is discussed in detail in section 14.3.

Court of Appeal

At the next level down in the hierarchy is the Court of Appeal which has two divisions: Civil and Criminal. Both divisions of the Court of Appeal are bound to follow decisions of the European Court of Justice and the Supreme Court. In addition, they must usually follow past decisions of their own; although there are some limited exceptions to this rule. Also the Court of Appeal (Criminal Division) is more flexible where the point involves the liberty of the subject. The position of the two divisions is discussed in detail in 14.4.

Divisional Courts

The three Divisional Courts (Queen's Bench, Chancery and Family) are bound by decisions of the European Court of Justice, the Supreme Court and the Court of Appeal. In addition, the Divisional Courts are bound by their own past decisions, although they operate similar exceptions to those operated by the Court of Appeal.

14.2.2 Courts of first instance

The term 'court of first instance' means any court where the original trial of a case is held. The appellate courts considered in section 14.2.1 do not hear any original trials. They only deal with appeals from decisions of other courts. Quite often an appeal will be about a point of law. This allows the appellate courts to decide the law and this is why the appellate courts are much more important than courts of first instance when it comes to creating precedent.

Court	Courts bound by it	Courts it must follow
European Court	All courts	None
Supreme Court	All other courts in the English legal system	European Court
Court of Appeal	Itself (with some exceptions) Divisional Courts All other lower courts	European Court Supreme Court
Divisional Courts	Itself (with some exceptions) High Court All other lower courts	European Court Supreme Court Court of Appeal
High Court	County Court Magistrates' Court	European Court Supreme Court Court of Appeal Divisional Courts
Crown Court	Possibly Magistrates' Court	All higher courts

County Court and Magistrates' Court do not create precedent and are bound by all higher courts

Figure 14.2 The courts and precedent

Courts of first instance rarely create precedent. They must follow the decisions of the courts above them.

The High Court

This is bound by decisions of all the courts above and in turn it binds the lower courts. High Court judges do not have to follow each others' decisions but will usually do so. In *Colchester Estates (Cardiff) v Carlton Industries plc* (1984) it was held that where there were two earlier decisions which conflicted, then, provided the first decision had been fully considered in the later case, that later decision should be followed.

Inferior courts

These are the Crown Court, the County Court and the Magistrates' Court. They are bound to follow decisions by all higher courts and it is unlikely that a decision by an inferior court can create precedent. The one exception is that a

ruling on a point of law by a judge in the Crown Court technically creates precedent for the Magistrates' Court. However, since such rulings are rarely recorded in the law reports, this is of little practical effect.

14.3 The Supreme Court (formerly the House of Lords)

The main debate about the former House of Lords was the extent to which it should follow its own past decisions, and the ideas on this changed over the years.

Originally the view was that the House of Lords had the right to overrule past decisions, but gradually during the nineteenth century this more flexible approach disappeared. By the end of that century, in *London Street Tramways v London County Council* (1898), the House of Lords held that certainty in the law was more important than the possibility of individual hardship being caused through having to follow a past decision.

So from 1898 to 1966 the House of Lords regarded itself as being completely bound by its own past decisions unless the decision had been made *per incuriam*, that is 'in error'. However, this idea of error referred only to situations where a decision had been made without considering the effect of a relevant statute.

This was not felt to be satisfactory. The law could not alter to meet changing social conditions and opinions, nor could any possible 'wrong' decisions be changed by the courts. If there was an unsatisfactory decision by the House of Lords, then the only way it could be changed was by Parliament passing a new Act of Parliament.

This happened in the law about intention as an element of a criminal offence. The House of Lords in *DPP v Smith* (1961) had ruled that an accused could be guilty of murder if a reasonable person would have foreseen that death or very serious injury might result from the accused's actions. This decision was criticised as it meant that the defendant could be guilty even if he had not intended to cause

Self-Test Questions

1. What part of a judgment forms a precedent for future cases?
2. What is the rest of the judgment known as?
3. What is meant by 'original precedent'?
4. What is meant by 'binding precedent'?
5. What effect do decisions of the Judicial Committee of the Privy Council have on future cases?
6. What is meant by a dissenting judgment?
7. Give two other types of persuasive precedent.
8. What is the highest court in the legal system in England and Wales?
9. Where a point of European law is involved, the decisions of which court must be followed?
10. Which courts do not create precedents?

death or serious injury, nor even realised that his actions might have that effect. Eventually Parliament changed the law by passing the Criminal Justice Act 1967.

14.3.1 The Practice Statement

It was agreed that the House of Lords should have more flexibility. So, in 1966, the Lord Chancellor issued a Practice Statement announcing a change to the rule in *London Street Tramways v London County Council* (1898). The Practice Statement said:

> Their Lordships regard the use of precedent as an indispensable foundation upon which to decide what is the law and its application to individual cases. It provides at least some degree of certainty upon which individuals can rely in the conduct of their affairs, as well as a basis for orderly development of legal rules.
>
> Their Lordships nevertheless recognise that the rigid adherence to precedent may lead to injustice in a particular case and also unduly restrict the proper development of the law. They propose, therefore, to modify their present practice and while treating former decisions of this House as normally binding, to depart from a previous decision when it appears right to do so.
>
> In this connection they will bear in mind the danger of disturbing retrospectively the basis on which contracts, settlement of property and fiscal arrangements have been entered into and also the especial need for certainty as to the criminal law. This announcement is not intended to affect the use of precedent elsewhere than in this House.

14.3.2 Use of the Practice Statement

From 1966 to 2009 (when the House of Lords was abolished and replaced by the Supreme Court), this Practice Statement allowed the House of Lords to change the law if it believed that an earlier case was wrongly decided. It gave the flexibility to refuse to follow an earlier case when 'it appears right to do so'. This phrase was, of course, very vague and gave little guidance as to when the House of Lords might overrule a previous decision. In fact the House of Lords was reluctant to use this power, especially in the first few years after 1966. The first case in which the Practice Statement was used was *Conway v Rimmer* (1968), but this only involved a technical point on discovery of documents.

The first major use did not occur until 1972 in *Herrington v British Railways Board* (1972).

Herrington v British Railways Board (1972)

Herrington was a boy aged six who had trespassed on a railway line and been severely injured. He had been able to get on to the railway line because the Railways Board had not maintained the fencing along the railway line properly. This case involved the law on the duty of care owed to a child trespasser. An earlier case of *Addie v Dumbreck* (1929) had decided that an occupier of land would only owe a duty of care for injuries to a child trespasser if those injuries had been caused deliberately or recklessly. In *Herrington*, the Lords held that social and physical conditions had changed since 1929, and the law should also change. The Railways Board owed a duty of care to child trespassers and was liable.

There was still great reluctance in the House of Lords to use the Practice Statement, as was shown by the case of *Jones v Secretary of State for Social Services* (1972). This case involved the interpretation of the National Insurance (Industrial Injuries) Act 1946 and four out of the seven judges hearing the

Key facts

1898	House of Lords decided in the case of *London Street Tramways* that it was bound to follow its own previous decisions
1966	Issue of the Practice Statement House of Lords would depart from previous decisions when 'it is right to do so'
1968	First use of Practice Statement in *Conway v Rimmer* Only involves technical law on discovery of documents
1972	First major use of Practice Statement in *Herrington v British Railways Board* on the duty of care owed to child trespassers
1980s and 1990s	House of Lords showed an increasing willingness to use Practice Statement to overrule previous decisions, e.g. *R v Shivpuri* (criminal attempts); *Pepper v Hart* (use of *Hansard* in statutory interpretation)
2003	Practice statement used to overrule the decision in *Caldwell* on recklessness in the criminal law

Figure 14.3 Key facts chart for the operation of judicial precedent in the House of Lords

case regarded the earlier decision in *Re Dowling* (1967) as being wrong. Despite this the Lords refused to overrule that earlier case, preferring to keep to the idea that certainty was the most important feature of precedent.

From the mid-1970s onwards the House of Lords showed a little more willingness to make use of the Practice Statement. For example, in *Miliangos v George Frank (Textiles) Ltd* (1976) the House of Lords used the Practice Statement to overrule a previous judgment that damages could only be awarded in sterling. Another major case was *Pepper v Hart* (1993) where the previous ban on the use of *Hansard* in statutory interpretation was overruled.

14.3.3 The Practice Statement in criminal law

The Practice Statement stressed that criminal law needs to be certain, so it was not surprising that the House of Lords did not rush to overrule any judgments in criminal cases. The first use in a criminal case was in *R v Shivpuri* (1986) which overruled the decision in *Anderton v Ryan* (1985)

on attempts to do the impossible. The interesting point was that the decision in *Anderton* had been made less than a year before, but it had been severely criticised by academic lawyers. In *Shivpuri* Lord Bridge said:

 I am undeterred by the consideration that the decision in Anderton v Ryan was so recent. The Practice Statement is an effective abandonment of our pretension to infallibility. If a serious error embodied in a decision of this House has distorted the law, the sooner it is corrected the better.

In other words, the House of Lords recognised that they might sometimes make errors and the most important thing then was to put the law right. Where the Practice Statement was used to overrule a previous decision, that past case was then effectively ignored. The law is now that which is set out in the new case.

Another important case on the use of the Practice Statement in criminal law was *R v R and G* (2003).

R v R and G (2003)

R and G were boys aged 10 and 11. They had set fire to some paper in a dustbin at the back of some shops. This fire had spread to the shops and caused over a million pounds' worth of damage. The boys were convicted of criminal damage to the shops under the law in the case of *Caldwell* (1982). In *Caldwell*, the House of Lords had ruled that recklessness included the situation where the defendant had not realised the risk of his actions causing damage, but an ordinary careful person would have realised there was a risk. In *R v R and G*, the House of Lords held that this was the wrong test to use. The Law Lords overruled *Caldwell* and held that a defendant was only reckless if he realised that there is a risk of damage and went ahead and took that risk. The boys' convictions were quashed.

Activity

Read the following passage which comes from an extra explanatory note which was given to the press when the Practice Statement was issued and answer the questions below.

'The statement is one of great importance, although it should not be supposed that there will frequently be cases in which the House thinks it right not to follow their own precedent. An example of a case in which the House might think it right to depart from a precedent is where they consider that the earlier decision was influenced by the existence of conditions which no longer prevail, and that in modern conditions the law ought to be different.

One consequence of this change is of major importance. The relaxation of the rule of judicial precedent will enable the House of Lords to pay greater attention to judicial decisions reached in the superior courts of the Commonwealth, where they differ from earlier decisions of the House of Lords. That could be of great help in the development of our own law. The superior courts of many other countries are not rigidly bound by their own decisions and the change in the practice of the House of Lords will bring us more into line with them.'

Questions

1. Why was the Practice Statement of great importance?
2. Does the note suggest that the Practice Statement was likely to be used often?
3. Do you agree that 'in modern conditions the law ought to be different'? Give reasons and examples to support your answer.
4. Why should the House of Lords (now the Supreme Court) want to consider decisions from Commonwealth countries? What authority do such decisions have in the English legal system?

14.3.4 The Supreme Court

When the Supreme Court replaced the House of Lords in 2009, the Practice Direction was considered to be part of the established jurisprudence relating to appeals. This meant that it was transferred to the Supreme Court under s 40 of the Constitutional Reform Act 2005.

In *Austin v London Borough of Southwark* (2010), which was about tenancy law, the Supreme Court confirmed that the Practice Statement still applied. However, they did not use it to depart from an earlier decision as they took the view that certainty in tenancy law was important.

14.4 The Court of Appeal

As already stated there are two divisions of this court (the Civil Division and the Criminal Division) and the rules for precedent are not quite the same in these two divisions.

14.4.1 Decisions of courts above it

Both divisions of the Court of Appeal are bound by decisions of the European Court of Justice and the Supreme Court. This is true even though there have been attempts in the past, mainly by Lord Denning, to argue that the Court of Appeal should not be bound by the then House of Lords. In *Broome v Cassell & Co Ltd* (1971) Lord Denning refused to follow the earlier decision of the House of Lords in *Rookes v Barnard* (1964) on the circumstances in which exemplary damages could be awarded.

Again, in the cases of *Schorsch Meier GmbH v Henning* (1975) and *Miliangos v George Frank (Textiles) Ltd* (1976) the Court of Appeal refused to follow a decision of the House of Lords in *Havana Railways* (1961) which said that damages could only be awarded in sterling (English money). Lord Denning's argument for refusing to follow the House of Lords' decision was that the economic climate of the world had changed, and sterling was no longer a stable currency; there were some situations in which justice could only be done by awarding damages in another currency. The case of *Schorsch Meier GmbH v Henning* was not appealed to the House of Lords, but *Miliangos v George Frank (Textiles) Ltd* did go on

appeal to the Lords, where it was pointed out that the Court of Appeal had no right to ignore or overrule decisions of the House of Lords. The more unusual feature of *Miliangos* was that the House of Lords then used the Practice Statement to overrule its own decision in *Havana Railways*.

Comment

Should the Court of Appeal have to follow Supreme Court/House of Lords' decisions?

The main argument in favour of the Court of Appeal being able to ignore Supreme Court/House of Lords' decisions is that very few cases reach the Supreme Court, so that if there is an error in the law it may take years before a suitable case is appealed all the way to that court. The cases of *Schorsch Meier* and *Miliangos* illustrate the potential for injustice if there had not been an appeal to the House of Lords.

What would have happened if the Court of Appeal in *Schorsch Meier* had decided that it had to follow the House of Lords' decision in *Havana Railways?* It is quite possible that the later case of *Miliangos* would not have even been appealed to the Court of Appeal. After all, why waste money on an appeal when there have been previous cases in both the Court of Appeal and the House of Lords ruling on that point of law? The law would have been regarded as fixed and it might never have been changed.

On the other hand, if the Court of Appeal could overrule the House of Lords (now the Supreme Court), the system of precedent would break down and the law would become uncertain. There would be two conflicting precedents for lower courts to choose from. This would make it difficult for the judge in the lower court. It would also make the law so uncertain that it would be difficult for lawyers to advise clients on the law. However, since the case of *Miliangos*, there has been no further challenge by the Court of Appeal to this basic idea (in our system of judicial precedent) that lower courts must follow decisions of courts above them in the hierarchy.

14.4.2 Human rights cases

Section 2(1)(a) of the Human Rights Act 1998 states that courts must take into account any judgment or decision of the European Court of Human Rights. In the case of *Re Medicaments (No 2), Director General of Fair Trading v Proprietary Association of Great Britain* (2001), the Court of Appeal refused to follow the decision of the House of Lords in *R v Gough* (1993) because it was slightly different to decisions of the European Court of Human Rights.

In *Kay v Lambeth LBC* (2006), the House of Lords pointed out that lower courts in the hierarchy were not strictly required to follow rulings of the European Court of Human Rights. This was because lower courts were bound to follow rulings of superior courts in our domestic court hierarchy.

However, the House of Lords also stated that it was unlawful for domestic courts to act in a way that was incompatible with a Convention right. So, in exceptional cases lower courts might be obliged to follow a ruling of the European Court of Human Rights rather than a ruling by a court above them in the domestic hierarchy.

14.4.3 The Court of Appeal and its own decisions

The first rule is that decisions by one division of the Court of Appeal will not bind the other division. However, within each division, decisions are normally binding, especially for the Civil Division. This rule comes from the case of *Young v Bristol Aeroplane Co Ltd* (1944) and the only exceptions allowed by that case are:

- Where there are conflicting decisions in past Court of Appeal cases, the court can choose which one it will follow and which it will reject.
- Where there is a decision of the Supreme Court/House of Lords which effectively overrules a Court of Appeal decision, the Court of Appeal must follow the decision of the Supreme Court/House of Lords.
- Where the decision was made *per incuriam*, that is carelessly or by mistake because a relevant Act of Parliament or other regulation has not been considered by the court.

The rule in *Young's case* was confirmed in *Davis v Johnson* (1979). The Court of Appeal refused to follow a decision made only days earlier regarding the interpretation of the Domestic Violence and Matrimonial Proceedings Act 1976. The case went to the House of Lords on appeal where the Law Lords, despite agreeing with the actual interpretation of the law, ruled that the Court of Appeal had to follow its own previous decisions and said that they 'expressly, unequivocally and unanimously reaffirmed the rule in *Young v Bristol Aeroplane*'.

Since this case the Court of Appeal has not challenged the rule in *Young's* case, though it has made some use of the *per incuriam* exception allowed by *Young's* case. For example in *Williams v Fawcett* (1986) the Court refused to follow previous decisions because these had been based on a misunderstanding of the County Court rules dealing with procedure for committing to prison those who break court undertakings. In *Rickards v Rickards* (1989) the court refused to follow a case it had decided in 1981. This was because of the fact that, in the previous case, it had misunderstood the effect of a House of Lords' decision. Even though the court did not follow its own previous decision Lord Donaldson said that it would only be in 'rare and exceptional cases' that the Court of Appeal would be justified in refusing to follow a previous decision. *Rickards v Rickards* was considered a 'rare and exceptional' case because the mistake was over the critical point of whether the court had power to hear that particular type of case. Also it was very unlikely that the case would be appealed to the House of Lords.

Activity

Read the following comments by Lord Scarman in his judgment in *Tiverton Estates Ltd v Wearwell Ltd* (1975) and answer the questions below.

'The Court of Appeal occupies a central, but intermediate position in our legal system. To a large extent, the consistency and certainty of the law depend upon it ... If, therefore, one division of the court should refuse to follow another because it believed the other's decision to be wrong, there would be a risk of confusion and doubt arising where there should be consistency and certainty.

The appropriate forum for the correction of the Court of Appeal's errors is the House of Lords, where the decision will at least have the merit of being final and binding, subject only to the House's power to review its own decisions. The House of Lords as the court of last resort needs this power of review; it does not follow that an intermediate court needs it.'

Questions

1. Why did Lord Scarman describe the Court of Appeal as occupying 'a central but intermediate position'?

2. Do you agree with his view that there would be a 'risk of confusion and doubt' if the Court of Appeal was not obliged to follow its own past decisions?

3. Describe the situations in which the Court of Appeal may refuse to follow its own past decisions.

4. Why does the House of Lords (now the Supreme Court) need the power of review?

Key facts

General rules for Court of Appeal	Comment
Bound by European Court of Justice	Since 1972 all courts in England and Wales are bound by the European Court of Justice.
Bound by Supreme Court and the former House of Lords	This is because the Supreme Court is above the Court of Appeal in the court hierarchy. Also necessary for certainty in the law. Court of Appeal tried to challenge this rule in *Broome v Cassell* (1971) and also in *Miliangos* (1976). The House of Lords rejected this challenge. The Court of Appeal must follow decisions of the Supreme Court/House of Lords.
Bound by its own past decisions	Decided by the Court of Appeal in *Young's* case (1944) though there are minor exceptions (see below). In *Davis v Johnson* (1979) the Court of Appeal tried to challenge this rule but the House of Lords confirmed that the Court of Appeal had to follow its own previous decisions.

Exceptions	Comment
Exceptions in *Young's* case	Court of Appeal need not follow its own previous decisions where: ● there are conflicting past decisions ● there is a Supreme Court/House of Lords' decision which effectively overrules the Court of Appeal decision ● the decision was made *per incuriam* (in error).
Limitation of *per incuriam*	Only used in 'rare and exceptional cases' (*Rickards v Rickards* (1989)).
Special exception for the Criminal Division	If the law has been 'misapplied or the misunderstood' (*R v Gould* (1968)).

Figure 14.4 Key facts chart for the Court of Appeal and the doctrine of precedent

14.4.4 The Court of Appeal (Criminal Division)

The Criminal Division, as well as using the exceptions from *Young's* case, can also refuse to follow a past decision of its own if the law has been 'misapplied or misunderstood'. This extra exception arises because in criminal cases people's liberty is involved. This idea was recognised in *R v Taylor* (1950). The same point was made in *R v Gould* (1968). Also in *R v Spencer* (1985) the judges said that there should not in general be any difference in the way that precedent was followed in the Criminal Division and in the Civil Division, 'save that we must remember that we may be dealing with the liberty of the subject and if a departure from authority is necessary in the interests of justice to an appellant, then this court should not shrink from so acting'.

14.5 Distinguishing, overruling and reversing

14.5.1 Distinguishing

This is a method which can be used by a judge to avoid following a past decision which he would otherwise have to follow. It means that the judge finds that the material facts of the case he is deciding are sufficiently different for him to draw a distinction between the present case and the previous precedent. He is not then bound by the previous case.

Two cases demonstrating this process are *Balfour v Balfour* (1919) and *Merritt v Merritt* (1971). Both cases involved a wife making a claim against her husband for breach of contract.

14.5.2 Overruling

This is where a court in a later case states that the legal rule decided in an earlier case is wrong. Overruling may occur when a higher court

---

Balfour v Balfour (1919)

The husband worked abroad. After they had been back in England for a period of leave, the wife was too ill to return with her husband. He agreed to pay her a certain amount of money each month while they were apart. He did not pay and she made a claim for the money. It was decided that the claim could not succeed because there was no intention to create legal relations; there was merely a domestic arrangement between a husband and wife and so there was no legally binding contract.

Merritt v Merritt (1971).

The husband and wife separated. They made a written agreement that the husband would pay the wife £40 a month and the wife would pay the mortgage. Also when the mortgage was paid off, the husband would transfer his share of the house to the wife. This second case was successful because the court held that the facts of the two cases were sufficiently different in that, although the parties were husband and wife, the agreement was made after they had separated. Furthermore, the agreement was made in writing. This distinguished the case from *Balfour*; the agreement in *Merritt* was not just a domestic arrangement but meant as a legally enforceable contract.

overrules a decision made in an earlier case by a lower court, for example, the Supreme Court overruling a decision of the Court of Appeal. It can also occur where the European Court of Justice overrules a past decision it has made; or when the Supreme Court overrules a past decision of its own.

14.5.3 Reversing

This is where a court higher up in the hierarchy overturns the decision of a lower court on appeal in the same case. For example, the Court of Appeal may disagree with the legal ruling of the High Court and come to a different view of the law; in this situation they reverse the decision made by the High Court.

Key facts

Concept	Definition	Comment
stare decisis	Stand by what has been decided	Follow the law decided in previous cases for certainty and fairness
ratio decidendi	Reason for deciding	The part of the judgment which creates the law
obiter dicta	Others things said	The other parts of the judgment – these do not create law
binding precedent	A previous decision which has to be followed	Decisions of higher courts bind lower courts
persuasive precedent	A previous decision which does not have to be followed	The court may be 'persuaded' that the same legal decision should be made
original precedent	A decision in a case where there is no previous legal decision or law for the judge to use	This leads to judges 'making' law
distinguishing	A method of avoiding a previous decision because facts in the present case are different	e.g. *Balfour v Balfour* not followed in *Merritt v Merritt*
overruling	A decision which states that a legal rule in an earlier case is wrong	e.g. in *Pepper v Hart* the House of Lords overruled *Davis v Johnson* on the use of *Hansard*
reversing	Where a higher court in the same case overturns the decision of the lower court	This can only happen if there is an appeal in the case

Figure 14.5 Key facts chart for Precedent and Acts of Parliament

14.6 Judicial law-making

Although there used to be a school of thought that judges did not actually 'make' new law but merely declared what the law had always been, today it is well recognised that judges do use precedent to create new law and to extend old principles. There are many areas of law which owe their existence to decisions by the judges.

Law of contract

Nearly all the main rules which govern the formation of contracts come from decided cases. Many of the decisions were made in the nineteenth century, but they still affect the law today.

Tort of negligence

The law of negligence in the law of tort is another major area which has been developed and refined by judicial decisions. An important starting point in this area of law was the case of *Donoghue v Stevenson* (1932) in which the House of Lords, when recognising that a manufacturer owed a duty of care to the 'ultimate consumer', created what is known as the 'neighbour test'. Lord Atkin in his judgment in the case said: 'You must take reasonable care to avoid acts or omissions which you can reasonably foresee would be likely to injure your neighbour.'

This concept has been applied by judges in several different situations, so that the tort of negligence has developed into a major tort. There have also been major developments in case law on liability for nervous shock where there has been negligence. The House of Lords laid down the guidelines for this area of law in the case of *Alcock v Chief Constable of South Yorkshire* (1991) which involved claims made by people who had lost relatives in the Hillsborough tragedy.

Criminal law

In the criminal law the judges have played a major role in developing the law on intention. For example, it is only because of judicial decisions that the intention for murder covers not only the intention to kill but also the intention to cause grievous bodily harm. Judicial decisions have also effectively created new crimes, as in *Shaw v DPP* (1962) which created the offence of conspiracy to corrupt public morals and *R v R* (1991) when it was decided that rape within marriage could be a crime.

However, there have been cases in which the House of Lords has refused to change the law, saying that such a change should only be made by Parliament. This happened in *C v DPP* (1995) when it refused to abolish the presumption that children between 10 and 14 were incapable of having the necessary intention to commit a crime. (This presumption meant that there always had to be evidence that the child knew he or she was doing something which was seriously wrong.) In fact the Government did change the law later in the Crime and Disorder Act 1998.

14.7 Precedent and Acts of Parliament

Although judges can and do make law, precedent is subordinate to statute law, delegated legislation and European regulations. This means that if (for example) an Act of Parliament is passed and that Act contains a provision which contradicts a previously decided case, that case decision will cease to have effect; the Act of Parliament is now the law on that point. This happened when Parliament passed the Law Reform (Year and a Day Rule) Act in 1996. Up to then judicial decisions meant that a person could only be charged with murder or manslaughter if the victim died within a year and a day of receiving his injuries. The Act enacted that there was no time limit, and a person could be guilty even if the victim died several years later, so cases after 1996 follow the Act and not the old judicial decisions.

Comment

Should judges make law?

It is argued that it is wrong for judges to make law. Their job is to apply the law, while it is for Parliament to make the law. Parliament is elected to do this but judges are not. This means that law-making by judges is undemocratic.

But, in reality judges have to make law in some situations. The first is where a case involves a legal point which has never been decided before. As there is no law on it, the judge in the case has to make a decision. After all, the parties in the case would not want the judge to refuse to deal with the case; they want the matter to be decided.

The second area is more controversial. This is where judges overrule old cases and in doing so create new law. It is important for the law to be updated in this way. Law for the twenty-first century needs to be based on today's society and values. Law decided 100 years or more ago may no longer be suitable. Ideally, Parliament should reform the law, but Parliament is sometimes slow to do this. If judges never overruled old cases, then the law might be 'out of date'.

An example of this is the case of *R v R* (1991). In this case a man was charged with raping his wife. The point the court had to decide was whether, by being married, a woman automatically consented to sex with her husband and could never say 'no'. The old law dated back to 1736 when it was said that 'by their mutual matrimonial consent the wife hath given up her herself in this kind to her husband, which she cannot retract'. In other words, once married, a woman was always assumed to consent and could not go back on this. This was still held to be the law in *R v Miller* (1954), even though the wife had already started divorce proceedings. Parliament had not done anything to reform this law.

So, when the case of *R v R* came before the courts, the judges had to decide whether to follow the old law, or whether they should change the law to match the ideas of the late twentieth century. In the House of Lords, the judges pointed out that 'the status of women and the status of a married woman in our law have changed quite dramatically. A husband and wife are now for all practical purposes equal partners in marriage'. As a result it was decided that if a wife did not consent to sex then her husband could be guilty of rape. The House of Lords stated that the common law (judge-made law) 'is capable of evolving in the light of changing social, economic and cultural developments'. This clearly recognised that judges in the House of Lords (now the Supreme Court) can, and will, change the law if they think it necessary.

14.8 Advantages and disadvantages of precedent

As can be seen from the previous sections there are both advantages and disadvantages to the way in which judicial precedent operates in England and Wales. In fact it could be said that every advantage has a corresponding disadvantage.

14.8.1 Advantages

The main advantages are:

1. Certainty
   Because the courts follow past decisions, people know what the law is and how it is likely to be applied in their case; it allows lawyers to advise clients on the likely outcome of cases; it also allows people to operate their businesses knowing that financial and other arrangements they make are recognised by law. The House of Lords' Practice Statement pointed out how important certainty is.

2. Consistency and fairness in the law
It is seen as just and fair that similar cases should be decided in a similar way, just as in any sport it is seen as fair that the rules of the game apply equally to each side. The law must be consistent if it is to be credible.

3. Precision
As the principles of law are set out in actual cases the law becomes very precise; it is well illustrated and gradually builds up through the different variations of facts in the cases that come before the courts.

4. Flexibility
There is room for the law to change as the Supreme Court can overrule its own previous decisions. The ability to distinguish cases also gives all courts some freedom to avoid past decisions and develop the law. However, the system could be made more flexible if the English courts adopt the same attitude to precedent as in some other countries. For example, in the United States of America a previous precedent is likely to be ignored if it fails to meet with academic approval. In other words, if there is considerable criticism of the decision by leading academic lawyers, judges in later cases are likely to take note of that criticism and rule differently. This has happened in England in the case of *R v Shivpuri* (1986), but this was a rare happening, while in America it occurs more frequently.

5. Time-saving
Precedent can be considered a useful time-saving device. Where a principle has been established, cases with similar facts are unlikely to go through the lengthy process of litigation.

The main advantages have been summed up very neatly as follows:

> The main advantages of the precedent system are said to be certainty, precision and flexibility. Legal certainty is achieved in theory at least, in that if the legal problem raised has been solved before, the judge is bound to adopt that solution. Precision is achieved by the sheer volume of reported cases containing solutions to innumerable factual situations. No code or statute could ever contain as much.
>
> Flexibility is achieved by the possibility of decisions being overruled and by the possibility of distinguishing and confining the operation of decisions which appear unsound.

14.8.2 Disadvantages

However, there are disadvantages as follows:

1. Rigidity
The fact that lower courts have to follow decisions of higher courts, together with the fact that the Court of Appeal has to follow its own past decisions, can make the law inflexible so that bad decisions made in the past may be perpetuated. There is the added problem that so few cases go to the Supreme Court. Change in the law will only take place if parties have the courage, the persistence and the money to appeal their case.

2. Complexity
Since there are over half a million reported cases it is not easy to find all the relevant case law, even with computerised databases. Another problem is in the judgments themselves, which are often very long with no clear distinction between comments and the reasons for the decision. This makes it difficult in some cases to extract the *ratio decidendi*; indeed in *Dodd's Case* (1973) the judges in the Court of Appeal said they were unable to find the *ratio* in a decision of the House of Lords.

3. Illogical distinctions
The use of distinguishing to avoid past decisions can lead to 'hair-splitting' so that

some areas of the law have become very complex. The differences between some cases may be very small and appear illogical.

4. Slowness of growth

   Judges are well aware that some areas of the law are unclear or in need of reform, but they cannot make a decision unless there is a case before the courts to be decided. This is one of the criticisms of the need for the Court of Appeal to follow its own previous decisions, as only about 50 cases go to the Supreme Court every year. Also, there may be a long wait for a suitable case to be appealed as far as the Supreme Court.

14.9 Law reporting

In order to follow past decisions there must be an accurate record of what those decisions were. Written reports have existed in England and Wales since the thirteenth century, but many of the early reports were very brief and, it is thought, not always accurate. The earliest reports from about 1275 to 1535 were called Year Books, and contained short reports of cases, usually written in French. From 1535 to 1865 cases were reported by individuals who made a business out of selling the reports to lawyers. The detail and accuracy of these reports varied

enormously. However, some are still occasionally used today.

In 1865 the Incorporated Council of Law Reporting was set up – this was controlled by the courts. Reports became accurate, with the judgment usually noted down word for word. This accuracy of reports was one of the factors in the development of the strict doctrine of precedent. These reports still exist and are published according to the court that the case took place in. For example, cases references abbreviated to 'Ch' stand for 'Chancery' and the case will have been decided in the Chancery Division; while 'QB' stands for 'Queen's Bench Division'.

There are also other well-established reports today, notably the All England series (abbreviated to 'All ER') and the Weekly Law Reports ('WLR'). Newspapers and journals also publish law reports, but these are often abbreviated versions in which the law reporter has tried to pick out the essential parts of the judgment.

14.9.1 Internet law reports

All High Court, Court of Appeal and Supreme Court cases are now reported on the internet. Some websites give the full report free, while others give summaries or an index of cases. There are also subscription sites which give a very comprehensive service of law reports.

 Internet Research

Search at least one website and find a recent law report. Some suggestions for websites are given below.

www.iclr.co.uk gives summaries of important cases.

www.supremecourt.gov.uk gives reports of Supreme Court cases.

www.bailii.org has cases from the Court of Appeal and below.

Examination Questions

Question 1. Read the source material below and answer parts (a) to (c) which follow.

Source A

The House of Lords has the power to overrule its own past decisions using the 1966 Practice Statement. The use of the Practice Statement is illustrated in the case of *A v Hoare* (2008). In this case the defendant was convicted of rape in 1989 and sent to prison. In 2004 he was released on licence and then won £7 million on the lottery. The claimant then sought to claim damages for the rape. Under the precedent decided in *Stubbings v Webb* (1993) the claimant would not be entitled to compensation because she had not started her claim in time. The House of Lords used the Practice Statement overruling *Stubbings v Webb* so as to give the courts flexibility in allowing cases to proceed in such circumstances.

The House of Lords' decision to overrule *Stubbings* does not come as a great surprise, the decision having been described as unbalanced by the Law Commission when reviewing this in 2001. It recommended a number of changes in this are. No steps were ever taken to implement any further legislation, perhaps, as Lord Hoffman suggests in the *Hoare* judgment, because the Commission's recommendations were not confined to the *Stubbings* inconsistency but proposed a completely new law. This has been a common problem for the Law Commission and its recommendations.

Extract adapted from
http:www.bevanbrittan.com/metis/article/
claims/col30/col30c_rick1.asp

Source B

The Law Commission was established in 1965 with the duty to keep the law under review. It has five full-time commissioners, all of whom are lawyers and are appointed by the Lord Chancellor. The Law Commission has made a significant impact on the development of the law but it has encountered many problems. One major issue involves the inconsistent implementation by Parliament of the Law Commission's proposals.

(a) With reference to Source A and other cases, describe the use of the Practice Statement. 15 marks

(b) Explain the power of the Supreme Court in the following situations:
 (i) A case similar to *A v Hoare* is about to be tried by the Supreme Court.
  5 marks
 (ii) The House of Lords is hearing an appeal in 1965. There is a previous precedent on this issue from the House of Lords in 1960. 5 marks
 (iii) A case comes before the Supreme Court. There is a previous decision by the Privy Council which conflicts with an earlier decision in the House of Lords.
  5 marks

(c) With reference to Source A and Source B and your own knowledge:
 (i) Describe the role of the Law Commission. 15 marks
 (ii) Discuss the problems encountered by the Law Commission in fulfilling its role. 15 marks

OCR G152 June 2010

Examination Questions

Question 2. Read the source material below and answer parts (a) to (c) which follow.

Source A

Stare decisis means to stand by what has been decided. It is central to the operation of the system of binding precedent. Through the hierarchy of the courts, the concept of *stare decisis* is reinforced in that higher courts should bind lower courts. However, strict adherence to this principle can cause problems for certain courts, like the Court of Appeal. By not allowing greater flexibility, it stops the development of the law as it cannot be adapted to social change quickly as it was in *Schorsch Meier*.

Source B

Should precedent created by the House of Lords (Supreme Court) be followed by the Court of Appeal? This was considered by Lord Denning in *Schorsch Meier GmbH v Henin* [1975]. On this occasion, the Court of Appeal was split. Lord Denning and Foster J agreed that a 1961 decision of the House of Lords had run its course and should not be followed and decided they would not follow it. Lawton J disagreed because he argued that the Court of Appeal does not have the power to ignore the House of Lords. This is because the Court of Appeal is bound by the House of Lords. The majority decision of the Court of Appeal, therefore, was to refuse to follow the decision of the House of Lords. This case was not appealed to the House of Lords.

The House of Lords soon had an opportunity to comment on this issue in a case named *Miliangos v George Frank (Textiles) Ltd* [1976]. The Court of Appeal in Miliangos chose to follow its own previous decision and not the relevant House of Lords precedent. When the case went before the House of Lords, their Lordships agreed to overrule their own previous decision but took the opportunity to criticise Lord Denning's approach in the *Schorsch Meier* case for ignoring the doctrine of *stare decisis*.

It is interesting to note Lord Greene's statement in *Young v Bristol Aeroplane Company Ltd* [1944] that the Court of Appeal is bound by its own previous decisions. The decision in *Young* allows the Court of Appeal to depart from its previous decisions only in three situations. Some argue that this is too rigid and restricts the proper development of the law, whilst others counter that this creates certainty within the legal system.

Adapted from '*Learning Legal Rules*', Holland and Webb, 7th edition

(a) Source A at line 1 refers to *stare decisis*

Describe the concept of *stare decicis* using the sources and other cases to illustrate your answer.   15 marks

(b) Source B refers to the powers of the Court of Appeal. Explain whether or not the Court of Appeal can depart from the previous decision(s) in each of the following situations using source B and your knowledge:

(i) A case concerning a medical operation is being heard by the Court of Appeal (Criminal Division). Two years earlier, a similar case was heard by the Court of Appeal (Civil Division).
                                    5 marks

(ii) A case concerning damages is being heard by the Court of Appeal. The only previous precedent was set by the Supreme Court.   5 marks

Examination Questions

(iii) A case involving breach of contract is being heard by the Court of Appeal (Civil Division). There are two conflicting previous precedents. These were set by the Court of Appeal and the Supreme Court. **5 marks**

(c) With reference to sources A and B:

(i) Describe the powers of the Court of Appeal within the doctrine of precedent using cases to illustrate your answer. **15 marks**

(ii) Discuss whether or not the powers of the Court of Appeal within the doctrine of precedent should be extended. **15 marks**

OCR G152 June 2012

Exam tips

As you can see from the question above, the tasks you are being asked to do are very different to those in G151 and you must use a range of skills to do well. First, identify which is the best question for you – read all parts of both questions and then make a considered decision. Do not rush at the first question and then discover later that you could have done a better job if you had answered the question on the other topic.

Once you have made your choice, read all the questions again and be sure you understand the focus they require in your response. Use your highlighter and go through the source material in detail. You can, and should, use the material to support your answer by picking out key words and phrases or linking your remarks to the appropriate lines in the material, but it does not mean that you should rewrite large chunks of the material.

When you are answering a question pay particular attention to what the question asks you to do: part (a) will require you to 'describe' – this means you need to give factual information; in part (b) you need to 'explain' – this means showing how you can apply your knowledge; and in part (c) (ii) you must 'discuss' – this means looking at the particular area you are given from more than one perspective.

In a precedent question the key to doing well is to use cases – after all, precedent is all about law evolved by judges through the cases. It is a big topic and the question will often focus on just one aspect – it might be to consider a particular court or specific tools the courts have at their disposal. Whatever the question you need to have the discipline to use the correct material rather than simply writing everything you know.

Finally, it is worth noting that this paper can focus on more than one source of law in a single question. Even though precedent is a sizeable topic in its own right, you might have to know about another source of law as well to score top marks. If this happens you need to think carefully whether this is the best question for you to do – an even performance across all the questions usually brings higher marks than doing one or two parts really well but having very little to say on others, especially if the parts you can't do well have a sizeable mark allocation.

Chapter 15

Acts of Parliament

I n today's world there is often a need for new law to meet new situations. Clearly, the method of judicial law-making through precedents is not suitable for major changes to the law, nor is it a sufficiently quick or efficient law-making method for a modern society. The other point to be made is that judges are not elected by the people and, in a democracy, the view is that laws should only be made by the elected representatives of society. So, today, the main legislative body in the United Kingdom is Parliament.

Laws passed by Parliament are known as Acts of Parliament or statutes, and this source of law is usually referred to as 'statute law'. About 60–70 Acts are passed each year. In addition to Parliament as a whole enacting law, power is delegated to Government Ministers and their departments to make detailed rules and regulations, which supplement Acts of Parliament. These regulations are delegated legislation (see Chapter 16) and are called statutory instruments.

15.1 Parliament

Parliament consists of the House of Commons and the House of Lords. Under the normal procedure both Houses must vote in favour of a Bill before it can become a new Act of Parliament.

15.1.1 The House of Commons

The people who sit in the House of Commons are referred to as Members of Parliament (MPs). These members of the House of Commons are elected by the public, with the country being divided into constituencies and each of these returning one

Member of Parliament (MP). Under the Fixed-term Parliament Act 2011, there must be a General Election every five years. In addition, there may be individual by-elections in constituencies where the MP has died or retired during the current session of Parliament. The Government of the day is formed by the political party which has a majority in the House of Commons.

15.1.2 The House of Lords

At the end of 2010 the House of Lords consisted of:

- about 90 hereditary peers
- about 650 life peers
- the most senior bishops in the Church of England.

The total number in the House of Lords is about 760, of which about 170 are women. Note that until 2009, the 12 most senior judges used to sit in the House of Lords. They no longer do so. They are now separate from Parliament and sit as the Supreme Court (see Chapter 9).

Originally most of the members of the House of Lords were hereditary peers. During the twentieth century the awarding of a title for life (a life peerage) became more common. The Prime Minister nominated people who should receive a title for their lifetime, but this title would not pass on to their children. The title was then awarded by the Monarch. In this way people who had served the country and were thought to be suitable members of the House of Lords were able to bring their expertise to the House. Most life peerages were given to former politicians who had retired from the House of Commons. For example, Margaret Thatcher, who had been Prime Minister in the 1980s, was made a life peer.

15.1.3 Reform of the House of Lords

Before 1999, there were over 1,100 members of the House of Lords, of whom 750 were hereditary peers. The Labour Government decided that in a modern society an inherited title should not automatically allow someone to participate in

The Houses of Parliament

making law. They felt that some of the members should be elected and some should be nominated. To help decide exactly what reforms should be made, a Royal Commission (known as the Wakeham Commission) was set up to consider how members of the House of Lords should be selected. In the meantime the right of most of the hereditary peers to sit in the House of Lords was abolished in November 1999. Only 92 hereditary peers were allowed to continue to be members of the House of Lords.

The Wakeham Commission reported in 2000 and recommended that one-third of the House should be elected. Also, there should be a limit on the system of political patronage whereby the Prime Minister nominates people to the House of Lords. The Commission recommended that an independent House of Lords Appointments Commission should be able to reject poorly qualified nominees and also be able to appoint 'people's peers'.

The House of Lords Appointments Commission was set up in 2001 and the first 'people's peers' were appointed to the House of Lords. These were supposed to be ordinary people who had been recommended by other ordinary people. However, the list was mainly of already famous people, rather than 'Mr Joe Public'.

This was meant to be a temporary solution while the Government consulted on the final make-up of the House of Lords. However, there have been major disagreements about how many members of the House of Lords should be elected by the general public and how many should be nominated (and by whom). As a result the reform of the House of Lords has not been completed.

15.2 Influences on parliamentary law-making

15.2.1 The Government programme

When a government is formed, it will have a programme of reforms it wishes to carry out. These will have been set out in its party manifesto on which it asked people to vote for it in the General Election. Also, at the start of each parliamentary session, the Government announces (in the Queen's Speech) what particular laws it intends to introduce during that session. So most new legislation is likely to arise from government policy.

15.2.2 European Union law

However, there are other influences on what law is enacted: European Union law can lead to new Acts of Parliament which are passed in order to bring UK law in line with the European law. This may be to implement a specific European Regulation or Directive, as in the case of the Consumer Protection Act 1987, or because a decision of the European Court of Justice has shown that our law does not conform with the Treaty of Rome, as with the Sex Discrimination Act 1986. The effect of European law is considered in more detail in Chapter 18.

15.2.3 Other influences

Other outside influences include proposals for law reform put forward by law reform agencies, commissions or inquiries into the effectiveness of existing law. These law reform agencies are dealt with in detail in Chapter 19. In addition specific events may also play a role in formulating the law. A particularly tragic example was the massacre in March 1996 of 16 young children and their teacher in Dunblane by a lone gunman. After this there was an inquiry into the laws on gun-ownership. By March 1997 Parliament passed the Firearms (Amendment) Act 1997 banning private ownership of most handguns.

Another major example of an event leading to new law was the terrorist attack on the World Trade Center in New York in September 2001. (This is often referred to as '9/11'.) Following this the UK Parliament passed the Anti-Terrorism, Crime and Security Act 2001.

Pressure groups

Pressure groups may also cause the Government to reconsider the law on certain areas. A clear example of the Government bowing to public opinion and the efforts of pressure groups was the introduction of the Disability Discrimination Act 1995. This Act gave disabled people certain rights in relation to employment. It also stated that they should have access to shops and hotels and other services.

More recently, the Government bowed to public opinion and the efforts of the pressure group, the League against Cruel Sports, and passed the Hunting Act 2004 which banned hunting foxes with dogs. In 2007 strict laws against smoking in public places were introduced because of public and medical opinion and the efforts of ASH, the anti-smoking pressure group.

15.3 The pre-legislative process

On major matters a Green Paper may be issued by the Minister with responsibility for that matter. A Green Paper is a consultative document on a topic in which the Government's view is put forward with proposals for law reform. Interested parties are then invited to send comments to the relevant government department, so that a full consideration of all sides can be made and necessary changes made to the Government's proposals. Following this the Government will publish a White Paper with its firm proposals for new law.

Activity

Read the following article and answer the questions below.

Judge reprieves Dempsey, the harmless pit bull

A High Court judge, who reprieved a pit bull terrier from death row yesterday, savaged the Dangerous Dogs Act (1991) which he said would have sent a 'perfectly inoffensive animal to the gas chamber'.

Dempsey, dubbed Britain's most expensive dog after a long legal battle to save her, will be returned to her overjoyed owner after Lord Justice Staughton and Mr Justice Rougier quashed a destruction order by Ealing Magistrates' Court in 1992.

Dempsey's only crime was being the wrong kind of dog, Judge Rougier said. Magistrates sentenced her to be destroyed after the nephew of her owner, Dianne Fanneran, took her muzzle off in public when she became ill, and she was spotted by a policeman.

Mr Justice Rougier said: 'It seems to me that, while acknowledging the need to protect the public ... the Dangerous Dogs Act bears all the hallmarks of an ill-thought-out piece of legislation, no doubt drafted in response to another pressure group ... '

The Act was rushed through in 1991 by the then Home Secretary, Kenneth Baker, after pit bull terriers attacked a man in Lincoln and a six-year-old girl in Bradford. It requires them to be put down unless they are neutered, tattooed, microchipped, registered, muzzled and kept on a lead in public.

Taken from an article by Clare Dyer in *The Guardian*, 23 November 1995
Copyright Guardian News & Media Ltd 1995

Questions

1. Why was the Dangerous Dogs Act 1991 passed?

2. Why was Dempsey in breach of the Act?

3. What did Mr Justice Rougier say about the Act?

4. How might this problem with the Act have been avoided by the Government when formulating the legislation?

Consultation before any new law is framed is valuable as it allows time for mature consideration. Governments have been criticised for sometimes responding in a 'knee-jerk' fashion to incidents and, as a result, rushing law through that has subsequently proved to be unworkable. This occurred with the Dangerous Dogs Act 1991.

15.4 Introducing an Act of Parliament

The great majority of Acts of Parliament are introduced by the Government – these are initially drafted by lawyers in the civil service who are known as Parliamentary Counsel to the Treasury. Instructions as to what is to be included and the effect the proposed law is intended to have, are given by the government department responsible for it.

15.4.1 Bills

When the proposed Act has been drafted it is published, and at this stage is called a Bill. It will only become an Act of Parliament if it successfully completes all the necessary stages in Parliament. Even at this early stage there are difficulties, as the draftsmen face problems in trying to frame the Bill. It has to be drawn up so that it represents the Government's wishes, while at the same time using correct legal wording so that there will not be any difficulties in the courts applying it. It must be unambiguous, precise and comprehensive. Achieving all of these is not easy, and there may be unforeseen problems with the language used, as discussed in Chapter 17. On top of this there is usually pressure on time, as the Government will have a timetable of when they wish to introduce the draft Bill into Parliament.

Public Bills

A public Bill involves matters of public policy which will affect either the whole country or a large section of it. Most Government Bills are in this category, for example the Constitutional Reform Act 2005, the Legal Services Act 2007, the Coroners and Justice Act 2009 and the Legal Aid, Sentencing and Punishment of Offenders Act 2012.

Private Bills

A small number of Bills are designed to pass a law which will affect only individual people or corporations. These do not affect the whole community. They are known as Private Bills. A recent example of such a Bill of this was the Whitehaven Harbour Bill which was passed by Parliament and is now the Whitehaven Harbour Act 2007. This transferred all rights and obligations in respect of the harbour from three separate companies to the Whitehaven Harbour Commissioners.

15.4.2 Private Members' Bills

Ballot

Bills can also be sponsored by individual MPs. The parliamentary process allows for a ballot each parliamentary session in which 20 private members are selected who can then take their turn in presenting a Bill to Parliament. The time for debate of Private Members' Bills is limited, usually only being debated on Fridays, so that only the first six or seven members in the ballot have a realistic chance of introducing a Bill on their chosen topic.

Relatively few Private Members' Bills become law, but there have been some important laws passed as the result of such Bills. A major example was the Abortion Act 1967 which legalised abortion in this country. More recent examples are the Marriage Act 1994, which was introduced by Giles Brandreth, the then MP for Chester. This allowed people to marry in any registered place, not only in Register Offices or religious buildings. Another example is the Household Waste Recycling Act 2003 which places local authorities under a duty to recycle waste.

Ten-minute rule

Backbenchers can also try to introduce a Bill through the 'ten-minute' rule, under which any MP can make a speech of up to ten minutes supporting the introduction of new legislation. This method is rarely successful unless there is no opposition to the Bill, but some Acts of Parliament have been introduced in this way; for example the Bail (Amendment) Act 1993 which gave the prosecution the right to appeal against the granting of bail to a defendant. Members of the House of Lords can also introduce Private Members' Bills.

15.5 The process in Parliament

In order to become an Act of Parliament, the Bill will usually have to be passed by both Houses of Parliament, and in each House there is a long and complex process (see Figure 15.1). A Bill may start in either the House of Commons or the House of Lords, with the exception of finance Bills which must start in the House of Commons. All Bills must go through the stages explained below:

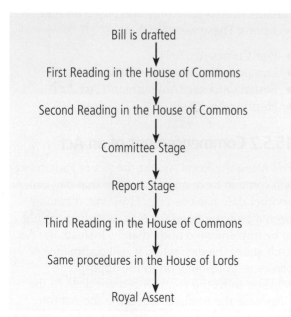

Bill is drafted

↓

First Reading in the House of Commons

↓

Second Reading in the House of Commons

↓

Committee Stage

↓

Report Stage

↓

Third Reading in the House of Commons

↓

Same procedures in the House of Lords

↓

Royal Assent

Figure 15.1 Passing an Act of Parliament, starting in the House of Commons

First Reading

This is a formal procedure where the name and main aims of the Bill are read out. Usually no discussion takes place.

Second Reading

This is the main debate on the whole Bill in which MPs debate the principles behind the Bill. The debate usually focuses on the main principles rather than the smaller details. Those MPs who wish to speak in the debate must catch the Speaker's eye, since the Speaker controls all debates and no one may speak without being called on by the Speaker. At the end of this a vote is taken; obviously there must be a majority in favour for the Bill to progress any further.

Committee Stage

At this stage a detailed examination of each clause of the Bill is undertaken by a committee of between 16 and 50 MPs. This is usually done by what is called a Standing Committee, which, contrary to its name, is a committee chosen specifically for that Bill. The membership of such a committee is decided 'having regard to the qualifications of those members nominated and to the composition of the House'. So, although the Government will have a majority, the opposition and minority parties are represented proportionately to the number of seats they have in the House of Commons. The members of Parliament nominated for each Standing Committee will usually be those with a special interest in, or knowledge of, the subject of the Bill which is being considered. For finance Bills the whole House will sit in committee.

Report Stage

At the Committee Stage amendments to various clauses in the Bill may have been voted on and passed, so this report stage is where the committee report back to the House on those amendments. (If there were no amendments at the Committee Stage, there will not be a 'Report'

@ Internet Research

Look to see what Bills are going through Parliament at the moment. You can find this at **www.parliament.uk.**

Try to find one Bill that is currently going through the House of Commons and a different Bill that is currently going through the House of Lords.

Stage – instead the Bill will go straight on to the Third Reading.) The amendments will be debated in the House and accepted or rejected. Further amendments may also be added. The Report Stage has been described as 'a useful safeguard against a small Committee amending a Bill against the wishes of the House, and a necessary opportunity for second thoughts'.

Third Reading

This is the final vote on the Bill. It is almost a formality since a Bill which has passed through all the stages above is unlikely to fail at this late stage. In fact in the House of Commons there will only be an actual further debate on the Bill as a whole if at least six MPs request it. However, in the House of Lords there may sometimes be amendments made at this stage.

The House of Lords

If the Bill started life in the House of Commons it is now passed to the House of Lords where it goes through the same five stages outlined above and, if the House of Lords makes amendments to the Bill, then it will go back to the House of Commons for it to consider those amendments. If the Bill started in the House of Lords then it passes to the House of Commons.

Royal Assent

The final stage is where the Monarch formally gives approval to the Bill and it then becomes an

Act of Parliament. This is now a formality and, under the Royal Assent Act 1967, the Monarch will not even have the text of the Bills to which she is assenting; she will only have the short title. The last time that a monarch refused assent was in 1707, when Queen Anne refused to assent to the Scottish Militia Bill.

15.5.1 The Parliament Acts 1911 and 1949

The power of the House of Lords to reject a Bill is limited by the Parliament Acts 1911 and 1949. These allow a Bill to become law even if the House of Lords rejects it, provided that the Bill is re-introduced into the House of Commons in the next session of Parliament and passes all the stages again there.

The principle behind the Parliament Acts is that the House of Lords is not an elected body, and its function is to refine and add to the law rather than oppose the will of the democratically elected House of Commons. In fact there have only been four occasions when this procedure has been used to bypass the House of Lords after they had voted against a Bill. Since 1949 the Parliament Acts have only been used on four occasions. These were for the:

- War Crimes Act 1991
- European Parliamentary Elections Act 1999
- Sexual Offences (Amendment) Act 2000
- Hunting Act 2004.

15.5.2 Commencement of an Act

Following the Royal Assent the Act of Parliament will come in force on midnight of that day, unless another date has been set. However, there has been a growing trend for Acts of Parliament not to be implemented immediately. Instead, the Act itself states the date when it will commence or passes responsibility on to the appropriate Minister to fix the commencement date. In the latter case the Minister will bring the Act into force by issuing a commencement order. This can cause problems of uncertainty, as it is difficult to

Key facts

Green Paper	Consultation document on possible new law
White Paper	Government's firm proposals for new law
First Reading	Formal introduction of Bill into the House of Commons
Second Reading	Main debate on Bill's principles
Committee Stage	Clause by clause consideration of the Bill by a select committee
Report Stage	Committee reports suggested amendments back to the House of Commons
Third Reading	Final debate on the Bill
Repeat of process in the House of Lords	All stages are repeated BUT if the House of Lords votes against the Bill, it can go back to the House of Commons and, under the Parliament Acts 1911 and 1949, become law if the House of Commons passes it for the second time (rare occurrence)
Royal Assent	A formality – normally Acts of Parliament come into force at midnight after receiving the Royal Assent

Figure 15.2 Key facts chart for the legislative process

discover which sections of an Act have been brought into force.

It may be that some sections or even a whole Act will never become law. An example of this is the Easter Act 1928, which was intended to fix the date of Easter Day. Although this Act passed all the necessary parliamentary stages, and was given the Royal Assent, it has never come into force.

It can be seen that with all these stages it usually takes several months for a Bill to be passed. However, there have been occasions where all parties have thought a new law is needed urgently and an Act has been passed in less than 24 hours. This happened with the Northern Ireland Bill in 1972.

15.5.3 Example of an Act

Figure 15.3 is a reproduction of the Law Reform (Year and a Day Rule) Act 1996. This shows what an Act of Parliament looks like. The name of the Act is given immediately under the Royal coat of arms and underneath the name '1996 CHAPTER 19' means that it was the nineteenth Act to be passed in 1996. Next follows a short statement or preamble about the purpose of the Act. Then there is a formal statement showing that the Act has been passed by both Houses of Parliament and received the Royal Assent; this is included in all Acts. After this comes the body of the Act, which is set out in sections; this is an unusually short Act as it has only three sections.

Section 1 abolishes the 'year and a day rule'. Note that the Act actually refers to it in those terms; this is because the rule was a part of the common law and was never written down in any statute. Section 2 sets out when the consent of the Attorney-General is needed before a prosecution can be started. The last section gives the name by which the Act may be cited and it also sets out that the Act does not apply to cases in which the incident which led to death occurred before the Act was passed. Section 3 is concerned with the commencement of the Act; this sets the

ELIZABETH II   c. 19

Law Reform (Year and a Day Rule) Act 1996

1996 CHAPTER 19

An Act to abolish the "year and a day rule" and, in consequence of its abolition, to impose a restriction on the institution in certain circumstances of proceedings for a fatal offence. [17th June 1996]

B E IT ENACTED by the Queen's most Excellent Majesty, by and with the advice and consent of the Lords Spiritual and Temporal, and Commons, in this present Parliament assembled, and by the authority of the same, as follows:—

1. The rule known as the "year and a day rule" (that is, the rule that, for the purposes of offences involving death and of suicide, an act or omission is conclusively presumed not to have caused a person's death if more than a year and a day elapsed before he died) is abolished for all purposes.

Abolition of "year and a day rule".

2.—(1) Proceedings to which this section applies may only be instituted by or with the consent of the Attorney General.

Restriction on institution of proceedings for a fatal offence.

(2) This section applies to proceedings against a person for a fatal offence if—

    (a) the injury alleged to have caused the death was sustained more than three years before the death occurred, or

    (b) the person has previously been convicted of an offence committed in circumstances alleged to be connected with the death.

(3) In subsection (2) "fatal offence" means—

    (a) murder, manslaughter, infanticide or any other offence of which one of the elements is causing a person's death, or

    (b) the offence of aiding, abetting, counselling or procuring a person's suicide.

2   c. **19**   *Law Reform (Year and a Day Rule) Act 1996*

(4) No provision that proceedings may be instituted only by or with the consent of the Director of Public Prosecutions shall apply to proceedings to which this section applies.

(5) In the application of this section to Northern Ireland—

(a) the reference in subsection (1) to the Attorney General is to the Attorney General for Northern Ireland, and

(b) the reference in subsection (4) to the Director of Public Prosecutions is to the Director of Public Prosecutions for Northern Ireland.

Short title, commencement and extent.

3.—(1) This Act may be cited as the Law Reform (Year and a Day Rule) Act 1996.

(2) Section 1 does not affect the continued application of the rule referred to in that section to a case where the act or omission (or the last of the acts or omissions) which caused the death occurred before the day on which this Act is passed.

(3) Section 2 does not come into force until the end of the period of two months beginning with the day on which this Act is passed; but that section applies to the institution of proceedings after the end of that period in any case where the death occurred during that period (as well as in any case where the death occurred after the end of that period).

(4) This Act extends to England and Wales and Northern Ireland.

© Crown copyright 1996

PRINTED IN THE UNITED KINGDOM BY MIKE LYNN
Controller and Chief Executive of Her Majesty's Stationery Office
and Queen's Printer of Acts of Parliament

Figure 15.3 The Law Reform (Year and a Day Rule) Act 1996

Self-Test Questions

1 What type of Paper may be issued by the Government before a new Bill is introduced into Parliament?
2 Who introduces the majority of Bills into Parliament?
3 By what two methods can a private MP introduce a Bill into Parliament?
4 Explain what is meant by a public Bill.
5 When a Bill is introduced into the House of Commons what stages does it have to pass before it goes to the House of Lords?
6 Which Acts limit the House of Lords' powers in respect of Bills?
7 Give two disadvantages of the Parliamentary system of law-making.

commencement date for s 2 at two months after the Act is passed. As s 1 is not specifically mentioned, the normal rule that an Act comes into effect on midnight of the date on which it receives the Royal Assent applies to that section.

Exam tips

An awareness of the forces that drive legislation and the process by which an idea can end up as an Act of Parliament is important, especially since we have an unwritten constitution.

The legislative process is a topic which lends itself to a flow chart format when you are revising and it is a good idea to have plenty of examples on which you can draw in response to a question on this area.

High marks come from being very clear on the different types of Bill, the range of sources that give rise to them and the ability to explain fully and clearly what happens at each stage of the process. This topic does not appear on exam papers very often but it is easy to manage and so it is a good topic to have tucked away, just in case. It could also link to another source and so it could be an important aid to a high score for you on this unit.

15.6 Criticisms of the legislative process

Many criticisms can be made about the legislative process. The Renton Committee in 1975 said there were four main categories of complaint:

1. The language used in many Acts was obscure and complex.

2. Acts were 'over-elaborate' because draftsmen tried to provide for every contingency.

3. The internal structure of many Acts was illogical with sections appearing to be out of sequence, making it difficult for people to find relevant sections.

4. There was a lack of clear connection between Acts, so that it was not easy to trace all the Acts on a given topic. In addition, the frequent practice of amending small parts of one Act by passing another increased the difficulty of finding out what the law was.

The Committee made 81 recommendations, but only about half of these have been fully implemented.

15.6.1 Lack of accessibility

Ideally, the laws of the land should be easily accessible to citizens but there are some major problems which create difficulties. As already mentioned, it is difficult to discover which Acts and/ or which sections have been brought into force.

An example of problems with knowing what sections are in force is the Criminal Justice Act 2003 which has 339 sections and several Schedules. Only 11 sections came into force when the Royal Assent was given. Some more came into force four weeks after the Royal Assent. Many of the other 300-plus sections have been brought into effect a few at a time over a period of time. Schedule 3, which concerned how certain cases would be transferred from the Magistrates' Courts to the Crown Court, was only brought into effect in 2012. However, some of the sections have still not been brought into effect.

Where sections are brought into effect at different times, it is difficult to know what the law is. This prevents law from being easily accessible.

@ Internet Research

Find the commencement section or schedule in an Act of Parliament.

This can be done on the internet at **www.legislation.gov.uk.** There is usually a list of contents at the start of an Act.

The Coroners and Justice Act 2009 is another example of where sections were brought into force at different times. In particular, the sections in regard to the partial defences to murder were not brought into effect until a year after the Act was passed. These sections redefined diminished responsibility, abolished the old defence of provocation and created a new partial defence, 'loss of control'.

15.6.2 Other problems

Many statutes are amended by later statutes so that it is necessary to read two or more Acts together to make sense of provisions. The law may also be added to by delegated legislation in the form of statutory instruments. All of this increases the difficulty of discovering the law that is actually in force.

The language used in Acts is not always easily understood and apart from the obvious difficulties this causes, it also results in many cases going to court. In fact about 75 per cent of cases heard by the Supreme Court/House of Lords each year involve disputes over the interpretation of Acts.

15.7 Parliamentary sovereignty

Parliamentary law is sovereign over other forms of law in England and Wales. This means that an Act of Parliament can completely overrule any custom, judicial precedent, delegated legislation or previous Act of Parliament. This is also referred to as parliamentary supremacy.

The concept of the sovereignty of parliamentary law is based on the idea of democratic law-making. A member of Parliament is elected by the voters in the constituency, so that in theory that MP is participating in the legislative process on the behalf of those voters. However, this is a very simplistic view since:

- MPs usually vote on party lines rather than how their particular constituents wish.
- Many MPs are elected by only a very small majority and if there were several candidates in the election, it may well be that the MP was

only actually voted for by about 30 per cent or even fewer of the voters.
- Parliamentary elections only have to take place once every five years, so that an MP who votes against the wishes of his constituents is not immediately replaced.

In addition, the ideal concept of democracy is lost because much of the drafting of parliamentary law is done by civil servants who are not elected. Finally, there is the point that the House of Lords is not an elected body.

15.7.1 Definition of parliamentary supremacy

The most widely recognised definition of parliamentary supremacy was given by A.V. Dicey in the nineteenth century. He made three main points:

1. Parliament can legislate on any subject-matter.
2. No Parliament can be bound by any previous Parliament, nor can a Parliament pass any Act that will bind a later Parliament.
3. No other body has the right to override or set aside an Act of Parliament.

Legislating on any subject-matter

There are no limits on what Parliament can make laws about. It can make any law it wants. For example, Parliament has changed the rule on who should succeed to the throne. This was in 1700, when Parliament passed the Act of Settlement which stated that the children of King James II (who were the direct line of the monarchy) could not succeed to the throne.

Parliament can also change its own powers. It did this with the Parliament Acts 1911 and 1949, which placed limits on the right of the House of Lords to block a Bill by voting against it (see section 15.5.1).

Cannot bind successor

Each new Parliament should be free to make or change what laws it wishes. Parliament cannot be bound by a law made by a previous Parliament, and can repeal any previous Act of Parliament.

There are, however, some laws that have become such an important part of the British constitution that they cannot realistically be repealed. For example, the Act of Settlement in 1700 changed the line of succession to the throne. It affected who was entitled to become king or queen. Realistically, after 300 years, this cannot now be repealed.

There are other modern limitations which have been self-imposed by Parliament. These are dealt with in section 15.7.2 below.

Cannot be overruled by others

This rule is adhered to, even if the Act of Parliament may have been passed because of incorrect information. This was shown by *British Railways Board v Pickin* (1974). A private Act of Parliament, the British Railways Act 1968, was enacted by Parliament. *Pickin* challenged the Act on the basis that the British Railways Board had fraudulently concealed certain matters from Parliament. This alleged fraud had led to Parliament passing the Act which had the effect of depriving *Pickin* of his land or proprietary rights. The action was struck out because no court is entitled to go behind an Act once it has been passed. A challenge cannot be made to an Act of Parliament even if there was fraud.

15.7.2 Limitations on parliamentary sovereignty

There are now some limitations on Parliament's sovereignty, but all these limits have been self-imposed by previous Parliaments. The main limitations are through:

● membership of the European Union
● the effect of the Human Rights Act 1998.

Membership of the European Union

The United Kingdom joined the European Union in 1973. In order to become a member, Parliament passed the European Communities Act 1972. Although, as Parliament passed that Act, it is theoretically possible for a later Parliament to pass an Act withdrawing from the European Union, political reality means that this is very unlikely. Membership of the EU affects so much of our law and political system.

Membership of the EU means that EU laws take priority over English law even where the English law was passed after the relevant EU law. This was shown by the Merchant Shipping Act 1988, which set down rules for who could own or manage fishing boats registered in Britain. The Act stated that 75 per cent of directors and shareholders had to be British. The European Court of Justice ruled that this was contrary to European Union law, under which citizens of all member states can work in other member states. The Merchant Shipping Act 1988 could not be effective so far as other EU citizens were concerned.

Human Rights Act 1998

This states that all Acts of Parliament have to be compatible with the European Convention on Human Rights. It is possible to challenge an Act on the ground that it does not comply with the Convention. Under s 4 of the Human Rights Act, the courts have the power to declare an Act incompatible with the Convention.

The first case this happened in was *H v Mental Health Review Tribunal* (2001). When a patient was making an application to be released, the Mental Health Act 1983 placed the burden of proof on the patient to show that he should be released. Human rights meant that it should be up to the state to justify the continuing detention of such a patient. The court made a declaration that the law was not compatible with human rights. Following this declaration of incompatibility, the Government changed the law.

However, a declaration of incompatibility does not mean that the Government has to change the law. Also, if Parliament wishes it can pass a new Act which contravenes the European Convention on Human Rights.

Exam tips

It is important to have a grasp of the issues which surround the legislative process and the wider issue of Parliamentary sovereignty. Even if such issues do not appear in their own right on the exam paper, they impact on other important areas such as statutory interpretation and topics on the G151 paper such as judges and the way in which they do their job.

In addition these ideas will become very important when you are studying Law at A2 level as many successes, and problems, in the

law are rooted in the adequacy, or otherwise, of legislation and the way in which judges interpret the law, based on their perception of their role.

Starting to engage with these ideas now is an important step in becoming a well-rounded Law student and it will make the subject more enjoyable as it takes you into the realms of politics and issues which will affect you as you become an adult with responsibilities such as the right to vote.

Examination Questions

1 Read the source material below and answer parts (a) to (c) which follow.

Exercise on Legislation and Delegated Legislation

Source A

Delegated legislation is made by some person or body other than Parliament under the authority of Parliament. This authority is given through an enabling Act. An enabling Act is created by Parliament through its normal processes, an example being the Police and Criminal Evidence Act. This Act will have been accepted by both Houses of Parliament and received the Royal Assent. By conferring powers on others, it allows Parliament to utilise expert advice, but Parliament must be careful when it creates an enabling Act because this sets out the limits of power.

Source B

STATUTORY INSTRUMENT (SI)

1991 No. 2687

Police and Criminal Evidence Act 1984

(Tape-recording of Interviews) (No. 1) Order 1991

Made	29th December 1991
Laid before Parliament	6th December 1991
Coming into force	1st January 1992

Now, therefore, in pursuance of the said section 60(1)(b), the Secretary of State hereby orders as follows:

2 This Order shall apply to interviews of persons suspected of the commission of indictable

Examination Questions

offences (serious offences eg murder) which are held by police officers at police stations in the police areas specified in the Schedule to this Order and which commence after midnight on 31st December 1991.

3 (1) Subject to paragraph (2) below, interviews to which this Order applies shall be tape-recorded in accordance with the requirements of the code of practice on tape-recording which came into operation on 29th July 1988 ...

3 (2) The duty to tape-record interviews under paragraph (1) above shall not apply to interviews – (a) where the offence of which a person is suspected is one in respect of which he has been arrested or detained under section 14(1)(a) of the Prevention of Terrorism (Temporary Provisions) Act 1989.

(a) Describe how an Act of Parliament is made with reference to source A and your knowledge of legislation.   15 marks

(b) Each of the following interviews was conducted by police officers and took place at a police station covered by Statutory Instrument 1991/2667 (source B), but none of the interviews was recorded.

Explain the lawfulness of each of the following interviews:

(i) On the 1st November 1991, Gemma was arrested for summary offences (not serious) and was interviewed.   5 marks

(ii) Carl was suspected of an indictable offence (serious) and was interviewed on 1st November 2000.   5 marks

(iii) Hank was detained under s14(1)(a) of the Prevention of Terrorism (Temporary Provisions) Act 1989 (see source B) and was interviewed in March 2000.   5 marks

(c) With reference to sources A and B and using your knowledge of delegated legislation:

(i) Describe the three different types of delegated legislation.   15 marks

(ii) Discuss the advantages and disadvantages of delegated legislation.   15 marks

OCR, G152, June 2011

(Note you will need information from Chapter 16 to answer questions c(i) and c(ii).)

Delegated legislation

Delegated legislation is law made by some person or body other than Parliament, but with the authority of Parliament. That authority is usually laid down in a 'parent' Act of Parliament known as an enabling Act which creates the framework of the law and then delegates power to others to make more detailed law in the area. An example of enabling Acts include the Access to Justice Act 1999 which gave the Lord Chancellor wide powers to alter various aspects of the legal funding schemes. Another example is the Criminal Justice Act 2003 which gives the Secretary of State the power to make delegated legislation in several areas. One of these powers enables a code of practice to be created for the use of conditional cautions. A conditional caution is used instead of taking an offender to court.

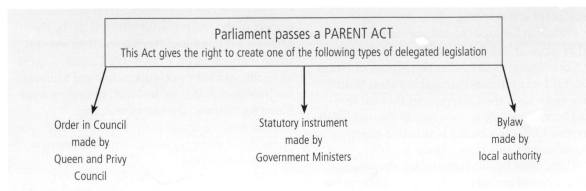

Figure 16.1 Different types of delegated legislation

16.1 Types of delegated legislation

There are three different types of delegated legislation. These are:

- Orders in Council
- statutory instruments
- bylaws.

16.1.1 Orders in Council

The Queen and the Privy Council have the authority to make Orders in Council. The Privy Council is made up of the Prime Minister and other leading members of the Government. So this type of delegated legislation effectively allows the Government to make legislation without going through Parliament.

Orders in Council can be made on a wide range of matters, especially:

- giving legal effect to European Directives
- transferring responsibility between Government departments; for example when the Ministry of Justice was created, the powers of the previous Department of Constitutional Affairs and some of the powers of the Home Office were transferred to this new ministry
- bringing Acts (or parts of Acts) of Parliament into force

In addition, the Privy Council has the power to make law in emergency situations under the Civil Contingencies Act 2004. This power will usually only be exercised in times of emergency when Parliament is not sitting.

Orders in Council can also be used to make other types of law. For example, in 2003 an Order in Council was used to alter the Misuse of Drugs Act 1971 so as to make cannabis a class C drug. Five years later, the Government decided that it had been a mistake to downgrade cannabis, and another Order in Council was issued changing cannabis back to a class B drug.

There must be an enabling Act allowing the Privy Council to make Orders in Council on the particular topic. For the change of category of cannabis, the enabling Act was the Misuse of Drugs Act 1971.

Another enabling Act giving power to make Orders in Council is the Constitutional Reform Act 2005. This allows the Privy Council to alter the number of judges in the Supreme Court.

 Internet Research

Look up recent Orders in Council on the Privy Council website at **www.privy-council.org.uk.**

On the Home page, click on Privy Council, then click on Privy Council Meetings. You should now see a series of dates on which meetings took place. Click on any of these dates and you should see a list of Orders made at that meeting.

Look to see which enabling Acts have allowed recent orders to be made. The enabling Act is usually given on the left-hand side of the list of orders.

16.1.2 Statutory instruments

The term 'statutory instruments' refers to rules and regulations made by Government Ministers. Ministers and government departments are given authority to make regulations for areas under their particular responsibility.

There are about 15 departments in the Government. Each one deals with a different area of policy and can make rules and regulations in respect of the matters with which it deals. The Minister for Work and Pensions will be able to make regulations on work-related matters, such as health and safety at work, while the Minister for Transport is able to deal with necessary road traffic regulations. The use of statutory instruments is a major method of law-making as about 3,000 statutory instruments are brought into force each year.

Statutory instruments can be very short, covering one point such as making the annual change to the minimum wage. However, other

2008 No. 3130

DANGEROUS DRUGS

The Misuse of Drugs Act 1971 (Amendment) Order 2008

Made	*10th December 2008*
Coming into force	*26th January 2009*

At the Court at Buckingham Palace, the 10th day of December 2008

Present,

The Queen's Most Excellent Majesty in Council

In accordance with section 2(5) of the Misuse of Drugs Act 1971 a draft of this Order has been laid before Parliament after consultation with the Advisory Council on the Misuse of Drugs and approved by a resolution of each House of Parliament.

Accordingly, Her Majesty, in exercise of the powers conferred upon Her by sections 2(2) and 2(4) of that Act, is pleased, by and with the advice of Her Privy Council, to order as follows:

Citation, commencement and revocation

1.—(1) This Order may be cited as the Misuse of Drugs Act 1971 (Amendment) Order 2008 and shall come into force on 26th January 2009.

(2) The Misuse of Drugs Act 1971 (Modification) (No. 2) Order 2003 is revoked.

Amendments to the Misuse of Drugs Act 1971

2.—(1) Schedule 2 to the Misuse of Drugs Act 1971 (which specifies the drugs which are subject to control under that Act) is amended as follows.

(2) In Part 2 (Class B drugs)

(a) in paragraph 1(a), after "Amphetamine" insert-

"Cannabinol

Cannabinol derivatives

Cannabis and cannabis resin";

(b) after paragraph 2 insert—

"**2A.**   Any ester or ether of cannabinol or of a cannabinol derivative."; and

(c) in paragraph 3, for "or 2" substitute ", 2 or 2A".

(3) In Part 3 (Class C drugs) the following words are repealed —

(a) in paragraph 1(a), "Cannabinol", "Cannabinol derivatives" and "Cannabis and cannabis resin"; and

(b) in paragraph 1(d), "or of cannabinol or a cannabinol derivative".

Judith Simpson
Clerk of the Privy Council

Figure 16.2 Example of an Order in Council

Definition of delegated legislation	Law made by bodies other than Parliament, but with the authority of Parliament through an enabling or parent Act		
	Types of delegated legislation	**Made by**	**Examples**
	Orders in Council	Made by Queen and Privy Council	The Misuse of Drugs Act 1971 (Amendment) Order 2008
	Statutory instruments	Made by Government Ministers	Codes of Practice under PACE
	Bylaws	Made by local authorities	Local parking regulations

Figure 16.3 Types of delegated legislation

statutory instruments may be very long with detailed regulations which were too complex to include in an Act of Parliament.

Examples of statutory instruments which include a lot of detail are:

- the Chemicals (Hazard Information and Packaging for Supply) Regulations 2009. This statutory instrument was made by the Minister for Work and Pensions under powers given in the European Communities Act 1972 and the Health and Safety at Work Act 1974.
- police codes of practice in relation to such powers as stop and search, arrest and detention. These were made by the Minister for Justice under powers in the Police and Criminal Evidence Act 1984.

The Legislative and Regulatory Reform Act 2006

In addition to specific Acts giving Ministers powers to make statutory instruments, the Legislative and Regulatory Reform Act 2006 gives Ministers power to make *any* provision by order if it will remove or reduce a 'burden' resulting from legislation. For this purpose a burden is defined as:

- a financial cost
- an administrative inconvenience

- an obstacle to efficiency, productivity or profitability
- a sanction which affects the carrying on of any lawful activity.

This means that Ministers can change Acts of Parliament, even though the original Act did not give them the power to do this. However, when the Legislative and Regulatory Reform Act was being discussed, the Government gave a clear undertaking that orders made under the Act would 'not be used to implement highly controversial reforms'.

16.1.3 Bylaws

These can be made by local authorities to cover matters within their own area; for example, Norfolk County Council can pass laws affecting the whole county, while a District or Town Council can only make bylaws for its district or town. Many local bylaws involve traffic control, such as parking restrictions.

Bylaws can also be made by public corporations and certain companies for matters within their jurisdiction which involve the public. This means that bodies such as the British Airports Authority and the railways can enforce rules about public behaviour on their premises.

Activity

Look at the following two sources and answer the questions below.

Source A

2009 No. 606

HEALTH AND SAFETY

The Health and Safety Information for Employees (Amendment) Regulations 2009

Made	*10th March 2009*
Laid before Parliament	*16th March 2009*
Coming into force	*6th April 2009*

The Secretary of State, in exercise of the powers conferred by sections 15(1), (2), (3)(a), (4) and (9) of, and paragraph 15(1) of Schedule 3 to, the Health and Safety at Work etc. Act 1974 ("the 1974 Act"), and for the purpose of giving effect without modifications to proposals submitted to him by the Health and Safety Executive under section 11(3) of the 1974 Act after the carrying out by the said Executive of consultation in accordance with section 50(3) of that Act, hereby makes the following Regulations:

Citation, commencement and interpretation

1.—(1) These Regulations may be cited as the Health and Safety Information for Employees (Amendment) Regulations 2009 and shall come into force on 6th April 2009.

(2) In these Regulations "the 1989 Regulations" means the Health and Safety Information for Employees Regulations 1989.

Amendment of the 1989 Regulations

2.—(1) The 1989 Regulations are amended as follows.

(2) In regulation 3(3) for "nine months" substitute "five years".

(3) After regulation 5(1)(b) insert the following—

"; or (c) information as to how any of his employees may obtain the information referred to in (a) and (b) above.".

(4) After regulation 5(3)(b) insert the following—

"; or (c) information as to how any of his employees may obtain the information referred to in (a) and (b) above.".

Extension outside Great Britain

3. These Regulations shall apply to and in relation to premises and activities outside Great Britain to the same extent as provided for in regulation 2(5) of the 1989 Regulations.

Jonathan Shaw
Parliamentary Under Secretary of State
Department for Work and Pensions
10th March 2009

Source B:

Alcohol free zones in Knowsley

Alcohol free zones are being set up in Knowsley to tackle crime and anti-social behaviour caused by binge drinking. The Safer Knowsley Partnership, which includes Merseyside Police and Knowsley Council, is taking the measure after successfully securing the borough's first Designated Public Place Orders back in 2008.

The orders have been approved in Wignall Park, Court Hey Park, Stadtmoers, Millennium Green and Henley Park, and will come into force on 16th July 2009. The orders will make it an offence for anyone to drink alcohol after being required by a police officer not to do so.

Police have the power to confiscate and dispose of alcohol and it is an arrestable offence to fail to co-operate, without reasonable excuse, with a police officer's request. The ban does not affect drinking in any licensed premises.

Reducing crime and disorder

Knowsley Council's Licensing Committee approved the orders on 25th June 2009. This is part of the Safer Knowsley Partnership's ongoing commitment to reduce alcohol-related crime and disorder and anti-social behaviour.

Taken from Mersey Police website July 2009

Questions

1. What type of delegated legislation is Source A?

2. Which Act is the enabling Act which allowed this delegated legislation to be made?

3. Which government department was responsible for producing the regulations?

4. To which type of delegated legislation does Source B refer?

5. Who made the orders referred to in the source?

6. What effect do these orders have?

Exam tips

Delegated legislation is an important topic because it is a well-used source of law-making. It can appear as an exam question in its own right but it also combines well with other sources, such as the way in which the law is reformed or the way law is made. It is certainly worth remembering that sources of law do not necessarily operate in isolation.

If a question focuses exclusively on delegated legislation then the information you will need breaks down into several areas, with the first being the different forms of delegated legislation. It is good to have examples of each type that you can use as illustrations; be very clear as to when each type is used as this may well be the focus of an application question. This material is relatively easy to organise and revise so it is a good topic if you prefer not to have to deal with a very extensive range of information.

16.2 The need for delegated legislation

1. Parliament does not have time to consider and debate every small detail of complex regulations.

2. In addition Parliament may not have the necessary technical expertise or knowledge required; for example, health and safety regulations in different industries need expert knowledge, while local parking regulations need local knowledge. Modern society has become very complicated and technical, so that it is impossible for members of Parliament to have all the knowledge needed to draw up laws on controlling technology, ensuring environmental safety, dealing with a vast array of different industrial problems or operating complex taxation schemes. It is thought that it is better for Parliament to debate the main principles thoroughly, but leave the detail to be filled in by those who have expert knowledge of it.

3. Ministers can have the benefit of further consultation before regulations are drawn up. Consultation is particularly important for rules on technical matters, where it is necessary to make sure that the regulations are technically accurate and workable. In fact, some Acts giving the power to make delegated legislation set out that there must be consultation before the regulations are created. For example, before any new or revised police Code of Practice under the Police and Criminal Evidence Act 1984 is issued, there must be consultation with a wide range of people including:

- persons representing the interests of police authorities
- the General Council of the Bar
- the Law Society.

4. As already seen, the process of passing an Act of Parliament can take a considerable time and in an emergency, Parliament may not be able pass law quickly enough. This is another reason why delegated legislation is sometimes preferred. It can also be amended or revoked easily when necessary, so that the law can be kept up to date, and Ministers can respond to new or unforeseen situations by amending or amplifying statutory instruments.

Self-Test Questions

1 What is an enabling Act?
2 Who can make Orders in Council?
3 Give an example of an Order in Council.
4 Who can make bylaws?
5 Who can make statutory instruments?
6 Give an example of a statutory instrument.

16.3 Control of delegated legislation

As delegated legislation in many instances is made by non-elected bodies and, since there are so many people with the power to make delegated legislation, it is important that there should be some control over this. Control is exercised by Parliament and by the courts. In addition there may sometimes be a public inquiry before a law is passed on an especially sensitive matter, such as planning laws which may affect the environment.

16.3.1 Control by Parliament

Parliament has different ways of controlling what delegated legislation is made. These are:

- the enabling Act
- Delegated Powers Scrutiny Committee
- laying before Parliament
- questions by MPs
- Scrutiny Committee.

Enabling Act

Parliament has the initial control over what powers are delegated as the enabling Act sets the boundaries within which the delegated legislation is to be made. All enabling Acts will state which Government Minister can make the regulations. It will also state the type of laws to be made and whether they can be made for the whole country or only for certain areas. The Act can also set out whether the Government department must consult other people before making the regulations.

Parliament also retains control over the delegated legislation as it can repeal the powers in the enabling Act at any time. If it does this then the right to make regulations ceases.

Delegated Powers Scrutiny Committee

A Delegated Powers Scrutiny Committee was established in 1993 in the House of Lords to consider whether the provisions of any Bills delegated legislative power inappropriately. It reports its findings to the House of Lords before the Committee stage of the Bill, but has no power to amend Bills.

Laying before Parliament

Statutory instruments must normally be laid before Parliament. This is normally done in one of two ways:

- affirmative resolution
- negative resolution.

Affirmative resolutions

A small number of statutory instruments will be subject to an affirmative resolution. This means that the statutory instrument will not become law unless specifically approved by Parliament. The need for an affirmative resolution will be included in the enabling Act. For example, an affirmative resolution is required before new or revised police Codes of Practice under the Police and Criminal Evidence Act 1984 can come into force. One of the disadvantages of this procedure is that Parliament cannot amend the statutory instrument; it can only be approved, annulled or withdrawn.

Negative resolutions

Most other statutory instruments will be subject to a negative resolution, which means that the relevant statutory instrument will be law unless rejected by Parliament within 40 days. Individual Ministers may also be questioned by MPs in Parliament on the work of their departments, and this can include questions about proposed regulations.

Questions in Parliament

Individual Ministers may also be questioned by MPs in Parliament on the work of their departments, and this can include questions about proposed regulations.

Scrutiny Committee

A more effective check is the existence of a Joint Select Committee on Statutory Instruments (formed in 1973), usually called the Scrutiny Committee. This committee reviews all statutory instruments and, where necessary, will draw the attention of both Houses of Parliament to points that need further consideration. However, the review is a technical one and not based on policy. The main grounds for referring a statutory instrument back to the Houses of Parliament are that:

- it imposes a tax or charge – this is because only an elected body has such a right
- it appears to have retrospective effect which was not provided for by the enabling Act
- it appears to have gone beyond the powers given under the enabling legislation or it makes some unusual or unexpected use of those powers
- it is unclear or defective in some way.

The Scrutiny Committee can only report back its findings; it has no power to alter any statutory instrument.

The two main problems are firstly, that the review is only a technical one limited to the points set out above. Secondly, even if the Committee discovers a breach of one of these points, the Committee cannot alter the regulations or stop them from becoming law. The Committee can only draw the attention of Parliament to the matter.

16.3.2 The Legislative and Regulatory Reform Act 2006

This Act sets out procedure for the making of statutory instruments which are aimed at repealing an existing law in order to remove a 'burden' (see section 16.1.2). Under s 13 of the Act, the Minister making the statutory instrument must consult various people and organisations. These include:

- organisations which are representative of interests substantially affected by the proposals
- the Welsh Assembly in relation to matters upon which the Assembly exercises functions
- the Law Commission, where appropriate.

Orders made under this power of this Act must be laid before Parliament. There are three possible procedures:

1. Negative resolution procedure:
   where the Minister recommends that this procedure should be used, it will be used unless within 30 days one of the Houses of Parliament asks for a super affirmative procedure. If the negative resolution procedure is adopted, the delegated legislation will not become law until it has been laid before Parliament for 40 days.

2. Affirmative resolution procedure:
   this requires both Houses of Parliament to approve the order: even though the Minister has recommended this procedure, Parliament can still require the super-affirmative resolution procedure to be used.

3. Super-affirmative resolution procedure:
   under this the Minister must have regard to:

   - any representations
   - any resolution of either House of Parliament
   - any recommendations by a committee of either House of Parliament who are asked to report on the draft order.

This super-affirmative resolution procedure gives Parliament more control over delegated legislation made under the Legislative and Regulatory Reform Act 2006. It is important that this is the position, as the Act gives Ministers very wide powers to amend Acts of Parliament.

CONTROL BY PARLIAMENT	Advantages	Disadvantages
Enabling Act	Parliament sets limits Parliament can amend or repeal Act	The powers in the Act may be very wide
Delegated Powers Scrutiny Committee	Looks at proposed powers before they are enacted Should ensure that only appropriate powers are given	Can only report – cannot amend Bill
Affirmative resolution	Means Parliament must agree with the regulations	Time-consuming: cannot be used for all SIs
Negative resolution	Gives MPs the opportunity to check SIs before they come into force	Unlikely that many SIs will be looked at under this procedure
Scrutiny Committee	Ensures ● do not impose taxes or ● go beyond the powers ● are not retrospective ● do not make unusual or unexpected use of powers ● are not unclear or defective	Only a technical check – cannot check substance of the SI Committee can only report to Parliament – it cannot make changes
CONTROL BY THE COURTS		
Judicial review	Anyone affected by the delegated legislation can ask for a judicial review	It is expensive to take court proceedings
Doctrine of *ultra vires*	Court can declare delegated legislation void	Can normally only do this if the correct procedure has not been followed OR if the delegated legislation goes beyond the power given by the enabling Act

Figure 16.4 Control of delegated legislation and the advantages and disadvantages of each control

16.3.3 Control by the courts

Delegated legislation can be challenged in the courts on the ground that it is *ultra vires*, that is, it goes beyond the powers that Parliament granted in the enabling Act. This questioning of the validity of delegated legislation may be made through the judicial review procedure, or it may arise in a civil claim between two parties, or on appeal (especially case-stated appeals).

Any delegated legislation which is ruled to be *ultra vires* is void and not effective. This was illustrated by *R v Home Secretary, ex parte Fire Brigades Union* (1995) where changes made by the Home Secretary to the Criminal Injuries Compensation scheme were held to have gone beyond the power given to him in the Criminal Justice Act 1988.

The courts will presume that unless an enabling Act expressly allows it, there is no power to do any of the following:

- make unreasonable regulations – in *Strickland v Hayes Borough Council* (1896) a bylaw prohibiting the singing or reciting of any obscene song or ballad and the use of obscene language generally, was held to be unreasonable and so *ultra vires*, because it was too widely drawn in that it covered acts done in private as well as those in public
- levy taxes
- allow sub-delegation.

It is also possible for the courts to hold that delegated legislation is *ultra vires* because the correct procedure has not been followed. For example in the *Aylesbury Mushroom* case (1972) the Minister of Labour had to consult 'any organisation ... appearing to him to be representative of substantial numbers of employers engaging in the activity concerned'. His failure to consult the Mushroom Growers' Association, which represented about 85 per cent of all mushroom growers meant that his order establishing a training board was invalid as against mushroom growers, though it was valid in relation to others affected by the order, such as farmers, as the minister had consulted with the National Farmers' Union.

In *R v Secretary of State for Education and Employment, ex parte National Union of Teachers* (2000) a High Court judge ruled that a statutory instrument setting conditions for appraisal and access to higher rates of pay for teachers was beyond the powers given under the Education Act 1996. In addition, the procedure used was unfair as only four days had been allowed for consultation.

Statutory instruments can also be declared void if they conflict with European Union legislation.

16.4 Advantages and disadvantages of delegated legislation

16.4.1 Advantages

Saves Parliamentary time

Parliament does not have time to consider and debate every small detail of complex regulations. Making such regulations through delegated legislation saves Parliamentary time.

Need for technical expertise

Parliament may not have the necessary technical expertise or knowledge required. It is impossible to expect MPs to have all the necessary knowledge to draw up laws on controlling technology, ensuring environmental safety, dealing with a vast array of different industrial problems or operating complex taxation schemes. It is better for Parliament to debate the main principles thoroughly, but leave the detail to the experts.

Allows consultation

Ministers can have the benefit of further consultation before regulations are drawn up. Consultation is particularly important for rules on technical matters, where it is necessary to make sure that the regulations are technically workable.

Key facts

		Comment or Case
Reasons for delegated legislation	• Knowledge and expertise • Saving of parliamentary time • Can be changed more quickly than Acts of Parliament	
Disadvantages of delegated legislation	• Undemocratic • Risk of sub-delegation • Large volume • Lack of publicity	
Control by Parliament	Negative resolution Affirmative resolution Scrutiny Committee Super-affirmative resolution	Becomes law unless within 40 days there is an objection Must be approved by both Houses of Parliament Reviews and can draw Parliament's attention to problems, but cannot amend Only for SIs made under Legislative and Regulatory Reform Act 2006
Control by the courts	Judicial review to decide: • if it is beyond the powers given in the enabling Act • unreasonable • failed to follow correct procedure	*R v Home Secretary, ex parte Fire Brigades Union* (1995) *Strickland v Hayes* (1896) *Aylesbury Mushroom case* (1972)

Figure 16.5 Key facts chart for delegated legislation

16.4.2 Disadvantages of the use of delegated legislation

1. The main criticism is that it takes law-making away from the democratically elected House of Commons and allows non-elected people to make law. This is acceptable provided there is sufficient control, but, as already seen, Parliament's control is fairly limited. This criticism cannot be made of bylaws made by local authorities since these are elected by local citizens.

2. Another problem is that of sub-delegation, which means that the law-making authority is handed down another level. This causes comments that much of our law is made by civil servants and merely 'rubber-stamped' by the Minister of that department.

3. The large volume of delegated legislation also gives rise to criticism since it makes it difficult to discover the present law. This problem is aggravated by a lack of publicity, as much delegated legislation is made in private in contrast to the public debates of Parliament.

4. Finally, delegated legislation shares with Acts of Parliament the same problem of obscure wording that can lead to difficulty in understanding the law. This difficulty of how to understand or interpret the law is dealt with in Chapter 17.

Self-Test Questions

1 Name three ways in which Parliament can control delegated legislation.
2 Give three advantages of these controls.
3 Give three disadvantages of these controls.
4 When can the courts declare that delegated legislation is void?
5 Give three advantages of using delegated legislation.
6 Give three disadvantages of using delegated legislation.

Exam tips

The other aspects of delegated legislation which are popular in exam questions are those of controls – by Parliament and the courts – and the advantages and disadvantages of this type of law-making. You will probably make use of material on the good and bad things about delegated legislation in a part (c) question as this is always a discussion. On the other hand, it is possible that the mechanisms for controlling delegated legislation could appear in:

• part (a) if you are required to describe what happens
• part (b) if you need to resolve which method of control works best in a particular factual situation
• part (c) if you need to discuss the merits of different methods of control.

This goes to show that when you are revising it is a good idea to work at methods of learning the information and then to consider how you would tailor what you have revised depending on the question. Working this out beforehand will pay dividends and give you a lot more flexibility in terms of the question you choose to answer when you are under pressure in the exam room.

Examination Questions

1 Read the source material below and answer parts (a) to (c) which follow.

Source

Delegated legislation is the description given to the vast body of orders in council, statutory instruments and bylaws created by subordinate bodies under specific powers delegated to those bodies by Parliament. The need for delegated legislation is that it enables regulations to be made and altered quickly. The powers delegated are frequently defined in the widest terms. An example is the Human Rights Act which empowers a minister to make such amendments to legislation, or subordinate legislation, as he considers appropriate in order to remove incompatibility with the European Convention on Human Rights.

The powers to delegate are subject to the control of Parliament but, where the legislative power is conferred on a minister, this may not be an effective control. Delegated legislation is valid if the right to make it is conferred by Parliament (*intra vires* – inside the powers). If it is not, it is said to be *ultra vires* (outside the powers) and is, in that event, invalid. However, unless and until declared *ultra vires* by a judgment in an action in court, it must be treated as part of the law and enforced accordingly. The courts treat delegated legislation differently from primary legislation.

Unlike an Act of Parliament, delegated legislation can be declared invalid, because it is *ultra vires*.

Adapted from '*Walker & Walker's English Legal System*', R. Ward, 8th edition, Butterworths

(a) Descibe the need for delegated legislation using the Source and your knowledge of delegated legislation.   15 marks

(b) Identify and explain the most suitable type of delegated legislation to implement law in the following situations:
  (i) To implement a European Union Directive quickly when Parliament is not sitting.   5 marks

  (ii) To allow a government department to issue regulations on education.   5 marks

  (iii) For a train company (a public corporation) to implement a ban on the use of mobile phones by passengers.   5 marks

(c) With reference to the Source and your knowledge of delegated legislation:

  (i) Descibe the controls on delegated legislation.   15 marks

  (ii) Discuss the effectiveness of the controls on delegated legislation.   15 marks

OCR G152 June 2010

Chapter 17

Statutory interpretation

As seen in Chapter 15, many statutes are passed by Parliament each year. The meaning of the law in these statutes should be clear and explicit but this is not always achieved. In order to help with the understanding of a statute, Parliament sometimes includes sections defining certain words used in that statute: such sections are called interpretation sections. In the Theft Act 1968, for example, the definition of 'theft' is given in s 1, and then ss 2–6 define the key words in that definition.

To help the judges with general words, Parliament has also passed the Interpretation Act 1978 which makes it clear that, unless the contrary appears, 'he' includes 'she', and singular includes plural.

17.1 The need for statutory interpretation

Despite the aids mentioned above, many cases come before the courts because there is a dispute over the meaning of an Act of Parliament. In such cases the court's task is to decide the exact meaning of a particular word or phrase. There are many reasons why the meaning may be unclear:

- A broad term
  There may be words designed to cover several possibilities; this can lead to problems as to how wide this should go. In the Dangerous Dogs Act 1991 there is a phrase: 'any dog of the type known as the pit bull terrier' which seems simple but has led to problems. What is meant by 'type'? Does it mean the same as 'breed'? In *Brock v DPP* (1993) this was the key point in dispute and the Queen's Bench Divisional

Activity

Read the following law report and answer the questions below.

Lurking policemen not 'passengers'

Cheeseman v Director of Public Prosecutions

Before Lord Justice Bingham and Mr Justice Waterhouse
[Judgment October 19]

Police officers who witnessed a man masturbating in a public lavatory were not 'passengers' within the meaning of section 28 of the Town Police Clauses Act 1847 when they had been stationed in the lavatory following complaints.

The Queen's Bench Divisional Court so held in allowing an appeal by way of case stated by Ashley Frederick Cheeseman against his conviction by Leicester City Justices of an offence of wilfully and indecently exposing his person in a street to the annoyance of passengers.

Section 81 of the Public Health Amendment Act 1902 extended the meaning of the word 'street' in section 28 to include, *inter alia*, any place of public resort under the control of the local authority.

Mr Stuart Rafferty for the appellant: Mr David Bartlett for the prosecution.

LORD JUSTICE BINGHAM, concurring with Mr Justice Waterhouse, said that *The Oxford English Dictionary* showed that in 1847 when the Act was passed 'passenger' had a meaning, now unusual except in the expression 'foot-passenger' of 'a passer by or through: a traveller (usually on foot); a wayfarer'.

Before the meaning of 'street' was enlarged in 1907 that dictionary definition of passenger was not hard to apply: it clearly covered anyone using the street for ordinary purposes of passage or travel.

The dictionary definition could not be so aptly applied to a place of public resort such as a public lavatory, but on a commonsense reading when applied in context 'passenger' had to mean anyone resorting in the ordinary way to a place for one of the purposes for which people would normally resort to it.

If that was the correct approach, the two police officers were not 'passengers'. They were stationed in the public lavatory in order to apprehend persons committing acts which had given rise to earlier complaints. They were not resorting to that place of public resort in the ordinary way but for a special purpose and thus were not passengers.

Solicitors: Bray & Bray, Leicester: CPS Leicester.
The Times Law Report, 2 November 1990

Questions

1. In this case the meaning of the word 'street' was important. How did the court discover the meaning of the word in this case?

2. The meaning of the word 'passenger' was also important. How did the court discover what this word meant in 1847?

3. The court decided that 'passenger' meant 'a passer by or through; a traveller (usually on foot); a wayfarer'. Why did that definition not apply to the police officers who arrested the defendant?

4. The defendant was found not guilty because of the way the court interpreted 'passenger'. Do you think this was a correct decision? Give reasons for your answer.

Court decided that 'type' had a wider meaning than 'breed'. It could cover dogs which were not pedigree pit bull terriers, but had a substantial number of the characteristics of such a dog.

- Ambiguity
  This is where a word has two or more meanings; it may not be clear which meaning should be used.
- A drafting error
  The Parliamentary Counsel who drafted the original Bill may have made an error which has not been noticed by Parliament; this is particularly likely to occur where the Bill is amended several times while going through Parliament.
- New developments
  New technology may mean that an old Act of Parliament does not apparently cover present day situations. This is seen in the case of *Royal College of Nursing v DHSS* (1981) where medical science and methods had changed since the passing of the Abortion Act in 1967. This case is discussed more fully in section 17.5.1.
- Changes in the use of language
  The meaning of words can change over the years. This was one of the problems in the case of Cheeseman v DPP (1990). The Times law report of this case is set out below in the activity section.

17.2 Literal approach versus purposive approach

The case of *Cheeseman* illustrates several of the problems of statutory interpretation. It is an example of the courts taking the words literally. However, it can be argued that the defendant was 'wilfully and indecently exposing his person in a street' and that he was caught doing that. Is it important whether the police officers were 'passengers'? After all, they were there because of previous complaints about this type of behaviour and presumably the defendant thought they were ordinary members of the public. Some people would argue that the whole purpose of the Act was to prevent this type of behaviour; this is the purposive approach to statutory interpretation – instead of looking at the precise meaning of each word, a broader approach is taken.

This conflict between the literal approach and the purposive approach is one of the major issues in statutory interpretation. Should judges examine each word and take the words literally or should it be accepted that an Act of Parliament cannot cover every situation and that the meanings of words cannot always be exact? In European law the purposive approach is taken. The Treaty of Rome sets out general principles but without explicit details. As Lord Denning said of the Treaty in *Bulmer Ltd v Bollinger SA* (1974):

> " It lays down general principles. It expresses its aims and purposes. All in sentences of moderate length and commendable style. But it lacks precision. It uses words and phrases without defining what they mean. An English lawyer would look for an interpretation clause, but he would look in vain. There is none. All the way through the Treaty there are gaps and lacunas. These have to be filled in by the judges. "

In fact, since European treaties, regulations and directives are issued in several languages it would be difficult, if not impossible, to take the meanings of words literally. It is not always possible to have an exact translation from one language to another.

In English law the judges have not been able to agree on which approach should be used, but instead, over the years they have developed three different rules of interpretation. These are:

- the literal rule
- the golden rule
- the mischief rule.

These rules take different approaches to interpretation and some judges prefer to use one rule, while other judges prefer another rule. This means that in English law the interpretation of a statute may differ according to which judge is hearing the case. However, once an interpretation has been laid down, it may then form a precedent for future cases under the normal rules of judicial precedent. Since the three rules can result in very different decisions, it is important to understand them.

17.3 The literal rule

Under this rule courts will give words their plain, ordinary or literal meaning, even if the result is not very sensible. This idea was expressed by Lord Esher in *R v Judge of the City of London Court* (1892) when he said:

> If the words of an act are clear then you must follow them even though they lead to a manifest absurdity. The court has nothing to do with the question whether the legislature has committed an absurdity.

The rule developed in the early nineteenth century and was the main rule used for the first part of the twentieth century. It is still used as the starting point for interpreting any legislation.

17.3.1 Cases using the literal rule

The rule was often used in old cases. But it could lead to absurd decisions or to possible injustice. Two examples are given below.

Whiteley v Chappell (1868)

The defendant was charged under a section which made it an offence to impersonate 'any person entitled to vote'. The defendant had pretended to be a person whose name was on the voters' list, but who had died. The court held that the defendant was not guilty since a dead person is not, in the literal meaning of the words, 'entitled to vote'. Using the literal rule in this case made the law absurd.

London & North Eastern Railway Co. v Berriman (1946)

A railway worker was killed while doing maintenance work, oiling points along a railway line. His widow tried to claim compensation because there had not been a look-out man provided by the railway company in accordance with a regulation under the Fatal Accidents Act which stated that a look-out should be provided for men working on or near the railway line 'for the purposes of relaying or repairing' it. The court took the words 'relaying' and 'repairing' in their literal meaning and said that oiling points was maintaining the line and not relaying or repairing so that Mrs Berriman's claim failed. In this case, the rule led to a harsh or unjust decision.

17.3.2 Advantages of the literal rule

The rule follows the words that Parliament has used. Parliament is our law-making body and it is right that judges should apply the law exactly as it is written. Using the literal rule to interpret Acts of Parliament means that unelected judges do not make law.

Using the literal rule should make the law more certain, as it should be interpreted exactly as it is written. This makes it easier for people to know what the law is and how judges will apply it.

17.3.3 Disadvantages of the literal rule

The literal rule assumes every Act will be perfectly drafted. In fact it is not always possible to word an Act so that it covers every situation that Parliament intended. This was seen in the case of *Whiteley v Chappell* (1868) where the defendant was not guilty of voting under another person's name (see 17.3.1 above).

Words may have more than one meaning, so that the Act is unclear. Often in dictionaries words are defined with several different meanings.

Following the words exactly can lead to unfair or unjust decisions. This was seen in *London & North Eastern Railway Co. v Berriman* (1946) (see 17.3.1 above).

With decisions such as *Whiteley v Chappell* and the *Berriman case,* it is not surprising that Professor Michael Zander has denounced the literal rule as being mechanical and divorced from the realities of the use of language.

17.4 The golden rule

This rule is a modification of the literal rule. The golden rule starts by looking at the literal meaning but the court is then allowed to avoid an interpretation which would lead to an absurd result. There are two views on how far the golden rule should be used. The first is very narrow and is shown by Lord Reid's comments in *Jones v DPP* (1962) when he said:

> **"** It is a cardinal principle applicable to all kinds of statutes that you may not for any reason attach to a statutory provision a meaning which the words of that provision cannot reasonably bear. If they are capable of more than one meaning, then you can choose between those meanings, but beyond this you cannot go. **"**

So under the narrow application of the golden rule the court may only choose between the possible meanings of a word or phrase. If there is only one meaning then that must be taken.

The second and wider application of the golden rule is where the words have only one clear meaning, but that meaning would lead to a repugnant situation (that is, a situation which the court feels that using the clear meaning would produce a result which should be allowed). In such a case the court will invoke the golden rule to modify the words of the statute in order to avoid this problem.

17.4.1 Cases using the golden rule

The narrow view of the golden rule can be seen in practice in *Adler v George* (1964).

Adler v George (1964)

In this case the Official Secrets Act 1920 made it an offence to obstruct Her Majesty's Forces 'in the vicinity' of a prohibited place. The defendants had obstructed HM Forces actually in the prohibited place. They argued they were not guilty as the literal wording of the Act did not apply to anyone in the prohibited place. It only applied to those 'in the vicinity', i.e. outside but close to it. The Divisional Court found the defendants guilty as it would be absurd if those causing an obstruction outside the prohibited place were guilty, but anyone inside was not. The words should be read as being 'in or in the vicinity of' the prohibited place.

A very clear example of the use of the wider application of the golden rule was the case of *Re Sigsworth* (1935).

Re Sigsworth (1935)

In this case the son had murdered his mother. The mother had not made a will, so normally her estate would have been inherited by her next-of-kin according to the rules set out in the Administration of Justice Act 1925. This meant that the murderer son would have inherited as her 'issue'.

There was no ambiguity in the words of the Act, but the court was not prepared to let a murderer benefit from his crime, so it was held that the literal rule should not apply, and the golden rule would be used to prevent the repugnant situation of the son inheriting. Effectively the court was writing into the Act that the 'issue' would not be entitled to inherit where they had killed the person from whom they would be inheriting.

17.4.2 Advantages of the golden rule

It respects the exact words of Parliament except in limited situations. Where there is a problem with using the literal rule, the golden rule provides an 'escape route'.

It allows the judge to choose the most sensible meaning where there is more than one meaning to the words in the Act. It can also provide sensible decisions in cases where the literal rule would lead to a repugnant situation. It would clearly have been unjust to allow the son in *Re Sigsworth* to benefit from his crime.

This shows how it can avoid the worst problems of the literal rule.

17.4.3 Disadvantages of the golden rule

It is very limited in its use, so it is only used on rare occasions. Another problem is that it is not always possible to predict when courts will use the golden rule.

Michael Zander has described it as a 'feeble parachute'. In other words, it is an escape route but it cannot do very much.

17.5 The mischief rule

This rule gives a judge more discretion than the other two rules. The definition of the rule comes from *Heydon's case* (1584), where it was said that there were four points the court should consider. These, in the original language of that old case, were:

1. 'What was the common law before the making of the Act?
2. What was the mischief and defect for which the common law did not provide?
3. What was the remedy the Parliament hath resolved and appointed to cure the disease of the commonwealth?
4. The true reason of the remedy.
   Then the office of all the judges is always to make such construction as shall suppress the mischief and advance the remedy.'

Under this rule therefore, the court should look to see what the law was before the Act was passed in order to discover what gap or 'mischief' the Act was intended to cover. The court should then interpret the Act in such a way that the gap is covered. This is clearly a quite different approach to the literal rule.

17.5.1 Cases using the mischief rule

The mischief rule was used in *Smith v Hughes* (1960) to interpret s 1(1) of the Street Offences Act 1959 which said 'it shall be an offence for a common prostitute to loiter or solicit in a street or public place for the purpose of prostitution'.

Smith v Hughes (1960)

The court considered appeals against conviction under this section by six different women. In each case the women had not been 'in a street'; one had been on a balcony and the others had been at the windows of ground floor rooms, with the window either half open or closed. In each case the women were attracting the attention of men by calling to them or tapping on the window, but they argued that they were not guilty under this section since they were not literally 'in a street or public place'. The court decided that they were guilty, with Lord Parker saying:

> For my part I approach the matter by considering what is the mischief aimed at by this Act. Everybody knows that this was an Act to clean up the streets, to enable people to walk along the streets without being molested or solicited by common prostitutes. Viewed in this way it can matter little whether the prostitute is soliciting while in the street or is standing in the doorway or on a balcony, or at a window, or whether the window is shut or open or half open.

A similar point arose in *Eastbourne Borough Council v Stirling* (2000).

> **Eastbourne Borough Council v Stirling** (2000)
>
> A taxi driver was charged with 'plying for hire in any street' without a licence to do so. His vehicle was parked on a taxi rank on the station forecourt. He was found guilty as, although he was on private land, he was likely to get customers from the street. The court referred to *Smith v Hughes* and said that it was the same point. A driver would be plying for hire in the street when his vehicle was positioned so that the offer of services was aimed at people in the street.

Another case in which the House of Lords used the mischief rule was *Royal College of*

Read the facts of the case set out below then apply the different rules of interpretation.

CASE: *Fisher v Bell* [1960] 1 QB 394

The Restriction of Offensive Weapons Act 1959 s 1(1)

'Any person who manufactures, sells or hires or offers for sale or hire or lends or gives to any other person – (a) any knife which has a blade which opens automatically by hand pressure applied to a button, spring or other device in or attached to the handle of the knife, sometimes known as a "flick knife" ... shall be guilty of an offence.'

FACTS: The defendant was a shopkeeper, who had displayed a flick knife marked with a price in his shop window; he had not actually sold any. He was charged under s 1(1) and the court had to decide whether he was guilty of offering the knife for sale. There is a technical legal meaning of 'offers for sale', under which putting an article in a shop window is not an offer to sell. (Students of contract law should know this rule!)

Questions

Consider the phrase 'offers for sale' and explain how you think the case would have been decided using:

(a) the literal rule

(b) the golden rule

(c) the mischief rule.

Note: The court's decision on the case is given in Appendix 1.

Key facts

Literal rule	Golden rule	Mischief rule
Words in their ordinary grammatical meaning	Can choose best interpretation of ambiguous words OR avoid an absurd/repugnant result	Looks at the gap in the law prior to the Act and interprets words to 'suppress the mischief'
Case: *LNER v Berriman* (1946) Not 'relaying or repairing' track, but was oiling points (maintenance) Literal approach – held maintenance was not within the literal meaning of the words 'relaying or repairing' Could not claim compensation	Case: *R v Allen* (1872) 'Marry' meant go through a ceremony of marriage Case: *Re Sigsworth* (1935) Son not allowed to inherit money from mother because he murdered her	Case: *Smith v Hughes* (1960) Prostitutes calling from a house to men in the street were 'soliciting in a street' This was the mischief that the Act was intended to prevent
Advantages of literal rule ● leaves law-making to Parliament ● makes law more certain	Advantages of golden rule ● respects the words of Parliament as only used in limited situations ● avoids the worst problems of the literal rule	Advantages of mischief rule ● fills in the gaps in the law ● promotes the purpose of the Act ● produces 'just' results
Disadvantages of literal rule ● assumes that every Act is perfectly drafted ● words have more than one meaning ● can lead to absurd results ● can lead to unjust decisions	Disadvantages of golden rule ● can only be used in limited situations ● a 'feeble parachute' (Zander)	Disadvantages of mischief rule ● risk of judicial law-making ● not as wide as the purposive approach ● limited to looking back to the law prior to the Act ● can make law uncertain

Figure 17.1 Key facts chart on the three 'rules' of statutory interpretation

Nursing v DHSS (1981). In this case the wording of the Abortion Act 1967 which provided that a pregnancy should be 'terminated by a registered medical practitioner', was in issue. When the Act was passed in 1967 the procedure to carry out an abortion was such that only a doctor (a registered medical practitioner) could do it. From 1972 onwards improvements in medical technique meant that the normal method of terminating a pregnancy was to induce premature labour with drugs. The first part of the procedure was carried out by a doctor, but the second part was performed by nurses without a doctor present. The court had to decide if this procedure was lawful under the Abortion Act. The case went to the House of Lords where the majority (three) of the judges held that it was lawful, while the other two said that it was not lawful.

The three judges in the majority based their decision on the mischief rule, pointing out that the mischief Parliament was trying to remedy was the unsatisfactory state of the law before 1967 and the number of illegal abortions. They also said that the policy of the Act was to broaden the grounds for abortion and ensure that they were carried out with proper skill in hospital. The other two judges took the literal view and said that the words of the Act were clear and that terminations could only be carried out by a registered medical practitioner. They said that the other judges were not interpreting the Act but 'redrafting it with a vengeance'.

It is clear that these three rules can lead to different decisions on the meanings of words and phrases. Below is an activity based on a real case in which the different rules could result in different decisions.

17.5.2 Advantages of the mischief rule

The mischief rule promotes the purpose of the law as it allows judges to look back at the gap in the law which the Act was designed to cover. The emphasis is on making sure that the gap on the law is filled. This is more likely to produce a 'just' result.

The Law Commission prefers the mischief rule and, as long ago as 1969, recommended that it should be the only rule used in statutory interpretation.

17.5.3 Disadvantages of the mischief rule

There is the risk of judicial law-making. Judges are trying to fill the gaps in the law with their own views on how the law should remedy the gap. The case of *Royal College of Nursing v DHSS* (see 17.5.1) shows that judges do not always agree on the use of the mischief rule.

Use of the mischief rule may lead to uncertainty in the law. It is impossible to know when judges will use the rule and also what result it might lead to. This makes it difficult for lawyers to advise clients on the law.

The mischief rule is not as wide as the purposive approach (see 17.6) as it is limited to looking back at the gap in the old. It cannot be used for a more general consideration of the purpose of the law.

17.6 The purposive approach

This goes beyond the mischief rule in that the court is not just looking to see what the gap was in the old law. The judges are deciding what they believe Parliament meant to achieve. The champion of this approach in English law was Lord Denning. His attitude towards statutory interpretation was shown when he said in the case of *Magor and St Mellons v Newport Corporation* (1950):

> We sit here to find out the intention of Parliament and carry it out, and we do this better by filling in the gaps and making sense of the enactment than by opening it up to destructive analysis.

However, his attitude was criticised by judges in the House of Lords when they heard the appeal in the case. Lord Simonds called Lord Denning's approach:

> a naked usurpation of the legislative function under the thin disguise of interpretation

and pointed out that:

> if a gap is disclosed the remedy lies in an amending Act.

Another judge, Lord Scarman, said:

> If Parliament says one thing but means another, it is not, under the historic principles of the common law, for the courts to correct it. The general principle must surely be acceptable in our society. We are to be governed not by Parliament's intentions but by Parliament's enactments.

This speech shows the problem with the purposive approach. Should the judges refuse to follow the clear words of Parliament? How do they know what Parliament's intentions were? Opponents of the purposive approach say that it impossible to discover Parliament's intentions; only the words of the statute can show what Parliament wanted.

17.6.1 Cases using the purposive approach

The purposive approach was used in *R v Registrar-General, ex parte Smith* (1990), where the court had to consider s 51 of the Adoption Act 1976 which stated:

> (1) Subject to subsections (4) and (6), the Registrar-General shall on an application made in the prescribed manner by an adopted person a record of whose birth is kept by the Registrar-General and who has attained the age of 18 years supply to that person ... such information as is necessary to enable that person to obtain a certified copy of the record of his birth ...

Subsection (4) said that before supplying that information the Registrar-General had to inform the applicant about counselling services available. Subsection (6) stated that if the adoption was before 1975 the Registrar-General could not give the information unless the applicant had attended an interview with a counsellor. The facts and decision in the case are given below.

R v Registrar-General, ex parte Smith (1990)

Charles Smith applied for information to enable him to obtain his birth certificate. Mr Smith had made his application in the correct manner and was prepared to see a counsellor. On a literal view of the Act the Registrar-General had to supply him with the information, since the Act uses the phrase 'shall ... supply'.

The problem was that Mr Smith had been convicted of two murders and was detained in Broadmoor as he suffered from recurring bouts of psychotic illness. A psychiatrist thought that it was possible he might be hostile towards his natural mother.

This posed a difficulty for the court; should they apply the clear meaning of the words in this situation? The judges in the Court of

---

Appeal decided that the case called for the purposive approach, saying that, despite the plain language of the Act, Parliament could not have intended to promote serious crime. So, in view of the risk to the applicant's natural mother if he discovered her identity, they ruled that the Registrar-General did not have to supply any information.

Another case which used the purposive approach is R *(Quintavalle) v Secretary of State* (2003).

R (Quintavalle) v Secretary of State (2003)

The House of Lords had to decide whether organisms created by cell nuclear replacement (CNR) came within the definition of 'embryo' in the Human Embryology and Fertilisation Act 1990.

Section 1(1)(a) of this Act states that 'embryo means a live human embryo where fertilisation is complete'. CNR was not possible in 1990 when the Act was passed and the problem is that fertilisation is not used in CNR. Lord Bingham said:

> [T]he court's task, within permissible bounds of interpretation is to give effect to Parliament's purpose ... Parliament could not have intended to distinguish between embryos produced by, or without, fertilisation since it was unaware of the latter possibility.

17.6.2 Advantages of the purposive approach

The purposive approach leads to justice in individual cases. It is a broad approach which

Literal approach	Purposive approach
Words taken in their ordinary grammatical meaning	Looks for the purpose of Parliament and interprets the law to ensure that purpose
Case: *LNER v Berriman* (1946) Not 'relaying or repairing' track, but was oiling points (maintenance) Literal approach – held maintenance was not within the literal meaning of the words 'relaying or repairing' Could not claim compensation	Case: *R (Quintavalle) v Sec of State for Health* (2003) Act stated embryo meant 'a live human embryo where fertilisation is complete' Embryos were created by cell nuclear replacement, so there was no fertilisation Purposive approach – Parliament could not have intended to distinguish between embryos The Act applied
Advantages of literal approach • leaves law-making to Parliament • makes law more certain	Advantages of purposive approach • leads to justice in individual cases • broad approach covering more situations • fills in the gaps in the law • allows for new technology
Disadvantages of literal approach • assumes that every Act is perfectly drafted • words have more than one meaning • can lead to absurd results • can lead to unjust decisions	Disadvantages of purposive approach • leads to judicial law-making • can make law uncertain • difficult to discover the intention of Parliament

Figure 17.2 Comparing the literal approach and the purposive approach

Self-Test Questions

1 Explain two reasons why it may be necessary to interpret an Act.
2 Define the literal rule and give a case in which it was used.
3 Give one advantage and one disadvantage of using the literal rule.
4 Define the golden rule and give a case in which it was used.
5 Give one advantage and one disadvantage of using the golden rule.
6 Define the mischief rule and give a case in which it was used.
7 Give one advantage and one disadvantage of using the mischief rule.
8 Define the purposive approach and give a case in which it was used.
9 Give one advantage and one disadvantage of using the purposive approach.
10 Compare the literal and the purposive approaches.

allows the law to cover more situations than applying words literally. This means it can fill in the gaps in the law.

The purposive approach is particularly useful where there is new technology which was unknown when the law was enacted. This is demonstrated by *R (Quintavalle) v Secretary of State*, the embryo case explained in 17.6.1. If the literal rule/approach had been used in that case, it would have been necessary for Parliament to make a new law to deal with the situation.

Exam tips

Statutory interpretation is a popular subject for questions for students and examiners alike. A top quality answer can shine through, starting with clear and detailed knowledge of the rules which judges can use. You need to be confident with each one, have some examples that you can use and then be able to discuss the advantages and disadvantages of the rules.

There are lots of case examples and your teacher will probably give some guidance but, if it is up to you, choose a selection that make different points and are ones you find easier to remember. Sometimes you can make a case work for you twice and *Royal College of Nursing v DHSS* (1981) is a good example where two different approaches are used as the case moves up the court hierarchy.

Also remember that the most important part of the case is the law and the way in which the judicial approach is demonstrated rather than simply a detailed account of the fact. A mind map with the principles of each rule in one colour, the cases in another and discussion points in a third colour might help you visualise this large and complex topic. Read the questions carefully and then use your highlighter to annotate the sources so that you have the flavour of the best material to use in your answer.

17.6.3 Disadvantages of the purposive approach

Using the purposive approach makes the law less certain. It also allows unelected judges to 'make' law as they are deciding what they think the law should be, rather than using the words that Parliament enacted.

Another problem with the purposive approach is that it is difficult to discover the intention of Parliament. There are reports of debates in Parliament in *Hansard* (see 17.7.2), but these give every detail of debates including those MPs who did not agree with the law that was under discussion. The final version of what Parliament agreed is the actual words used in the Act.

It also leads to uncertainty in the law. It is impossible to know when judges will use this approach or what result it might lead to. This makes it difficult for lawyers to advise clients on the law.

17.7 Finding Parliament's intention

There are certain ways in which the courts can try to discover the intention of Parliament and certain matters which they can look at in order to help with the interpretation of a statute.

17.7.1 Intrinsic aids

These are matters within the statute itself that may help to make its meaning clearer. The court can consider the long title, the short title and the preamble (if any). Older statutes usually have a preamble which sets out Parliament's purpose in enacting that statute. Modern statutes either do not have a preamble or contain a very brief one, for example the Theft Act 1968 states that it is an Act to modernise the law of theft. The long title may also explain briefly Parliament's intentions.

The other useful internal aids are any headings before a group of sections, and any schedules attached to the Act. There are often also marginal notes explaining different sections, but these are not generally regarded as giving Parliament's intention as they will have been inserted after the parliamentary debates and are only helpful comments put in by the printer.

17.7.2 Extrinsic aids

These are matters which are outside the Act – it has always been accepted that some external sources can help explain the meaning of an Act. These undisputed sources are:

- previous Acts of Parliament on the same topic
- the historical setting
- earlier case law
- dictionaries of the time.

As far as other extrinsic aids are concerned, attitudes have changed. Originally the courts had very strict rules that other extrinsic aids should not be considered; however, for the following three aids the courts' attitude has changed. These three main extrinsic aids are:

- *Hansard*: the official report of what was said in Parliament when the Act was debated
- reports of law reform bodies, such as the Law Commission, which led to the passing of the Act
- international Conventions, Regulations or Directives which have been implemented by English legislation.

The use of *Hansard*

Until 1992 there was a firm rule that the courts could not look at what was said in the debates in Parliament. Some years earlier Lord Denning had tried to attack this ban on *Hansard* in *Davis v Johnson* (1979), which involved the interpretation of the Domestic Violence and Matrimonial Proceedings Act 1976. He admitted that he had indeed read *Hansard* before making his decision, saying:

> Some may say ... that judges should not pay any attention to what is said in Parliament. They should grope about in the dark for the meaning of an Act without switching on the light. I do not accede to this view.

In the same case the House of Lords disapproved of this and Lord Scarman explained their reasons by saying:

> Such material is an unreliable guide to the meaning of what is enacted. It promotes confusion, not clarity. The cut and thrust of debate and the pressures of executive responsibility ... are not always conducive to a clear and unbiased explanation of the meaning of statutory language.

However, in *Pepper v Hart* (1993) the House of Lords relaxed the rule and accepted that *Hansard* could be used in a limited way. This case was unusual in that seven judges heard the appeal, rather than the normal panel of five. These seven judges included the Lord Chancellor, who was the only judge to disagree with the use of *Hansard*. The majority ruled that *Hansard* could be consulted. Lord Browne-Wilkinson said in his judgment that:

> the exclusionary rule should be relaxed so as to permit reference to parliamentary materials where: (a) legislation is ambiguous or obscure, or leads to an absurdity; (b) the material relied on consists of one or more statements by a minister or other promoter of the Bill together if necessary with such other parliamentary material as is necessary to understand such statements and their effect; (c) the statements relied on are clear. Further than this I would not at present go.

Key facts

	BRIEF DEFINITION	CASE EXAMPLES
Literal approach	● Approaching problems of statutory interpretation by taking the words at their face value	*Fisher v Bell* (1960)
Purposive approach	● Looking at the reasons why a law was passed and interpreting the words accordingly	*R v Registrar-General, ex parte Smith* (1990)
The 'three rules' Literal rule	● Words given ordinary, plain, grammatical meaning	*Whiteley v Chappell* (1868)
Golden rule	● Avoids absurd or repugnant situations	*Adler v George* (1964)
Mischief rule	● Looks at the gap in the previous law and interprets the words 'to advance the remedy'	*Smith v Hughes* (1960)
Rules of language *Ejusdem generis*	● General words which follow a list are limited to the same kind	*Hobbs v CG Robertson* (1970)
Expressio unius	● The express mention of one thing excludes others	*Tempest v Kilner* (1846)
Noscitur a sociis	● A word is known by the company it keeps	*IRC v Frere* (1965)
Presumptions	● No change to common law ● Crown not bound ● *Mens rea* required ● No retrospective effect	*Leach v R* (1912) *Sweet v Parsley* (1970)
Aids to finding Parliament's intention	● Intrinsic – within the Act, e.g. interpretation section ● Extrinsic– outside the Act, e.g. *Hansard* ● Law Commission Reports	*Pepper v Hart* (1993) *Black Clawson* case (1975)

Figure 17.3 Key facts chart for statutory interpretation

So *Hansard* may be considered but only where the words of the Act are ambiguous or obscure or lead to an absurdity. Even then *Hansard* should only be used if there was a clear statement by the Minister introducing the legislation, which would resolve the ambiguity or absurdity. The Lord Chancellor opposed the use of *Hansard* on practical grounds, pointing out the time and cost it would take to research *Hansard* in every case.

The only time that a wider use of *Hansard* is permitted is where the court is considering an Act that introduced an international convention or European Directive into English law. This was pointed out by the Queen's Bench Divisional Court in *Three Rivers District Council and others v Bank of England (No 2)* (1996). In such a situation it is important to interpret the statute purposively and consistently with any European materials and the court can look at ministerial statements, even if the statute does not appear to be ambiguous or obscure.

Since 1992 *Hansard* has been referred to in a number of cases, even sometimes when there did not appear to be any ambiguity or absurdity. The Lord Chancellor's predictions on cost have been confirmed by some solicitors, with one estimating that it had added 25 per cent to the bill. On other occasions it is clear that *Hansard* has not been helpful or that the court would have reached the same conclusion in any event.

Law reform reports

As with *Hansard*, the courts used to hold that reports by law reform agencies should not be considered by the courts. However this rule was relaxed in the *Black Clawson* case in 1975, when it was accepted that such a report should be looked at to discover the mischief or gap in the law which the legislation based on the report was designed to deal with (see Chapter 19 for more detail on law reform agencies).

International conventions

In *Fothergill v Monarch Airlines Ltd* (1980) the House of Lords decided that the original convention should be considered as it was possible that in translating and adapting the convention to our legislative process, the true meaning of the original might have been lost. The House of Lords in that same case also held that an English court could consider any preparatory materials or explanatory notes published with an international convention. The reasoning behind this was that other countries allowed the use of such material, known as *travaux préparatoires*, and it should therefore be allowed in the UK in order to get uniformity in the interpretation of international rules.

Example of use of extrinsic aids

Several extrinsic aids were considered in *Laroche v Spirit of Adventure (UK) Ltd* (2009).

Laroche v Spirit of Adventure (UK) Ltd (2009)

The claimant had been injured as the result of a sudden landing of a hot air balloon in which he was travelling. The meaning of the word 'aircraft' was important. Was a hot air balloon within the definition of 'aircraft'? If so, then the claim would fail as it had not been made within two years of the accident.

In deciding the case the Court of Appeal first looked at the definition of 'aircraft' in the Pocket Oxford Dictionary. This defined 'aircraft' as 'aeroplane(s), airship(s) and balloon(s)'. The court also looked at the Air Navigation Order 2000 (a statutory instrument). This supported the view that a hot air balloon should be regarded as an 'aircraft'.

In addition, the court pointed out that the English law had to be interpreted in a similar way to international carriage by air which is ruled by an international convention, the Warsaw Convention.

As a result of considering these three extrinsic aids, the court ruled that a hot air balloon was regarded as an 'aircraft'. This meant that the claim failed as it not been brought within the two years' time limit.

17.8 The effect of EU law

The purposive approach is the one preferred by most European countries when interpreting their own legislation. It is also the approach which has been adopted by the European Court of Justice (see Chapter 18) in interpreting European law.

Since the United Kingdom became a member of the European Union in 1973 the influence of the European preference for the purposive approach has affected the English courts in two ways. Firstly, they have had to accept that, at least for law which has been passed as a result of having to conform to a European law, the purposive approach is the correct one use. Secondly, the fact that judges are having to use the purposive approach for European law is making them more accustomed to it and, therefore, more likely to apply it to English law.

17.8.1 Interpreting EU law

Where the law to be interpreted is based on European law, the English courts must interpret it in the light of the wording and purpose of the European law. This is because the Treaty of Rome, which sets out the duties of European member states, says that all member states are required to:

 take all appropriate measures … to ensure fulfilment of the obligations.

The European Court of Justice in the *Marleasing* case (1992) ruled that this included interpreting national law in the light and the aim of the European law.

An example of the English courts interpreting law by looking at the purpose of the relevant European Union law is *Diocese of Hallam Trustee v Connaughton* (1996). This case is discussed in full in Chapter 18, at 18.2.1.

17.9 The effect of the Human Rights Act 1998

Section 3 of the Human Rights Act says that, so far as it is possible to do so, legislation must be read and given effect in a way which is compatible with the rights in the European Convention on Human Rights. This applies to any case where one of the rights is concerned, but it does not apply where there is no involvement of human rights.

An example of the effect of the Human Rights Act on interpretation is *Mendoza v Ghiadan* (2002). In this case the Court of Appeal ignored a House of Lords' judgment which had been made prior to the implementation of the Human Rights Act.

The Rent Act 1977 applied where a person who had the tenancy of a house or flat died. If the tenant had been living in the property with their spouse, then the spouse had the right to take over the tenancy. The Rent Act also allowed unmarried partners to succeed to the tenancy as it stated that 'a person who was living with the original tenant as his or her wife or husband shall be treated as the spouse of the original tenant'.

In *Mendoza v Ghaidan* the question was whether same sex partners had the right to take over the tenancy. A House of Lords' decision, made before the Human Rights Act came into effect, had ruled that same sex partners did not have the right under the Rent Act to take over the tenancy.

The Court of Appeal held that the Rent Act had to be interpreted to conform to the European Convention on Human Rights which forbids discrimination on the ground of gender. In order to make the Act compatible with human rights, the Court of Appeal read the words 'living with the original tenant as his or her wife or husband' in to mean 'as *if they were* his or her wife or husband'. This allowed same sex partners to have the same rights as unmarried opposite sex couples.

The Court of Appeal pointed out the importance of conforming to the Convention rights when they said:

 In order to remedy this breach of the Convention the court must, if it can, read the Schedule so that its provisions are rendered compatible with the Convention rights of the survivors of same-sex partnerships.

In 2004 the House of Lords confirmed the Court of Appeal's decision in this case.

17.10 Rules of language

Even the literal rule does not take words in complete isolation. It is common sense that the other words in the Act must be looked at to see if they affect the word or phrase which is in dispute. In looking at the other words in the Act the courts have developed a number of minor rules which can help to make the meaning of words and phrases clear where a particular sentence construction has been used. These rules, which also have Latin names, are:

- the *ejusdem generis* rule
- the express mention of one thing excludes others
- a word is known by the company it keeps.

17.10.1 The *ejusdem generis* rule

This states that where there is a list of words followed by general words, then the general words are limited to the same kind of items as the specific words. This is easier to understand by looking at cases.

Hobbs v CG Robertson Ltd (1970)

A workman had injured his eye when brickwork which he was removing splintered. He claimed compensation under the Construction (General Provision) Regulation 1961. These regulations made it a duty for employers to provide goggles for workmen when 'breaking, cutting, dressing or carving of stone, concrete, slag or similar material'. The court held that brick did not come within the term 'a similar material'. Brick was not ejusdem generis with stone, concrete, slag. The reason was that all the other materials were hard, so that bits would fly off them when struck with a tool, whereas brick was a soft material. This ruling meant that the workman's claim for compensation failed.

There must be at least two specific words in a list before the general word or phrase for this rule to operate. This is illustrated by *Allen v Emmerson* (1944).

Allen v Emmerson (1944)

The court had to interpret the phrase 'theatres and other places of amusement' and decide if it applied to a funfair. As there was only one specific word, 'theatres', it was decided that a funfair did come under the general term 'other places of amusement' even though it was not of the same kind as theatres.

17.10.2 *Expressio unius exclusio alterius* (the mention of one thing excludes others)

Where there is a list of words which is not followed by general words, then the Act applies only to the items in the list.

Tempest v Kilner (1846)

The court had to consider whether the Statute of Frauds 1677 (which required a contract for the sale of 'goods, wares and merchandise' of more than £10 to be evidenced in writing) applied to a contract for the sale of stocks and shares. The list 'goods, wares and merchandise' was not followed by any general words, so the court held that only contracts for those three types of things were affected by the statute; because stocks and shares were not mentioned they were not caught by the statute.

17.10.3 *Noscitur a sociis* (a word is known by the company it keeps)

This means that the words must be looked at in context and interpreted accordingly; it involves looking at other words in the same section or at other sections in the Act. Words in the same section were important in *Inland Revenue Commissioners v Frere* (1965).

Inland Revenue Commissioners v Frere (1965)

The case involved interpreting a section which set out rules for 'interest, annuities or other annual interest'. The first use of the word 'interest' on its own could have meant any interest paid, whether daily, monthly or annually. Because of the words 'other annual interest' in the section, the court decided that 'interest' only meant annual interest.

Other sections of the Act were considered by the House of Lords in *Bromley London Borough Council v Greater London Council* (1982).

Bromley London Borough Council v Greater London Council (1982)

The issue in this case was whether the GLC could operate a cheap fare scheme on their transport systems, where the amounts being charged meant that the transport system would run at a loss. The decision in the case revolved around the meaning of the word 'economic'. The House of Lords looked at the whole Act and, in particular, at another section which imposed a duty to make up any deficit as far as possible. As a result they decided that 'economic' meant being run on business lines and ruled that the cheap fares policy was not legal since it involved deliberately running the transport system at a loss and this was not running it on business lines.

Self-Test Questions

1 Explain what is meant by an internal aid to statutory interpretation.
2 What is Hansard?
3 Which case allowed Hansard to be used for statutory interpretation?
4 What are the limitations on the use of Hansard in statutory interpretation?
5 Give two other aids to interpretation.
6 What approach does European law use in statutory interpretation?
7 How does the Human Rights Act 1998 affect interpretation in cases which involve human rights?
8 Explain the ejusdem generis (of the same kind) rule.
9 Explain one other rule of language.
10 Give two presumptions that are made when interpreting an Act.

17.11 Presumptions

The courts will also make certain presumptions or assumptions about the law, but these are only a starting point. If the statute clearly states the opposite, then the presumption will not apply and it is said that the presumption is rebutted. The most important presumptions are:

1. A presumption against a change in the common law
    In other words it is assumed that the common law will apply unless Parliament has made it plain in the Act that the common law has been altered. An example of this occurred in *Leach v R* (1912), where the question was whether a wife could be made to give evidence against her husband under the Criminal Evidence Act 1898. Since the Act did not expressly say that this should happen, it was held that the common law rule that a wife could not be compelled to give evidence still applied. If there had been explicit words saying that a wife was compellable then the old common law would not apply. This is now

the position under s 80 of the Police and Criminal Evidence Act 1984, which expressly states that in a crime of violence one spouse can be made to give evidence against the other spouse.

2. A presumption that *mens rea* is required in criminal cases
    The basic common law rule is that no one can be convicted of a crime unless it is shown that they had the required intention to commit it. In *Sweet v Parsley* (1970) the defendant was charged with being concerned with the management of premises which were used for the purposes of smoking cannabis. The facts were that the defendant was the owner of premises which she had leased out and the tenants had smoked cannabis there without her knowledge. She was clearly 'concerned in the management' of the premises and cannabis had been smoked there, but because she had no knowledge of the events she had no *mens rea*. The key issue was whether *mens rea* was required; the Act did not say there was any need for knowledge of the events. The House

of Lords held that she was not guilty as the presumption that *mens rea* was required had not been rebutted.

3. A presumption that the Crown is not bound by any statute unless the statute expressly says so.

4. A presumption that legislation does not apply retrospectively
   This means that no Act of Parliament will apply to past happenings; each Act will normally only apply from the date it comes into effect.

Examination Questions

Read the source material below and answer parts (a) to (c) which follow.

Source A

"I have been long and deeply impressed with the wisdom of the rule now, I believe, universally adopted, at least in the courts of law, that in construing statutes, the grammatical and ordinary sense of the words is to be adhered to, unless that would lead to some absurdity, or some repugnance or inconsistency, in which case the grammatical and ordinary sense of the words may be modified, so as to avoid the absurdity, but no farther.

According to the golden rule, therefore, the court is supposed to follow the literal rule unless it produces absurdity (and perhaps inconvenience or inconsistency), in which case it should find some other meaning."

Adapted from Lord Wensleydale,
Grey v Pearson, 1857

Source B

Meah v Roberts [1978] 1 All ER 97, DC

A customer ordering lemonade for his children in an Indian restaurant was served with caustic soda, which was used for cleaning the beer pipes and had been stored in a lemonade bottle under the bar. The restaurant manager was convicted under section 8(1) Food and Drugs Act 1955 of selling food intended but not fit for human consumption (which under the statute expressly includes drink). Dismissing his appeal, the Divisional Court using the golden rule said the supply of something purporting to be lemonade was a supply of food for the purposes of the Act.

Adapted from: *www.francisbennion.com*

(a) Source A refers to the literal rule.

Describe the literal rule using source A and cases to illustrate your answer.   15 marks

(b) Consider whether any of the following are guilty under section 8(1) Food and Drugs Act 1955 (source B) of selling food unfit for but intended for human consumption using source B and the rules of statutory interpretation:

(i)   Mark, a butcher, is knowingly selling chickens which are two weeks out of date.   5 marks

(ii) Lucy, a restaurant manager, sells a customer what she believes to be water, but is in fact bleach.   5 marks

(iii) Sunhill, a bar manager, is having a charity barbeque. He gives a free burger to all those who attend. The burgers are contaminated.   5 marks

(c) Sources A and B illustrate the golden rule.

(i)   Describe the golden rule using the sources and other cases to illustrate your answer.   15 marks

(ii) Discuss the advantages and disadvantages of the golden rule.   15 marks

OCR G152 January 2011

Exam tips

It is important to learn about the other tools judges can use when they are interpreting statutes. Accurate knowledge is important and you can try to learn the Latin names if you like, but being able to explain how the rules are applied will work too. Examples are crucial as they will raise the quality of an answer, as does referring to relevant points in the sources – you can best do this by using the line numbers as a point of reference rather then copying out information.

Questions refer you to the source so don't ignore this material – it really is important and teaches you legal skills as a lawyer's view will always be informed by evidence based on the law. This topic also requires you to understand the relationship between the law made in England and Wales with that made by the EU, as well as the impact the Human Rights Act 1998 has had on law making. This is an interesting area and allows you to see the bigger picture, which is an important aspect of being a good law student; our law cannot operate in isolation of other responsibilities. In a discussion question you might be asked to explore the relationship between the judge and Parliament and here you can link back to some of the analytical points you considered when looking at the doctrine of precedent and the role of the judges.

There are lots of case examples so it is worth having some which illustrate different perspectives in your answer. Use past paper questions too as these can give some guidance and offer useful practice for the part (b) application questions – these might seem like very small questions but they add up to 15 marks out of a total of 60 and doing them well can make a considerable difference to your overall grade. Make sure you give yourself enough time for each part of the question and focus on what you are being asked to do so that you tailor what you write appropriately.

Chapter 18

European law

O n 1 January 1973 the United Kingdom joined what was then the European Economic Community, and another source of law came into being: European law. Since then it has had increasing significance as a source of law. The European Economic Community was originally set up by Germany, France, Italy, Belgium, the Netherlands and Luxembourg in 1957 by the Treaty of Rome. The name 'European Union' was introduced by the Treaty of European Union in 1993. Denmark and Ireland joined at the same time as the United Kingdom. In the 1980s and 1990s Greece, Spain, Portugal, Austria, Finland and Sweden joined. Then on 1 May 2004 another ten countries joined the EU. These were Cyprus, Czech Republic, Estonia, Hungary, Latvia, Lithuania, Malta, Poland, Slovak Republic and Slovenia. The most recent members are Bulgaria and Romania who joined on 1 January 2007. There are now 27 Member States (see Figure 18.1).

In 2009 the Treaty of Lisbon restructured the European Union. There are now two treaties setting out its rules. These are:

- Treaty of European Union (TEU)
- Treaty of the Functioning of the European Union (TFEU).

18.1 The institutions of the European Union

In order to implement the aims of the treaties, the European Union has a vast and complex organisation with institutions. The main institutions which exercise the functions of the Union are:

- the Council of the European Union
- the Commission
- the European Parliament
- the Court of Justice.

Date	Countries joining	Comment
1957	Belgium France Germany Italy Luxembourg The Netherlands	These are the founder members Treaty of Rome signed
1973	Denmark Ireland United Kingdom	UK passes the European Communities Act 1972 on joining
1981	Greece	
1986	Portugal Spain	
1995	Austria Finland Sweden	
2004	Cyprus, Czech Republic, Estonia, Hungary, Latvia, Lithuania, Malta, Poland, Slovak Republic and Slovenia	
2007	Bulgaria Romania	

Figure 18.1 Chart showing the Member States of the European Union

18.1.1 The Council

The Government of each nation in the Union sends a representative to the Council. The Foreign Minister is usually a country's main representative, but a government is free to send any of its Ministers to Council meetings. This means that usually the Minister responsible for the topic under consideration will attend the meetings of the Council, so that the precise membership will vary with the subject being discussed. For example, the Minister for Agriculture will attend when the issue to be discussed involves agriculture. Twice a year government heads meet in the European Council or 'Summit' to discuss broad matters of policy. The Member States take it in turn to provide the President of the Council, each for a six-month period.

The Council is the principal decision-making body of the Union. Voting in the Council is on a weighted basis with each country having a number of votes roughly in proportion to the size of its population.

18.1.2 The Commission

This consists of 27 Commissioners who are supposed to act independently of their national origin. Each Member State has one Commissioner.

The Commissioners are appointed for a five-year term and can only be removed during this term of office by a vote of censure by the European Parliament. Each Commissioner heads a department with special responsibility for one area of Union policy, such as economic affairs, agriculture or the environment.

The Commission as a whole has several functions as follows:

- It is the motive power behind Union policy as it proposes policies and presents drafts of legislation to the Council for the Council's consideration. In its own booklet on Union law, the European Union says the relationship between the Commission and the Council can be briefly summarised by saying 'the Commission proposes and the Council disposes'.

- The Commission is also the 'guardian' of the treaties. It ensures that treaty provisions and other measures adopted by the Union are properly implemented. If a Member State has failed to implement Union law within its own country, or has infringed a Provision in some way, the Commission has a duty to intervene and, if necessary, refer the matter to the Court of Justice of the European Union. The Commission has performed this duty very effectively, and as a result there have been judgments given by the Court against Britain and other Member States.
- It is responsible for the administration of the Union and has executive powers to implement the Union's budget.

Internet Research

Use the internet to find out more about the European Commission. Find out who is the Commissioner for the United Kingdom. Try http://europa.eu.

elections which take place once every five years. Within the Parliament the Members do not operate in national groups, but form political groups with those of the same political allegiance. The Parliament meets on average about once a month for sessions that can last up to a week. It has standing committees which discuss proposals made by the Commission and then report to the full Parliament for debate. Decisions made by the Parliament are not binding, though they will influence the Council of Ministers.

The main criticism is that the Parliament has no real power. However, the assent of Parliament is required to any international agreements the Union wishes to enter into. This allows it an important role in deciding whether new members should be admitted to the Union. It also has some power over the Union budget, especially in non-compulsory expenditure, where it has the final decision on whether to approve the budget or not.

Figure 18.2 Map showing countries of the European Union

18.1.3 The European Parliament

The European Parliament has no direct law-making authority. Its main function is to discuss proposals put forward by the Commission. The members of the European Parliament are directly elected by the people of the Member States in

18.2 The Court of Justice of the European Union

Its function is set out in Art 19 of the Treaty of the European Union (TEU). This states that the Court must 'ensure that in the interpretation and application of the Treaty the law is observed'. The court sits in Luxembourg and has 27 judges, one from each Member State. For a full court, 11 judges will sit, but it also sits in chambers of five judges or three judges. Judges are appointed from those who are eligible for appointment to the highest judicial posts in their own country or who are leading academic lawyers. Each judge is appointed for a term of six years, and can be

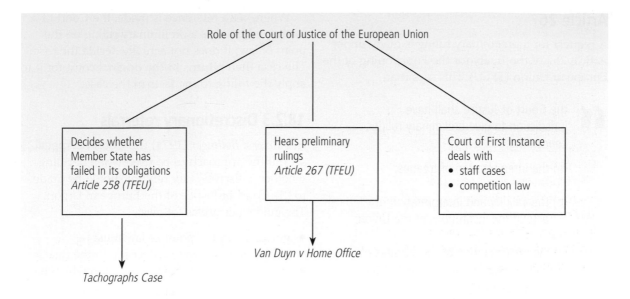

Figure 18.3 Role of the Court of Justice of the European Union

re-appointed for a further term of six years. The judges select one of themselves to be President of the Court.

The Court is assisted by nine Advocates General who also hold office for six years. Each case is assigned to an Advocate General whose task is to research all the legal points involved and 'to present publicly, with complete impartiality and independence, reasoned conclusions on cases submitted to the Court of Justice with a view to assisting the latter in the performance of its duties'.

18.2.1 Role of the court

The court's task is to ensure that the law is applied uniformly in all Member States (see Figure 18.3) and it does this by performing two key roles:

- hearing cases to decide whether Member States have fulfilled their obligations
- hearing references under Art 267 (TFEU) from national courts for preliminary rulings on a point of EU law.

Hearings in respect of Member States' obligations

Such actions are usually initiated by the European Commission, although they can also be started by another Member State. An early example of such a case was *Re Tachographs: The Commission v United Kingdom* (1979) in which the court held that the United Kingdom had to implement a Council Regulation on the use of mechanical recording equipment (tachographs) in road vehicles used for the carriage of goods (see 18.2.2 for further information on the effect of Regulations).

18.2.2 Article 267 rulings

The second key function is that it hears references from national courts for preliminary rulings on points of European law. This function is a very important one since rulings made by the Court of Justice are then binding on courts in all Member States. This ensures that the law is indeed uniform throughout the European Union.

Article 267

A request for a preliminary ruling is made under Article 267 of the Treaty for the Functioning of the European Union (TFEU). This says that:

 the Court of Justice shall have jurisdiction to give preliminary rulings concerning:

(a) the interpretation of treaties;

(b) the validity and interpretation of acts of the institutions of the Union;

(c) the interpretation of the statutes of bodies established by an act of the Council, where those statutes so provide.

Article 267 goes on to state that where there is no appeal from the national court within the national system, then such a court *must* refer points of European Law to the Court of Justice. Other national courts are allowed to make an Art 267 reference, but as there is still an appeal available within their own system, such courts do not have to do so. They have a discretion (that is, they can choose whether or not to refer the case).

Applied to the court structure in England and Wales, this means that the Supreme Court must refer questions of European law, since it is the highest appeal court in our system. However, the Court of Appeal does not have to refer questions. It has a choice: it may refer if it wishes or it may decide the case without any referral. The same is true of all the lower courts in the English court hierarchy.

However, even courts at the bottom of the hierarchy can refer questions of law under Article 267, if they feel that a preliminary ruling is necessary to enable a judgment to be given. An example of this was in *Torfaen Borough Council v B & Q* (1990) when Cwmbran Magistrates' Court made a reference on whether the restrictions which then existed on Sunday were in breach of the Treaty of Rome.

Whenever a reference is made, the Court of Justice only makes a preliminary ruling on the point of law; it does not actually decide the case. The case then returns to the original court for it to apply the ruling to the facts in the case.

18.2.3 Discretionary referrals

In *Bulmer v Bollinger* (1974) the Court of Appeal set out the approach to be used when deciding whether a discretionary referral should be made to the Court of Justice of the European Union. The guidelines are as follows:

- guidance on the point of law must be necessary to come to a decision in the case
- there is no need to refer a question which has already been decided by the Court of Justice in a previous case
- there is no need to refer a point which is reasonably clear and free from doubt; this is known as the *'acte clair'* doctrine
- the court must consider all the circumstances of the case
- the English court retains the discretion on whether to refer or not.

The first case to be referred to the Court of Justice of the European Union by an English court was *Van Duyn v Home Office* (1974).

18.2.4 How the court operates

When compared with English courts there are several major differences in the way in which the Court of Justice of the European Union operates. First the emphasis is on presenting cases 'on paper'. Lawyers are required to present their arguments in a written form and there is far less reliance on oral presentation of a case. This requirement is, of course, partly because of the wide range of languages involved, though French is the traditional language of the Court. It also represents the traditional method of case presentation in other European countries. An interesting point to note is that the English system in some areas is now beginning to use this 'paper' submission.

Key facts

Council	• Consists of Ministers from each Member State • Responsible for broad policy decisions • Under Art 288 (TFEU) can issue regulations, directives and decisions
Commission	• 27 Commissioners whose duty it is to act in Union's interest • Proposes legislation • Tries to ensure the implementation of the Treaties and can bring court action against Member States who do not comply with EU law
European Parliament	• Members voted for by electorate in each of the Member States • Consultative body, has limited powers
Court of Justice	• Judges from each Member State, assisted by Advocates-General • Rules on European law when cases are referred under Art 267 (TFEU)

Figure 18.4 Key facts chart on the institutions of the European Union

The Court of Justice of the European Union

Advocates-General

A second major difference is the use of Advocates-General. This independent lawyer is not used in the English system. However in the Court of Justice the Advocate-General who was assigned to the case will present his findings on the law after the parties have made their submissions. The court, therefore, has the advantage of having all aspects of the law presented to them.

One judgment

The deliberations of the judges are secret and where necessary the decision will be made by a majority vote. However, when the judgment is delivered, again in a written form, it is signed by all the judges who formed part of the panel, so that it is not known if any judges disagreed with the majority. This contrasts strongly with the English system, whereby a dissenting judge not only makes it known that he disagrees with the majority, but also usually delivers a judgment explaining his reasoning.

Not bound by own decisions

The other points to be noted are that the Court of Justice of the European Union is not bound by its own previous decisions and that it prefers the purposive approach to interpretation (see 17.6 for an explanation of the purposive approach).

Use of extrinsic material

The court has wide rights to study extrinsic material when deciding the meaning of provisions and may study preparatory documents. The Court of Justice is important, not only because its decisions are binding on English courts, but also because its attitude to interpretation is increasingly being followed by English courts. The Court of Justice pointed this out in *von Colson v Land Nordrhein-Westfalen* (1984) when it said:

 national courts are required to interpret their national law in the light of the wording and the purpose of the directive. 🙷

Self-Test Questions

1 When did the UK join the EU (the European Economic Community, as it was then called)?
2 Briefly explain the role of the Commission.
3 How many judges are there in the Court of Justice of the European Union?
4 Under which Article of which Treaty can national judges refer a point of EU law to the Court of Justice for a preliminary ruling?
5 Which court in the UK *must* refer a case to the Court of Justice for a preliminary ruling if there is an unclear point of EU involved?
6 Which other courts in the UK *may* refer a case to the Court of Justice for a preliminary ruling on a point of EU law?
7 Explain two differences in the working of the Court of Justice of the European Union and courts in England and Wales.

Exam tips

EU Law is of fundamental importance – after all, your studies elsewhere will have shown you that, where it is relevant, it is our most important source! However, students often find it is a difficult area to master; this is a shame as it covers some interesting issues and it regularly appears on the exam paper. Think of the topic in two parts – the first being the institutions which make up the EU, and their various roles, and the second being the types of law making and the impact these have on the English legal system. The terminology might be different but the institutions do jobs you will recognise from elsewhere in your studies. It is worth focusing on getting the detail right – using correct Article numbers is a prime example – and knowing the number of people involved in any institution and having a clear sense of the job they do will improve your answer.

The EU has a website, http://europa.eu, which gives you excellent links to information which can help you get to grips with this topic. As in other questions on G152, use the source to guide your answer and it will also give you valuable triggers from which you can develop your own points. This is a topic which it is worth persevering with – you can do well and if you go on to study Law at university it will be a compulsory component of your degree, so it's worth getting started now.

18.3 European sources of law

These are classed as primary and secondary sources of law. Primary sources are mainly the Treaties, the most important of which is the Treaty of the European Union. Secondary sources are legislation passed by the Institutions of the Union under Art 267 (TFEU). This secondary legislation is of three types: regulations, directives and decisions, all of which are considered below.

18.3.1 Treaties

So far as our law is concerned all treaties signed by our head of government become part of English law automatically. This is as a result of the European Communities Act 1972, s 2(1) which states that:

> All such rights, powers, liabilities, obligations and restrictions from time to time created or arising by or under the Treaties and all such remedies and procedures from time to time provided for by or under the Treaties, as in accordance with the Treaties *are*

without further enactment to be given legal effect or used in the United Kingdom, shall be recognised and available in law and be enforced, allowed and followed accordingly.

Direct effect

This not only makes European Union law part of our law but also allows individuals to rely on it. In the case of *Van Duyn* v *Home Office* (1974) the Court of Justice held that an individual was entitled to rely on Art 39 (now Art 45 TFEU) giving the right of freedom of movement. The Article had direct effect and conferred rights on individuals which could be enforced not only in the Court of Justice, but also in national courts.

This means that citizens of the United Kingdom are entitled to rely on the rights in the treaties, even though those rights may not have been specifically enacted in English law. This is clearly illustrated by the case of *Macarthys Ltd v Smith* (1980).

Macarthys Ltd v Smith (1980)

Wendy Smith's employers paid her less than her male predecessor for exactly the same job. As the two people were not employed at the same time by the employer there was no breach of English domestic law. However, Wendy Smith was able to claim that the company which employed her was in breach of Art 141 of the Treaty of Rome (now Art 157 (TFEU)) over equal pay for men and women, and this claim was confirmed by the Court of Justice.

The growing influence of European law is shown in that British courts are prepared to apply European Treaty law directly rather than wait for the Court of Justice to make a ruling on the point. This is illustrated in *Diocese of Hallam Trustee v Connaughton* (1996). In this case the Employment Appeal Tribunal had to consider facts which had some similarity to the Wendy Smith case.

Diocese of Hallam Trustee v Connaughton (1996)

Josephine Connaughton was employed as director of music by the Diocese of Hallam from 1990 to September 1994, at which time her salary was £11,138. When she left the position, the post was advertised at a salary of £13,434, but the successful applicant, a man, was actually appointed at a salary of £20,000. In other words, where in Wendy Smith's case she had discovered that her male predecessor was paid more than she was, in the *Connaughton* case it was the immediate successor who was receiving considerably higher pay.

The Employment Appeal Tribunal considered Art 141 of the Treaty of Rome and decided as a preliminary point that its provisions were wide enough to allow Miss Connaughton to make a claim, saying:

 We are sufficiently satisfied as to the scope of Article 141 so as to decide this appeal without further reference to the European Court of Justice.

Similarly the House of Lords in *R v Secretary of State, ex parte EOC* (1994) decided, without referring the case to the Court of Justice, that the longer period of qualification for redundancy for those working less than 16 hours a week discriminated against women and was contrary to Art 141.

18.3.2 Regulations

Under Art 288 (TFEU) the European Union has the power to issue regulations which are

 binding in every respect and directly applicable in each Member State.

Such regulations do not have to be adopted in any way by the individual states, as Art 288 makes it clear that they automatically become law in each member country.

This 'direct applicability' point was tested in *Re Tachographs: Commission v United Kingdom* (1979).

Re Tachographs: Commission v United Kingdom (1979)

A regulation requiring mechanical recording equipment to be installed in lorries was issued. The United Kingdom Government of the day decided not to implement the regulation, but to leave it to lorry owners to decide whether or not to put in such equipment. When the matter was referred to the Court of Justice it was held that Member States had no discretion in the case of regulations. The wording of Art 288 was explicit and meant that regulations were automatically law in all Member States.

States cannot pick and choose which regulations they will implement. In this way regulations make sure that laws are uniform across all the Member States.

Direct effect

Regulations have direct effect. This means that, provided a regulation is clear and gives rights to individuals, the regulation can be relied on by an individual in any case in the UK. Individuals can enforce the rights given by a regulation against both the State and any other person or business.

18.3.3 Directives

Directives are the main way in which harmonisation of laws within Member States is reached. There have been directives covering many topics including company laws, banking, insurance, health and safety of workers, equal rights, consumer law and social security.

As with regulations, it is Art 288 (TFEU) that gives the power to the Union to issue directives. There is, however, a difference from regulations in that Art 288 says such directives

 bind any Member State to which they are addressed as to the result to be achieved, while leaving to domestic agencies a competence as to form and means.

Key facts

Type of law	Effect	Source
Treaties	Directly applicable	Section 2(1) of the European Communities Act 1972
	Have direct effect (both vertically and horizontally) if give individual rights and are clear	*Macarthys v Smith* (1979)
Regulations	Directly applicable	Article 288 (TFEU)
	Have direct effect (both vertically and horizontally) if give individual rights and are clear	
Directives	NOT directly applicable	Article 288 (TFEU)
	Have vertical direct effect if give individual rights and are clear	*Marshall* case (1986)
	NO horizontal direct effect	*Duke v GEC Reliance* (1988)
	But individual can claim against State for loss caused by failure to implement	*Francovich v Italian Republic* (1991)

Figure 18.5 Key facts chart showing effect of EU laws

This means that Member States will pass their own laws to bring directives into effect (or implement them) and such laws have to be brought in within a time limit set by the European Commission.

Implementation

The usual method of implementing directives in the United Kingdom is by Statutory Instrument. An example is the Unfair Terms in Consumer Contracts Regulations 1994, which implemented a directive aimed at giving consumers protection from unfair terms in contracts. Directives can, however, be implemented by other law-making methods. An example is the Consumer Protection Act 1987. A directive on liability for defective products was issued in July 1985. (This was some nine years after the proposal had first been put forward by the Commission!) The Directive had to be implemented by 30 July 1988. This was done in the UK by Parliament passing the Consumer Protection Act 1987, which came into force on 1 March 1988.

Directives can also be implemented by an order in Council made by the Privy Council.

Working Time Directive

Another example of a directive is the Working Time Directive which was issued in 1993. This directive gave detailed instructions of the maximum number of hours that should be worked, the rest periods and the amount of paid holiday to which workers were entitled. It should have been implemented by November 1996 but the UK Government did not implement it until October 1998, with the Working Time Regulations 1998.

Direct effect

Where Member States have not implemented a directive within the time laid down, the Court of Justice of the European Union has developed the concept of 'direct effect'.

If the purpose of a directive is to grant rights to individuals and that directive is sufficiently clear, it may be directly enforceable by an individual against the Member State. This will be so even though that State has not implemented the directive, or has implemented it in a defective way. The important point is that an individual who is adversely affected by the failure to implement only has rights against the State. This is because of the concepts of vertical effect and horizontal effect (see Figure 18.6).

Vertical direct effect

A case illustrating vertical direct effect is *Marshall v Southampton and South West Hampshire Area Health Authority* (1986).

> *Marshall v Southampton and South West Hampshire Area Health Authority* (1986)
>
> Miss Marshall was required to retire at the age of 62 whereas men doing the same work did not have to retire until aged 65. Under the Sex Discrimination Act 1975 in English law this was not discriminatory. However, she was able to succeed in an action for unfair dismissal by relying on the Equal Treatment Directive 76/207. This Directive had not been fully implemented in the United Kingdom but the Court of Justice held that it was sufficiently clear and imposed obligations on the Member State. This ruling allowed Miss Marshall to succeed in her claim against her employers because her employers were 'an arm of the state'; that is, they were considered as being part of the State. The Directive had vertical effect, allowing her to rely on it and take action against them.

The concept of the State for these purposes is quite wide, as it was ruled by the Court of Justice in *Foster v British Gas plc* (1990) that it was:

> ❝ a body, whatever its legal form, which has been made responsible, pursuant to a measure adopted by the State, for providing a public service under the control of the State and has for that purpose special powers beyond those which result from the normal rules applicable in relations between individuals. ❞

In view of this wide definition the House of Lords decided that British Gas, which at the time was a nationalised industry, was part of the State, and Foster could rely on the Equal Treatment Directive.

The concept of vertical effect means that a Member State cannot take advantage of its own failure to comply with European law and implement a directive. Individuals can rely on the directive when bringing a claim against the State.

This concept of vertical effect was also used in the case of *Gibson v East Riding of Yorkshire Council* (1999).

> *Gibson v East Riding of Yorkshire Council* (1999)
>
> Mrs Gibson was employed as a part-time swimming instructor. She did not get paid holidays. The Employment Appeal Tribunal held that under the Working Time Directive she was entitled to four weeks' paid holiday from November 1996, the date that the directive should have been implemented. Her employers were an 'emanation of the State' and could not rely on the lack of domestic legislation to defeat her claim.

Horizontal direct effect

Directives which have not been implemented do not, however, give an individual any rights against other people. So, in *Duke v GEC Reliance Ltd* (1988), Mrs Duke was unable to rely on the Equal Treatment Directive as her employer was a private company. This illustrates that directives do not have horizontal effect and this has been confirmed by an Italian case, *Paola Faccini Dori v Recreb Srl* (1994), in which the Italian

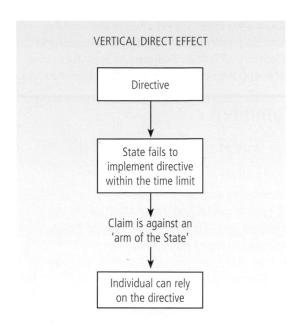

Figure 18.6 Vertical and horizontal direct effect

Government failed to implement Directive 85/447 in respect of consumer rights to cancel certain contracts. Dori could not rely on the directive in order to claim a right of cancellation against a private trader.

Duty to interpret national law in the light of directives

Even where a directive has not been implemented, national courts have a duty to interpret their national law in the light of the wording and purpose of any relevant directive.

This was pointed out by the Court of Justice in the earlier case of *von Colson v Land Nordrhein-Westfalen* (1984) that

> national courts are required to interpret their national law in the light of the wording and the purpose of the directive.

Actions against the State for failure to implement a directive

Clearly it is unfair that these conflicting doctrines of vertical and horizontal effect should give rights to individuals in some cases and not in others. The Court of Justice has developed another strategy under which it may be possible to take an action to claim damages against the Member State which has failed to implement the European directive. This was decided in *Francovich v Italian Republic* (1991) where the Italian Government failed to implement a directive aimed at protecting wages of employees whose employer became insolvent. As a result when the firm for which Francovich worked went into liquidation owing him wages, he sued the State for his financial loss. The Court of Justice held that he was entitled to compensation. The court said that:

> Community law required the Member States to make good damage caused by a failure to transpose a directive, provided three conditions were fulfilled;
>
> First, the purpose of the directive had to be to grant rights to individuals.
>
> Second, it had to be possible to identify the content of those rights on the basis of the provisions of the directive.
>
> Finally, there had to be a causal link between the breach of the State's obligations and the damage suffered.

In *R v HM Treasury, ex parte British Telecommunications plc* (1996) the Court of Justice held that although a directive on telecommunications had been incorrectly implemented in English law, compensation was not payable as the breach of European Union law was not sufficiently serious.

The principle of Member States being liable to pay compensation has been extended to other breaches by Member States of European Union law.

This was seen in the joined cases of *Brasserie du Pêcheur SA v Federation of Republic of Germany* and *R v Secretary of State for Transport, ex parte Factortame Ltd (No 4)* (1996) which are considered below in 18.4.

Self-Test Questions

1 Which Act of Parliament makes EU treaties automatically part of our law?
2 Treaties have direct effect. Explain what is meant by 'direct effect' in this context.
3 Give a case in which a UK citizen relied on a treaty provision.
4 Which Article of which Treaty gives power to the EU to issue regulations and directives?
5 If a directive is not implemented by the national government, when can an individual rely on it?
6 Explain the difference between 'vertical direct effect' and 'horizontal direct effect'.
7 What did the case of *Francovich v Italian Republic* decide?

Comment

The importance of rulings of the Court of Justice

The development of the concept of direct effect has been a very important one for the effectiveness of EU law. If the Court of Justice had not developed this concept citizens of Member States would not have been able to enforce the rights given to them.

In particular where the Government has not implemented a directive, the rights of individuals in many important areas, especially employment law and discrimination, would have been lost. The rulings of the Court of Justice have allowed individuals to rely on EU law in claims against the State or an arm of the State, and also forced the Government to implement EU law more fully.

The development of the *Francovich* principle has provided citizens with a remedy against the State, when otherwise they would not have had one. However, this brings its own problems as the Court of Justice has no mechanism for enforcing its judgments.

Activity

Below in Source A are set out extracts from Arts 1 and 2 of the Equal Treatment Directive 76/207. Read these and then apply them, giving reasons for your decision, to the facts set out in Source B.

Source A

Council Directive No. 76/207

Article 1
1. The purpose of this Directive is to put into effect in the Member States the principle of equal treatment as regards access to employment, including promotion, and to vocational training and as regards working conditions ... This principle is hereinafter referred to as the 'principle of equal treatment'.

Article 2
1. For the purposes of the following provisions, the principle of equal treatment shall mean that there shall be no discrimination

whatsoever on the grounds of sex either directly or indirectly by reference in particular to marital or family status.

2. This Directive shall be without prejudice to the right of Member States to exclude from its field of application those occupational activities and, where appropriate, the training leading thereto, for which, by reason of their nature or the context in which they are carried out, the sex of the worker constitutes a determining factor.

3. This Directive shall be without prejudice to provisions concerning the protection of women, particularly as regards pregnancy and maternity.

4. This Directive shall be without prejudice to measures to promote equal opportunity for men and women, in particular by removing existing inequalities which affect women's opportunities in the areas referred to in Article 1(1).

Source B

CASE FACTS: Amy Austin and Ben Bowen are employed by Green Gardens Ltd. There is a vacancy for a promotion to section manager, and both have applied for the post. Green Gardens have interviewed Amy and Ben and decided that both are equally qualified for the position. In this situation, if there are fewer women employed at the relevant level, Green Gardens have a policy of appointing the female applicant.

Ben complains that this is discriminatory and contrary to the Equal Treatment Directive.

18.4 Conflict between European law and national law

European law takes precedence over national law. This was first established in *Van Gend en Loos* (1963) which involved a conflict of Dutch law and European law on customs duty. The Dutch Government argued that the Court of Justice had no jurisdiction to decide whether European law should prevail over Dutch law; that was a matter for the Dutch courts to decide. However, the European Court rejected this argument. In *Costa v ENEL* (1964) the Court of Justice held that even if there was a later national law it did not take precedence over the European law. In this case the Court of Justice said:

> the Member States have limited their sovereign rights, albeit within limited fields, and have thus created a body of law which binds both their nationals and themselves.

This conflict was seen clearly in the *Factortame* case (1990) when the Court of Justice decided that Britain could not enforce the Merchant Shipping Act 1988. This Act had been passed to protect British fishermen by allowing vessels to register only if 75 per cent of directors and shareholders were British nationals. It was held that this contravened the Treaty of Rome.

This breach of European Union law has had another effect as the Court of Justice held in a later action in the joined cases of *Brasserie du Pêcheur SA v Federation of Republic of Germany* and *R v Secretary of State for Transport, ex parte Factortame Ltd (No 4)* (1996) that governments were liable for financial loss suffered as a result of their breach of European law. In *Brasserie du Pêcheur* a French company claimed that it was forced to discontinue exports of beer to Germany, because the German authorities considered that the beer did not comply with the purity requirements laid down in German law. In *Factortame* European fishermen claimed that they had been deprived of the right to fish as result of the Merchant Shipping Act 1988. In both cases there was a claim for compensation from the State concerned.

The Court of Justice held that EU law did give the right to compensation provided that three conditions were met. These were:

- the rule of EU law infringed must be intended to confer rights on individuals
- the breach must be sufficiently serious
- there must be a direct causal link between the breach of the obligation resting on the State and the damage sustained by the injured parties.

18.4.1 The effect of European law on the sovereignty of Parliament

From the cases given above it can be seen that Member States, including Britain, have definitely transferred sovereign rights to a Union created by them. None of the Member States can rely on its own law when it is in conflict with European Union Law.

It is also a principle of the Treaty of the European Union that no Member State may call into question the status of Union law as a system of uniformly and generally applicable law throughout the European Union. It therefore follows from this, that EU law has priority over any conflicting law of Member States. This is true both of national laws which were enacted before EU law and also of national laws which were enacted after the relevant EU law.

While Britain is member of the European Union it is therefore true to say that the sovereignty of Parliament has been affected and that, in the areas it operates, European law has supremacy over national law.

Key facts

	Cases	Important decisions
1963	*Van Gend en Loos*	Court of Justice has right to decide whether EU law or national law prevails
1964	*Costa v ENEL*	European law takes precedence over national law
1974	*Van Duyn v Home Office*	Principle of direct applicability Citizens can rely directly on an article of the treaties which confer rights on individuals
1986	*Marshall v Southampton etc Health Authority*	Vertical direct effect of directives In an action against the State individuals can rely on a directive which has not been implemented
1991	*Francovich v Italy*	Individual can claim compensation from State for its failure to implement directive
1996	*Brasserie du Pêcheur, ex parte Factortame No 4*	State liable to compensate for breaches of EU law

Figure 18.7 Key facts chart of some important decisions of the Court of Justice of the European Union

Examination Questions

1 Read the source material below and answer parts (a) to (c) which follow.

Exercise on European Union (EU) Law

Source A

European Union law can be classified into primary and secondary sources of law. Primary sources are mainly the Treaties. Secondary sources are legislation passed by the institutions and include regulations, directives and decisions.

The two most important treaties of the European Union (EU) are the Treaty of Rome (as amended) and the Treaty of Lisbon. These and other treaties have laid down the framework and given the legal authority to the institutions of the EU. The main institutions which exercise the functions of the EU are:

• The Commission
• The European Parliament
• The European Court of Justice (ECJ)

Each of these institutions has a different but essential role with regard to the smooth running and development of the EU. The Council of Ministers is the principal decision-making body; its decision making is sometimes made more difficult due to national interests. The Commission has a range of functions but its two key roles involve proposing legislation and acting as the guardian of the Treaties.

The ECJ has two key functions: judicial and supervisory. The ECJ, through a series of landmark judgments, has ensured that EU legislation has been consistently enforced. In *Francovich v Italy*, the ECJ paved the way for individuals to claim compensation when a Member State had failed to live up to its obligations. This approach conferred on individuals key benefits which would have been lost without the judgment of the ECJ. The ECJ has also ensured that Treaty obligations have been followed in landmark judgments such as *Factortame*. This case clearly highlights that EU law is supreme and must be followed if there is a conflict with national law.

(a) Source A at lines 18–22 refers to the Council of Ministers and the Commission. Describe the role and composition of both the Council of Ministers and the Commission using source A and other examples to illustrate your answer.
                                                             15 marks

(b) Identify and explain the most appropriate source of European Union law in the following situations using source A:
(i) The EU wishes to alter the Treaty of Rome.   5 marks
(ii) The EU wishes to harmonise the law on banking.   5 marks
(iii) The EU wishes to pass a law on insurance that will be instantly and identically applied in all member states.   5 marks

(c) Source A at line 25 refers to the European Court of Justice (ECJ):
(i) Describe the role and composition of the ECJ using source A and other examples to illustrate your answer.   15 marks
(ii) Discuss the impact of ECJ decisions on the enforcement of EU legal rights.   15 marks

OCR G152 January 2012

Exam tips

The second aspect of this topic focuses on the different types of law-making. You can revise these through a mind map; make sure you can use case examples for each type of law-making. Some students get nervous as they find the names long and complicated, but most of the time a shorter name can be used; for example, if you use the name *Factortame* rather than the longer *Brasserie du Pêcheur, ex parte Factortame No 4* the examiner will know exactly which case you mean!

Perhaps the trickiest area of all is the concept of direct effect, but if you can master this, and using the flow charts in this chapter will help you, then you can answer a question on EU law with confidence. The areas of direct applicability and direct effect can also be tackled in part (b) and so it is worth trying to learn how the law works through practical examples.

In a discussion topic you are likely to need to consider the relationship between EU law and the English legal system, so you should prepare some points on this beforehand. However, you need to think about this from the context of the institution making the law and the effect the various types of law-making can have. The key is to think about the issue from different perspectives so that you can be flexible and precise in the material you use depending on the exam question.

Chapter 19

Law reform

19.1 Influences on law reform

It is important to keep the law under review and make sure that it is reformed when necessary. There are many influences on the way our law is formed and the impetus for reform can come from a number of sources. Some of these will have more effect than others. It is also possible that in some situations there may be conflicting interests about the way that the law should be reformed.

19.1.1 Parliament

Throughout any session of Parliament, the Government has the major say on what new laws will be put before the House of Commons and the House of Lords for discussion.

Queen's Speech

At the opening of each session of Parliament (usually once a year) the Government announces its plans for new laws in that session. This is done in the Queen's Speech. This speech is written for the Queen by the Prime Minister and other senior Ministers. This is shown in the speech as the Queen will often use the words 'my Government will … '.

However, there is a problem of the amount of time available in Parliament. A lot of time has to be given to financial matters such as budgets and taxation; foreign policy is also discussed in Parliament, particularly at times of crisis, such as after the terrorist attacks in London in July 2005.

Other topics including education and health must also be given parliamentary time, so the time left for 'pure' law reform is limited.

19.1.2 Judges

When judges decide points of law in cases, they sometimes have to decide a new point. This allows them to 'make' law. Decisions by judges over the years have created the tort of negligence. This is the law that allows you to claim compensation when you have been injured by another person's negligence (see Chapter 14, 14.6). In the criminal law the judges have sometimes created new offences. An important example was when they created the offence of marital rape in *R v R* (1991) (see 14.6).

The House of Lords can use the Practice Statement to alter the law when they think it is right to do so. This power is not used very often. However, it has been used when there has been a change of opinion or social values over several years so that the law did not match current expectations. An example of this use of the Practice Statement was *Herrington v BRB* (1972) (see 14.3.2).

However, judges only create or reform law in a very small number of cases. Their job is to apply the law.

19.1.3 Public opinion

Where there is strong public opinion about a change to the law, the Government may bow to such opinion. This is more likely towards the end of a term of government when there will be a General Election soon and the Government wants to remain popular with the majority of people.

Media

The media play a large role in bringing public opinion to the Government's attention. Where an issue is given a high profile on television and in the newspapers, it is brought to the attention of other members of the public; this may add to the weight of public opinion.

However, in some cases this can be seen as the media manipulating the news and creating public opinion.

19.1.4 Pressure groups

An example of the Government bowing to public opinion and the efforts of a pressure group was the passing of the Hunting Act 2004 which banned hunting foxes with dogs.

Sometimes pressure groups will campaign against a proposed change to the law. This was seen when the Government tried to restrict the right to trial by jury. Pressure groups such as Justice and Liberty campaigned against this as they thought the changes infringed human rights.

There are also occasions when two pressure groups have conflicting interests and want opposing things. This was seen when the ban against fox hunting was considered. The League against Cruel Sports wanted it to be banned, but the Countryside Alliance wanted it to be allowed to continue.

Lobbying

Some pressure groups try to persuade individual Members of Parliament to support their cause. This is called lobbying (because members of the public can meet MPs in the lobbies of the House of Commons). If a pressure group is successful, it may persuade an MP to ask questions in Parliament about a particular problem. It is also

possible that a backbench MP may use the Private Members Bill session (see 15.4.2) to introduce a Bill trying to reform the law in the way that the pressure group wants. However, it is very unlikely that such a Bill will be passed by Parliament unless there is widespread support for it.

 Internet Research

Look up websites of pressure groups such as Liberty **www.liberty-human-rights.org.uk** or Justice **www.justice.org.uk** or Greenpeace **www.greenpeace.org.uk**. Choose one and write a brief summary of any changes in the law it is suggesting, or any success that it has had in changing the law.

19.2 The need for an independent law reform body

The problem with the above methods of law reform is that they do not look at the law as whole. The Government has a political agenda. It will want certain policies for taxation, education etc. Governments are less interested in 'pure' law reform. 'Pure' law means the law on different areas such as contract law, land law or criminal law.

Judges can only deal with the question of law in the case they are trying. They cannot deal with wider reforms of the law, although in some cases judges have commented on the need for the Government to change the law.

Public opinion is not always based on accurate information. Also the topics that arouse public interest are unlikely to include technical areas of law. Pressure groups are concerned with specific, and usually quite narrow, issues. Also pressure groups may be campaigning for opposite aims, as happened with fox hunting.

It is clear there needs to be an agency to consider reform of the law in a wider way. For this reason the Law Commission was created.

19.3 The Law Commission

The Law Commission was set up in 1965 by the Law Commissions Act. It is a full-time body and consists of a chairman, who is a High Court judge, and four other Law Commissioners. There are also support staff to assist with research and four parliamentary draftsmen who help with the drafting of proposed Bills.

The Commission considers areas of law which are believed to be in need of reform. The role of the Law Commission is set out in s 3 of the Law Commissions Act which states:

> It shall be the duty of each of the Commissions to take and keep under review all the law with which they are respectively concerned with a view to its systematic development and reform, including in particular the codification of such law, the elimination of anomalies, the repeal of obsolete and unnecessary enactments, the reduction of the number of separate enactments and generally the simplification and modernisation of the law ...

19.3.1 The way in which the Law Commission works

The actual topics may be referred to it by the Lord Chancellor on behalf of the Government, or it may itself select areas in need of reform and seek governmental approval to draft a report on them.

The Law Commission works by researching the area of law that is thought to be in need of reform. It then publishes a consultation paper seeking views on possible reform. The consultation paper will describe the current law, set out the problems and look at options for reform (often including explanations of the law in other countries).

Following the response to the consultation paper, the Commission will then draw up positive proposals for reform. These will be presented in a report which will also set out the research that led to the conclusions. There will often be a draft Bill attached to the report with the intention that this is the exact way in which the new law should be formed. Such a draft Bill must, of course, go before Parliament and go though the necessary parliamentary stages if it is to become law.

@ Internet Research

Look at the Law Commission's website (www.lawcom.gov.uk) and make a list of three areas of law which the Law Commission is currently researching.

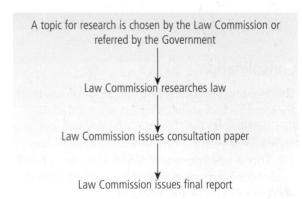

A topic for research is chosen by the Law Commission or referred by the Government

Law Commission researches law

Law Commission issues consultation paper

Law Commission issues final report

Figure 19.1 How the Law Commission works

19.3.2 Repeal and consolidation

Repeal

There are many very old and sometimes ridiculous statutes which are still on the statute book, but have long since ceased to have any relevance. In order to remove out of date statutes, the Law Commission prepares a Statute Law (Repeals) Bill for Parliament to pass. Through this, more than 2,500 out-of-date Acts have been completely repealed. In addition, parts of thousands of other Acts have also been repealed.

Date	Event
2004	The Law Commission brings out a report on partial defences to murder: *Partial Defences to Murder* (2004) (Law Com 290)
2005	The Government asks the Law Commission to consider the law on murder
2005	The Law Commission issues a consultation paper, *A new Homicide Act for England and Wales* (Consultation Paper 177)
2006	The Law Commission's Report, *Murder, Manslaughter and Infanticide* (Law Com 304) is published
2008	The Government accepts the proposals for reforming the partial defences to murder and publishes a consultation paper, *Murder, Manslaughter and Infanticide: Proposals for Reform of the Law*
	NB The Government rejects the Law Commission's proposals for a completely new definition of murder
2009	Parliament passes the Coroners and Justice Act. This redefines diminished responsibility, abolishes the previous defence of provocation and replaces it with a new defence, 'loss of control'

Figure 19.2 Examples of the working of the Law Commission

This 'tidying-up' of the statute book helps to make the law more accessible.

Consolidation

This is needed because in some areas of law there are a number of statutes which set out a small part of the total law. The aim of consolidation is to draw all the existing provisions together in one Act. This is another way in which the law is being made more accessible. For example, before 2000, the law on sentencing offenders under the age of 17 had been amended ten times and it was necessary to consult each of these Acts to get a full picture of the law. Much of the law on sentencing was consolidated in the Powers of the Criminal Courts (Sentencing) Act 2000.

The Law Commission produces about five Consolidation Bills every year, though it is perhaps true to say that as soon as one area is consolidated, another area is being fragmented by further Acts of Parliament! This has certainly happened with sentencing as, only months after the Powers of the Criminal Courts (Sentencing) Act 2000 brought most of the law together in one Act, Parliament passed the Criminal Justice and Courts Services Act 2000, altering some of the available sentences and creating new ones. More changes were made by the Criminal Justice Act 2003, yet more by the Criminal Justice and Immigration Act 2008 and yet more by the Legal Aid, Sentencing and Punishment of Offenders Act 2012.

19.3.3 Codification

Codification involves bringing together all the law on one topic into one source. Codification was specifically referred to by s 3 of the Law Commissions Act 1965 as part of the Law Commission's role.

Indeed, when the Law Commission was first formed in 1965 an ambitious programme of codification was announced, aimed at codifying family law, contract law, landlord and tenant laws and the law of evidence. However, the Law Commission has gradually abandoned these massive schemes of codification in favour of what might be termed the 'building-block' approach. Under this it has concentrated on codifying small sections of the law that can be added to later.

19.3.4 Effectiveness of the Law Commission

In the first ten years of the Law Commission's existence, it had a high success rate, with 85 per cent of its proposals being made law by Parliament. During the next ten years, however, only 50 per cent of its suggested reforms became law. This lack of success was due to the lack of parliamentary time and an apparent disinterest by Parliament in technical law reform. The rate hit an all-time low in 1990, when not one of its reforms was made law by Parliament.

Since then, matters have improved and different governments have enacted more reforms put forward by the Law Commission. Examples include:

- the Land Registration Act 2002 which was important for anyone selling or buying a house, flat or any other building or land, as it modernised and simplified the method of registering land
- the Fraud Act 2006 which reformed the law on fraud and deception offences
- the Corporate Manslaughter and Corporate Homicide Act 2007 which made corporations and other organisations liable for deaths caused through gross negligence.

However, there are still many reports awaiting implementation. Every year the Law Commission publishes an Annual Report in which it lists the reports that have been implemented and those that have not. In 2012, 15 reports were awaiting implementation. Some of these had been accepted by the Government and were supposed to be implemented 'when parliamentary time becomes available'.

Criminal law

The reform of the criminal law has been slower than reform of other areas. Originally the Law Commission hoped to create a criminal code which would cover large areas of the criminal law. They produced a draft Code in 1985 and a full Code in 1989. Because the Code was so large, it was obvious that Parliament would not have the time to deal with the whole of it at one time. In fact, in 2008 the Law Commission finally abandoned the project of having a complete criminal Code.

The Law Commission has published reports suggesting reform on parts of the criminal law. Some of these have become law, for example the Fraud Act 2006 and the Corporate Manslaughter and Corporate Homicide Act 2007 which establishes when a corporation is liable for manslaughter.

Other areas have either not been accepted by the Government or have not yet been made law. For example, the law on offences against the person is still awaiting reform. The Law Commission set out the lack of action in its annual report for 2006–07 when it wrote:

> Fourteen years ago [1993] the Law Commission published a report and draft Bill recommending an overhaul of the current legislation, which dates back to Offences Against the Person Act 1861. In 1997 the Home Office partially accepted these recommendations in principle. In 1998 the Home Office published a consultation paper setting out their initial proposals for reforming the law in this area, based on the Commission's report. In 2003, the Court of Appeal referred to the "need for radical reform" of section 20 of the 1861 Act.

By the time of writing this edition in 2013, the law on offences against the person had still not been reformed. This shows how slow Parliament can be in taking action on the Law Commission's proposals. Clearly, the Law Commission can only be effective if the Government and Parliament are prepared to find time to enact reforms.

Even when the Law Commission has produced reports on smaller areas of criminal law, the Government has been slow to implement them. In 2012, the Lord Chancellor stated in his annual report on implementation, which he has to make under the Law Commission Act 2009, that the Report on Participating in Crime (2007) (Law Com 305) and the Report on Conspiracy and Attempts (2009) (Law Com 318) were not priority areas and would not be implemented during the lifetime of the current Parliament which will last until 2015. This is yet another example of the Government's slowness in reforming the criminal law.

19.4 Other reform agencies

19.4.1 Royal Commissions

For some aspects of the legal system, the Government will set up a Royal Commission (a temporary committee) to investigate and report. For these Commissions, people with expertise in the area are consulted on the law. Once the Royal Commission has reported, its task is over and it is then disbanded.

Key facts

Set up	By the Law Commissions Act 1965
Personnel	Chairman and four other Commissioners Support staff including Parliamentary draftsmen
Function	To 'keep the law under review' s 3 Law Commissions Act 1965
Effectiveness	First ten years – 85% of proposals enacted by Parliament Second ten years – 50% of proposals enacted 1990 – no reports enacted 1991 to 2012 – more reports enacted, but some still awaiting implementation
Recent reforms	Land Registration Act 2002 Fraud Act 2006 Corporate Manslaughter and Corporate Homicide Act 2007

Figure 19.3 Key facts chart on the Law Commission

Self-Test Questions

1 Apart from the Law Commission, name two other influences which may lead to law reform.
2 Give two reasons why the Law Commission was needed.
3 Which Act set up the Law Commission?
4 Outline the way in which the Law Commission works in order to produce recommendations for reform of the law.
5 As well as recommending reform of the law, the Law Commission is responsible for proposing (a) repeals and (b) consolidation of the law. Briefly explain what is meant by these.
6 Name two Acts of Parliament which have brought in reforms proposed by the Law Commission.
7 What is the main problem faced by the Law Commission in turning its proposals into law?

Some Royal Commissions have led to important changes in the law. For example, the Royal Commission on Police Powers (the Phillips Commission) reported in 1981 and many of its recommendations were put into effect by the Police and Criminal Evidence Act 1984.

However, the Government has not always implemented recommendations by Royal Commissions. In 1978, the Pearson Commission on Personal Injury made far-reaching proposals for changes to the way in which people are compensated for injuries. These recommendations have never been implemented.

In some cases the Government will bring in some proposals but not the full report. This happened with the Runciman Commission on Criminal Justice.

19.4.2 Reviews by judges

An individual judge may be asked to lead an investigation into technical areas of law and make proposals for reform. A key example of this was the Woolf Report on the civil courts system. This report led to major changes to the civil justice system in 1999 (see 2.6).

19.4.3 Other reviews

As well as using judges to carry out reviews of areas of law, the Government has in recent times asked business people to review the workings of some areas of the justice system. For example, Sir David Clementi was asked to report on the legal profession. His report was published in 2004 and led to the Legal Services Act 2007 (see Chapter 10) which alters the way in which legal businesses are structured and the systems for dealing with regulation and complaints.

Examination Question

1 See part (c) of question 1 at the end of Chapter 14.

Exam tips

Law reform is a key part of the English legal system as there must be mechanisms to bring about change if the law is to develop and reflect the needs of society. This means it is an important topic and one which appears with some regularity on exam papers. It inter-links well with other areas of the specification, such as precedent and legislation, and so it is worth revising thoroughly as it may accompany one of those two key topics. The law reform element is likely to be worth a good number of marks, possibly 15 or even 30 of the 60 marks available, and so it can make a real difference when you are choosing which question to answer.

The key body is the Law Commission and you need to have a good range of factual information about them at your fingertips and some examples of their work, perhaps those connected to the area of law you will study at A2 level.

A wider awareness of the issues which drive law reform and the other bodies who have a role is also important as part of a good understanding of the whole process of changing the law. Whilst the focus of the question could be factual you should consider the wider issues which affect law reform bodies in terms of their effectiveness and the problems they face in getting support for their proposals as this may be the basis of a discussion question. Looking at the history of a reform can help you with this – for example the Coroners and Justice Act 2009 is a new piece of legislation which has finally been passed after several reports; it has taken a number of years for the new law to be enacted.

Appendix 1

This appendix gives help with the Activities on pages 7 and 248.

Distinguishing between civil and criminal cases (page 7)

Question 1 answer

Sources A and C are criminal cases. Sources B and D are civil cases. This information helps with the remainder of the questions in the activity.

Statutory interpretation and the case of *Fisher v Bell* (page 248)

The court used the literal rule in coming to the decision in this case. The court considered a technical legal meaning of 'offer for sale' and used this meaning in its literal sense. This meant that literally displaying knives in the window was not offering them for sale. As a result the court came to the decision that the knives were not 'offered for sale', and since they had not been sold or hired or lent either, the shopkeeper had not committed any offence under the Act. He was found not guilty.

Index

Note: Page numbers in **bold** refer to key facts